NATIONAL ASSOCIATION OF
School Psychologists

SCHOOL PSYCHOLOGIST AS COUNSELOR

A Practitioner's Handbook

Cynthia A. Plotts, PhD
Jon Lasser, PhD

Second Edition

From the NASP Publications Board Operations Manual
The content of this document reflects the ideas and positions of the authors. The responsibility lies solely with the authors and editors and does not necessarily reflect the position or ideas of the National Association of School Psychologists.

Published by the National Association of School Psychologists

Copyright © 2020 by the National Association of School Psychologists.

All rights reserved. No part of this publication may be reproduced or distributed in any form or by any means, electronic, mechanical, photocopying, recording, scanning, or otherwise, except as permitted under the United States Copyright Act of 1976, or stored in a database or retrieval system, without the prior written permission of the publisher, or authorization through payment of the appropriate per-copy fee to the Copyright Clearance Center, 222 Rosewood Drive, Danvers, MA 01923, 978-750-8400, fax 978-750-4474, www.copyright.com. Requests to the Publisher for permission should be addressed to Copyright Permissions, National Association of School Psychologists, 4340 East West Highway, Suite 402, Bethesda, MD 20814, 301-657-0270, fax 301-657-0275, email: publications@naspweb.org.

Copies may be ordered from:
NASP Publications
4340 East West Highway, Suite 402
Bethesda, MD 20814
301-657-0270
301-657-0275, fax
866-331-NASP, Toll Free
email: publications@naspweb.org
www.nasponline.org

ISBN 978-0932955-23-4

Printed in the United States of America

21 22 23 24 25 26   10 9 8 7 6 5 4 3 2

Dedication

To Kent, Betty, Jessie, Sam, and Joshua
–C.P.

To Illysa, Jasmine, and Sage
–J.L.

Contents

Preface...1

Chapter 1: The Counseling Role in School Psychology............................3

Chapter 2: The Counseling Process..29

Chapter 3: Counseling Within Multitiered Systems of Support...................47

Chapter 4: Techniques for Systems Consultation...............................67

Chapter 5: Family Interventions..85

Chapter 6: Nondirective Approaches..111

Chapter 7: Mindfulness..129

Chapter 8: Directive Approaches...139

Chapter 9: Therapeutic Responses to Trauma, Loss, and Crisis.................169

Chapter 10: Substance Abuse, Delinquency, and Psychopharmacology.............193

Chapter 11: Practical Applications and Resources............................219

Chapter 12: Self-Knowledge and Self-Care....................................237

Appendix A: Behavioral, Social, and Emotional Concerns......................253

Appendix B: Eligibility for Counseling as a Related Service.................255

Index...259

Preface

In this second edition, we maintained the focus on realistic and practical guidance for school psychologists who intend to provide counseling in school settings. Using feedback from our graduate students who used the first edition of this text in coursework, and practitioners who used the text in their work, we revised this book in several ways.

New content in this edition was included to achieve the following:

- Update information based on recent research.
- Describe and discuss approaches and techniques that have received increased emphasis over the past few years, for example, multitiered systems of support (MTSS), mindfulness, dialectical behavior therapy, trauma-informed therapy, motivational interviewing, and psychopharmacology.
- Emphasize practical applications through case examples and references to specific resources.
- Acknowledge that self-awareness and self-care are integral to competent practice.

We reordered and organized chapters to reflect our conceptualization of the needs of the school psychologist in a counseling role. Each chapter contains an overview, learning objectives, and discussion questions presented at the end of each chapter.

In Chapters 1 and 2, we cover foundational material, including the counseling role, counseling relationship, and counseling process, keeping in mind the constraints of school-based practice and legal and ethical mandates. New information about the importance of the counseling relationship to successful outcomes was added to Chapter 1.

Chapters 3 through 10 are organized within the framework of primary, secondary, and tertiary interventions as they apply to the counseling role. This framework, while not mapping fully onto the tiered frameworks of response to intervention (RTI) and MTSS, parallels these intervention models. In Chapters 3, 4, and 5, we emphasize the primacy of interventions informed by systems theory and models (MTSS, consultation, and family systems).

The next group of chapters (6, 7, and 8) is intended to present secondary interventions, those approaches that can effectively target student problems that have been identified as amenable to counseling. Chapter 6 describes nondirective methods such as play therapy and sandtray techniques,

Chapter 7 covers mindfulness-based techniques, and Chapter 8 addresses directive approaches, including cognitive–behavioral therapy and related techniques.

Chapter 9 (on trauma and crisis) and Chapter 10 (on substance abuse, delinquency, and psychopharmacology) delve into intensive counseling considerations that may involve systems and interventions to treat emotional and behavioral problems within and beyond the school setting.

Finally, we provide concluding chapters that address practical applications and resources for the busy school psychologist (Chapter 11) and practitioners' self-care (Chapter 12).

As experienced practitioners and trainers, we humbly acknowledge that no text, including this one, covers all theories, models, or techniques of counseling for children and adolescents. We elected to include content that has earned empirical support and seemed most likely to prove useful to school psychologists. Readers will have a range of training and practice; consultation and supervision are encouraged when experience is lacking.

We wish to acknowledge the contributions and assistance of our graduate students who helped make this book possible. Feedback from readers of the first edition proved to be incredibly helpful as we engaged in the process of revising and reorganizing the text. Moreover, we are grateful to the children and adolescents with whom we have worked, as we have learned much from them about counseling. Finally, we wish to acknowledge Liz Hjort for contributing case studies, and Cristina Palmer for her mentoring and generous sharing of ideas.

Chapter 1

The Counseling Role in School Psychology

OVERVIEW

Are you already, or do you aspire to be, a school psychologist who provides counseling services? In this chapter, we establish the need for counseling interventions in schools, explore the history that informs the school psychologist's unique preparation for this role, and review relevant training standards and ethical guidelines. Further, we introduce the concept of evidence-based practice and explore the significance of the counseling relationship through an empirical lens. The chapter also includes an overview of multitiered models of intervention and a framework for selection of counseling techniques.

First we give an overview of how we have organized this book to create a logical flow of information that will make it easier for readers to find what they are looking for. The book is designed around five dimensions, focusing on approaches that are evidence based:

- The foundations of counseling, in Chapters 1 and 2, include the role of counseling and processes used in schools.
- The primary or universal interventions, presented in Chapters 3, 4, and 5, include counseling within multitiered systems of support, systems consultation (consultation that fosters open communication in the school), and family interventions.
- Secondary or targeted interventions, covered in Chapters 6, 7, and 8, include nondirective approaches, mindfulness, and directive approaches.
- Tertiary, intensive, or individualized interventions include crisis and trauma-informed counseling (Chapter 9) and substance abuse, delinquency, and psychopharmacology considerations (Chapter 10).
- Practical considerations covered in Chapters 11 and 12 give case studies, measurement of outcomes, self-knowledge, and self-care.

OBJECTIVES

After reading this chapter, readers should be able to do the following:

- Recognize the growing need for counseling interventions in schools.
- Describe how the counseling role fits within the scope of school psychology services.
- Recognize how the history of school psychology has informed counseling practice.
- Identify the current training standards with respect to counseling skills for school psychologists.
- Apply relevant ethical principles to possible counseling situations.
- Define *evidence-based practice* for counseling services.
- Describe the centrality of the counselor–counselee relationship to counseling outcomes.
- Explain how response to intervention and multitiered systems of support can be applied to a range of counseling activities in a school setting.
- Recognize considerations of client characteristics in the choice of counseling techniques.

The Need for Counseling

Educational systems cannot ignore concerns about and considerations of the mental and behavioral health of children and adolescents. A survey conducted by the Substance Abuse and Mental Health Services Administration (SAMHSA) in 2017 revealed that the lifetime prevalence of any mental disorder among adolescents is 49.1%, with severe impairment occurring in 22.2% of individuals. In 2017, suicide was the second leading cause of death among individuals ages 10 to 24 years, exceeded only by unintentional injury. An estimated 3.2 million adolescents ages 12 to 17, or 13.3% of the U.S. population, had at least one major depressive episode (National Institute of Mental Health, 2018).

SAMHSA and administrators from the Centers for Medicaid and CHIP Services (CMS) prepared a *Joint Informational Bulletin* to provide guidance to states and school systems on addressing mental health and substance abuse issues in schools (SAMHSA & CMS, 2019). They reported that an estimated 10% of children and adolescents in the United States have a serious emotional disturbance, but approximately 80% do not receive needed services. Further, over 16% of adolescents ages 12 to 17 reported illicit drug use during 2017, with 4% meeting criteria for a substance use disorder.

In a review of mental health interventions in schools, Fazel et al. (2014) report that findings from epidemiological studies of high-income countries indicate that 8–18% of school-age children have psychiatric disorders, while many more children have psychological distress with lower levels of impairment. They maintain that disruptive behavior and anxiety are the most common disorders in school-age children, with separation anxiety and oppositional defiant disorder seen mainly in primary school children (ages 4–10 years). Generalized anxiety, conduct disorder, and depression are more common in secondary school students (ages 11–18 years). The incidence of eating disorders and psychosis increases rapidly from midadolescence on. Attention deficit hyperactivity disorder (ADHD) and autism spectrum disorders create notable difficulties for children in the school environment. Childhood psychiatric disorders are associated with educational failure and a range of additional adverse outcomes, such as risk-taking behavior and increased likelihood of entering the criminal justice system.

Schools have a critical role in both identifying children and adolescents with mental health and substance use disorders and connecting them with treatment and other services (NASP, 2015). As observed by Hughes and Minke (2014), "school psychologists are situated in real time in the biopsychosocial system where children spend 35 hours or more a week" (p. 29). School psychologists are specifically trained and uniquely placed to address the mental health needs of children and adolescents.

Definitions

Many school psychologists have developed an interest in counseling activities and have been able to incorporate counseling into the broader professional role and function, particularly as the critical need for prevention and early intervention has become apparent (NASP, 2019). Before we explore historical foundations of counseling and school psychology, we distinguish counseling as a school psychologist from the counseling roles of other professionals.

For the school psychologist, counseling refers to the set of interventions designed to promote the social, emotional, and behavioral well-being of children and adolescents. Although individual and group counseling sessions are the most direct way of addressing these aspects of functioning, they are not the only ways that school psychologists function as counselors. Of the broad, traditional roles of the school psychologist (assessment, intervention, and consultation), counseling would seem to fit squarely in the intervention role. As we will see later, the lines are less rigid than they may seem.

Counseling, *psychotherapy*, and *therapy* are terms that are used in the literature to describe interventions, and there may be some confusion about the proper use of these terms. The confusion is exacerbated by the fact that the terms are sometimes used interchangeably, and they may be conceptualized differently across disciplines.

Counseling is sometimes characterized as brief, focused, and advice oriented, whereas therapy or psychotherapy is often described as a treatment for more chronic or serious problems (with the implication that those providing psychotherapy may require more specialized training). Some professionals use terminology that matches their training and licensure, and some licensing bodies may restrict the use of some terminology (e.g., a jurisdiction may prohibit the use of "counseling" in advertising for those who are not licensed as counselors).

Just as there are turf issues among mental health professions regarding training requirements and the appropriate range of services, there are professional title issues. For example, the licensure of professional counselors (who may have different titles across states) is considered distinct from the certification or licensure of school counselors (American Counseling Association, n.d.). Similarly, state certification and licensure for school psychologists is regulated by different agencies than are school counselors or licensed professional counselors. Professional terminology and titles do not necessarily predict differences in interventions.

These distinctions may not be useful for a number of reasons. Because the terms *counseling* and *psychotherapy* are indeed used interchangeably, the distinctions can be confusing or meaningless to consumers. School psychologists are not infrequently asked, "Are you a school counselor?" The confusion in terms among parents and school staff is understandable! Moreover, if duration of services is used as a differentiating factor (e.g., counseling is brief, psychotherapy is not), then the emergence of *brief psychotherapy* or *single-session therapy* raises reasonable questions. Both the therapeutic approach and other constraints (e.g., insurance coverage, available time and personnel, concurrent interventions) may affect duration of counseling services, distinct from the severity of the emotional or behavioral problems. Individuals who report that they provide counseling, therapy, or psychotherapy may come from a variety of disciplines and training backgrounds. A psychologist may call herself a counselor or a psychotherapist, a social worker may say that he provides psychotherapy, and a licensed professional counselor may offer brief psychotherapy.

To avoid confusion in this text, we will use the term *counseling* to describe the interventions used by school psychologists (and other mental health professionals) to improve the social, emotional, and behavioral functioning of children and adolescents. We do not intend to define counseling so broadly as to encompass advice from peers, mentoring from teachers, or disciplinary action from school administrators. Rather, we limit the use of the term to planned and structured activities by trained professionals in the context of a specified relationship with clear boundaries and goals and objectives.

Counseling services in schools are designed to meet specific, measurable goals and objectives. Clinical psychologists, clinical or school social workers, school counselors, and counseling psychologists are also invested in achieving these goals and consequently overlap with school psychologists' role and function (Fagan & Wise, 2007). What differentiates school psychologists from some other mental health professionals is the context of the school and the emphasis on supporting the overall educational goals of students. Moreover, in some school districts, school psychologists may be those responsible for delivering counseling services that are part of a student's Individualized Education Program (IEP), while school counselors may be more focused on the general education population. Students with an IEP receive special education services, and counseling may be provided as a related service to support the IEP. In such cases, the counseling duration and number of sessions may be specified in a legal document, the IEP.

The school psychologist as counselor, even though operating under systemic constraints in schools, has discretion to use a wide range of therapeutic approaches, methods, and activities to further counseling goals. These may include, but are not limited to, individual and group therapy (using a variety of theoretical orientations and techniques); assessment to determine a need for counseling and to monitor counseling progress; consultation with parents, teachers, and other professionals; crisis prevention and intervention; social skills training; family therapy (though this may be less common); and referrals to and coordination with other services or professionals. Given the wide variety of activities that fall under the counseling role, we find it preferable to describe counseling by its goals, with an understanding that there are many ways to reach those goals.

History

School psychology as a profession began in the early 1900s with the child study movement (Phillips, 1990). The first individuals to identify as school psychologists were primarily concerned with identification of learning difficulties and intellectual disabilities, with an associated emphasis on formal assessment tools. These pioneers were not typically trained as school psychologists. Over time, the role and function of the school psychologist expanded, training standards developed, and school psychology matured into a more clearly defined profession.

Psychological Service for School Problems, written in 1930 by Gertrude Hildreth, emphasized application of the science of psychology to address school-related problems. Hildreth's focus was squarely on applied educational psychology to improve learning outcomes, with counseling services mentioned in passing. Hildreth listed 11 problems that can be solved by applying psychological techniques. Among the problems she listed were instructional problems in the classroom, assessment of achievement, interpretation of test results, instructional groupings of students for optimal outcomes, vocational guidance, curriculum development, and "investigation of the problems presented by exceptional pupils, including the mentally subnormal, the gifted, the specially talented, the physically handicapped, the nervous, and the delinquent" (p. 9). While terminology may have changed, these exceptionalities continue to be focused upon in training programs for school psychologists.

Hildreth's book comes closest to addressing counseling as a professional role in the context of what she called "mental hygiene" and "a program of reëducation [sic]." Though counseling receives relatively scant attention, notions of addressing students' self-confidence, fears, and repressions predominate, along with the importance of collaborating with teachers and families. Foreshadowing more current thinking, she also advocated for comprehensive assessment of the child and his or her ecosystemic context preceding intervention.

By the 1950s, the counseling role of the school psychologist came into sharper focus, and the words "counseling" and "therapy" began to appear in the professional literature. The 1954 Thayer Conference in West Point, New York, focused on school psychologists' roles, function, and training. The American Psychological Association's published report of the conference (the Thayer report), edited by Norma Cutts, identifies counseling as part of the school psychologist's role. "His [sic] training should give him a special part in assisting in the development of mental health and sound emotional attitudes. He can help children solve personal and social problems and learn to live with others" (Cutts, 1955, p. 29). Still, many school psychologists at the time focused their energies on assessment and referred counseling interventions to agencies. Citing a New York State report on school psychology (and psychiatry), the Thayer report identified school psychologists as potentially instrumental in the prevention of mental illness and recognized the need for individual work with students.

A more detailed discussion of the school psychologist as counselor emerged in the late 1960s and early 1970s, as evidenced by the more detailed discussion of training, competencies, and models (Bardon & Bennett, 1974; Smith, 1967). At the time, training standards varied from state to state, and, as today, not all school psychologists were trained to provide counseling. Those with counseling competencies engaged in individual, group, and crisis counseling. Bardon and Bennet expressed preference for the word *counseling* over *psychotherapy* for school psychology because the latter suggests a medical model of treatment for illness. Moreover, they noted concern that children served by school psychologists would be perceived as ill if the term *psychotherapy* were used.

The late 1960s and early 1970s were also defined by growing pains. Smith (1967) recognized an increased interest in counseling and psychotherapy, as well as controversy regarding training standards, titling and range of practice issues, and economic competition (not to mention status and ego). Given the increasingly specialized nature of counseling skills and techniques, Smith advised against a rigid role definition of the school psychologist as counselor. Rather, he suggested "some tentative guidelines to follow" that take a practical approach to counseling's application in the unique setting of the school (p. 143). In other words, Smith recognized that schools are unlike other settings and that counseling in school must consider context. For example, Smith noted that schools "cannot be all things to all children" in his discussion of the appropriateness of short-term versus long-term therapy in the schools (p. 149).

Nevertheless, in many respects psychology melds naturally with school practice. Why? Early intervention has better outcomes, children are reliably present in schools, both learning and behavior can be assessed and monitored across settings, and developmental norms are somewhat established by age and grade reference groups so that significant deviations from typical development are apparent. NASP (2015) documents that mental and behavioral wellness is associated with, among other things, positive student achievement and prevention of disciplinary incidents, risky behaviors, and substance abuse. In the Elementary and Secondary Education Act (2001), school psychologists are recognized as school-based mental health service providers. In the Affordable Care Act (ACA) of 2010, school psychologists are also recognized as "qualified health professionals" (Public law 111-148, Section 5203, Subpart 3, Sec. 775) and "mental health service professionals" (Public law 111-148, Section 5002, Definitions) if they are licensed or certified at the doctoral and/or specialist level.

The experiences of today's school psychologists vary greatly, with some fully engaged in counseling services as their primary role and others who have little to no opportunity to function as counselors. The results from the 2015 NASP membership survey indicated that 71.6% of respondents employed full-time in schools engaged in individual counseling for behavior/mental health problems, while 43.8% engaged in group counseling for these issues (McNamara et al., 2019). These results are similar to findings obtained in the 2010 survey, with engagement in group counseling somewhat increased over the 5 years between surveys. Consistent with past survey results, school psychologists continue to report substantial engagement in evaluations and reevaluations for special education and related services, with more than 90% of respondents involved in this role.

Although NASP promotes the role of school psychologists as mental and behavioral health providers, training programs vary in the degree to which they emphasize counseling as part of their preparation for future school psychologists. Typically, specialist-level programs, with required coursework covering broad content completed within 3 years, offer fewer opportunities for intensive counseling training and supervision, compared with doctoral-level programs, though there may be some exceptions.

Results from the 2015 NASP membership survey indicated that there is a relationship between the degree of engagement in behavioral and mental health services, particularly the use of school-wide services, and school psychologist-to-student ratios. Respondents from schools with student ratios that exceed 1:2,000 were significantly less likely to report involvement in system-level or school-wide behavioral and mental health activities. With ratios below 1:1,000, school psychologists reported significantly greater engagement in mental and behavioral health services and crisis intervention (McNamara et al., 2019). The NASP Practice Model, discussed in the following section, recommends a ratio for schools of one school psychologist to 500–700 students to best and most efficiently use school psychologists' skills and expertise.

Today's school psychologists' roles are diverse, but national training standards have brought greater uniformity to the preparation of practitioners. Although substantial advocacy efforts are needed to build acceptance for the broad range of professional activities of school psychologists, present-day counseling services are characterized by two related trends: an increased emphasis on evidence-based practices and an integration of counseling services within the framework of response to intervention (RTI) and multitiered systems of support (MTSS). Consequently, today's school psychologists serving in the counseling role provide services that have demonstrated efficacy in the peer-reviewed literature. Moreover, best practices stipulate that counseling services be provided at tiered levels of intensity appropriate to the magnitude of concern. These are covered in greater depth later in the chapter.

Training Standards

In 2020, the National Association of School Psychologists (NASP) approved its updated *Model for Comprehensive and Integrated School Psychological Services* (the NASP Practice Model) to continue to improve consistency in the implementation of school psychological services nationwide. Building on more than 30 years of work to establish training standards, the NASP Practice Model delineates 10 domains of practice in which school psychologists should be trained.

Along with the NASP Practice Model, the set of four integrated yet separate documents of the Professional Standards (NASP, 2020b) identify NASP's training and credentialing standards and ethical guidelines. These documents include the *Standards for Graduate Preparation of School Psychologists, Standards for the Credentialing of School Psychologists*, and *Principles for Professional Ethics*.

The NASP 2020 Professional Standards refer to counseling as part of school psychologists' roles and functions and underscore the importance of addressing counseling skills in the preparation and credentialing of school psychologists. We discuss the ethical issues related the school psychologist as counselor later in this chapter. The American Psychological Association's *Standards of Accreditation for Health Service Psychology* (APA, 2018), which provides guidelines for school psychology programs seeking APA accreditation at the doctoral level of training, addresses counseling in the curriculum of training programs only in the broad, general sense of intervention:

> "[H]ealth service psychology" is defined as the integration of psychological science and practice in order to facilitate human development and functioning. Health service psychology includes the generation and provision of knowledge and practices that encompass a wide range of professional activities relevant to health promotion, prevention, consultation, assessment, and treatment for psychological and other health-related disorders. (p. 2)

Although both NASP and APA view preparation to treat psychological disorders as integral to graduate training programs, NASP standards are more specific to the training for and practice of school psychology.

Ethical Guidelines

Professional school psychology has two primary sources for ethical standards and principles: the American Psychological Association's 2017 Ethics Code and NASP's 2020 *Principles for Professional Ethics*. These documents guide practitioners through professional expectations of ethical conduct and apply broad principles, among them competence, to the services that school psychologists provide for children, adolescents, families, and other professionals. As the profession matures and evolves, these ethical codes are revised to meet the changing needs of the field.

To assist with the application of ethical guidelines to practice, the NASP Ethics and Professional Practices Board has created an easily accessed series of problem-solving steps, ranging from informal resolution of concerns to formal adjudication of complaints (https://www.nasponline.org/standards-and-certification/professional-ethics). In this chapter, we highlight ethical principles and standards that are germane to the counseling role. Readers also can find a comprehensive review of ethical issues related to the counseling role of school psychologists found in a number of resources, including *Ethics and Law for School Psychologists* (Jacob et al., 2016), *Professional Ethics for School Psychologists: A Problem-Solving Casebook* (Armistead et al., 2011), and *School Psychology for the 21st Century: Foundations and Practices* (Merrell, Ervin, & Peacock, 2012).

Contemporary school service delivery models endorse a tiered approach that can present unique challenges to school psychologists as they conduct screening, consultation, and observation. Those activities might not always appear to be psychological services, and they might also be conducted by other professionals. Nevertheless, school psychologists who are engaged in screening and targeted interventions (Tier 1 and Tier 2), if practicing under a school psychology certification or license, are expected to abide by ethical guidelines for the profession.

The *Principles for Professional Ethics* (NASP, 2020a) is organized around four broad themes: (a) respecting the dignity and rights of all persons; (b) professional competence and responsibility; (c) honesty and integrity in professional relationships; and (d) responsibility to schools, families, communities, the profession, and society. What follows is a brief overview of these themes, and of the principles and standards that characterize them, with examples specific to the counseling role of the school psychologist.

Respecting the Dignity and Rights of All Persons

School psychologists are called upon to respect all individuals equally, including their privacy, autonomy, and self-determination. Respecting the dignity and rights of others is broad but fairly straightforward. However, determining the ethical course of action in specific situations can be challenging. This discussion moves from the more general themes to specific standards.

Principles and standards that apply to respecting the dignity and rights of others. Three principles fall under the theme of respecting others' dignity and rights: autonomy and self-determination (consent and assent); privacy and confidentiality; and fairness, equity, and justice. The first of these principles, *autonomy and self-determination* (Principle I.1), concerns the rights of individuals to participate in the decisions that affect them. The standards related to autonomy and self-determination reflect the reality that school psychologists work with minors and that parents and guardians participate in the decision-making and consent process.

For the school psychologist as counselor, autonomy and self-determination become most salient in the context of informed consent and assent. The *Principles for Professional Ethics* (2020) requires that an individual providing consent for school psychological services be fully informed about (a) the nature and scope of services offered, (b) assessment and intervention goals and procedures, (c) any foreseeable risks, (d) the cost of services to the parent or student (if any), (e) alternatives to the services proposed, and (f) benefits that reasonably can be expected.

The practitioner's explanation must include a discussion of the limits of confidentiality, who will have access to information about assessment or intervention outcomes, and the possible consequences of the psychological services being offered. Parents or caregivers may want to know what was said in counseling sessions, but school psychologists typically report progress in general terms without disclosing specific content. If appropriate, available alternative services are identified. Language and cultural differences, cognitive capabilities, developmental level, age, and other relevant factors must be taken into account to ensure that any consent is fully informed. Written or oral consent must be documented. Further, any psychological service provided by interns, practicum students, or other trainees must be explained and agreed to in advance, along with the identity and responsibilities of the supervising school psychologist.

Essentially, the school psychologist must provide parents with sufficient information about counseling services (not just get their signature on a form), including the opportunity to ask questions, so that parents can make informed choices.

The *Principles* encourages seeking student assent, but that may be omitted if the service is considered to be of direct benefit to the student or is required by law. The notion of "direct benefit" may be slippery, as not all parties may agree about purported benefits. Additionally, bypassing assent to provide counseling to an unwilling student may limit one's capacity to realize the desired benefits. The *Principles* notes that if assent is sought and the student refuses services, the student's wishes should be respected; however, practitioners should not rotely accept the student's refusal if they did not overtly solicit the student's assent.

These elements can be incorporated into a letter or form for parents to read before deciding whether they give their consent. Ideally any such letter or consent form should be preceded by face-to-face contact to discuss the behaviors of concern observed in school. A sample letter is provided in the example below.

EXAMPLE: SAMPLE INFORMED CONSENT LETTER

Dear Parent,
I would like consent for your child to participate in a counseling group that will meet every week after lunch with five other children to improve anxiety management skills. I am recommending this service because your child's teacher has observed behaviors indicating that anxiety may be interfering with your child's academic and/or social adjustment, and the group may help teach better coping skills. Although I anticipate that this group interaction will be successful, unwanted outcomes could include: disclosure of sensitive information, discomfort with discussion of anxiety, or temporary increase in anxious feelings or behaviors in the group. Potential benefits include decreased anxiety and improved social and academic adjustment. We are planning eight sessions during which I will lead the group in fun activities, relaxation techniques, and discussions about coping with anxiety. Your child will miss fourth period each day they attend the group. If you have any questions, you may contact me by phone or email. By signing below, you are indicating that you understand this letter and agree to your child's participation in the group.

Informed consent should be voluntary. In some cases, parents may feel pressure from interpersonal dynamics in the context of the IEP committee or student support team meetings, so school psychologists should be aware of such pressures and work to minimize them (Lasser & Klose, 2007). It would be unethical to coerce parents into consenting to a psychological service that they would otherwise refuse. Further, it would be unethical to obtain parents' consent without providing adequate information and opportunity to ask questions. Parental consent forms associated with IEPs (e.g., consent for special education services, including counseling) will not likely meet all the elements of informed consent as described above. It is the school psychologist's ethical obligation, not the responsibility of the IEP team, to ensure informed consent for counseling. If counseling services are included in a student's IEP, the IEP team would need to reconvene if a student consistently refuses to participate in counseling sessions.

Parental refusal of services should be honored, and in such cases it is recommended that school psychologists consider other forms of intervention (e.g., consultation, mentoring) that may be more acceptable to the family.

There may be some cases in which students are provided counseling services without parental consent, but these situations are rare and should be approached carefully. For example, the *Principles for Professional Ethics* (NASP, 2020a) notes that a school psychologist may ethically provide counseling without parental notice or consent in emergency situations or if there is reason to believe a student may pose a danger to others; is at risk for self-harm; or is in danger of injury, exploitation, or maltreatment. Of course, practitioners must also take school district policies and state law into consideration. The *Principles* also recommends that school districts make it known to all parents, such as through handbooks or websites, that emergency counseling without parental notification or consent may be provided.

Counseling also is ethical when provided to self-referred minors for one or several meetings to assess the need for services and the degree to which the minor may be in danger. School psychologists should consult their own state law and district policy for guidance on self-referral by minors. Counseling also may continue without parental consent if permitted by district policy and state law. In the absence of such provisions, parents must be notified, and consent must be obtained to continue. Alternatively, minors can be referred for services that do not require parental consent outside of the school district. However, in rural populations, referral sources may be very limited or nonexistent. In any case, the competent school psychologist should become familiar with mental health resources in the community.

The second principle that falls under the theme of respecting the dignity and rights of others involves *privacy and confidentiality* (Principle I.2). Privacy is a right of students and families, whereas confidentiality is the ethical obligation of school psychologists. When facilitating counseling groups, school psychologists also ask group members to maintain confidentiality. At its most basic level, this principle allows individuals to self-determine whether their private information will be disclosed. Of course, young children may have limited understanding of this principle and will need concrete examples to guide protection of privacy.

Practitioners must safeguard private information, but also should collect only information that is relevant to the provision of services. The school psychologist as counselor should not seek information that is not needed and must be thoughtful about recording information that is not pertinent, particularly if the disclosure of such information to a third party could place the student or family at risk. For example, a history of alcoholism or addiction in the extended family may be relevant to the issues presented by the child in counseling; however, recording or reporting information about specific family members or personal family details may intrude upon their privacy and would typically be outside the realm of the school counseling record.

At the outset of services, the school psychologist should, as part of the informed parental consent and student assent process, explain the limits of confidentiality to students and parents. Typically, these limits are related to disclosures of harm to self or others and subpoenas. Also, the explanation to children must be developmentally appropriate and in language that can easily be understood. For example, the school psychologist seeking informed assent from a 12-year-old child might say, "Everything we talk about in counseling will be kept private; I won't tell anyone what you tell me. However, because I care about you, I have to tell someone if you have been hurt, or if you plan on hurting someone else or yourself. Sometimes a court may also require me to share private information. If I do need to talk about anything you tell me with parents or anyone else, I will talk with you about it first." The school psychologist should also check with the student to ensure that the explanation was understood. Informing students and families about the limits of confidentiality should occur not only at the outset of services, but also on an ongoing basis as needed.

States differ with regard to reporting requirements in situations involving danger to self or others. School psychologists are advised to seek out specific reporting guidelines for the state in which they practice. The welfare of the client is a guiding ethical principle, along with legal reporting requirements, that will help the school psychologist work through dilemmas related to limits of confidentiality. Most states have laws that require professionals working with children to report suspected neglect and/or abuse (Child Welfare Information Gateway, 2019), though the requirements vary across states. Failure to report suspected neglect and/or abuse may result in fines, imprisonment, and disciplinary action from licensing and certification boards. The identity of the reporter is generally kept confidential, though some states permit the release of the reporter's identity in certain circumstances.

School psychologists do not reveal confidential information to third parties without the consent of adult students or parents or guardians. For example, if a child's psychiatrist called and asked you for the child's counseling records, you could not provide those records to the psychiatrist without the parent's or guardian's written consent (or an adult student's written consent). Conveying confidential information orally by telephone, or via email or text, would also require written consent from parents, guardians, or adult students. The assent of students should be sought before releasing confidential information to a third party, including information to be shared with the student's parents.

In school settings, confidential information may be shared with other school professionals on a need-to-know basis; for example, psychological test results may be shared in an IEP team meeting. Caution should be exercised with sensitive information that is shared in confidential counseling sessions. The counselor has the burden of exercising caution and judgment when determining what should or should not be shared with others in the school setting. Soliciting the student's assent may help in determining what should be disclosed to others. The integrity of the counseling relationship depends on the student's confidence that the counselor can be trusted with private information and abides by the guidelines set forth in the informed consent/assent process.

The *Principles* acknowledges that the sexual orientation, gender identity, and/or transgendered status of a student, parent, or employee is particularly sensitive information. The *Principles* unambiguously states that such information is never shared without the student's, parent's, or employee's consent. For example, the school psychologist would not disclose a student's sexual orientation to their parents without the student's consent.

The final area addressed under privacy and confidentiality is sensitive health information. The *Principles* recommends that school psychologists consult state laws and departments of public health for guidance if they believe that a student poses a health risk to others, but it generally advises that sensitive health information should not be disclosed without an individual's (or parent's) consent. Moreover, school psychologists must respect the privacy of students, family members, and colleagues regarding sensitive health information. For example, a school psychologist should not disclose to others that a colleague has HIV. Drug or alcohol abuse or addiction is also sensitive health information; while there are disciplinary procedures on school campuses regarding substance possession and use, the student's disclosure of a substance abuse disorder is not subject to reporting to school personnel or law enforcement. Determination of imminent harm would be a guiding principle for decisions regarding disclosure of sensitive health information to parents or others.

Also under the theme of respecting dignity and rights is the principle of fairness and justice (Principle I.3). This principle calls for school psychologists to promote a safe and welcoming school climate for all persons, and to treat others fairly in words and actions. The *Principles* specifically mentions that discrimination should not be based on a number of characteristics, including race; ethnicity; color; religion; ancestry; national origin; immigration status; socioeconomic status; primary language; gender; sexual orientation, gender identity, or gender expression; mental, physical, or sensory disability; or any other distinguishing characteristics.

The *Principles* goes beyond mere nondiscrimination. School psychologists must educate themselves about the ways in which diversity factors may affect learning, behavior, and development. The school psychologist as counselor should attend to cultural differences in communication, expression of feelings, nonverbal gestures, and acculturation. School psychologists must avoid stereotyping yet also be aware of cultural trends and patterns, which may require that they research unfamiliar cultures and practices. Ultimately, those with whom we work should first and foremost be understood as unique individuals. Careful and sensitive assessment can reveal the extent to which diversity factors play a role.

School psychologists are also asked to address injustices when they observe them and to take corrective action. For example, discriminatory school policies should be corrected. Such practices may adversely affect students, parents, or employees, and school psychologists may not sit by passively when they are aware of injustices. In line with this concept, school psychologists also work to ensure equal opportunities for children and families, as well as equal access to psychological services, including counseling. For example, recent controversy around the issue of immigration from Latin American countries has created the potential for discriminatory practices in public schools. It is incumbent upon school psychology training programs and on practicing school psychologists to recognize and address any discrimination or injustice in delivery of school services (Vega et al., 2015).

Professional Competence and Responsibility

School psychologists strive to benefit others through their work and to avoid harm. Doing so involves practicing according to the five principles within this second theme. Those that are relevant here include striving for and working within the limits of personal competence, accepting responsibility for actions, using responsible assessment and intervention practices, and practicing responsible school-based record keeping. The fifth principle, adhering to responsible use of materials, is not discussed here since it relates primarily to test security and respect for intellectual property.

The first principle under this theme, *competence* (Principle II.1), simply states that school psychologists limit their practice to activities for which they are qualified and competent. A school psychologist who has received no training, supervision, or experience in counseling should not provide counseling services until appropriate training and supervision are obtained. This raises important questions about competence. For example, how much training is enough when qualifying to be a school psychologist? If a practitioner's training in counseling is limited to cognitive–behavioral therapy, can they provide nondirective play therapy? The standards listed under this principle address such details. The standards also state that school psychologists assess their own capacities and seek supervision or consultation with colleagues as needed (or refer to another professional). Essentially, professional school psychologists bear the responsibility to reflect on their training and experience and to determine whether activities are within their level of competence.

Some types of competence extend beyond clinical skills and include cultural competence, or an understanding of the diverse languages, practices, values, and beliefs of those we serve. The *Principles* notes that school psychologists either must have the knowledge and experience necessary to serve diverse clients, or must obtain the necessary training and supervision or refer their client to a competent practitioner. For example, a second-grade girl who recently migrated from Guatemala has been referred to the school psychologist for counseling, but the school psychologist has no experience working with children or families from Guatemala and knows very little about Latin American culture. Further, she is not informed about conditions in Guatemala or the circumstances of the immigration. The school psychologist needs to learn more about this child's language, culture, and immigration experience to provide competent counseling. She is advised to conduct further research, consult with a colleague who has such competency, or refer the child to another professional with relevant experience.

Competence is not static, and school psychologists must recognize when personal problems limit their capacity to be helpful to others. In such situations, school psychologists seek assistance from others so that children and families receive effective services. For example, a school psychologist who is going through a divorce and is distressed about her own children's adjustment may not be in a good position to lead a support group for children of divorced parents. It is the school psychologist's responsibility to recognize interference in or impairment of the ability to provide effective services and to seek support from colleagues.

School psychologists are lifelong learners who continuously update their knowledge and skills. Attending workshops, seeking continuing education opportunities, and attending trainings help maintain and enhance competence to provide high-quality services to children and families.

Credentialing bodies require school psychologists to document appropriate continuing education to maintain licensure and certification.

The second principle under the *Principles'* broad theme of competence and responsibility concerns accepting responsibility for one's actions (Principle II.2). When practitioners write reports or sign documents, they must check for accuracy. Signing the report indicates approval of and responsibility for the contents of the document. For example, a school psychologist conducts an assessment to determine whether an adolescent is eligible for counseling as a related service, but the report contains errors with respect to reported scores on behavior rating scales. Though the report had already been distributed to members of the team, the school psychologist can add a dated and signed addendum to the report to correct the error.

Another way that school psychologists take responsibility is by monitoring the implementation of recommendations and interventions. When providing counseling services, school psychologists must collect data to determine whether counseling interventions are effective. If the data indicate that progress is not being made, school psychologists have an ethical responsibility to change or discontinue the intervention and/or seek consultation or supervision. Because the ethical guidelines do not specify how long an intervention should be tried before it is modified or discontinued, school psychologists must exercise clinical judgment to make such determinations. Some counseling interventions (for example, a manualized program for depression or anxiety) may have a specific number of sessions after which an evaluation of the outcome is conducted. Similarly, IEPs may specify a duration for counseling intervention, at which time decisions can be made to discontinue, modify, or continue the counseling intervention. When indicated on the basis of clinical judgment, changes can be made before the intended evaluation point. The IEP team must be informed and reach a consensus if an IEP-mandated intervention is significantly changed or discontinued.

Sometimes school psychologists make recommendations that lead to unanticipated negative outcomes. For example, a school psychologist as counselor may recommend that the parents conduct regular family meetings to encourage their child's more open expression and acceptance of feelings, but the child reacts to the change in family dynamics with increased anxiety. In this case, the school psychologist should take responsibility for the unanticipated negative outcomes and work closely with the parents to develop a less risky home intervention or refer the family for counseling, if warranted.

Responsibility also extends to school psychologists supervising graduate students, and the *Principles* notes that supervisors take responsibility for the work of their students. In the context of assessments conducted by a graduate student, a supervisor reads a student's report closely, and by signing the report, indicates approval and responsibility for the work. The counseling context may not be as clear. Though school psychologists and graduate students may cofacilitate counseling groups, graduate students may provide counseling services in the absence of their supervisor and then discuss cases later in supervisory meetings. In such cases, it may be more challenging for the supervisor to take responsibility for the student's work. The burden is then on the supervisor to take the necessary precautions or actions to ensure that responsibility is taken. For example, the supervisor could meet with the referred child, review the evaluation for counseling, participate in writing the counseling IEP, help with selection of techniques and materials, and review with the supervisee the progress toward goals and objectives. Should counseling inadvertently produce negative outcomes (e.g., worsening of social, emotional, or behavioral concerns), the supervisor must take responsibility and work to address these concerns. It should also be recognized that initially negative (and temporary) changes are sometimes part of counseling progress and not necessarily indicators of ineffective intervention.

The third principle under the theme of competence and responsibility concerns responsible assessment and intervention practices (Principle II.3). Most of the standards related to this principle concern assessment, though some standards directly address counseling services as well. Because school psychologists conduct assessments to determine the need for counseling services and to evaluate the efficacy of the services provided, this section begins with a brief overview of the assessment-oriented standards and then focuses more closely on the counseling activities. In general, the following standards apply: (a) assessment should incorporate valid and reliable instruments; (b) school psychologists should evaluate computer-assisted scoring systems for accuracy and validity; (c) standardized administration procedures should be followed; and (d) school psychologists should always consider the effects of current instruction and behavior management practices before diagnosing or classifying children.

With respect to intervention, school psychologists use intervention, counseling and therapy procedures, consultation techniques, and other direct and indirect services that are judged by the profession to be responsible, research-based practice (NASP, 2020a). Consistent with this approach, school psychologists employ a data-based, problem-solving approach that relies on published, scientifically proven methods. Moreover, the *Principles* also states that school psychologists involve parents in interventions and link efforts at home and at school (taking into account ethnic and cultural differences and family resources). Also, in consideration of autonomy and assent, school psychologists communicate with students about intervention plans and, when appropriate, collaborate with students in the development of interventions. Thus, competent and responsible intervention is characterized by carefully selected and developed plans and activities that are evidence based and collaborative, connected to the home, and in alignment with the child's or adolescent's needs.

Within this broad theme of professional competence and responsibility, responsible school-based record keeping is critically important in the delivery of psychological services (Principle II.4). School psychologists keep records to facilitate treatment and transfer of care, to document activities, and to monitor progress. Because records contain private information, school psychologists have an ethical responsibility to maintain the confidentiality of records. To this end, school psychologists ensure that records are not released to other agencies or individuals without parents' or adult students' consent in writing. School psychologists also limit access to private records to only those school professionals who have a legitimate educational interest.

Some school psychologists keep private notes apart from a student's official school or counseling records when the professional does not want the information in the private note to be part of the student's records. These notes, sometimes referred to as *sole possession records* (because the practitioner is the only one with access to such records), are often used by professionals as a memory aid. The *Principles* states that it is ethically permissible to keep private notes; however, all information that is used to make educational decisions about a student must be accessible to parents and adult students. Moreover, a court may subpoena private notes. In school settings, private notes may be of little use to school psychologists and could inadvertently result in the disclosure of sensitive information. Therefore, those who might want to keep private notes should carefully consider the implications of that choice.

Honesty and Integrity in Professional Relationships

Of the four themes within in the NASP *Principles for Professional Ethics*, the theme of honesty and integrity is the broadest and encompasses the ideas of telling the truth, meeting professional commitments, and avoiding multiple relationships. The accurate presentation of professional qualifications (Principle III.1) is integral to honesty and integrity. When interacting with children, families, school personnel, and other professionals, school psychologists must always represent themselves accurately with respect to competence, education, training, experience, and certification and licensing credentials. Graduate students should represent themselves as students under supervision rather than licensed or credentialed professionals. School psychologists should not convey competence in an area for which they have minimal or no training and experience. For example, if parents ask whether a school psychologist can help their child who has a severe posttraumatic stress disorder, the school psychologist who lacks training and experience in this area should make a referral to a qualified practitioner. When a third party misrepresents the qualifications of a school psychologist (e.g., refers to an intern as a school psychologist or to a nondoctoral-level practitioner as doctor), the school psychologist must correct the error. Blatant misrepresentation is clearly unethical, but so are subtle exaggerations of competencies or skills.

According to the *Principles* (III.2), school psychologists are forthright in explaining professional services, roles, and priorities. As with informed consent, they must explain services, roles, and competencies in a clear and understandable manner. When collaborating with others, they must clearly define their role while simultaneously respecting the roles of others. School psychologists communicate their commitment to prioritizing the rights and welfare of children to those with whom they collaborate. Because loyalties can become conflicted, school psychologists make an effort to communicate their priorities and commitments in advance to avoid misunderstandings.

School psychologists work with a wide range of professionals, including but not limited to teachers, administrators, nurses, social workers, counselors, paraprofessionals, and administrative support personnel. When working with other professionals, school psychologists are cooperative and respectful (Principle III.3). Collaboration and mutual respect help meet children's needs effectively and promote the use of all available resources. Often, children receive similar services from more than one professional (e.g., a school psychologist in a counseling role and a school counselor), and in such cases the school psychologist should work to coordinate services. Coordination may require special care to avoid redundancies, align goals, streamline services, and avoid confusion.

Referral is an important part of collaboration, and it is guided by ethical principles. School psychologists referring children and families to other professionals should provide multiple appropriate referral options from which clients can choose. When a student is referred to another professional, all relevant and appropriate individuals, including the client, are notified of the change and reasons for the change. For example, a school psychologist is working with a student to address depression and the student discloses that he was sexually abused. The school psychologist does not have training or experience in working with individuals who have been sexually abused and transfers the student's care to another professional who is competent in this specialized area. It may be possible for the school psychologist to support the student's access to the curriculum by supporting skills to alleviate anxiety and depression while coordinating with a community-based specialist. The referring school psychologist should notify the student and parents of the referral and why it is being made. Checking the accuracy of referral contact information, availability of appointments, and likely duration of a wait list will help build credibility when making referrals.

Mutual respect of others extends to reports written by other professionals. Outside of a supervisory role with graduate students, school psychologists do not make changes to other professionals' reports. Should a school psychologist want someone's report to be altered, they should discuss the concern with the other professional in a respectful manner.

Multiple relationships and other conflicts of interest should be avoided to prevent harm (Principle III.4). Though the NASP *Principles* addresses the issue of multiple relationships, the American Psychological Association's (2017) Ethics Code provides a more detailed overview:

> **APA Ethics Code, Ethical Standard 3.05: Multiple Relationships** (a) A multiple relationship occurs when a psychologist is in a professional role with a person and (1) at the same time is in another role with the same person, (2) at the same time is in a relationship with a person closely associated with or related to the person with whom the psychologist has the professional relationship, or (3) promises to enter into another relationship in the future with the person or a person closely associated with or related to the person. A psychologist refrains from entering into a multiple relationship if the multiple relationship could reasonably be expected to impair the psychologist's objectivity, competence, or effectiveness in performing his or her functions as a psychologist, or otherwise risks exploitation or harm to the person with whom the professional relationship exists. Multiple relationships that would not reasonably be expected to cause impairment or risk exploitation or harm are not unethical.

The school psychologist as counselor may be in a multiple relationship when providing counseling services (professional role) to a child who is also on a softball team the school psychologist coaches outside of school (other role). Note that neither the NASP *Principles* nor the APA code prohibits multiple relationships, but rather state that they should be avoided if there is potential for exploitation or harm. Harm may result from impaired objectivity or efficacy. Multiple relationships can often be avoided by simply referring clients to other practitioners, though opportunities to do so may be very limited in small communities, where multiple relationships may be common. Should multiple relationships present problems, school psychologists can acknowledge the multiple relationship and make every effort to resolve the concern in a way that brings a benefit (the opportunity for counseling) and avoids harm to the client.

Some of the standards that fall under Principle III.4 are not directly related to multiple relationships and conflicts of interest but are nevertheless significant. For example, it is noted that the *Principles* guides professional, rather than private, conduct. In their private lives, school psychologists are free to pursue their personal interests, except to the degree that those interests compromise professional effectiveness.

Sometimes a school psychologist's religious or personal beliefs influence the nature of services provided. For example, a school psychologist who believes that abortion is a sin may be conflicted about working with an adolescent who seeks counseling about her unwanted pregnancy. The *Principles* states that in such cases the school psychologist should inform clients of this fact. When personal beliefs or other conflicts of interest pose a risk of interfering with effectiveness, it is up to the school psychologist to request reassignment of responsibilities or to guide the client to alternative services (though options may be limited in some communities). Of course, protection of the client's confidentiality is of utmost importance when seeking consultation or supervision.

Responsibilities to Schools, Families, Communities, the Profession, and Society

This last theme may not appear to be directly related to the school psychologist's counseling role, but the emphasis on prevention and early intervention is consistent with tiered service delivery and contemporary models of social–emotional support and intervention.

From an ecosystemic perspective, healthy school, family, and community environments contribute to healthy outcomes for individuals. In keeping with Principle IV.1, school psychologists therefore work to promote safe and healthy systems by collaborating, partnering, and coordinating across those systems.

School psychologists also have knowledge of and respect the laws pertaining to school psychology and must consider both the laws and the *Principles* when selecting a course of action. When school psychologists encounter conflicts between the law and ethics, they work to resolve such conflicts using positive, respected, and legal channels.

The *Principles* was developed, in part, to maintain the public's trust in school psychologists. To address this concern, school psychologists monitor their own behaviors and those of colleagues with respect to ethical standards. Therefore, school psychologists understand the *Principles*, apply them to real work scenarios, and consult with colleagues when they encounter challenging ethical dilemmas. When school psychologists suspect that their colleagues are behaving unethically, they first try to informally resolve the concern through a collegial problem-solving process. Though not defined in the *Principles*, this process typically involves discussing the concern with a colleague for clarification (perhaps there was a misunderstanding), education (perhaps the colleague was unaware that the behavior in question was unethical), and collaboration (perhaps together they can develop a plan for corrective action). If this problem-solving approach is not effective, it may be necessary to bring the concern to a supervisor, the state ethics committee, or NASP, through a formal complaint.

Evidence-Based Practice

In a 2005 policy statement, the American Psychological Association defined evidence-based practices as "the synthesis of empirical evidence, clinical expertise, and patient values in implementing treatments." This statement identifies three components of evidence-based practice: empirical evidence, clinical expertise, and patient values. Educators and social service providers are increasingly being asked to demonstrate that the services they provide are evidence based (or, alternatively, research based or empirically based). Definitions of these terms vary, yet they appear to be used interchangeably in some contexts.

The Individuals with Disabilities Education Act 2004 Reauthorization requires a student's Individualized Education Program (IEP) to include "a statement of the special education service and related services and supplementary aids and services, based on peer-reviewed research to the extent practicable, to be provided to the child…" (20 U.S.C. § 1414(d)(1)(a)(1)(IV)). IDEA does not define "peer-reviewed research," nor does it provide an explanation of "to the extent practicable." Nevertheless, the spirit of the law suggests that schools should use interventions that have met some empirical criteria or standards.

Faced with ambiguity, where can a practitioner turn for guidance with respect to evidence-based counseling interventions? The U.S. Department of Education's Coalition for Evidence-Based Policy (2003) published its guide to evidence-supported educational practices, which presents three basic levels: strong evidence, possible evidence, and no evidence. An intervention that meets the criteria for strong evidence is one that is supported with randomized controlled trials that are well designed and implemented and show effectiveness in at least two school settings (including a setting similar to that of the school or classroom in which you would like to use the intervention). Interventions that have been studied but fall short of the strong evidence criteria (e.g., meta-analyses and pre–post studies) fall into the possible evidence category. The document provides additional details and definitions of terms as well as some examples.

A number of websites maintain databases of evidence-based mental health interventions, with descriptions of standards for inclusion of interventions and research that support them. The What Works Clearinghouse (https://ies.ed.gov/ncee/wwc/FWW) provides a link to evidence-based interventions specifically for behavioral problems. SAMHSA's Evidence-Based Practices Resource Center (https://www.samhsa.gov/ebp-resource-center) contains a collection of science-based resources for mental health, including fact sheets, toolkits, and resource guides. The Promising Practices Network on Children and Families (http://www.promisingpractices.net) also provides information about evidence-based practices (this website is no longer updated because of funding constraints but is archived online).

Shernoff, Bearman, and Kratochwill (2017) describe the use of evidence-based mental health practices as essential to the training and practice of school psychologists. However, they identify several barriers to implementation:

- They may be packaged in a way that is not readily accessible or useful in school practice; for example, they focus on only one referral concern, with manualized interventions that reflect that focus).
- They typically target direct, pullout counseling services that may better match practices in clinical or agency settings rather than school settings, where a team approach and indirect consultation services are needed.
- They may be based on research with relatively homogeneous samples that do not reflect the ethnic and cultural diversity found in public schools.
- They tend to be more narrow in scope (e.g., directed at intensive or Tier 3 referral problems), whereas school psychologists should be prepared to intervene more broadly according to tiered models of practice.

Shernoff et al. (2017) propose solutions to these challenges, including (a) adapting current training standards to ensure greater uniformity in exposure to evidence-based mental health practices in graduate programs, (b) strengthening the link between consultation and dissemination of evidence-based practices to other key service providers, (c) tailoring interventions based on individual student responses by using feedback systems, and (d) increasing trainees' skills as evidence-based service providers.

Multiple standards exist for evidence-based intervention, and meeting one set of standards does not necessarily mean that all other sets of standards have been met. Ultimately, it is the practitioner who is responsible for the selection and implementation of interventions. Using the resources at their disposal, school psychologists should select interventions that are supported by research.

The Counseling Relationship

Any discussion of empirically based interventions must include the counseling relationship as a variable that affects outcomes. Efforts to promote evidence-based treatments without considering the counseling relationship are incomplete and potentially misleading. Norcross and Lambert (2018), in their introduction to a special issue of the journal *Psychotherapy* that was devoted to evidence-based psychotherapy relationships, maintain that decades of research that converge with clinical evidence to conclude that the counseling relationship substantially and consistently contributes to psychotherapy outcomes, independent of the therapeutic approach. Theoretical orientation, technique, setting, and materials reciprocally interact with the therapeutic relationship to determine outcomes. According to Norcross and Lambert (2018, citing Gelso and Carter's 1994 operational definition of the therapeutic relationship), it can be described as "the feelings and attitudes that the therapist and the client have toward one another, and the manner in which these are expressed" (p. 2).

School psychologists who feel they have been given limited time to study and practice the theories and techniques learned in their graduate training program, or who have limited access to ideal counseling rooms and materials, may take comfort in knowing the power of their relationship with the client to effect change.

Norcross and Lambert (2018) describe the essential elements of this relationship. Citing meta-analytic results of 16 studies they included in the special issue, they assert that the following are "demonstrably effective" elements of the counseling relationship, including those relevant to counseling with children and adolescents: alliance with both youth and their parents; collaboration; goal consensus; empathy, positive regard, and affirmation; and collection and delivery of client feedback. Elements of the relationship determined to be "probably effective" include congruence/genuineness, emotional expression, cultivating positive expectations, promoting treatment credibility, and repairing alliance ruptures. The elements of self-disclosure and immediacy were found to be promising predictors of outcomes, but insufficient research was done on effectiveness.

Although some of these terms may be more familiar to clinical psychologists than school practitioners, Norcross and Lambert's (2018) findings on the importance of the therapeutic relationship must be considered when engaging in the counseling role. At a minimum, the school psychologist as counselor should focus on the establishment and maintenance of alliances (for example, through informed consent/assent and reliable communication), empathy, goal consensus and collaboration, positive regard and affirmation, and genuineness when establishing counseling relationships.

Response to Intervention and Multitiered Systems of Support

Schools are increasingly using tiered systems of prevention and intervention that are tailored to meet the needs of all students. Response to intervention (RTI) provides high-quality educational practices for all students (e.g., instruction, prevention programs, and social–emotional learning). MTSS addresses systematic barriers and conditions for both students and educators, including attention to the social, emotional, behavioral, and academic aspects of learning to promote equitable access. Although the terms are often used interchangeably in educational settings, MTSS tends to be broader in its conceptualization and implementation than RTI.

Most students should benefit from universal, or Tier 1, prevention practices. When students are identified as being at risk, as indicated by academic and behavioral outcomes, they are provided targeted, or Tier 2, evidence-based interventions, with the expectation that most at-risk students will benefit from the intervention. Ongoing progress monitoring helps assess the degree to which interventions are working, and practitioners use the progress monitoring data to modify interventions as needed. Students who do not improve following intervention are provided more intensive Tier 3 intervention (National Center on Response to Intervention, 2010).

Although the lion's share of RTI attention has been devoted to academic skills, social, emotional, and behavioral skills are increasingly being addressed through RTI and MTSS models (Fazel et al., 2014). For example, the Boston public school system launched an MTSS approach to address social, emotional, and behavioral issues titled *The Comprehensive Behavioral Health Model* in 2012–2013 (Figure 1.1).

The three-tiered model includes partnerships with hospitals, the community, universities, and mental health organizations, with a recent annual report documenting improved academic and behavioral outcomes. (The model and its implementation are described in Pearrow et al., 2016.)

Selection of Techniques

This book was designed with the practitioner in mind. We have made every effort to provide readers with current research regarding effective mental health interventions for school-age children from a *school psychology* perspective. To the extent possible, we report evidence-based practices and consider tiered levels of prevention and intervention. When considering techniques for the specific needs of counseling clients, we propose the following general framework based on our practical experience, within which we explore evidence-based interventions.

Children and adolescents vary widely in their cognitive, verbal, and interpersonal skills. School psychologists often have access to psychological assessment reports or counseling eligibility reports that detail individual characteristics that can guide the counseling approach. These techniques, which are not mutually exclusive nor limited to these subgroups, will be described and elaborated in subsequent chapters. Examples suggest approaches for students with the following characteristics:

FIGURE 1.1. Comprehensive Behavioral Health Model

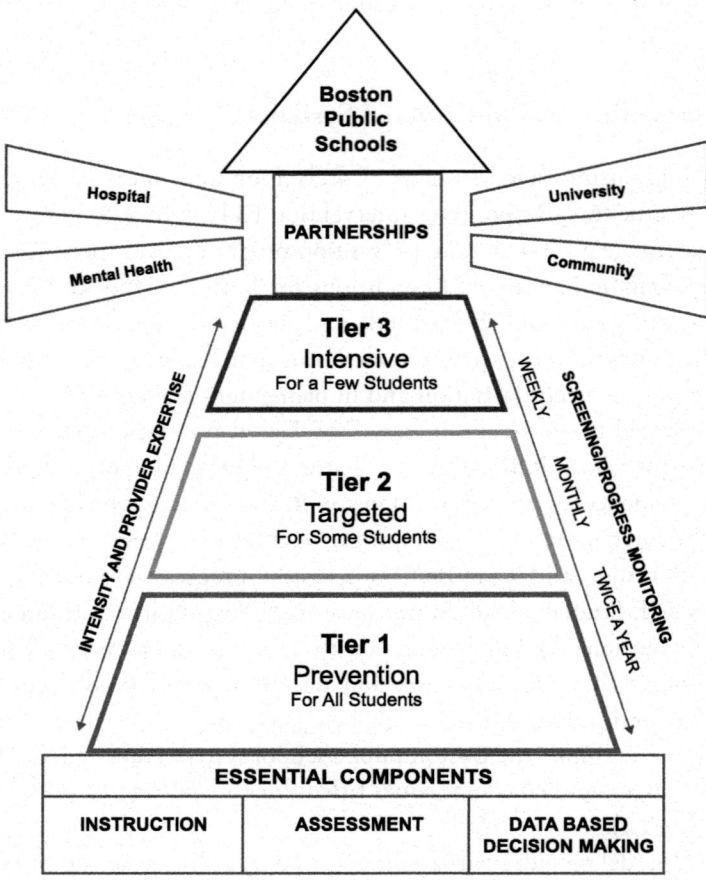

Note. From *Comprehensive Behavioral Health Model*, by Boston Public Schools Behavioral Health Services, 2020 (https://cbhmboston.com/what-is-cbhm/). Copyright 2020 Boston Public Schools. Reprinted with permission.

- *Low cognitive/low verbal abilities.* Students might respond best to (a) behavioral approaches for specific behavior deficits or excesses that are closely coordinated with home efforts; (b) art and play activities with low verbal demand to build a sense of safety; and (c) a counseling relationship that focuses on reliability, acceptance, respect, and fun.
- *High cognitive/low verbal abilities.* Students can benefit from (a) nondirective approaches with low verbal demand, such as sandtray therapy; (b) social modeling techniques, including technology such as movie clips and interactive web activities; and (c) bibliotherapy and interactive games.
- *High cognitive and high verbal abilities.* Students may respond well to (a) cognitive–behavioral techniques that require metacognition, practice, and discussion; (b) reality therapy and solution-oriented therapy techniques that require recollection of past events and conceptualization of future events; and (c) behavioral activation and motivational interviewing, which tap into the ability to conceptualize choices and their outcomes.

Of course, individual characteristics may guide the school psychologist as counselor to select a mix of techniques and materials that is then modified based on the client's response. As we noted earlier, the quality of the relationship is fundamental to successful outcomes, and having flexibility of techniques within the context of goals and objectives is key to achieving that quality!

SUMMARY

In this chapter we have introduced the counseling role of the school psychologist. We traced the history of counseling in school psychology and identified the relative importance of counseling activities in the contemporary professional literature. Ethical standards and principles relevant to counseling were discussed, followed by a review of evidence-based practice guidelines, and including response to intervention and multitiered systems of support as they apply to the counseling role. The counseling relationship was described as an essential component of evidence-based interventions. We also introduced a framework for conceptualizing counseling interventions that takes into account individual characteristics. In subsequent chapters, we will focus on specific theoretical orientations, techniques, and unique child and adolescent circumstances that may warrant counseling services. Of the multitude of counseling theories and related techniques, we selected for inclusion those approaches that appear to offer the most solid empirical foundation and practical tools for practicing school psychologists. Chapter 11 will provide additional tools and resources.

KEY POINTS FOR DISCUSSION

- Why has counseling historically been less emphasized than assessment in professional school psychology?
- How is the counseling role reflected in the ethics and standards for school psychologists?
- How would you approach a colleague who is providing counseling without obtaining informed consent?
- Under what circumstances might a school psychologist justify the use of counseling interventions that do not have an established evidence base?
- How does the school psychologist develop an effective counseling relationship?
- What are the benefits of applying a tiered approach to counseling services in the schools?
- How might you begin to conceptualize counseling sessions for students with limited verbal abilities? For verbally gifted students?

REFERENCES

American Counseling Association. (n.d.). State licensing of professional counselors. Retrieved from https://www.counseling.org/knowledge-center/licensure-requirements/overview-of-state-licensing-of-professional-counselors

American Psychological Association. (2005). Policy statement on evidence-based practice in psychology. Retrieved from https://www.apa.org/practice/guidelines/evidence-based-statement

American Psychological Association. (2017). *Ethical principles of psychologists and code of conduct.* Retrieved from https://www.apa.org/ethics/code/?item=6#305c

American Psychological Association. (2018). *Standards of accreditation for health service psychology and accreditation operating procedures.* Washington, DC: Author.

Armistead, L., Williams, B. B., & Jacob, S. (2011). *Professional ethics for school psychologists: A problem-solving casebook* (2nd ed.). Bethesda, MD: National Association of School Psychologists.

Boston Public Schools Behavioral Health Services. (2020). *Comprehensive behavioral health model.* https://cbhmboston.com/

Bardon, J. I., & Bennett, V. C. (1974). *School psychology.* Englewood Cliffs, NJ: Prentice-Hall.

Child Welfare Information Gateway. (2019). Mandatory reporters of child abuse and neglect: Summary of state laws. Retrieved from https://www.childwelfare.gov/topics/responding/reporting/

Coalition for Evidence-Based Policy. (2003). *Identifying and implementing educational practices supported by rigorous evidence: A user friendly guide.* Washington, DC: U.S. Department of Education, Institute of Education Sciences, & National Center for Education Evaluation and Regional Assistance. Retrieved March 19, 2011, from http://www2.ed.gov/rschstat/research/pubs/rigorousevid/rigorousevid.pdf

Cutts, N. E. (Ed.). (1955). *School psychologists at mid-century.* Washington, DC: American Psychological Association.

Elementary and Secondary Education Act, 20 U.S.C. § 4155 et seq. (2001).

Fagan, T. K., & Wise, P. S. (2007). *School psychology: Past, present, and future.* Bethesda, MD: National Association of School Psychologists.

Fazel, M., Hoagwood, K., Stephan, S., & Ford, T. (2014). Mental health interventions in schools 1: Mental health interventions in schools in high-income countries. *Lancet Psychiatry, 1*(5), 377–387. https://doi.org/10.1016/S2215-0366(14)70312-8

Gelso, C. J., & Carter, J. A. (1994). Components of the psychotherapy relationship: Their interaction and unfolding during treatment. *Journal of Counseling Psychology, 41,* 296–306.

Hildreth, G. H. (1930). *Psychological service for school problems.* Yonkers-on-Hudson, NY: World Book.

Hughes, T., & Minke, K. (2014). Blueprint for health-service-psychology education and training: School psychology response. *Training and Education in Professional Psychology, 8,* 26–30. https://doi.org/10.1037/tep0000019

Individuals with Disabilities Education Improvement Act, 20 U.S.C. § 1400 (2004).

Jacob, S., Decker, D. M., & Lugg, E. T. (2016). *Ethics and law for school psychologists* (7th ed.). Hoboken, NJ: John Wiley & Sons.

Lasser, J., & Klose, L. M. (2007). The impact of social psychological phenomena on ethical decision-making. *School Psychology Review, 36,* 484–500.

McNamara, K. M., Walcott, C. M., & Hyson, D. (2019). *Results from the NASP 2015 membership survey, part two: Professional practices in school psychology [Research report].* Bethesda, MD: National Association of School Psychologists.

Merrell, K. W., Ervin, R. A., & Peacock, G. G. (2012). *School psychology for the 21st century: Foundations and practices* (2nd ed.). New York, NY: Guilford Press.

National Association of School Psychologists. (2015). School psychologists: Qualified health professionals providing child and adolescent mental and behavioral health services. [White paper]. Bethesda, MD: Author

National Association of School Psychologists. (2020a). *Principles for professional ethics.* Bethesda, MD: Author.

National Association of School Psychologists (2020b). *The professional standards of the National Association of School Psychologists.* Bethesda, MD: Author.

National Center on Response to Intervention. (2010). *Essential components of RTI: A closer look at response to intervention.* Washington, DC: U.S. Department of Education, Office of Special Education Programs. Retrieved from https://www.rti4success.org/resource/essential-components-rti-closer-look-response-intervention

National Institute of Mental Health. (2018). Mental illness. https://www.nimh.nih.gov/health/statistics/mental-illness.shtml

Norcross, J. C., & Lambert, M. J. (2018). Psychotherapy relationships that work III. *Psychotherapy, 55*(4), 303–315. http://dx.doi.org/10.1037/pst0000193

Pearrow, M. M., Amador, A., & Dennery, S. (2016). Boston public schools' comprehensive behavioral health model. *Communiqué, 45*(3), 1, 20–22.

Phillips, B. N. (1990). *School psychology at a turning point: Ensuring a bright future for the profession.* San Francisco, CA: Jossey-Bass.

Shernoff, E. S., Bearman, S. K., & Kratochwill, T. R. (2017). Training the next generation of school psychologists to deliver evidence-based mental health practices: Current challenges and future directions. *School Psychology Review, 46*(2), 219–232.

Smith, D. C. (1967). Counseling and psychotherapy in the school setting. In J. F. Magary (Ed.), *School psychological services* (pp. 142–170). Englewood Cliffs, NJ: Prentice-Hall.

Substance Abuse and Mental Health Services Administration. (n.d.). *Evidence-based practice resource center.* https://www.samhsa.gov/ebp-resource-center

Substance Abuse and Mental Health Services Administration and Center for Medicaid and CHIP Services. (2019, July 1). *Joint informational bulletin: Guidance to states and school systems on addressing mental health and substance use issues in schools.* https://store.samhsa.gov/product/guidance-states-and-school-systems-addressing-mental-health-and-substance-use-issues

Vega, D., Lasser, J., & Plotts, C. (2015). Global migration: The need for culturally competent school psychologists. *International School Psychology, 36*(4), 358–374. https://doi.org/10.1177/0143034315587011

Chapter 2

The Counseling Process

OVERVIEW

This chapter provides a practical approach to the counseling process for school psychologists as it focuses on systematic, procedural issues with an emphasis on the unique nature of the school setting. It discusses referrals for counseling services, the problem-solving process, assessment to determine eligibility for counseling services, methods for planning and conducting the Individualized Education Program (IEP) assessment, development of a counseling IEP, informed consent, treatment planning, progress monitoring, and termination.

Because school counseling service delivery models and procedures are different across states and districts, this chapter provides a general set of guidelines and recommendations that can be adapted to meet a variety of needs. Some school psychologists may provide related services under the IDEA category of "psychological services," whereas others may provide "counseling as a related service." Some prefer the former because it is broad and may be used more flexibly, whereas others prefer the latter because it aligns more closely with counseling. In many cases, the language used reflects tradition or preference in a school district rather than meaningful distinctions. We use the terms interchangeably here and encourage school psychologists to consider which may be most appropriate for their unique settings.

The request for counseling as a related service or as part of psychological services is often initiated by a child's teacher, parent, IEP team, or problem-solving team. Related services are available only to students who are served under IDEA, so the assessment to determine eligibility for the related service is usually done in conjunction with an initial full individual evaluation or as a part of a special request.

OBJECTIVES

After reading this chapter, readers should be able to do the following:

- Describe the process of referring a child for counseling as a related service, with an emphasis on prereferral or problem-solving activities.
- Explain how an assessment to determine eligibility for counseling services is conducted.
- Develop measurable counseling goals and objectives based on a referral scenario.
- Discuss the importance of treatment planning for counseling cases.
- Determine whether individual or group counseling services are appropriate.
- Make data-based decisions for a student's dismissal from counseling services.
- Develop a plan to ensure that students have adequate supports in place following dismissal from counseling services.

Referral

The need for counseling services may come to the attention of school psychologists in a variety of ways. A child or adolescent may self-refer, though this scenario has historically been rare. In more recent years, with decreased social stigma around mental health and psychotherapy, mental health professionals have observed an increase in students self-referring. Even so, most referrals are initiated when teachers or parents express concerns about a child's social, emotional, or behavioral functioning. Many parents and teachers may be eager for the referred child to begin receiving services right away, but the first step should be a meeting with the school psychologist, parents, and teachers to discuss a possible problem-solving process. Data-based decision-making and tiered (response to intervention) procedures are central to this process. Through engagement in the problem-solving process, the school psychologist, parents, and teachers may collaboratively ensure that the student's needs are addressed with services that are appropriate for the level and nature of the concerns. We provide more detailed information on counseling in the context of multitiered systems of support (MTSS) in Chapter 3.

School psychologists may use a structured or semistructured interview format to gather data about the initial concerns. (Appendix A has a sample form, *Addressing Behavioral, Social, and Emotional Concerns*, that may be adapted for this purpose.) Ideally the school psychologist will meet with a problem-solving team and the child's parents to address the following questions:

- What is the nature of the concern?
- Does the concern appear to be primarily social, emotional, or behavioral?
- When did you first become aware of this concern?
- How often does this concern present itself?
- Under what circumstances is the concern most likely to appear?
- Under what circumstances is the concern least likely to appear?

- What has been tried at home and school to prevent or eliminate this concern? (If strategies were tried, when were they tried? For how long were they implemented? What was the outcome?)
- Has this concern been brought to the attention of any professionals outside the school setting?

This line of questioning is quite deliberate, and the framing of the referral as a *concern* avoids diagnostic terminology and opens the possibility that the concern may be amenable to a briefer, targeted intervention, thereby avoiding an unnecessarily lengthy commitment of time and resources. While team members may use diagnostic language (e.g., "he's depressed," or "he has bipolar disorder"), the school psychologist may validate those concerns while simultaneously steering the conversation toward the identification of observable behaviors that are measurable and tied to outcome goals. The focus is on problem identification rather than referral for services, and a structured approach for the meeting may be helpful in guiding the team through a systematic process.

During the problem-solving meeting, the school psychologist will be interested in what has already been tried. In keeping with a tiered model of service delivery, counseling services would be recommended only after other options have been tried with integrity (i.e., the intervention was delivered as it was designed without being abandoned prematurely) and have failed to yield the desired outcomes. Many social, emotional, and behavioral concerns can be adequately addressed with minimal changes at home and school without time-intensive interventions such as counseling. A child should not be pulled out of the classroom to receive counseling services—thereby decreasing opportunities for academic engagement—if the concern can be addressed within the classroom, perhaps with changes to instructional delivery methods, and through modifications to the home environment, such as establishing regular sleeping patterns.

Inquiring about the nature of the concern (social, emotional, or behavioral) provides the school psychologist with useful information about the way others think about the referral. For example, a child who bothers other students may be seen by parents and teachers as (a) a child who finds bothering others more rewarding than academic work (behavioral), (b) poor at reading or responding to the social cues of peers (social), or (c) poor at regulating their feelings (emotional). Understanding the theoretical orientation of those who work with the child helps the school psychologist predict the acceptability of those recommendations. It may be helpful to acknowledge that social, emotional, and behavioral concerns are not mutually exclusive categories (i.e., a child's emotional difficulties may manifest in behavioral problems). When there appears to be consensus among the team members, the team can then develop goals to address the concerns and a plan for interventions to achieve those goals. For example, if the team members see the problem as social, then a goal might be to see an increase in a particular social skill and to create a plan to develop that skill.

Parents are a valuable source of information in such meetings and should be encouraged to share their experiences and perspectives. They may have information that can assist school personnel in understanding and dealing with the concern. Through effective partnering, the family and school together may be more effective in addressing their concerns than if either were doing so alone (Lines et al., 2011). Parents who are included in discussions about their children may also feel supported by the school, as illustrated in the case example of Pedro.

CASE EXAMPLE: PEDRO

Pedro Ramirez is a fifth-grade student at Park Elementary School. He is a tall, athletic boy who is well liked by his peers. He has a history of math difficulties and was identified as a student with a disability (learning disability in mathematics calculation) in the third grade. He currently receives special education support. Pedro's teacher, Ms. Toole, has been concerned about Pedro for several weeks. In class he seemed withdrawn and apathetic, and he "has not been himself" since he returned from the spring break. She would like him to receive counseling services to address these concerns.

Ms. Black, the school psychologist, visited with Ms. Toole to discuss her concerns, and they agreed to schedule a meeting with Pedro's parents and other teachers to share information and develop a plan. Prior to the meeting, Ms. Black contacted Pedro's parents and received their informed consent to observe him at school. At the meeting, Ms. Black shared her observations and, in a semistructured format, guided the team through questions similar to those found in Appendix A.

In preparation for the meeting, Ms. Toole spent additional time thinking about her concerns so that she could provide more detailed information to the team. She stated that Pedro was not initiating conversations with other students as he had in the past, and he no longer seemed to take an interest in activities that used to give him pleasure. For example, he had previously participated in a Jeopardy-style current events game in his social studies class, but he no longer seemed at all interested in playing. He also stared off into space and needed frequent redirection.

Pedro's parents reported that they also noted a change in Pedro ever since his uncle died in a car accident over spring break. His mother reported that the loss has been hard for the family and that it has taken an especially heavy toll on Pedro. At home he has been spending most of his time in his room, saying very little to his parents and siblings.

Ms. Black solicited information from the other teachers who were present (art, physical education, and music) and received consistent reports across subject areas. She synthesized the information with her observations of Pedro in the classroom, on the playground, and in the cafeteria and offered the hypothesis that Pedro's change in behavior and mood is likely a manifestation of his grieving process. The other team members agreed.

Next, Ms. Black asked team members what had been tried so far to address this concern. Pedro's teachers reported that they were previously unaware of Pedro's uncle's death but had tried to be patient and encouraging in response to his withdrawal. They reported no improvement. Pedro's parents shared that a social worker visited the family once after the funeral to offer support but that Pedro did not speak with her.

Ms. Black proposed that Pedro be referred to the school guidance counselor for a brief series of grief counseling sessions and that the team meet again to evaluate the efficacy of these sessions. If the desired changes were not observed in response to the counseling, the team would meet again to make additional recommendations. The team members agreed to the proposal, and Ms. Black introduced Pedro's parents to the school counselor to begin initiating counseling services.

The plan for Pedro in the example reflects several key points. First, the team was using data to inform their decisions. Data may be quantitative or qualitative or both (in the example provided, the data were qualitative), but the emphasis here is that the process is being guided by relevant information from key players. Second, the meeting was collaborative and reflected family–school partnering. Third, the team took a tiered approach, trying less intensive interventions before considering more time- and energy-intensive solutions.

A fourth consideration for this example is the idea of goal setting. How will the problem-solving team know whether the grief counseling intervention was successful? The team was acting in Pedro's best interests and wanted him to be more successful, but the results of this plan have yet to be operationalized, that is, the criteria for success have not been identified in such a way that it can be measured. The importance of developing clear, measurable, and realistic counseling goals is discussed later in the chapter. For now our focus is on encouraging problem-solving teams to determine the criteria for success before implementing interventions.

Fifth, if Pedro's work with the school counselor did not yield the desired outcomes, the problem-solving team may explore the provision of counseling as a related service or psychological services. Related services such as counseling can be provided to children who have been identified with disabilities under the Individuals with Disabilities Education Improvement Act (2004 IDEA Reauthorization), provided that certain conditions are met. Because Pedro has been identified with a disability, he has met one criterion to qualify for related services such as occupational therapy, counseling, psychological services, and physical therapy. An additional criterion for related services under IDEA is the student's need to receive counseling or psychological services in order to benefit from instructional services in special education, in Pedro's case, in math computation.

Being identified as a student with a disability is necessary but not sufficient for the provision of related services. Eligibility for the related service must be based on data from an assessment by the school psychologist or another professional who will provide the related service.

Assessment to Determine Eligibility for Counseling Services

An assessment to determine eligibility for counseling as a related service requires answers to a number of questions. Some of these questions are directly related to the eligibility requirements of related services, whereas others are more useful in the planning and delivery of counseling services. Although specific questions will likely vary across students, the following list is representative of a typical set of questions:

- What is the history of the social, emotional, and behavioral concerns? (For example, when did they first emerge, when did they become a problem?)
- What is the student's present level of performance in the area of social, emotional, and behavioral functioning? (Note strengths and deficits.)
- What are the student's competencies and how do they suggest a capacity to benefit from counseling as a related service? (For example, note that the student is able to express thoughts and feelings, is motivated to improve behavior, and has the capacity to work well with adults.)
- Does the student need counseling as a related service to benefit from her educational program?
- What are the antecedents and consequences of the problem?
- What is the frequency of the concern?
- When is the student most successful?
- What interventions have been tried so far to address the concerns?
- How long were interventions tried?
- To what extent have interventions been successful?

- If counseling is indicated, what are the treatment goals? (Goals may be general at the assessment stage but will need to become more specific when a treatment plan is put into place.)

These questions are similar to the questions asked at the initial problem-solving stage, discussed earlier in this chapter. In fact, the notes from the initial problem-solving process may be used as a source of data for the assessment.

The next step is to identify additional sources of data that should be considered when conducting an assessment to determine eligibility for counseling as a related service. School psychologists rely on multiple sources of data and a variety of data collection methods—for example, observations, interviews, rating scales, and other norm-referenced measures of social, emotional, and behavioral functioning—in the interest of conducting high-quality assessments. Moreover, assessment methods should be consistent with the Standards for Educational and Psychological Testing (American Educational Research Association, American Psychological Association, & National Council on Measurement in Education, 2014) and relevant ethical guidelines (American Psychological Association, 2017; National Association of School Psychologists, 2010).

Students who receive special education services will have already been assessed to determine whether they have a disability and are eligible for special education services, and their records will contain a significant amount of information that will be helpful to the school psychologist who is assessing to determine eligibility for psychological services or counseling as a related service. Therefore, a good place for the school psychologist to start the assessment process is with a review of existing records. The following may be helpful: the student's full individual evaluation, disciplinary records, attendance records, medical records, private psychological evaluations, records from previous interventions (both in and out of school), and notes and records from problem-solving or RTI team meetings.

A student's records give the school psychologist a better understanding of the background and history, particularly with regard to past intervention outcomes, but they rarely provide sufficient information to capture the child's current functioning and recent history. One of the best ways to gather data about the presenting concern, as well as the child's strengths and other assets, is to conduct interviews with individuals who know the child well and can provide reliable information (typically parents or guardians, the student, and teachers). Although school psychologists can use any number of structured interview formats, they also can easily develop individualized, semistructured interviews to gather the most useful information. The interview has some clear advantages over other methods, such as behavior rating scales. Interviews give the school psychologist and the student some face-to-face time during which trust and rapport are built. A semistructured interview also gives the student an opportunity to ask questions and provide information that may not have been anticipated. Moreover, the interview format tends to generate rich, detailed responses that are not available from rating scales. Some students may articulate their own goals in an interview, and these may later become part of the IEP. Interview questions should be crafted that will answer the assessment questions listed earlier in this section.

Norm-referenced data also play an important role in the assessment, and a number of published, norm-referenced measures are available. For example, a school psychologist may consider any of the following (or some combination) in this brief list when conducting an assessment to determine eligibility for counseling as a related service:

- Behavior Assessment System for Children, Third Edition (BASC-3; Reynolds & Kamphaus, 2015)
- Children's Depression Inventory 2 (CDI-2; Kovacs, 2010)
- Revised Children's Manifest Anxiety Scale, Second Edition (RCMAS-2; Reynolds & Richmond, 2008)
- Vineland Adaptive Behavior Scales, Third Edition (Vineland-II; Sparrow, et al., 2016)
- Social Skills Improvement System (SSIS; Gresham & Elliott, 2008)

Standardized, norm-referenced measures allow the school psychologist to determine the degree to which the child's reported behavior deviates from established norms. For example, in interviews, parents and teachers may express concerns about anxious behaviors, but BASC-3 and RCMAS-2 data may indicate that behaviors associated with anxiety are within normal limits.

Ratings from teachers, parents, and other informants do not always align, and the novice practitioner may find the lack of concordance disconcerting. For example, norm-referenced data collected from Teacher A suggest clinically significant depression, but Teacher B's ratings suggest that the same behaviors are within normal limits. Ratings on the same student from the parent suggest clinically significant attention problems, but no depression. Naturally, a consistent endorsement of items in the area of depression would suggest a clear diagnostic picture, and divergent ratings may appear to call the validity of the assessment into question.

School psychologists recognize that informants in different roles (e.g., teacher, parent, student) have unique perspectives and frequently report divergent data. Therefore, the lack of concordance is an *expected* finding, particularly when informants interact with the student in different settings (e.g., classroom, home). The responses from multiple informants may also show that the behaviors are present in some, but not all, settings (and that expectations, rules, antecedents, and consequences vary across settings).

Information regarding the administration, scoring, and interpretation of measures used in an assessment are beyond the scope of this book but are part of the broader training in school psychology. As with other kinds of assessment, the school psychologist integrates the findings into a written report that can be easily understood by parents and other members of the IEP team. The report should communicate whether the student is eligible for counseling as a related service and make recommendations. Part of the eligibility criteria includes the determination that the child's symptoms interfere with their educational experience, and that counseling as a related service is needed. If the team determines that the student is not eligible for counseling services, then the school psychologist should indicate what available services might be appropriate as alternatives (e.g., general education counseling, behavior management, community-based family services, or consultation).

For those students who are eligible for psychological services or counseling as a related service, the recommendations in the report should be used in the development of IEP goals. For example, the report may recommend social skills training to address deficits, and goals may be developed to address those concerns. Recommendations in the report do not need to be as specific as IEP goals, but they should communicate the general focus of the intervention. For example, a school psychologist might recommend that counseling interventions focus on decreasing withdrawal and increasing academic engagement with peers and teachers. Appendix B shows an example of a report, though the content and organization of such reports will vary across school districts.

The completed report should be shared with the parents or guardians and members of the IEP team, who ultimately decide whether to initiate counseling as a related service and develop the IEP goals and objectives. Typically, the individual providing the service (in many cases the school psychologist) will independently develop a draft of a counseling IEP and then seek input from members of the IEP team. Some school psychologists may also share the draft IEP with the student for input, which may help motivate the student to engage in the counseling process. The process of seeking student input will vary depending on the developmental characteristics of the student, but it may look something like this:

School psychologist: Hi Amanda, I wanted to show you something I've been working on.
Amanda: What's that?
School psychologist: Well, now that I've gotten to know you better and talked with your parents and teachers, it seems that you have a lot of strengths, like that way you're able to communicate your needs and how well you get along with your teachers.
Amanda: That's true.
School psychologist: I also learned that one of your challenges is getting along with other kids. Is that something you'd like to improve?
Amanda: Yeah, I would like to have more friends.
School psychologist: That's something we can work on. Look, I wrote this goal for counseling (*shows the goal to Amanda*). Is that something you'd be willing to aim for?
Amanda: Sure.
School psychologist: What other goals do you have?
Amanda: I'd like to be better at controlling my anger.
School psychologist: Sounds like that's an important goal to you. May I add it to this other one?
Amanda: Yeah, that would be good.
School psychologist: Great, if it's ok with you I'll share this with your IEP team and get their input.
Amanda: OK thanks.

Once consensus regarding the counseling goals is reached, the IEP team will formally adopt the final version of the counseling IEP. The team will also be charged with responsibility for determining how much time will be dedicated to counseling services, projecting an end date, and selecting a method of evaluation to determine whether the intervention is effective.

Development of Counseling IEP Goals and Objectives

The goals and objectives of a counseling IEP must follow the same requirements as any other IEP outlined in the 2004 IDEA Reauthorization. According to that statute, the IEP must include the following:

(I) A statement of the child's present levels of academic achievement and functional performance . . .

(II) A statement of measurable annual goals, including academic and functional goals designed to (aa) meet the child's needs that result from the child's disability to enable the child to be involved in and make progress in the general education curriculum; and (bb) meet each of the child's other educational needs that result from the child's disability;

(III) A description of how the child's progress toward meeting the annual goals described in subclause II will be measured, and when periodic reports on progress the child is making toward meeting the annual goals (such as through the use of quarterly or other periodic reports concurrent with the issuance of report cards) will be provided. (Pub. L. 108-446, 118 Stat. 2708)

A good starting point for the development of a counseling IEP is the statement of the student's present level of performance with respect to social, emotional, and behavioral functioning. For the counseling IEP, this statement should indicate not only the concerns that warrant counseling but also the student's assets. The statement may be brief, as in the following example:

> *Amanda's frequent angry outbursts and difficulty getting along with peers have a significant negative effect on her academic progress and development of socialization skills. She has a strong desire to please adults and is motivated to improve her social, emotional, and behavioral functioning.*

The statement of the student's present level of performance can come from the information that was gathered and organized in the assessment for determining eligibility for counseling services. The eligibility report should contain the details regarding the student's present level of performance.

The next step is to develop the IEP goals and objectives. In keeping with the 2004 IDEA Reauthorization, goals and objectives need to be written in a way that supports educational needs. Some find this paradoxical, because counseling goals seem to be distinct from educational goals. However, a helpful way to frame the relationship is to think about aspects of the present level of performance that interfere with the student's education. Children who are depressed, anxious, withdrawn, or aggressive have obstacles that interfere with their learning. If counseling can address the social, emotional, and behavioral concerns, then learning is more likely to occur. Though this may seem obvious, the fact that counseling goals support learning may not always be apparent to all members of the IEP team, so it may be helpful for school psychologists to underscore this important relationship.

IEP annual goals are broad and are designed to be achieved by the end of the school year, whereas objectives are more specific and short-term. A useful framework for conceptualizing goals involves categorizing them by social, emotional, and behavioral domains. This distinction is not to suggest that social goals are not also behavioral (e.g., a frequent goal is to increase social behaviors). Rather, the classification is a way of thinking about the emphasis, such as social skills versus emotional regulation versus compliance. In the example above, in Amanda's present level of performance, her angry outbursts and difficulty getting along with peers were the primary concerns. The angry outbursts may be addressed through emotional goals, and the peer relations may be addressed through social goals, as follows:

Annual Goal. Amanda will make measurable progress in the area of emotional functioning.

Annual Goal. Amanda will make measurable progress in the area of social functioning.

Two observations can be made about these goals. First, they are written very broadly because the objectives will set out specific ways of moving toward goal completion. Second, the word *measurable* is deliberate and important. The school psychologist will gather data throughout the intervention to track progress toward the completion of the goal. If the goals and objectives are not measurable, the team cannot know whether the intervention is effective.

The statement of objectives is much more specific and includes criteria for mastery. The statement also includes the methods that will be used to evaluate progress, as shown for Amanda's first annual goal.

Annual Goal. Amanda will make measurable progress in the area of emotional functioning.

- Objective 1: Amanda will accurately identify signs that she is getting angry before she has an outburst (effective at identifying signs four out of five times).
- Objective 2: Amanda will use appropriate ways of expressing her anger (expresses anger in appropriate ways three out of five times).
  Methods for evaluating: Observation, counselor-developed measurement tool, BASC-3.

At this stage, the counseling IEP does not yet indicate what kind of intervention will be used. The goals and objectives identify the destination, but the school psychologist can use many ways to get there. Given the same goals and objectives, one school psychologist may use a cognitive–behavioral approach, whereas another may rely on a play therapy approach. For some students, group counseling may be indicated, whereas others may benefit from individual sessions (a topic we discuss in more detail later in this chapter). The IEP team develops and approves the goals and objectives, but it generally allows the service provider to make decisions regarding the intervention.

The mastery criteria (set at 4/5 for the first objective and 3/5 for the second objective) are set using the assessment data that have been collected. The criteria will be different for each student based on the current level of functioning. Amanda's objectives show that at the time her counseling IEP was developed, she was accurately identifying signs that she was getting angry two out of five times. Similarly, she was employing appropriate ways of expressing her anger fewer than three out of five times. In other words, the objective strives for an improvement from the baseline.

Progress on Amanda's objectives will be measured with a variety of data sources—observation, a counselor-developed measurement tool, and BASC-3. These methods give the school psychologist an opportunity to gather both quantitative and qualitative data, and the notation lets the IEP team know at the outset how progress will be measured.

Writing unique, specific objectives for each student can be challenging, but using generic objectives for students fails to address their individual needs. Moreover, when school psychologists use the same objectives for all students, IEP team members recognize that the process is not individualized. However, school psychologists do not have to start with a blank slate each time they sit down to write goals and objectives. Many districts have developed banks or libraries from which objectives can be selected and then modified to fit the unique needs of the student. The following are additional examples of counseling objectives:

Annual Goal. The student will make measurable progress in the area of behavioral functioning.

- Objective: The student will follow school rules as evidenced by a decrease in disruptive behaviors (fewer than two disruptive behaviors per week).

Annual Goal. The student will make measurable progress in the area of emotional functioning.

- Objective: The student will demonstrate coping strategies for dealing with stress through a decrease in compulsive behavior (positive response to redirection 90% of the time).

Annual Goal. The student will make measurable progress in the area of social functioning.

- Objective: The student will demonstrate self-control in social situations by decreasing negative statements to others (no more than 10% of statements are negative).

Treatment Planning

Once the IEP team has adopted a set of counseling goals and objectives, the school psychologist begins to plan the intervention. Having a clear plan based on the goals and objectives helps maintain a focused approach to counseling and can be used for the transfer of care if needed. For some school psychologists, a written treatment plan may be required by the licensing or certifying agency (e.g., the state entity that credentials school psychologists). Treatment plans do not need to be elaborate, but they should be fairly specific. In addition to treatment goals and selected methods, the plan should include an estimated number of sessions needed to meet the counseling goals. The school psychologist should review the treatment plan with parents or guardians as part of the informed consent process.

The treatment plan serves as both compass and map. School psychologists new to the job or under training supervision may feel "stuck" on one or more of their counseling cases. They will have met with the child several times and established rapport, yet they are not sure that the sessions are going anywhere. In many cases, this problem is the result of neglecting to pay attention to the treatment plan and goals. When practitioners refocus on the original goals and objectives, they can see more clearly in what direction they need to move the counseling.

The treatment plan does not lock the school psychologist into a course of action that cannot be changed. In fact, school psychologists must pay attention to the effects of the intervention and of any changes in the student's environment and adjust the treatment as needed. For example, if a student does not respond to a structured, verbal approach to counseling, the school psychologist may try a play-based approach. Any changes made to the treatment plan must be documented to maintain accurate and current records.

Informed Consent

Informed consent must be obtained both for the assessment and for the counseling services themselves. School counselors and school psychologists may handle informed consent differently, partly because of their different ethical codes and training—the American School Counselor Association and the National Association of School Psychologists, respectively—but perhaps also because of differences in policies and procedures related to special education. What follows is an overview of informed consent for counseling services consistent with the practice of school psychology.

School psychologists always obtain informed consent from parents and assent from the student before they assess a student to determine eligibility for counseling services and before they provide counseling services to children or adolescents. However, in some emergency situations, such as suicidal intent or a suicide attempt, they may provide immediate services without consent and then follow a more formal consent process after the situation stabilizes. (See Chapter 1 for a more thorough discussion of informed consent.)

Because informed consent is required by organizational (e.g., NASP, APA, etc.) codes of ethics, as well as by school district policy and state licensing and certification boards, some practitioners focus disproportionately on the technical requirements and overlook the therapeutic elements of informed consent, or even neglect to think of informed consent as part of the counseling process. However, informed consent is more than compliance with requirements and, if done well, can contribute to a successful counseling relationship.

One of the ways that informed consent and assent facilitate the counseling process is by building trust with students and their families. When the school psychologist spends time with children and adolescents explaining the purpose of counseling and the approach and activities that will be used in counseling, students are likely to feel more comfortable and trusting of the school psychologist. Similarly, parents may take a more active role as partners with a school psychologist who takes the time to provide them with detailed information about counseling. In Chapter 1, we noted that forming an alliance with students and their parents predicts positive outcomes.

Informed consent may also provide the school psychologist with important information that can be useful for the development of a treatment plan. For example, during the course of the informed consent process, parents may communicate new details about the child. The school psychologist may tell the parents that she intends to use a variety of expressive arts media (paints and clay) with the child, and the parents tell her that the child has always had an aversion to touching clay. Occasionally, a child may even be allergic to the dyes or additives in art materials. Knowing this, the school psychologist can avoid those mediums and ask the parents for suggestions. In this regard, informed consent can be an opportunity for information to flow in both directions. For this reason, school psychologists are encouraged to have a face-to-face meeting with families rather than send a form home to be signed and returned. Also, the school psychologist providing the counseling services should handle the informed consent process, rather than delegate the task to another individual.

Over the course of treatment, the school psychologist monitors the student's progress; consults with teachers, families, and others; and revisits informed consent as needed for changes in the treatment. Moreover, using informed consent as a process (rather than a discrete event) gives others who have an interest in the child's progress an opportunity to share new information and ask questions. For psychological services or counseling as a related service, significant changes in goals, techniques, number of sessions, or other procedures will require that the IEP team meet to revise the counseling IEP.

Individual Versus Group Counseling

Students may benefit from individual or group counseling, and school psychologists may consider a number of factors when deciding on the most appropriate treatment modality. Generally speaking, taking a close look at the student's characteristics and variables will help the school psychologist determine what kind of approach will be most helpful to the student and maximize the likelihood that the counseling goals will be reached. In this section we consider not only student characteristics but also some features of individual and group counseling that may be taken into account.

Some students may be good candidates for group counseling, whereas others may be better suited for individual counseling. The school psychologist may consider the following list of student characteristics, though the list should not be used in a formulaic if–then decision-making scheme. Rather, school psychologists are encouraged to think carefully about these variables when making decisions about the counseling format:

- Student's capacity to listen to others
- Turn-taking abilities
- Need for privacy
- Willingness to adhere to group rules
- Language development (receptive and expressive)
- Severity of the student's emotional or behavioral interference
- History of aggression
- Nature of the student's IEP goals (e.g., social, emotional, behavioral)
- Student's cognitive development
- Student's desire to receive services in individual or group format
- Parental support for group work

Using the list above, consider Danielle, a ninth-grade student who receives special education services under the classification traumatic brain injury. Her IEP counseling goals focus primarily on improving her social skills, and Danielle has expressed great interest in receiving group counseling over individual counseling. Since her brain injury she has had difficulty with impulse control and has demonstrated some aggression toward peers and adults. Her receptive language is much better than her expressive language. The school psychologist may believe that group counseling is often a good modality for social skills development but may also worry that Danielle's aggressive behavior and impulse control challenges could be disruptive to the group. Additional information from parents and teachers may help the school psychologist determine the best course of action.

In addition to thinking carefully about unique student variables, contemplating the advantages and disadvantages of individual and group counseling also becomes a critical part of the decision-making process. Though group counseling may appear to be a more efficient use of time (e.g., I can see eight students in one session instead of eight individual sessions), saving time isn't a good reason to provide services in a group format, particularly if the student's goals and characteristics align poorly with that modality. So what are some reasons why groups may be appropriate? The follow list includes some advantages to consider:

- Group members can share common goals.
- They have opportunities to help each other.
- Group members experience *universality*, or the idea that they are less likely to feel alone when they recognize that others are overcoming similar challenges.
- Social skills with peers can be practiced safely with a skilled counselor present.
- Students can receive immediate peer feedback and a therapeutic setting.
- Members can practice relating with others and increase their ability to listen and share.
- Group interactions allow members to generalize new skills to real-world challenges.

Though there are many benefits to group work, school psychologists must always be cautious when forming groups to ensure group members' safety and confidentiality. Not all students are comfortable in groups, and some may have a hard time respecting the privacy of others. Moreover, students who are likely to harm other members of the group may not be good candidates. To minimize these risks, school psychologists may initially meet with each potential group member individually to discuss group rules, confidentiality, safety, and so on. The school psychologist may ask questions such as the following: Is participation in a group something that you would like to try? Are you able to follow these group rules? Do you understand that what is said in the group stays in the group? Naturally, the questions would be adapted to meet the language and developmental needs of potential group members.

A final consideration is competency. Group work requires a set of skills and experiences that not all school psychologists have, so it's the responsibility of the school psychologist to ensure that he has the training and skills to deliver group counseling, or that he has appropriate supervision and consultation while building these skills. The development of group counseling skills may also be supported by reading, attending workshops, and participating in trainings.

In the next section, we consider how school psychologists move from newly developed IEPs for psychological services or counseling services to preparing for the delivery of services. Whether delivering individual or group counseling, school psychologists must be organized and prepared, collaborative, and mindful of the goals and objectives.

Strategies for Organizing Sessions and Cases

This section discusses some practical considerations for planning, coordinating, and carrying out counseling sessions in school. Because of the diversity of school settings, these examples may not apply equally well to all situations, but they can provide ideas for adaptation.

In the private practice setting, the psychologist frequently works in isolation with a great deal of autonomy. They schedule sessions with the parent, see the child, and maintain their own records for their own use. Alternatively, school systems are much more complex and require greater coordination and collaboration among interconnected parties. Consequently, the school psychologist must work with teachers and administrators and parents to identify the most appropriate times to work with students. For example, without careful planning and coordination, a student who struggles with math may miss critical instructional opportunities if removed from math class for counseling sessions each week. Therefore, school psychologists must work closely with families and school personnel to develop a counseling schedule that considers the needs of all parties. Ideally, the student is seen on a consistent, predictable basis, though situations such as fire drills, absences, crises, or benchmark testing may require flexibility.

The complexities aside, counseling in school settings has advantages as well: children are there every day, all day; the context is naturalistic, in that the child interacts with peers and authority figures within different learning contexts; and opportunities exist for observing and evaluating the transfer and maintenance of new skills, to name a few advantages. School psychologists working in the schools also have the opportunity to collaborate with teachers, administrators, specialists, and parents to support the student's progress on counseling goals.

The first session brings with it many opportunities. In this session the school psychologist can communicate to the student details about the counseling process, answer any questions that the student may have, and build rapport with the student. The first session is important because it sets the tone and expectations. Every school psychologist has their individual personality and style, so the first session is a chance for the student to get to know the counselor as a person. Similarly, the first session is an opportunity for the school psychologist to get to know the child outside of the context of referral and assessment. This is an opportunity to see the child beyond a diagnosis or classification and appreciate the child as a person.

The first session can be used to build rapport through conversation, a game, or any other method that seems developmentally appropriate for the student. The counselor may also use this time to review the student's goals and objectives, discuss methods or techniques, and enlist the student's commitment to collaboration. If the counseling methods being considered have a strong psychoeducational component, such as cognitive–behavioral therapy or reality therapy, this discussion is especially important. Some students also may need more time dedicated to rapport building than others. The student's development and cognitive and language skills may drive some of the school psychologist's decisions about how to conduct the first session.

The bulk of the work rests between the bookends of the first session, described above, and the end of counseling, described later. The work that falls in the middle is an ongoing process of intervention and progress monitoring. The school psychologist provides counseling services and periodically collects data to assess the effect that the intervention is having, then uses this formative assessment to adjust the treatment plan. Progress will be measured using the methods that the team identified in the IEP.

Because the counseling services described in this chapter are being delivered through the IEP plan, the counselor must report on progress to parents and other members of the IEP team at least as often as report cards are sent home (typically every 6 or 9 weeks, though the interval may be determined by the IEP team). Progress reports, as shown here, should provide some information about the counseling process and movement toward the student's treatment plan goals. If the counselor does not anticipate achieving the goals by the end of the year, then the IEP team must meet to address the concern.

SAMPLE PROGRESS REPORT

Annual Goal 1. Jamie will make measurable progress in the area of behavioral functioning.

- Objective: Demonstrate productive behavior in academic situations by increasing task completion (90% completion).

Annual Goal 2. Jamie will make measurable progress in the area of emotional functioning.

- Objective: Jamie will demonstrate adaptive coping strategies when facing stressors (70% of coping strategies are adaptive).

Progress Report

Jamie received six counseling sessions this reporting period. Consultation with teachers and his mother played an instrumental role in monitoring and modifying his behavior. He has demonstrated greatly improved coping strategies (65% are adaptive) and significant gains in assignment completion (80% completion). We anticipate that Jamie will meet his annual IEP counseling goals by the end of the school year.

Dismissal and Termination

A student may be dismissed from psychological services (or counseling as a related service) when goals and objectives are met or if the counselor determines that the interventions have been ineffective. The decision to terminate individual counseling must be a data-based decision, so the school psychologist must be prepared to share data with the IEP team to support dismissal. The data collection methods should be consistent with those identified in the IEP and progress reports.

In some cases, members of the IEP team may not support dismissal from counseling. When the school psychologist's recommendation for dismissal from counseling is met with resistance, they should listen carefully to those dissenting opinions. The role of the school psychologist in the IEP team is not to persuade others to follow recommendations, but rather to provide useful information so that team members, and parents or guardians in particular, can make informed choices (Lasser & Klose, 2007). Often concerns about dismissal are tied to a belief that the student will not succeed without the support of counseling, or that termination will result in the removal of a safety net. In the spirit of providing accurate and helpful information to team members, the school psychologist may share the following with the IEP team:

- Data documenting the achievement of goals and objectives
- Information about support services available to the student if IEP counseling is discontinued
- A reminder that the initial goal of counseling was ultimately dismissal from counseling (or, alternatively stated, the goal was for the student to manage their behavior, emotions, and social skills with greater independence)
- Assurance that the student's needs are being met in the least restrictive environment

If the IEP team decides to continue counseling, that decision should also be based on data from the progress monitoring assessment. When team members interpret the data differently, they must collaborate to develop an appropriate program for the student.

Should the team support the decision to discontinue counseling, the school psychologist has a responsibility to ensure that the student understands that services will end and to prepare the student for that conclusion. For many students, ending counseling services does not present a challenge, and the transition out of counseling is unremarkable. Others may become attached to the counselor and be disappointed that the counseling is ending. The school psychologist should make every effort to encourage the student's successful transition by preparing the student in advance (e.g., "We will have three more sessions."), framing the final session as an achievement or accomplishment (e.g., "Congratulations! You've met all of your goals."), and developing a plan for support should difficulties resurface (e.g., consulting, a behavioral intervention plan, or family referrals). For many students, planning a special event for the final session encourages the sense of accomplishment and closure. For example, the school psychologist and student may decide to have lunch in the counseling office, play a favorite game, or create an art project to take away from the counseling relationship.

In school settings, most children easily adjust to the discontinuation of counseling services. They are accustomed to getting new teachers each year and are quite adaptable. The school psychologist should not assume that termination will be devastating for a child but should observe and monitor (largely through consultation) to ensure that the child is doing well after counseling ends. Moreover, as counseling sessions are coming to an end, the school psychologist should promote the student's independence and capacity to self-regulate. For some children, gradual discontinuation of counseling may be used, with longer periods between sessions or brief check-in sessions to reduce dependence and monitor adjustment.

SUMMARY

This chapter has provided a practical guide to counseling as a related service. It described the referral process, assessment to determine eligibility for counseling services, and the development of a counseling IEP, plus the ways school psychologists monitor and report progress, change counseling approaches as needed, and discontinue counseling services when the data indicate that termination is appropriate.

KEY POINTS FOR DISCUSSION

- How does the provision of counseling services through an IEP differ from counseling services provided through general education?
- In what ways is the assessment to determine eligibility for counseling services similar to and different from other assessments?
- How does the school psychologist as counselor collaborate with other professionals and parents or guardians?
- What can school psychologists do to ensure that children who are dismissed from counseling continue to receive support?

REFERENCES

American Educational Research Association, American Psychological Association, & National Council on Measurement in Education. (2014). *Standards for educational and psychological testing*. Washington, DC: American Educational Research Association.

American Psychological Association. (2017). *Ethical principles of psychologists and code of conduct*. Retrieved from http://www.apa.org/ethics/code/ethics-code-2017.pdf

Gresham, F. M., & Elliott, S. N. (2008). Social Skills Improvement System. Minneapolis, MN: NCS Pearson.

Individuals with Disabilities Education Improvement Act of 2004. Pub. L. No. 108-446, § 302, 118 Stat. *2647* (2004).

Kovacs, M. (2010). Children's Depression Inventory 2. New York, NY: Multi-Health Systems.

Lasser, J., & Klose, L. (2007). School psychologists' ethical decision making: Implications from selected social psychological phenomena. *School Psychology Review, 36*, 484–500.

Lines, C., Miller, G. E., & Arthur-Stanley, A. (2011). *The power of family-school partnering (FSP): A practical guide for school mental health professionals and educators*. New York, NY: Routledge.

National Association of School Psychologists. (2010). *Principles for professional ethics*. Bethesda, MD: Author.

Reynolds, C. R., & Kamphaus, R. W. (2015). Behavior Assessment System for Children, Third Edition. Bloomington, MN: PsychCorp.

Reynolds, C. R., & Richmond, B. O. (2008). Revised Children's Manifest Anxiety Scale, Second Edition (RCMAS-2). Los Angeles, CA: Western Psychological Services.

Sparrow, S. S., Cicchetti, D. V., & Saulnier, C. A. (2016). Vineland Adaptive Behavior Scales, Third Edition (Vineland-3). San Antonio, TX: Pearson.

Chapter 3

Counseling Within Multitiered Systems of Support

OVERVIEW

Counseling interventions always occur in a context. In school systems, this context includes other prevention and problem-solving models. This chapter takes a look at a broader role of the school psychologist as counselor, with a focus on problem-solving teams and special education rules, procedures, and processes. Chapter 2 addressed the counseling process and discussed eligibility for counseling as a related service, Individualized Education Program (IEP) goals and objectives for counseling, and progress monitoring and evaluation. This chapter focuses more directly on school-based counseling in the context of multitiered systems of support (MTSS). It considers how counseling services are delivered in the context of MTSS or response to intervention (RTI) and positive behavioral intervention and support (PBIS), as well as counselor roles that go beyond the direct services of individual and group counseling.

OBJECTIVES

After reading this chapter, readers should be able to do the following:

- Describe the relationship between counseling and psychological assessment.
- Identify systems and parameters that shape the school psychologist's counseling activities.
- List the steps of the problem-solving model.
- Explain how counseling fits within the MTSS/RTI framework.
- Demonstrate how school psychologists facilitate the transition from counseling in general education to special education.

- Describe how the school psychologist as counselor can use PBIS to promote positive social, emotional, and behavioral outcomes.
- Discuss the ways in which the school psychologist collaborates with the IEP team and other systems.
- Recognize the roles, beyond the provision of individual and group counseling, that are available to the school psychologist as counselor.

Introduction

School psychologists have a degree of freedom and latitude in defining their roles and functions, but laws, policies, standards, and procedures place some limits and parameters on school psychologists' activities (as do time constraints, ethical guidelines, personal competencies, and so on). Moreover, schools are complex systems and subsystems that present challenges to professional educators (Kershner & McQuillan, 2016; Schaughency, Alsop, & Dawson, 2010; Tschannen-Moran & Gareis, 2014).

Although one can easily view the complexities and challenges of psychology in the schools as obstacles to effective practice, the school psychologist has the potential to work at multiple levels to effect positive change within systems, a flexibility not typically characteristic of community-based providers who are constrained by billing and insurance requirements. This chapter describes some of the possible opportunities for the school psychologist as counselor, with an emphasis on the ways the role interfaces with teams and systems.

Over time, the traditional line between general education and special education has blurred with the increased application of the problem-solving process and MTSS/RTI. Whereas historically educators drew clear boundaries between general and special education activities (through funding, programming, eligibility, and policies), more school systems are recognizing that services can be more effectively and efficiently delivered when problems are conceptualized not through the framework of special education eligibility, but rather through a problem-solving model. Some practitioners may continue to feel bound by the "test and place" model that has historically dominated school psychology practice; however, we advocate for a broader role for the school psychologist. By gathering data to determine the most appropriate interventions for students based on their needs, schools that use problem-solving strategies can serve all children effectively and efficiently.

Ervin, Peacock, and Merrell (2010) summarize this approach concisely, stating that "the problem-solving school psychologist focuses on behaviors that are amenable to change and clearly identifies these, ensures that measurable outcomes are in place, and uses data to continually guide the process" (p. 7). The problem-solving approach does not focus on eligibility, nor is it limited to addressing problems at the level of the individual. As this chapter shows, the problem-solving approach also gives the school psychologist opportunities to engage in prevention and intervention at the systems level.

At the heart of MTSS lies a conviction that many problems can be prevented, and that effective MTSS has the potential to identify concerns when they emerge and intervene before they become more serious, enduring problems (Brown-Chidsey & Bickford, 2016). This prevention orientation may feel unfamiliar to those who provide counseling services, which are typically considered to be intervention oriented. In this model, prevention works proactively and intervention represents a reactive response. This chapter proposes an alternative conceptualization of counseling as a set of services that is much broader than individual and group therapy, extending to preventive practices that are part of the school psychologist's larger role.

The field of public health is full of prevention examples that can be applied to the general population in an effort to decrease the prevalence of disease. Vaccinations, exercise, and nutrition education are all promoted to prevent poor health outcomes (Brown-Chidsey & Bickford, 2016). Similarly, school psychologists have the capacity to focus some of their efforts on the prevention of poor outcomes in the areas of social, emotional, and behavioral functioning.

Problem Solving and Counseling

This book includes counseling techniques for individuals and groups that come from a variety of theoretical orientations (e.g., cognitive, play-based, behavioral). A problem-solving approach is compatible with any counseling theory or method because it is a general, overarching model. Tilly (2008) provides four questions that guide the school psychologist's decision making with this approach:

- What is the problem?
- Why is it occurring?
- What can be done about it?
- Did the approach work?

Tilly notes that the questions reflect a logical, practical approach that many professionals already use. In fact, problem solving's roots are in the scientific method (Clark & Tilly, 2010). Problem solving can be applied to an individual (e.g., Max's aggressive behavior) or to larger units (e.g., a high school's pervasive bullying problem) and is sometimes framed in terms of problem identification, problem analysis, intervention planning and implementation, and intervention plan evaluation (e.g., Hoff & Sawka-Miller, 2010). The particular names of the steps are less important than the overall process, which is a data-based, systematic approach to improving outcomes.

School psychologists as counselors can apply a problem-solving approach to their work for effective prevention and intervention in the areas of students' social, emotional, and behavioral well-being. The problem-solving approach is data driven, outcome focused, ecologically oriented, and collaborative (Ervin et al., 2010). The first case example shows how this model can be applied to counseling.

CASE EXAMPLE 1: ALEJANDRA

Michelle Guzman was surprised to see the failing grades on her daughter's report card. Prior to this reporting period, Alejandra had been making As and Bs in all her classes and had not exhibited any difficulties. Alejandra, a freshman at Johnson High School, did not have a history of academic problems. Michelle called the school psychologist, David Rainwater, to discuss the grades and ask what could be done to address the concerns. The counselor pulled up Alejandra's records on the computer and told Michelle that Alejandra had a high number of absences, tardies, and missing assignments. Michelle was completely surprised by this information, as she had assumed that Alejandra had been attending school regularly and completing all assignments. Michelle also expressed frustration at the school for not notifying her of concerns when they first emerged.

David listened to Michelle carefully and apologized for failing to notify her about Alejandra's academic and attendance difficulties sooner. He expressed concern about Alejandra and proposed that a meeting be held with the problem-solving team to develop and implement solutions. He also stated that Michelle's participation in the meeting would be helpful and asked for some days and times that they would be available to meet. Following his conversation with Michelle, David scheduled a meeting and began to prepare.

David began collecting and reviewing existing data, including Alejandra's attendance records, standardized test scores, grades, and disciplinary referrals. He also provided her teachers with a brief questionnaire on which they could report their impressions of her assets and areas of concern. He also contacted Michelle to collect some information over the phone prior to the meeting (e.g., a brief developmental, social, health, and academic history). David invited Alejandra to attend the meeting, but she declined.

The meeting was attended by Michelle, David, an assistant principal, two of Alejandra's teachers, and the school's social worker. David welcomed everyone and made introductions, and then shared the meeting's agenda. Using the problem-solving approach, David asked team members to collaboratively identify the problem. Not surprisingly, Michelle and the teachers expressed concerns about attendance and academic work. Alejandra had missing assignments in all of her classes and had been absent for more than two dozen school days. Records also indicated that she was tardy to at least one class almost every day. Using the information that he had collected prior to the meeting in conjunction with what was shared at the meeting, David summarized by stating that the central problem appeared to be poor and tardy attendance and failure to complete academic work. To make the problem identification specific, David noted the precise numbers of absences (14), tardy arrivals (20), and missing assignments (16).

David stated that the next step of the problem-solving model would be to determine why the problem was occurring. David solicited information from team members, noting that it is difficult to know why a problem is occurring but that the team could develop hypotheses and later test those hypotheses. Alejandra's English teacher said that she did not know why Alejandra was attending school irregularly and rarely completing assignments, but she thought that apathy may be the underlying problem. Her biology teacher reported that although Alejandra at times appeared to be interested in the subject matter, she seemed to have given up on trying to succeed academically. Michelle reported that Alejandra seemed to have fallen under the influence of a new peer group, and suspected that Alejandra was skipping school with her new friends and adopting their values (e.g., school is not important).

To bring the meeting to an end, David summarized what was discussed and noted that some progress was made in identifying the problem and developing hypotheses. Upon learning that no one had yet spoken to Alejandra about her perception of the problem, he proposed that he follow up on the hypotheses by meeting with Alejandra and then scheduling another team meeting to formulate a plan. The team members agreed and thanked David for taking a leadership role.

The next day, David met with Alejandra and shared with her what transpired in the team meeting and described the concerns expressed by her mother and other members of the team. Initially, Alejandra was resistant to talking, but as she became more comfortable, she disclosed that she had been uneasy about the changes that David noted. She shared that her new peer group was initially part of the problem, but that once she started to experience academic failure, it seemed too late to catch up. "I felt bad when my grades started to drop, but I didn't think I could really do anything about it once I got so far behind." David thanked her for talking about her situation, assured her that she could get back on track, and asked if she was willing to put in the effort to do so. Alejandra, sensing that David was there to help, agreed that she would meet with him again.

At the follow-up meeting, David shared the new information that Alejandra provided. Team members reflected on the hypotheses that had been generated and now came to a better understanding of Alejandra's situation: she had developed a sense of hopelessness about her academic status and had ceased to put forth effort. David notified the team that they would need to come up with a plan to address the problem. The assistant principal proposed an approach that would involve most members of the team. David was to meet with Alejandra to support her directly by helping her to establish realistic goals and organize her work to reach them; teachers said they would work closely with Michelle to monitor Alejandra's attendance, grasp of content, and assignment completion. The team set the following goal: Alejandra will have no more than two absences over the next 6 weeks and will complete 90% of her assignments. David volunteered to monitor progress on the goals weekly and to report to team members.

Over the next 6 weeks, David and Alejandra met weekly and reviewed the progress monitoring data together. Alejandra said that she was motivated to improve and seemed pleased when they reviewed the attendance and homework completion data. David also provided weekly summaries to team members by email. By all accounts, the intervention appeared to be effective. However, David was troubled by the fact that Michelle had not initially been notified of Alejandra's absences and missing assignments until the report cards were issued. He decided that, after evaluating the effectiveness of the intervention with Alejandra, he would work with the problem-solving team to develop a school-wide system for detecting students who are falling behind and to intervene earlier.

In the case example, the problem-solving approach was used to address attendance and task completion for a ninth-grade student, but it also revealed the need for an intervention at the system level to address early detection and intervention failure. The problem-solving approach underscores the relationship between assessment and intervention, because intervention decisions are based on data collected during the assessment phase.

Assessment and intervention are often thought of as separate processes, but assessment and intervention are best considered to be interrelated parts of a larger whole. Assessment informs intervention, and psychologists continue to assess changes to determine whether an intervention is effective. Moreover, many intervention methods and techniques (e.g., sandtray, thought records) generate useful data that become part of ongoing assessment.

As the profession moves away from dichotomous thinking about assessment and intervention, the increased potential in linking these activities becomes obvious. For example, Tharinger and colleagues (2009) have reported on the potential benefits to children and family systems of an assessment–intervention hybrid called therapeutic assessment (TA). Conceived in the 1990s, TA "is a method of assessment that is collaborative, is guided by consumers' questions, and uses psychology assessment as the centerpiece of a potent, short-term intervention" (Tharinger et al., 2009, p. 238). Sometimes referred to as TA-C (therapeutic assessment for families with children), it facilitates parental understanding of the child and promotes improved attitudes and interactions (Aschieri, Fantiti, & Bertrando, 2012). TA has also been adapted for school settings (Tharinger et al., 2011). This idea that assessment not only informs intervention but also is an intervention suggests that there may be opportunities for school psychologists to reexamine the role and function of assessment in a new context. The following section considers how prevention and intervention are integrated into RTI and PBIS.

MTSS and Counseling in the Schools

Though many school psychologists are familiar with the use of multitiered systems of support (MTSS), most applications of this model involve academic skills. Even so, schools are increasingly considering ways in which MTSS can prevent and address social, emotional, and behavioral concerns. This section briefly reviews how counseling and MTSS may be integrated to promote students' success in all areas.

Building a solid foundation to implement MTSS in schools begins with Tier 1, also called universal screening or core instruction. The intent is that all students, through general education activities, are provided with high-quality instruction to build social, emotional, and behavioral skills for success. This core curriculum may include but is not limited to building competencies in the areas of self-awareness, social awareness, and self-management (CASEL, 2018). Most MTSS models suggest that if Tier 1 is done well, this kind of competency building should result in 80% of students achieving success (which is to say, 80% of students will not require additional services to address social, emotional, or behavioral concerns). Just as hand washing can prevent the spread of infection, building students' self-regulation, empathy, and teamwork skills can prevent social and behavioral problems. Consistent with the MTSS model, schools are moving toward teaching these skills explicitly so that students can practice them in the academic, behavioral, and social arenas in which they routinely function at school.

Establishing a strong Tier 1 is essential to ensuring a strong foundation for MTSS. Although such an investment in universal prevention may take significant time and resources, it is designed to save resources in the future by preventing serious problems, including school violence and severe mental health crises. Even so, school systems that are committed to building greater Tier 1 capacity in the social and emotional learning (SEL) domain do not need to reinvent the wheel but may look to districts that have already established programs as models (see Austin Independent School District, 2018). The Collaborative on Academic, Social, and Emotional Learning (CASEL) also provides excellent resources (www.casel.org). When done well, explicit instruction in SEL gives children the skills they need in order to do well in schools, homes, and communities.

School psychologists may play many roles in Tier 1 SEL work, including the following:

- Identifying resources such as SEL curricula, tools, and strategies that have empirical support.
- Providing professional development around SEL to teachers, administrators, and other school employees.
- Working with schools to build SEL competencies, either through consultation or primary prevention efforts.

In a school district that does not have a comprehensive Tier 1 SEL foundation in place, school psychologists may be in an ideal position to review evidence-based programs that could be implemented to achieve district goals and forming an MTSS team. For example, Hart (2012) summarized programs and interventions that have demonstrated evidence of promoting emotional regulation. In some districts, the role of the school psychologist is associated primarily with reactive rather than proactive work; their work parameters only allow them to respond to student or classroom concerns rather than prevent them. School psychologists interested in initiating prevention activities might work with district administrators to begin the transformation, with the understanding that the shift toward a tiered system may take 3–5 years to become established.

Schools implementing MTSS also use universal screening to determine the degree to which prevention efforts are working. The idea of screening also comes from the public health model, which focuses on indicators or risk factors rather than diagnostics (Brown-Chidsey & Bickford, 2016). Many school psychologists are familiar with academic screening tools such as DIBELS or FAST Bridge, but they may be less familiar with behavioral screeners such as the Student Risk Screening Scale (SRSS) or the School-Wide Information System (SWIS). Such tools can help determine which students reap the benefits of Tier 1 prevention and identify those who may need additional support. Screening tools should be carefully selected to ensure that they are valid for the intended use (Pierce, Lambert, & Alamer, 2016).

Though most students (about 80%) are expected to benefit from Tier 1 prevention efforts, some (about 15%) will demonstrate a need for greater support when screened for social, emotional, or behavioral concerns. When the MTSS team determines that a student needs more than Tier 1 prevention, school psychologists work collaboratively with team members to select appropriate, evidence-based Tier 2 interventions. Collaborating with others to review data and make important decisions about intervention may be challenging, so we provided a semistructured format for facilitating a conversation with teams about next steps in Chapter 2 and included a form in Appendix A that may be adapted for such purposes.

When selecting Tier 2 interventions, school psychologists may draw on a number of resources to assist in their planning and execution. For example, Shinn and Walker's (2010) *Interventions for Achievement and Behavior Problems in a Three-Tier Model Including RTI* and Rathvon's (2008) *Effective School Interventions* are excellent resources and provide many evidence-based interventions. However, school psychologists need not limit themselves to interventions listed in books. As consumers of research, school psychologists may look to peer-reviewed research articles for the latest scholarship on interventions for social, emotional, and behavioral challenges. Tier 2 interventions in the social, emotional, and behavioral domain may include conjoint behavioral consultation, group counseling, check-in/check-out, or environmental changes to learning settings.

The goal of Tier 2 intervention is to target the concern with a focused, evidence-based response to either eliminate the problem or keep it from becoming more severe. In fact, most students receiving Tier 2 interventions are expected to respond favorably and therefore not require more intensive approaches. Following MTSS methods based on data-based decision making, school psychologists collect data to determine whether students are responding to Tier 2 interventions and collaborate with members of the MTSS team to review the findings and make decisions.

Just as some students need more support than what Tier 1 offers, some will need more than what is provided by Tier 2. When the data demonstrate that Tier 2 interventions have been implemented with integrity, and when sufficient time has passed without achieving the desired results, the MTSS team may recommend a Tier 3 intervention. Ideally, with excellent Tier 1 and Tier 2 efforts in place, a very small proportion (about 5%) of the whole student body will require Tier 3 interventions. This last tier may aim to ""limit and ameliorate the negative effects of a problem, even if the problem itself cannot be eliminated" (Brown-Chidsey & Bickford, 2016, p. 16). The problems demonstrated by the student have been resistant to change and require more intensive, individualized, focused resources (Tillery et al., 2010). This advanced level of intervention may include individual counseling, a functional behavior assessment (FBA), behavior intervention plan (BIP), and more systematic collaboration across home and school systems. Many of the effective counseling interventions that are appropriate for Tier 3 are discussed later in this book.

Positive Behavioral Support

Emerging in the 1980s as an alternative to using reactive and punitive methods to deal with behavioral concerns, positive behavioral intervention and support (PBIS) represents a proactive and supportive approach (Scott et al., 2002). Bambara and Kern (2005) describe it as a "problem-solving approach to understanding reasons for problem behavior and designing comprehensive interventions that are matched to hypotheses about why problem behavior is occurring and to the individual's social, environmental, and cultural milieu" (p. 3). In this respect, PBIS differs from systems that merely punish behavior without trying to understand it. Whereas traditional approaches are consequence based and short term, PBIS is growth based, functional, and long term.

PBIS is characterized by its focus on long-lasting, systemic change rather than short-term solutions. By focusing on prevention, altering environmental conditions that contribute to problem behaviors, teaching students prosocial and functional ways of behaving, and using recognition systems to encourage desirable adult and student behavior, PBIS promotes long-term behavioral improvement rather than simply punishing misbehavior (Bambara & Kern, 2005). This positive view of individuals and their capacity to grow comes from a person-centered paradigm, and the systematic problem-solving approach in PBIS can be traced to applied behavioral analysis. PBIS involves the use of universal screening to identify students who may benefit from tiered supports. Such universal screening may identify, early on, children who may need assessment for emotional–behavioral disorders; when prevention and intervention through general education do not yield improvements, PBIS may be considered as providing early assessment data (Burke et al., 2016).

For example, a screening model developed by Walker, Severson, and Feil (2014) involves a multiple-gating procedure consisting of three sequentially arranged stages or "gates" for elementary-age children. The process, Systematic Screening for Behavior Disorders (SSBD), begins with Gate 1 by requiring general education teachers to screen all students on internalizing and externalizing behavioral dimensions using a rank-order procedure. In Gate 2, the students who characterize the extremes on these two dimensions are targeted to be evaluated by teachers using rating scales. These scales assess specific critical behaviors and their frequencies. Students who exceed the normative criteria on these scales move on to Gate 3, which requires direct observation of the

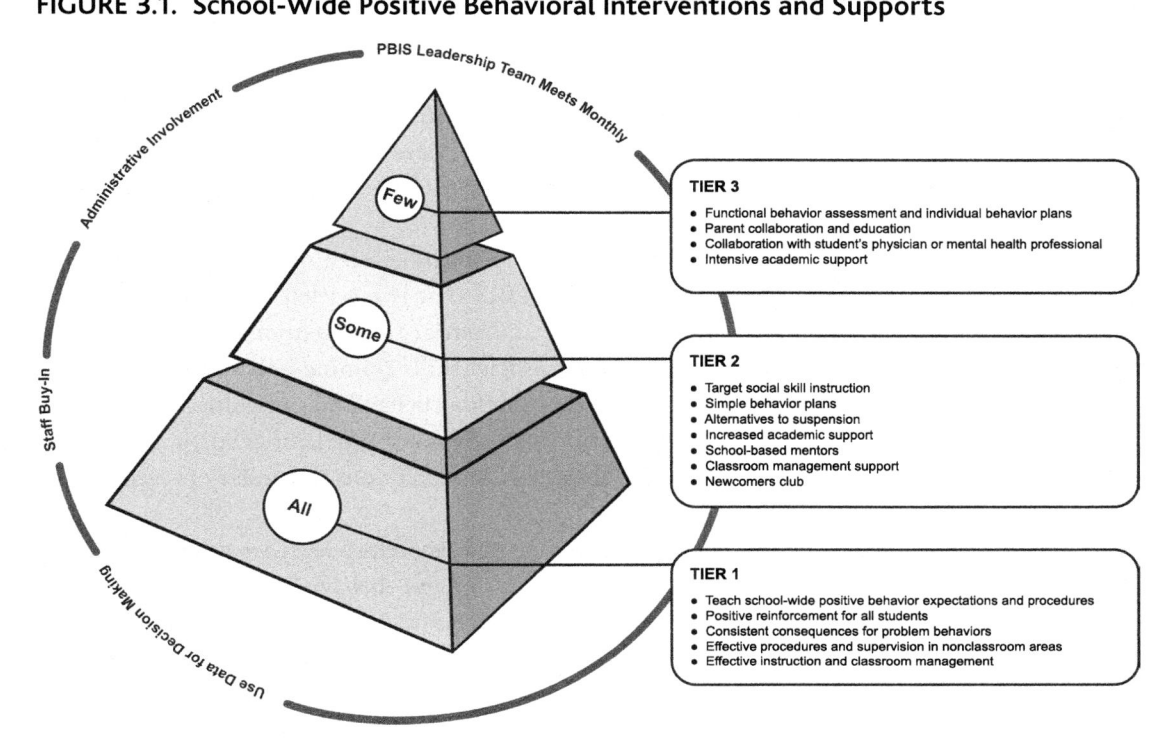

FIGURE 3.1. School-Wide Positive Behavioral Interventions and Supports

Surrounding the pyramid: PBIS Leadership Team Meets Monthly · Administrative Involvement · Staff Buy-In · Use Data for Decision Making

Pyramid levels (bottom to top): All · Some · Few

TIER 3
- Functional behavior assessment and individual behavior plans
- Parent collaboration and education
- Collaboration with student's physician or mental health professional
- Intensive academic support

TIER 2
- Target social skill instruction
- Simple behavior plans
- Alternatives to suspension
- Increased academic support
- School-based mentors
- Classroom management support
- Newcomers club

TIER 1
- Teach school-wide positive behavior expectations and procedures
- Positive reinforcement for all students
- Consistent consequences for problem behaviors
- Effective procedures and supervision in nonclassroom areas
- Effective instruction and classroom management

Note. From *School-Wide Positive Behavioral Interventions and Supports: Implementation Guide 2010* (p. 4), by the Office of Special Education, Michigan Department of Education, 2010, Author. Copyright 2010 by the Michigan Department of Education. Reprinted with permission.

students in the classroom and other settings. Behaviors targeted for teacher observation are academic engaged time in the classroom and amount and quality of social interaction during free time or recess. Students who exceed normative criteria applied to these observations are considered for prereferral interventions or may be referred to the multidisciplinary team for formal evaluation. School psychologists should determine when consent is required in their jurisdiction for prereferral assessment activities.

The problem-solving approach and PBIS fit together nicely, as both are data based and ecosystemic. They both also promote prevention, sustainable change over time, team-based collaboration, and progress monitoring. So similar are these two approaches that PBIS could be used as a problem-solving approach to promoting and sustaining positive behaviors for all students. In fact, figures depicting positive behavioral interventions and supports, such as the school-wide PBIS in Figure 3.1, are very similar to MTSS/RTI models, sharing the same tiered logic. Additional information about behavioral approaches can be found in Chapter 8.

RTI and the Transition From General to Special Education Support

One of the biggest challenges for mental health professionals in the schools is balancing the need to prevent poor outcomes in the areas of social, emotional, and behavioral functioning with the responsibility to respond to existing problems, particularly those that are acute and severe. Unfortunately, many school systems have been operating on inefficient models in which there is little coordination between prevention, screening, and intervention. Such models have a rigid boundary between general and special education services such that students who would benefit from brief, targeted intervention are deemed ineligible for services until their problems escalate to a level that is considered severe enough to qualify for services. The result of such a model is an approach that is reactive rather than proactive.

Walker and colleagues (2010) describe a system of universal screening for social, emotional, and behavioral problems in the context of RTI and PBIS that is modeled after the U.S. public health system of classification (primary, secondary, and tertiary intervention). At the universal level (primary prevention), all students are provided social skills training and school-wide rules, with 80–90% of students expected to succeed without serious behavioral difficulties. All students are screened to determine whether any are at risk for behavioral problems, and those who are deemed at risk are provided group or individual targeted interventions (secondary prevention) to remediate and prevent problems from worsening.

Those who fail to benefit from the interventions at the secondary level are referred for more specialized, intensive services to address chronic or intense behavioral problems (tertiary prevention). Throughout the process, assessment informs intervention, and services are calibrated to match the intensity of students' needs. Such systems are designed to efficiently promote positive behaviors and provide early, effective interventions to prevent problems from becoming more severe over time. Figure 3.2 demonstrates how the tiered service delivery model can be applied to both academic and behavioral systems.

A tiered approach to problem solving has received a significant amount of attention in the literature, but the focus has been primarily on academic outcomes. However, more recently, interest in applying these models to behavioral systems has increased (Hawkins, Barnett, Morrison, & Musti-Rao, 2010; NASP, 2016). For example, the pupil assistance model has integrated RTI and PBIS to address both the academic and behavioral needs of all students, and a growing body of research is demonstrating that such an approach, if implemented early, can prevent a number of behavioral and health risks (Walker et al., 2010). Similarly, Low, Frey, and Brockman (2010) reported a decrease in relational aggression (malicious gossip on elementary school playgrounds) following a universal prevention program, giving support to the notion that school psychologists can play an important role in promoting the development of adaptive social skills of all children.

The combined approach of RTI and PBIS has several advantages over the "refer, test, place" approach of the traditional special education paradigm. Rather than wait for student behavior to become sufficiently problematic to qualify for services, school personnel meet students' needs proactively and early. School personnel are more likely to be invested in the success of all students when RTI and PBIS are in place, as opposed to the differentiated approach (e.g., "He's not one of my students, because I'm a general education teacher"). Interventions are more likely to be matched to students' needs when RTI is employed with PBIS, which results in greater efficiency. Finally, the collaborative approach promotes shared responsibility across all parties (e.g., parents, teachers, administrators, and other professionals).

FIGURE 3.2. Multitiered Services and Parallel Interventions for Academic and Behavioral Systems

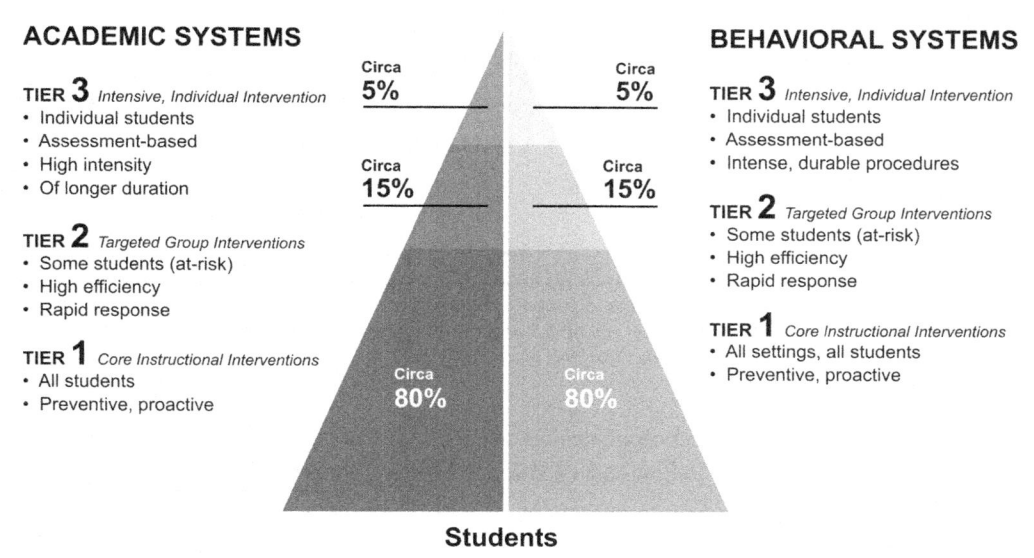

ACADEMIC SYSTEMS

TIER **3** *Intensive, Individual Intervention*
- Individual students
- Assessment-based
- High intensity
- Of longer duration

TIER **2** *Targeted Group Interventions*
- Some students (at-risk)
- High efficiency
- Rapid response

TIER **1** *Core Instructional Interventions*
- All students
- Preventive, proactive

Circa 5%
Circa 15%
Circa 80%

Circa 5%
Circa 15%
Circa 80%

BEHAVIORAL SYSTEMS

TIER **3** *Intensive, Individual Intervention*
- Individual students
- Assessment-based
- Intense, durable procedures

TIER **2** *Targeted Group Interventions*
- Some students (at-risk)
- High efficiency
- Rapid response

TIER **1** *Core Instructional Interventions*
- All settings, all students
- Preventive, proactive

Students

Note. From "Behaviorally Effective School Environments," by G. Sugai, R. H. Horner, & F. Gresham, 2002, in M. R. Shinn, H. M. Walker, & G. Stoner (Eds.), *Interventions for Achievement and Behavior Problems II: Preventive and Remedial Approaches*, p. 320, Bethesda, MD: National Association of School Psychologists. Copyright 2002 by the National Association of School Psychologists. Adapted with permission.

Collaboration Within Teams

The school psychologist as counselor may work with a variety of teams: crisis prevention and intervention teams, student assistance teams, IEP teams, and so forth. Serving as a member of school-based teams represents both opportunities and challenges for the school psychologist, but the experience ultimately expands their capacity to promote the social, emotional, and behavioral well-being of all students.

Teams are often formed because of the belief that people can accomplish more when they work together than when they work as individuals (Platt, cited in Rosenfield & Gravois, 1999, p. 1025). Thus, the student assistance team that consists of a school psychologist, teachers, parents, and administrators has the potential to function well because each member of the team brings unique skills, knowledge, and perspectives that, when combined, can solve problems effectively. Conversely, individuals acting in isolation may be less effective or even work at cross purposes if they lack the skills, knowledge, and perspectives that exist in the team. Moreover, parents whose student is struggling in school may be rightly frustrated when they are contacted by multiple school personnel who are not in communication with each other.

Working with teams as opposed to addressing problems in isolation has a number of other benefits as well. For example, when diverse team members share ownership and responsibility for a concern, specialized information is pooled for maximum benefit. Sheridan et al. (2010) summarize some of the elements and benefits of effective teams, as shown in Table 3.1.

TABLE 3.1. Elements and Benefits of Effective Teams

Element	Benefit
• Clear roles and expectations • Mutual goals • Shared responsibility and ownership • Regular communication among team members • Supportive leadership	• Prevents replication of services. • Defines and drives the team's primary purpose. • Maximizes team productivity. • Leads to sharing of information across disciplines, leading to better provision of services. • Gives team members a sense of ongoing support.

Note. Adapted from "Collaboration Across Systems to Support Children and Families," by S. M. Sheridan, K. L. Magee, C. A. Blevins, & M. S. Swanger-Gagné, 2010, *Practical Handbook of School Psychology: Effective Practices for the 21st Century*, edited by G. G. Peacock, R. A. Ervin, E. J. Daly, & K. W. Merrell, pp. 531–547, New York, NY: Guilford Press.

In some cases, the school psychologist takes a leadership role on the team, particularly when the referral is meant to address behavioral or mental health concerns (Sheridan et al., 2010). In such cases, the school psychologist as counselor uses their knowledge and skills in the areas of adaptive behavior, developmental expectations, and school and community resources to efficiently structure the process. The school psychologist "may guide the team by outlining relevant questions, pooling information from multiple sources, and sharing recommendations based on all available data" (Sheridan et al., 2010, p. 533). In this respect, the school psychologist requires both the interpersonal skills of a facilitator and the specialized knowledge of a clinician.

School psychologists may also contribute to teams by sharing their knowledge and skills regarding data-based decision making, particularly in the areas of monitoring progress on social, emotional, and behavioral goals. For example, school psychologists may help problem-solving teams collect baseline data and monitor how a student responds to an intervention by using Goal Attainment Scaling (GAS; Coffee & Ray-Subramania, 2009). By identifying expected levels of behavior and constructing a scale ranging from "somewhat less than expected" to "much more than expected," school psychologists can record baseline data and observe over time to track progress toward goals. This is just one of many ways school psychologists can bring their specialized training, knowledge, and skills to collaborate with MTSS teams.

Teamwork also involves parallel processes of business tasks and team maintenance (Rosenfield & Gravois, 1999). The business tasks are the functions of the team (e.g., scheduling meetings, reviewing cases, and problem solving), whereas the maintenance process focuses on the interactions between team members (e.g., communicating, giving and receiving feedback, and training). The school psychologist's training and background in interpersonal skills may be particularly useful for assisting with team maintenance activities. Active listening skills are among of the most powerful counseling strategies and can enhance the productivity of teamwork.

The School Psychologist as Counselor: Roles Beyond Direct Service

Given the vast and diverse behavioral and mental health needs in the schools, direct service roles such as individual and group counseling cannot alone remedy all problems. In fact, many in the field have argued that in the absence of prevention efforts, direct services merely treat the symptoms of larger underlying problems. Therefore, the school psychologist as counselor is advised to consider other ways to promote positive social, behavioral, and emotional functioning in addition to direct services.

McIntosh, Reinke, and Herman (2010) argue that a school psychology service delivery model predicated on the diagnosis and treatment of disorders is outmoded, and that contemporary models permit school psychologists to identify students who are at risk early so that they will not need to be diagnosed and treated later. The school psychologist, using a MTSS/RTI approach, may employ an expanded set of activities that include the following:

- "Identifying and clarifying the core behavioral curriculum provided to all students
- Assessing outcomes of school-wide efforts to reduce problem behavior and promote prosocial behavior
- Ensuring that services provided at all tiers are exemplary
- Screening students to determine which students need more (or less) support than they are currently receiving" (p. 136)

In this model, the school psychologist effectively uses data, such as systematically collected office referrals, to make decisions about how best to prevent behavior problems from emerging and to reduce existing behavior problems. If effective, these activities should result in a decrease in the number of students requiring more intensive intervention.

The promotion of social competence is another way that school psychologists as counselors can work toward preventing student problems. Merrell, Levitt, and Gueldner (2010) describe universal strategies, including social and emotional learning (SEL) programs, to teach skills that can be generalized across various settings (e.g., classroom, playground, home, and community), and they use the Strong Kids/Strong Teens curriculum as an example of such a program. Because not all children will benefit from primary prevention efforts, secondary and tertiary strategies must also be in place. The school psychologist plays an important role in coordinating the tiered approach, carefully selecting programs that are supported in the literature, and ensuring that prevention and intervention efforts meet students' and families' needs across settings.

The school psychologist as counselor may also create and promote collaborations across settings by facilitating communication among schools, families, and community service providers. In this role, the school psychologist must know about the environments that students occupy when not in school, cultural factors, community resources, and the best ways of integrating these components to maximize the benefits to students. Many students benefit from wraparound services that support students both at school and in their communities (Merrell et al., 2010). Interventions that fall under this paradigm require coordination for consistency and efficacy.

Another framework for collaboration to promote students' success across settings is family–school partnering (Lines, Miller, & Arthur-Stanley, 2010). Based on a body of research demonstrating better outcomes for children when schools and families work together, the family–school partnering model recognizes that sustained, ongoing collaboration across school, family, and community systems has great potential for addressing academic, social, emotional, and behavioral concerns. Following the 2002 multisite conferences on the Future of School Psychology, the Task Force on

Family–School Partnerships was established to develop evidence-based materials for use by trainers, practitioners, and students. (The task force's resources, which include presentations, videos, bibliographies, and other materials, are available at http://fsp.unl.edu/future_index.html.)

Family–school partnering can take many forms and is as much about attitudes as actions (Christenson, 2004). The approach is prevention and solution oriented, with an emphasis on high-quality relationships between schools and families. The model also assumes that "both families and educators are *essential* and provide resources for children's learning and progress in school" (p. 84). School psychologists who embrace family–school partnering have an opportunity to collaborate with families around common goals and to share the responsibility of promoting social and emotional growth for all children. For the school psychologist as counselor, family–school partnering presents an opportunity to look beyond the immediacy of child behaviors and work with the systems and environments that contribute to those behaviors.

School psychologists can integrate many of the ideas discussed in this chapter by implementing SEL programs (CASEL, 2018). Coordinated, developmentally appropriate, school-wide SEL curricula can teach students the skills necessary for successful social, emotional, and behavioral functioning. The core SEL competencies are self-awareness, responsible decision making, relationship skills, social awareness, and self-management. Promoting SEL competencies can result in positive learning and social environments that benefit children, schools, and families.

Other Considerations

In their discussion of future trends in school psychology, Fagan and Wise (2007) note that mental health needs in schools historically have not received sufficient attention, and that school psychologists who traditionally have focused their efforts on supporting students in the area of academic achievement may be challenged by the task of addressing the social, emotional, and behavioral needs of students. This difficulty may in part be due to training deficiencies, but it also reflects a practical matter of time constraints. Consequently, training of school psychologists may be moving toward greater specialization and clearly defined responsibilities. This shift may result in strands or cognates being available to graduate students pursuing degrees in school psychology, allowing students to choose from a variety of emphases (e.g., counseling, neuropsychology, autism).

School psychologists who wish to expand their roles to incorporate more counseling, prevention, and behavior management on a systems level may seek additional training in the form of continuing education, supervision, and consultation. Role expansion will require administrative support for the integration of new activities and functions. Therefore, school psychologists who wish to shift their activities toward mental health prevention and intervention may consider developing some talking points to lobby for administrative support. Such points may include the following:

- Prevention work in the area of social, emotional, and behavioral support can save time and money.
- Improved behavioral functioning is associated with improved academic success.
- Gains in behavioral outcomes are likely to improve teacher morale and retention.

Funding limitations may also be perceived as an obstacle to expanding mental health work in schools, but advocates are quick to point out that a tremendous cost is associated with not addressing mental health needs.

CASE EXAMPLE 2: SCHOOL PSYCHOLOGY INTERN

Amrita Goli is the school psychology intern in a large urban school district on the East Coast. In the first month of her internship she became oriented to the system and, with the support of her supervisor, began to think critically about the school district's service delivery model, which has remained essentially unchanged for several years. Her supervisor, Barry Johnston, conceded that the practice of school psychology in the district is "less than ideal" and welcomed Amrita's fresh perspective. In collaboration with Amrita's university supervisor, Barry and Amrita began the task of identifying ways in which school psychologists in the district may become more effective at reaching their goals.

After their initial meeting about Amrita's interest in studying the district's service delivery model, she and Barry agreed that the project needed a focus. Amrita's interest in behavior and social skills guided the process of narrowing the focus, and Barry advised her to interview a variety of stakeholders to learn more about perceived strengths and weaknesses in the district. Amrita planned to interview parents, teachers, campus- and district-level administrators, and school psychologists.

After spending several weeks collecting information from various stakeholders, Amrita again conferred with Barry. They noted some similarities that cut across many of the interviews and identified some patterns. Almost everyone interviewed acknowledged serious problems across the district with respect to behavior management, and many expressed frustration regarding the failure of programs that had been implemented (some at great expense) with few signs of improvement. Amrita summarized her key findings in a list that she presented to Barry:

- The district seems to lack a consistent set of behavioral expectations that is communicated to students and parents.
- Teachers' responses to students' behavior are inconsistent.
- Outcomes of behavior support programs are not measured.
- Students placed in self-contained behavior support classrooms tend to remain in those settings (i.e., they do not return to general education settings as a result of making progress).
- Although some programs have reported some success, the gains appear to be limited to the intervention settings (e.g., counseling groups) and do not generalize to the classrooms, let alone home and community settings.

Amrita and Barry considered the list and recognized that the problems were systemic and pervasive. Amrita felt overwhelmed by the problem and told Barry that she did not even know how one could begin to address these issues. Barry encouraged Amrita to break the problem into smaller parts and to solicit other collaborators. He asked her whether anyone that was interviewed would be interested in serving on a committee to address behavior at a systems level. Amrita readily identified a teacher, a parent, and an administrator, all from the same elementary school, who seemed interested in working toward solutions. With Barry's support, Amrita formed a committee to begin exploring solutions.

Amrita decided to apply the problem-solving model to the committee's work and took a leadership role in facilitating the committee. She organized the meeting around key questions: What is the problem? Why is it occurring? What can be done about it?

Amrita explained to committee members that these questions could not be readily answered without sufficient data. For the first question, the initial response from committee members was that the campus's efforts to manage behavior were inadequate. Amrita asked them to define the problem more specifically. As she sought more information from committee members, she learned that teachers appeared to have difficulty managing behavior in the classroom and that they would send noncompliant students to the office when efforts in the classroom fail. This pattern of office referrals did not seem to be effective and was possibly even counterproductive. Unfortunately, the school did not consistently maintain records on office referrals.

With the cooperation of the administrator, Amrita instituted a system to record and store important details about each office referral. She explained to committee members that one of their next tasks would be to analyze the data generated by the office referrals so that they could determine the extent of the perceived problem and identify some factors that might be causing the problem.

Results from the office referral data collection indicated some patterns. Most of the referrals came from fifth-grade teachers, and the students who had been referred had been referred multiple times (there were very few instances of students who were referred only once or twice). Most referrals were written near the end of the school day and were for noncompliance and aggression.

The committee's next task was to ask the third problem-solving question: What can be done about it? The committee decided to approach the problem on multiple fronts. Clear behavioral expectations were developed and presented to students and teachers. The school's guidance counselor and Amrita taught the rules to each fifth-grade classroom and provided the classroom teachers with some specialized training in behavior management techniques. The parent on the committee shared the new behavioral expectations with the Parent–Teacher Association and encouraged parents to reinforce appropriate behaviors at home. Finally, a behavior specialist worked with teachers to alter the physical environment of the classrooms in a way that would eliminate some antecedents of misbehavior.

Once the plan was in place, Amrita ensured that data from the office referrals were still being collected so that the plan's success could be evaluated. This helped the committee answer the final question: Did it work?

Over the course of the school year, the committee noted a drop in the number of office referrals. Teachers reported that they liked the new plan and were pleased with the results. However, the committee observed that parents did not report a decrease in behavior problems at home, and Amrita recognized the need to build in a component to generalize the behavioral improvements to nonschool settings. She reported the committee's findings to Barry, who expressed great admiration for Amrita's and the committee's accomplishments, noting that the collaborative, proactive approach to behavior management had a significant, positive effect.

PRACTICE: FAMILY–SCHOOL PARTNERING TO IMPROVE OUTCOMES

Bobby Reyes is a school psychologist in a growing South Texas school district. Over the past several years the Hispanic population of the school has been growing steadily, though Hispanic parental involvement has not increased proportionally. In recent months, the RTI team at Bobby's elementary school has received a number of referrals for learning and behavior concerns, but anecdotal data suggest that parents and teachers do not necessarily share with each other their own perceptions of the issues students face.

Bobby and the members of the RTI team feel frustrated by the increase in referrals and the perception that parents are not involved in the process. He would like to be more helpful to students, parents, and teachers but is not sure how to proceed. What steps can Bobby take at the systems level to promote efficient prevention and intervention services? What factors should he consider in developing a plan? As you develop your response to this case, consider the following:

- What cultural factors may be relevant to the decision-making process?
- How can Bobby's efforts be informed by the problem-solving model?
- How can Bobby simultaneously address the need for both prevention and intervention?
- What resources, both within and outside of the district, can Bobby draw on for support?
- What measures of success can be established so that Bobby can determine whether his efforts resulted in the desired outcomes?

SUMMARY

This chapter focused on ways the school psychologist as counselor can interact with systems, teams, and processes. It reviewed the interface between counseling as a related service (counseling delivered as part of the IEP) and RTI and PBIS and how school psychologists partner with families and educators to meet the social, emotional, and behavioral needs of students. In doing so, it has shown that the roles and functions of school psychologists as counselors go well beyond the provision of direct services to students.

KEY POINTS FOR DISCUSSION

- What are some specific activities in which school psychologists can promote positive behavioral support at the school level?
- Aside from providing individual and group counseling services, how can school psychologists as counselors become involved with MTSS/RTI in the areas of social, emotional, and behavioral functioning?
- Which aspects of training prepare school psychologists to take a lead role in problem-solving teams?
- How might the school psychologist as counselor use data to promote positive behaviors?

REFERENCES

Aschieri, F., Fantini, F., & Bertrando, P. (2012). Therapeutic assessment with children in family therapy. *Australian and New Zealand Journal of Family Therapy, 33*(4), 285–298. https://doi.org/10.1017/aft.2012.37

Austin Independent School District. (2018). Department of Social Emotional Learning Website. Retrieved from https://www.austinisd.org/sel

Bambara, L. M., & Kern, L. (2005). *Individualized supports for students with problem behaviors.* New York, NY: Guilford Press.

Brown-Chidsey, R., & Bickford, R. (2016). *Practical handbook of multi-tiered systems of support: Building academic and behavioral success in schools.* New York, NY: Guilford Press.

Burke, M. D., Rispoli, M., Clemens, N. H., Lee, Y.-H., Sanchez, L., & Hatton, H. (2016). Integrating universal behavioral screening within program-wide positive behavioral interventions and supports. *Journal of Positive Behavior Interventions, 18,* 5–16. https://doi.org/10.1177/1098300715580993

Christenson, S. L. (2004). The family-school partnership: An opportunity to promote the learning competence of all students. *School Psychology Review, 33,* 83–104.

Clark, J. P., & Tilly, W. D. (2010). *The evolution of response to intervention.* In J. P. Clark & M. E. Alvarez (Eds.), *Response to intervention: A guide for school social workers* (pp. 3–18). New York, NY: Oxford University Press.

Coffee, G., & Ray-Subramanian, C. E. (2009). Goal attainment scaling: A progress monitoring tool for behavioral interventions. *School Psychology Forum, 3*(1), 1–12.

Collaborative for Academic, Social, and Emotional Learning (CASEL). (2018). *What is SEL?* http://www.casel.org

Ervin, R. A., Peacock, G. G., & Merrell, K. W. (2010). *The school psychologist as problem-solver in the 21st century: Rationale and role definition.* In G. G. Peacock, R. A. Ervin, E. J. Daly, & K. W. Merrell, (Eds.), *Practical handbook of school psychology: Effective practices for the 21st century* (pp. 3–12). New York, NY: Guilford Press.

Fagan, T. K., & Wise, P. S. (2007). *School psychology: Past, present, and future* (3rd ed.). Bethesda, MD: National Association of School Psychologists.

Hart, S. R. (2012). *Promoting emotion-related regulation.* In S. E. Brock & S. R. Jimerson (Eds.), *Best practices in school crisis prevention and intervention.* Bethesda, MD: National Association of School Psychologists.

Hawkins, R. O., Barnett, D. W., Morrison, J. Q., & Musti-Rao, S. (2010). *Choosing targets for assessment and intervention: Improving important student outcomes.* In G. G. Peacock, R. A. Ervin, E. J. Daly, & K. W. Merrell, (Eds.), *Practical handbook of school psychology: Effective practices for the 21st century* (pp. 13–30). New York, NY: Guilford Press.

Hoff, K. E., & Sawka-Miller, K. D. (2010). *Self-management interventions.* In G. G. Peacock, R. A. Ervin, E. J. Daly, & K. W. Merrell, (Eds.), *Practical handbook of school psychology: Effective practices for the 21st century* (pp. 337–352). New York, NY: Guilford Press.

Kershner, B., & McQuillan, P. (2016). Complex adaptive schools: Educational leadership and school change. *Complicity: An International Journal of Complexity and Education, 13,* 4–29. https://doi.org/10.29173/cmplct23029

Lines, C., Miller, G., & Arthur-Stanley, A. (2010). *The power of family-school partnering (FSP): A practical guide for school mental health practitioners and educators.* New York, NY: Routledge.

Low, S., Frey, K. S., & Brockman, C. J. (2010). Gossip on the playground: Changes associated with universal intervention, retaliation beliefs, and supportive friends. *School Psychology Review, 39,* 536–551.

McIntosh, K., Reinke, W. M., & Herman, K. C. (2010). *Schoolwide analysis of data for social behavior problems: Assessing outcomes, selecting targets for intervention, and identifying need for support.* In G. G. Peacock, R. A. Ervin, E. J. Daly, & K. W. Merrell, (Eds.), *Practical handbook of school psychology: Effective practices for the 21st century* (pp. 135–156). New York, NY: Guilford Press.

Merrell, K. W., Levitt, V. H., & Gueldner, B. A. (2010). *Proactive strategies for promoting social competence and resilience.* In G. G. Peacock, R. A. Ervin, E. J. Daly, & K. W. Merrell, (Eds.),

Practical handbook of school psychology: Effective practices for the 21st century (pp. 254–273). New York, NY: Guilford Press.

National Association of School Psychologists. (2016). *Integrated model of academic and behavioral supports* [Position statement]. Bethesda, MD: Author.

Office of Special Education, Michigan Department of Education. (2010). *School-wide positive behavioral interventions and supports: Implementation guide 2010*. Retrieved from http://www.lcisd.k12.mi.us/UserFiles/Servers/Server_78652/File/specialed/PBIS/SchoolwidePBIS Michigan.pdf

Pierce, C. D., Lambert, M., & Alamer, H. (2016). Convergent, criterion and social validity of the emotional and behavioral screener. *Journal of Child and Family Studies, 25*, 77–85. https://doi.org/10.1007/s10826-015-0206-7

Rathvon, N. (2008). *Effective school interventions* (2nd ed.). New York, NY: Guilford Press.

Rosenfield, S., & Gravois, T. A. (1999). *Working with teams in the school*. In T. Gutkin & C. Reynolds (Eds.), *Handbook of school psychology* (3rd ed., pp. 1025–1040). New York, NY: Wiley.

Schaughency, E., Alsop, B., & Dawson, A. (2010). *The school psychologist's role in assisting school staff in establishing systems to manage, understand, and use data*. In G. G. Peacock, R. A. Ervin, E. J. Daly, & K. W. Merrell, (Eds.), *Practical handbook of school psychology: Effective practices for the 21st century* (pp. 548–565). New York, NY: Guilford Press.

Scott, T. M., Nelson, C. M., Liaupsin, C. J., Jolivette, K., Christle, C. A., & Riney, M. (2002). Addressing the needs of at-risk and adjudicated youth through positive behavior support: Effective prevention practices. *Education and Treatment of Children, 25*, 532–551.

Sheridan, S. M., Magee, K. L., Blevins, C. A., & Swanger-Gagné, M. S. (2010). *Collaboration across systems to support children and families*. In G. G. Peacock, R. A. Ervin, E. J. Daly, & K. W. Merrell, (Eds.), *Practical handbook of school psychology: Effective practices for the 21st century* (pp. 531–547). New York, NY: Guilford Press.

Shinn, M. R., & Walker, H. M. (2010). *Interventions for achievement and behavior problems in a three-tier model including RTI*. Bethesda, MD: National Association of School Psychologists.

Tharinger, D. J., Finn, S. E., Gentry, L., Hamilton, A., Fowler, J., Matson, M., … Walkowiak, J. (2009). Therapeutic assessment with children: A pilot study of treatment acceptability and outcome. *Journal of Personality Assessment, 91*, 238–244. https://doi.org/10.1080/00223890902794275

Tharinger, D. J., Krumholz, L. S., Austin, C. A., & Matson, M. (2011). *The development and model of therapeutic assessment with children: Application to school-based assessment*. In M. A. Bray & T. J. Kehele (Eds.), *The Oxford handbook of school psychology* (pp. 224–259). New York, NY: Oxford University Press.

Tilly, W. D. (2008). *The evolution of school psychology to science-based practice: Problem solving and the three-tiered model*. In A. Thomas & J. Grimes (Eds.), *Best practices in school psychology V* (pp. 17–36). Bethesda, MD: National Association of School Psychologists.

Tillery, A. D., Varjas, K., Meyers, J., & Collins, A. S. (2010). General education teachers' perceptions of behavior management and intervention strategies. *Journal of Positive Behavior Interventions, 12*, 86–102. https://doi.org/10.1177/1098300708330879

Tschannen-Moran, M., & Gareis, C. R. (2014). Faculty trust in the principal: An essential ingredient in high-performing schools. *Journal of Educational Administration, 53*, 66–92. https://doi.org/10.1108/JEA-02-2014-0024

Walker, H. M., Severson, H. H., & Feil, E. G. (2014). *Systematic Screening for Behavior Disorders (SSBD) technical manual: Universal screening for PreK–9* (2nd ed.). Eugene, OR: Pacific Northwest.

Walker, H. M., Severson, H. H., Naquin, G., D'Atrio, C., Feil, E. G., Hawken, L., & Sabey, C. (2010). *Implementing universal screening systems within an RtI-PBIS context*. In B. Doll, W. Pfohl, & J. Yoon, (Eds.), *Handbook of prevention science* (pp. 96–120). New York, NY: Routledge.

Chapter 4

Techniques for Systems Consultation

OVERVIEW

Within a complex system, such as a school district, communication patterns will greatly affect all intervention outcomes. Open communication channels and healthy boundaries will reduce staff and student stress and contribute to positive intervention outcomes. In this chapter, we focus on consultation as collateral to the counseling role, with a focus on facilitating open communication among the service providers and family members that make up the student's ecosystem. Consultation can be effective before counseling begins, during the counseling intervention, and after counseling has been terminated. Although consultation has emerged as a specialty area within school psychology, this chapter focuses on consultation as it contributes to effective counseling. We integrate consultation models with multitiered systems of support, addressing selected relevant models of consultation. Salient ethical issues include informed consent, limits of confidentiality, multiple relationships, and time constraints of the school psychologist.

OBJECTIVES

After reading this chapter, readers should be able to do the following:

- Identify distinctions between the specialty of school consultation and consultation as adjunct to individual or group counseling.
- Consider situations in which consultation may enhance the effects of counseling.
- Identify specific techniques that may be used by the school psychologist in consultation with a student's significant individuals.

- Identify ethical issues associated with school-based consultation in the context of a counseling case.
- Develop a specific consultation plan to increase the effectiveness of counseling interventions for identified problems.

Introduction

Although consultation has long been a focus of school psychology training, this role has become more prominent in the context of multitiered systems of support. School psychologists are ideally involved in primary prevention or school-wide systems of support, such as positive behavioral supports (Tier 1), secondary targeted interventions (Tier 2), and intensive individual interventions (Tier 3). At each level, effective consultation will establish the school psychologist's visibility, reliability, and competence. Counseling effectiveness will be proportional to the quality of communication within the larger school system. Blocked communication channels, such as between teachers and administrators, may lead to a sense of isolation and resentment or blame among various stakeholders for seemingly intractable problems. Consultation provided by school psychologists who are trained in communication and listening skills can facilitate problem solving among parties who serve the same student or students in a safe and supportive context.

With respect to the counseling role, consultation may serve as an effective and efficient technique for identifying students needing counseling, determining goals and objectives, and generalizing newly acquired skills for student clients as well as adults who work with students. Because consultation theory, research, and practice literature are broad and deep, this discussion will be necessarily limited to an overview of concepts and techniques likely to benefit the school psychologist in the counseling role. A brief review of selected consultation models will orient the reader to the options for using consultation to support the counseling role. This discussion illustrates parallels between the counseling and consultation models that share theoretical foundations. These parallels can work to the advantage of the school psychologist who employs both counseling and consultation interventions. For an in-depth discussion of school consultation training and practice, see *Building Competence in School Consultation: A Developmental Approach*, by Newman and Rosenfield (2019), and *Handbook of Research in School Consultation*, by Erchul and Sheridan (2014).

Consultation Models

Consultation is an indirect, interactive model of service delivery that requires at least two interdependent (not independent) participants. Collaborative consultation involves communicating and sharing perspectives across disciplines, without a hierarchy of roles. Collaborative consultation is a means to an end, the means being the collaborative generation of effective and creative interventions, with the end being improved functioning for a target child or children, and ultimately generalization of techniques by teachers or other school professionals to help other children in a school. As observed by Shernoff, Bearman, and Kratochwill (2017), consultation with teachers can be viewed as a universal intervention (Tier 1) to improve overall classroom health and climate, thus preventing the emergence of new mental health problems. For students at risk for serious mental health problems, consultation with teachers, parents, and other school staff

(Tier 2) may reduce referrals for more intensive individual counseling. Campus-based school psychologists who are integrated into the campus community can be readily available for consultation at the request of teachers, administrators, and/or parents. For the itinerant school psychologist who serves several campuses, consultation opportunities may result from family–school meetings, such as student support team meetings, or from crises. For example, the collaborative consultant might work with a teacher to determine whether a child in his classroom could benefit more from a classroom-based behavioral intervention, such as a behavioral contract or token economy, than from individual counseling. In this case, consultation might be part of the assessment of educational need for counseling, to first measure the response to less intensive intervention.

Within the various consultation models, the approach may be client centered (focused on the individual or system of concern) or consultee centered (focused on the teacher, parent, administrator, or others who will work directly with the student). Although most school consultation models are collaborative, there are specific distinctions among models as discussed below. Instructional (typically academic) consultation, a prominent model of service delivery in school psychology, is not addressed here because the focus on instruction is tangential to the counseling intervention.

Expert consultation, though not typically emphasized in school psychology training models, may be useful in Tier 1 activities. For example, a school district may be affected by an increase in suicides. A school psychologist who has specialty training in suicide prevention, intervention, and postvention, particularly with respect to social media issues (Niznik, Poland, & Lieberman, 2019), might be the ideal consultant for helping to develop a system-wide plan for addressing this concern by working with system administrators, teachers, parents, counselors, community mental health providers, news organizations, and law enforcement. Similarly, the school district might contact a school psychologist with specific expertise in screening for emotional–behavioral problems to be an expert consultant to the district to design and implement a tiered model for promoting mental health.

School psychologists, who typically have much more training in mental health interventions than other school personnel, should not shy away from the expert consultant role when appropriate, while acknowledging the expertise of others. The school psychologist also can provide workshops or training for teachers, parents, or other school psychologists as a form of expert consultation in which, to quote Elliott (2014), the school psychologist can "give psychology away" (p. 15). Taking on an expert role in specific areas does not equate to hierarchical authority over other professionals and fits within a collaborative framework. This role can help to reduce unnecessary referrals for counseling by addressing teachers' and other school professionals' needs for information and skills.

Behavioral consultation refers to the application of specific problem-solving steps to increase or decrease a specific, well-defined behavior. In the consultation framework, the school psychologist consultant might work with the teacher, parent, or administrator to (a) define a problem in behavioral terms, (b) assess the function of the behavior and the mechanisms that reinforce it, (c) develop a targeted intervention, and (d) evaluate the effectiveness of the intervention. This framework has obvious similarities to behavioral approaches in counseling, with manipulation of environmental variables to increase or decrease selected behaviors. Consultation could be used to help others in the child's everyday environment reinforce new behaviors learned in counseling. In contrast to counseling, behavioral consultation is an indirect method whereby the child is helped by the increased skills of the teacher or parent. Collateral benefits accrue to other students with whom the teacher engages once new skills have been acquired. Warren (2018) offers an extension of this model to encompass cognitive–behavioral consultation in schools. He presents an evidence-based approach for delivering collaborative consultation in K–12 schools. Current emphasis on evidence-based interventions and accountability for student outcomes means that school psychologists using behavioral consultation effectively must have foundations in applied behavior analysis and the empirical basis for selected interventions (Martens et al., 2014).

Conjoint behavioral consultation refers to an extension of behavioral consultation so that caregivers at school and home are included in the problem-solving collaboration (Sheridan, Clarke, & Ransom, 2014). In this model, the process of collaboration among parties is viewed as just as important as the outcome of the collaboration. Conjoint behavioral consultation is useful in home–school partnerships because it addresses concerns from both settings and generalizes skills to both settings. In this collaborative model, knowledge and perspectives can be shared across settings, with gains expected in the generalization of new skills. As with behavioral consultation, conjoint behavioral consultation uses a data-based approach with structured steps, in a naturalistic setting, under guidance from the school psychologist or other consultant. Such consultation might be accomplished through family–school meetings, where the importance of the entire ecological system surrounding the student is stressed, and where the parents, teachers, and consultant participate in all aspects of the problem-solving process. Having agreement among the perceptions of involved parties positively affects outcome (Klose, Plotts, & Lasser, 2010). Sheridan and others (2019), in a study of conjoint behavioral consultation for disruptive behaviors in rural schools, reported that immediate effects, as measured by parent-rated adaptive and social skills and teacher-rated school problems, were maintained when followed up after 1 year.

A recent study (Love et al., 2019) evaluated the impact of a social–cognitive teacher consultation intervention, COMPASS (a collaborative model for promoting competence and success), on teachers' intrapersonal factor of self-efficacy. Teachers who received the consultation intervention reported higher levels of self-efficacy for teaching students with autism spectrum disorder. Further, results indicated that self-efficacy for teaching students with autism spectrum disorder was significantly and positively correlated with teacher engagement and student outcomes, and negatively correlated with teacher stress.

Mental health consultation, perhaps most like counseling in its attention to intrapersonal variables (internal communication or perceptions), has a long tradition of use both within and outside of schools. Mental health consultation, as described and elaborated by Caplan and Caplan (1993), has its roots in child psychiatry in post-World War II Israel, where improving the skill and judgment of child guidance professionals resulted in protective benefits for the larger population of students and teachers rather than just the individual. This consultation model focuses on addressing the personal needs of both the adult providers (teachers or parents who are consultees) and the child receiving counseling services (client), with an emphasis on preventive strategies. The purpose and goal of the consultee-focused consultation is to improve the professional's functioning by strategically addressing the beliefs, attitudes, judgments, and skills that influence their work with students. According to Caplan and Caplan (1993), four sources of difficulty may interfere with a consultee's professional functioning: (a) lack of skill, (b) lack of knowledge, (c) lack of confidence, or (d) lack of objectivity. In a school setting, for example, a teacher who struggled with depression and suicidal ideation in adolescence, with a lack of intervention by the adults in their life, may believe that all struggling students should receive counseling from the school psychologist. In this example, the teacher is demonstrating what Caplan and Caplan termed "theme interference," or a lack of objectivity resulting from the teacher's emotional interference, which may result in excessive referrals to the school psychologist. The mental health consultant in this case might work with the teacher to clarify roles and boundaries, thus improving objectivity in their referral decisions. For the consulting school psychologist, it is important to distinguish between consultee-centered consultation, in which the emphasis is on the attributes of teachers that affect outcomes of students, and adult counseling, which would typically be conducted outside the school setting by another mental health practitioner.

A newer model of mental health consultation that is more aligned with school needs and structure may be described as *consultee-centered consultation* (Knotek & Hylander, 2014). In this model, interventions are nonprescriptive rather than prescriptive; that is, they develop as the consultation process evolves. The consultant does not assume a lack of objectivity on the part of the teacher, and the consultation process contributes to new knowledge that makes problems possible to resolve.

In an *ecological systems approach* to consultation (Bronfenbrenner, 1979), the focus is on evaluation of behavior, cognition, and environment, including the multiple and interacting systems within which the client as student and the teacher as consultee function. It may be preferred in schools where counseling approaches emphasize an ecosystemic understanding of behaviors of concern as occurring in a systems context. The school psychologist in the consultant role is likely to be a direct participant in evaluation of environmental variables using direct observation, checklists, and interviews with multiple consultees (teachers, administrators, parents, and other involve adults) and the student.

Organizational consultation might be viewed as a specialty training area within school psychology. In reality, school psychologists operating in a school system in which response to intervention (RTI), multitiered systems of supports, positive behavioral supports, and empirically based interventions are implemented will find themselves in an organizational or systems consultant role by virtue of participation on child study teams, crisis intervention teams, and IEP teams, for example (Crothers, Hughes, & Morine, 2008). However, formal organizational consultation involves not only advanced training for the school psychologist but also having an institution that acknowledges the need for change and is ready to do so, a sanctioned opportunity for the consultant and mode of entry into the system, access to stakeholders and resources, and trust and credibility, discussion of which is beyond the scope of this text.

Development of a general consultation model can help practitioners conceptualize their options for consulting in different levels of intervention and the sequence of steps they will follow. Figure 4.1 provides a sample consultation model to facilitate this process, taking into account that school consultation services are provided in "contextualized, nested settings that are by nature interdependent" (Erchul & Sheridan, 2014, p. 1192).

FIGURE 4.1. Consultation Model

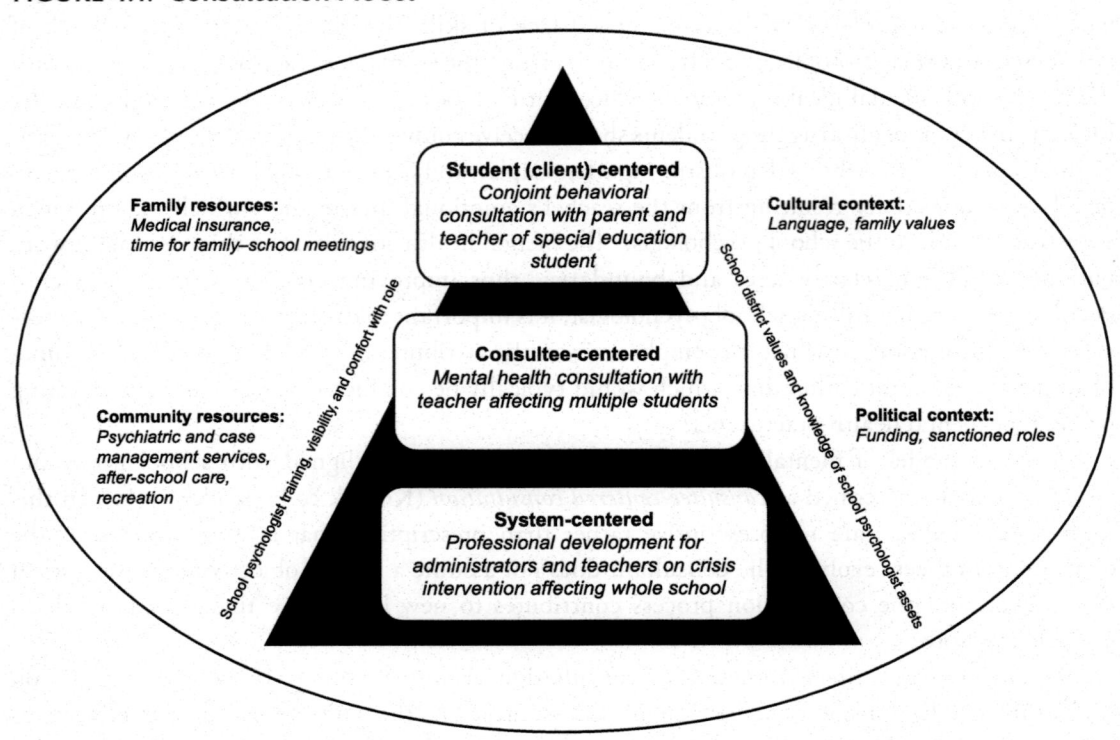

Note. Adapted from *School Psychologist as Counselor: A Practitioner's Handbook* (p. 155), by C. A. Plotts & J. Lasser, 2013, National Association of School Psychologists. Copyright 2013 by the National Association of School Psychologists. Adapted with permission.

Specific Applications

Consultation as adjunctive to counseling is best understood as it applies to the daily work of school psychologists as they collaborate with school personnel, family members, and other professionals.

Teachers, Administrators, and School Staff

Most consultation conducted by school psychologists who are counselors will be conducted in the client-centered model, typically with a teacher as the consultee. Examples might include prereferral consultations to implement an intervention as part of RTI prior to a special education referral. In such cases, behavioral or instructional consultation models would provide the school psychologist with knowledge about the student's emotional, behavioral, and academic status. The consultant might work with the teacher or parent beyond the interviews and initial data collection to develop realistic interventions and assess outcomes before moving to more direct services for the student.

Alternatively, a child may be the focus of consultation even if referral for special education or reevaluation for eligibility is not considered. For example, a child who returns to school following a traumatic event might be the focus of a consultation with the child's teacher to help the teacher who feels less able to deal with stress and grief management.

School administrators may also consider consultation regarding the needs of a particular student or teacher. For example, one of the authors was asked by a principal to consult with a teacher regarding a particularly difficult student. The teacher voluntarily agreed to the consultation arrangement; however, as the process evolved, it became clear that the teacher did not have a general classroom management strategy and the target student was one of several who were defying the teacher. The focus shifted from the student-centered approach to the consultee-centered approach, and the teacher agreed to collaborate on a classroom management plan. The teacher, students, and administrator all experienced relief, and the target student's behavior improved as well. This example illustrates how the collaborative consultation may lead to a shift both in the goals and in the approach used to achieve them. The consultant in such a situation might use a social–cognitive consultation model (e.g., rearranging the classroom seating, introducing classroom rules and consequences, and reinforcing incompatible alternative behaviors). For consultation strategies, the consultant might provide modeling of specific strategies, observe and provide feedback, and use encouragement.

The school psychologist as consultant might work with other school staff, such as hall monitors and other personnel, to plan for management of space and crowds in case a student with a seizure disorder has a seizure in the hallway or cafeteria or on the playground. School psychologists might also consult with other school mental health professionals, such as school counselors or social workers who need a second opinion when dealing with challenging situations. The complexity of students' emotional and behavioral needs routinely creates opportunities for consultation that most school staff welcome. Of course, the school psychologist should be attuned to ethical issues regarding confidentiality and multiple relationships, which are discussed later in this chapter.

For the school psychologist who uses consultation to complement and support other roles, their visibility, accessibility, recognition of role differences and peer equality, and respect for boundaries and confidential communications will go a long way in establishing credibility within school systems.

Parents, Siblings, and Extended Family

The busy school psychologist may have limited natural opportunities to engage with family members in a consultation role. Some events lend themselves to family consultation, including the following:

- Child support team or other prereferral or RTI meeting
- Interviews for history gathering when a child is referred for special education
- Family–school meetings, which are held on some campuses to do conjoint behavioral consultation around specific student needs
- Professional development meetings when presentations on specific topics are requested (e.g., restorative discipline models)

The topic of working with families in the context of counseling services is addressed in greater detail in Chapter 5, on family systems.

Other Professionals and Community Resources

Consultation with individuals outside of the school setting is challenging because most days are filled with school-based activities. Consultation with other professionals who provide services to students can also make the school psychologist's work more efficient such as by avoiding redundant services and coordinating interventions, as in the following examples:

- Medical consultation when a physician is treating a child whose school functioning may be affected by the medication.
- Treatment consultation when a student is receiving services from more than one mental health professional. Ethically, school psychologists are obligated to coordinate with other service providers who work with the same children.
- Transition for students who are leaving the school system for college, employment, or another school. IDEA requires that transition plans, which include coordination with community resources, be in place for all secondary special education students.
- Coordination of services for students with special medical or psychiatric needs, including those who are coming from or going to rehabilitation centers after traumatic brain injuries, or going to or from hospitals before or following medical or crisis interventions.

The school psychologist's visibility, accessibility, and willingness to initiate and maintain collaborative working relationships will reap benefits for children who receive school-based counseling. Routine and efficient completion of basic consultation tasks—such as telephone and email contacts, fulfillment of records requests, and obtaining of pertinent records—will help to establish credibility for the school psychologist in the consultant role. It may be tempting to assume that other school staff will communicate with outside professionals and community resources; however, essential communications fall through the cracks and are not done at all if not explicit in a job description. The school psychologist who hopes to enhance the consultation role might welcome such tasks, in addition to scheduling time to visit hospitals, rehabilitation centers, and so on, to make valuable connections.

Specific Techniques

Consultation is likely to enhance counseling interventions when school psychologists employ empirically supported techniques such as those described in this section.

Relationship Building

Research on the effectiveness of consultation is consistent with findings regarding counseling. Both conclude that the relationship between the consultant and the consultee is probably the most important variable in predicting outcomes (Crothers, Hughes, & Morine, 2008). How does the school psychologist develop a productive consultative relationship? The elements are probably familiar to most school psychologists, paralleling those skills that have proved successful in interviewing, counseling, and assessment relationships. For example, alliances with youth and parents are predictors of successful counseling outcomes. Also, attending behaviors (eye contact, open body language), active listening skills (reflection, paraphrasing), and higher-order skills (reflection of feeling, focusing, encouraging, summarizing) can go a long way toward establishing a working relationship. As always, being on time, reliable, and good humored foster comfort and trust.

Problem-Solving Model

In collaborative consultation, four basic steps are common to most problem-solving models: problem identification, problem assessment, intervention, and evaluation. These four steps have been elaborated, added to, and variously defined in the consultation models discussed earlier. Although the sequence is typically linear, the steps are not rigid and may be returned to during the consultation process.

The school psychologist who uses a behavioral model, also called a problem-solving model, will define the problem differently than one who selects a consultee-centered consultation model. For the teacher or parent who has difficulty with an impulsive first grader, behavioral consultation would help the teacher to define the behavior of most concern in concrete, behavioral terms; in contrast, the consultee-centered or mental health consultant might explore the teacher's past experience with similar problems, how they managed the problem, and similarities or differences between the current and former problems with a student.

Given that most school psychologists have time constraints that make consultation difficult, such as their assessment case load and travel among campuses, exploring options for service delivery is warranted. Fischer et al. (2017) compared the effectiveness of conducting the problem identification interview using a face-to face format and a videoconferencing format. Using four indices of effectiveness from a consultation analysis record, videoconference interviews were found to have higher content relevance, process effectiveness, and message control, but lower content focus. The authors concluded that their results provided initial support for the effectiveness of consultation delivered via videoconferencing. Technology for videoconferencing is available on many school campuses and could be a useful medium for collaborating with parents, teachers, and outside service providers.

Ecological Model

A useful perspective for conceptualizing the interplay between counseling and consultation in schools comes from Bronfenbrenner's ecological model of child development (1979), which describes the child as developing within a nested set of contexts that can be visualized as concentric circles, with the child at the center (Figure 4.2).

Each of the layers of context has dynamic interplay with other layers, including the microsystem of the child. This model has proved useful for conceptualizing interventions that take into account systemic variables affecting a child's functioning. Specific to this context, an ecological systems model could help inform the school psychologist who implements a counseling intervention in the context of family and classroom variables that can either confound or improve treatment outcomes. For example, the school psychologist who provides individual counseling that is focused on anger management will need to adapt to changes in the system when the child is removed from the parents' home by child protective services. In this case, the context for triggers of behavior and generalization of skills learned in counseling has changed. To maintain the child's safety net, the

FIGURE 4.2. Bronfenbrenner Model

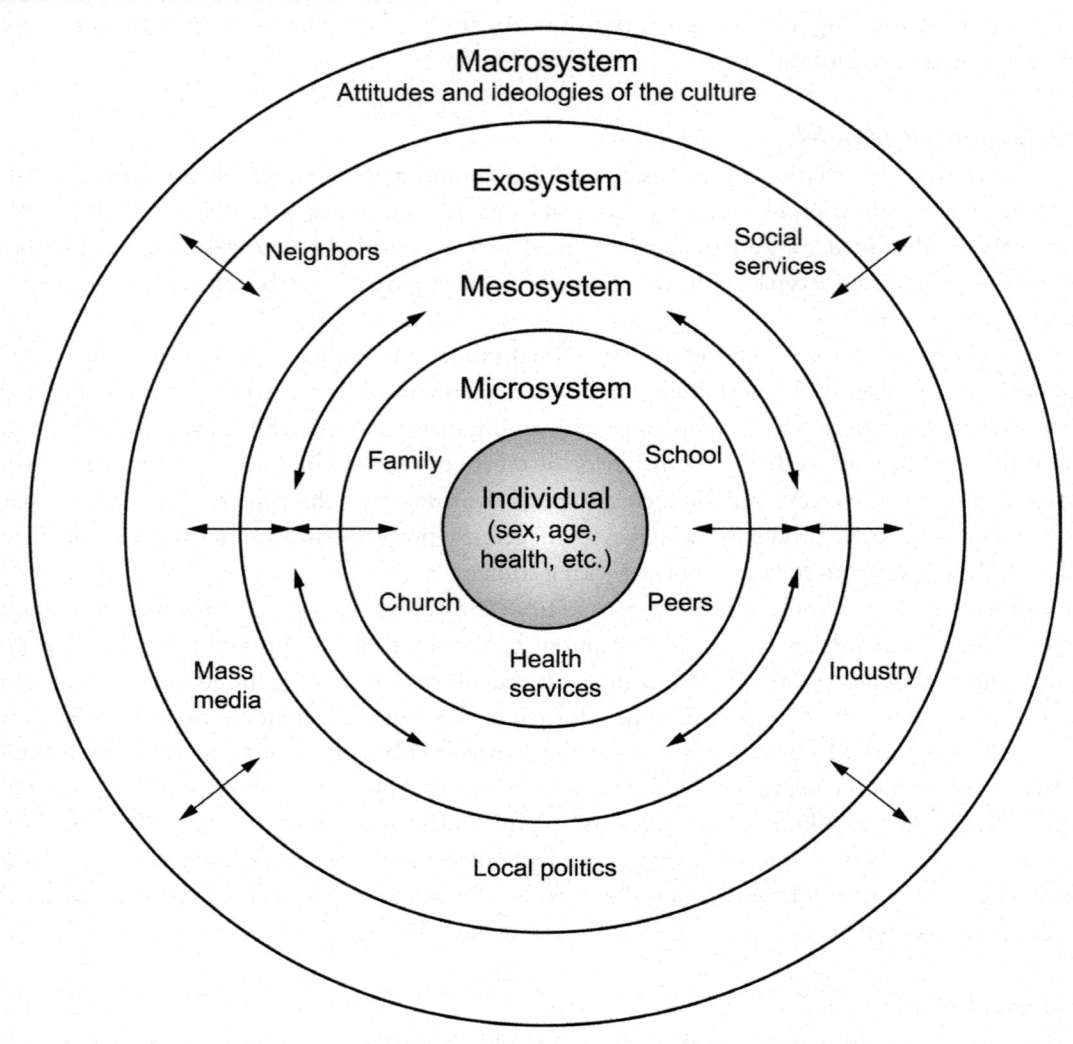

[Diagram of Bronfenbrenner's ecological systems model showing concentric circles from innermost to outermost: Individual (sex, age, health, etc.); Microsystem (Family, School, Peers, Health services, Church); Mesosystem; Exosystem (Neighbors, Social services, Mass media, Industry, Local politics); Macrosystem (Attitudes and ideologies of the culture).]

Note. Reprinted from *School Psychologist as Counselor: A Practitioner's Handbook* (p. 160), by C. A. Plotts & J. Lasser, 2013, National Association of School Psychologists. Copyright 2013 by the National Association of School Psychologists. Reprinted with permission.

school psychologist can consult with teachers, outside service providers, and family members to assess support resources and maintain open communication about the child's adjustment across settings.

Wellness Model and Positive Psychology

A wellness model and positive psychology orientation are strengths-based approaches that can help clients face complex challenges and problems with hope and an expectation for a positive outcome. Positive psychology can be defined as the scientific study of strengths and virtues that build resiliency and enable people to thrive (Seligman, 2019). These approaches are holistic in that they consider the individual in connection with family, community, and the world (Ivey, Ivey, & Zalaquett, 2014). From this perspective, change in any part of the system, if positive, can benefit the whole person. The school psychologist as counselor may recognize that the student has resources within the family or community that can contribute to more rapid benefits from counseling. For example, a student in foster care may have supportive extended family or church members who can provide a safety network during the crisis. A musically talented student who is struggling with social anxiety may find a safe place in the school band, choir, or other music group, to make positive connections and receive reinforcement for their contributions. Unless the school psychologist explores individual, family, community, and school strengths and resources, the focus may remain on deficits rather than strengths and resources.

Other Techniques

Most often, mental health professionals rely on verbal communication in counseling and consultation, especially when the clients are older adolescents and adults. However, individuals of all ages can benefit from the use of visual techniques such as drawings, charts, or graphs to convey information and to depict context. Ecological systems models, for example, depict the "world" of a specific child, and genograms or sociograms can help the school psychologist better understand the child's family and community systems.

The Bronfenbrenner (1979) model described earlier can be used with students, parents, and teachers to generate a diagram that informs all parties about variables influencing a child's functioning and development. Such a diagram can also maintain the focus of an intervention, especially when environmental or setting variables might change as part of the intervention. Development of such diagrams, which requires gathering information from multiple informants, encourages involvement of all relevant parties in the intervention.

Weiss et al. (2014) describe a social executive functioning model that is derived in part from Bronfenbrenner's ecological systems model. In the social executive functioning graphic, the individual child, with their own executive functioning processes, is at the center. Around that, concentric circles include significant individuals, contextual resources and dangers, and the community context. Ideally, the child's system includes self-regulating adults who model and support the child's development of executive functions, including developmentally appropriate emotional and behavioral self-regulation.

Weiss et al.'s (2014) social executive functioning model reflects their position that better coordination among children's significant individuals is needed to improve school and family collaboration. The model was designed to demonstrate how adults inside and outside the child's home can work together to improve the child's educational outcomes. From a consultation perspective, this model might be used to visualize the context within which a student is developing and to identify and connect resources to promote healthy development. Understanding the supports, and stressors, around a student can help the school psychologist design realistic and empathetic approaches to intervention.

A genogram is a graphic representation of a family tree that displays detailed data on relationships among individuals. A sociogram is a visual model for displaying relationships among groups, such as classrooms, counseling groups, and school personnel. Both have been used in counseling and therapy across mental health disciplines and can aid in consultation in the following ways:

- Eliciting information in a nonthreatening, engaging activity format.
- Using the information generated by the activity as a prompt to enhance understanding, expression of feelings, and problem solving.
- Sharing student-produced models with parents and teachers (with appropriate consent) to develop insight and understanding.
- Using the information generated by the diagram to conceptualize the case, guide consultation, and assess the convergence of perceptions across parties.
- Using a wellness approach to identify resources that might be overlooked when approaching a student's presenting problems.

Several online programs are available for generating genograms and sociograms (see http://www.genopro.com/genogram/family-systems-theory/, https://www.edrawsoft.com, and http://www.sussex.ac.uk/Users/robinb/socio.html).

Ethical Considerations

When consultation techniques and counseling are employed with the same student client, several ethical considerations come to mind, including confidentiality, informed consent, triangulation in communication, multiple relationships, and competence.

Confidentiality, described as the protection of private information disclosed by a client, can be challenging when multiple parties are involved. For example, the student who is receiving counseling may be the client, while the teacher, parent, administrator, and community professional might all be consultees. All parties would be receiving psychological services when counseling and consultation are used together, and for each individual there would be relationship and confidentiality considerations. In general, a consultation approach requires that some core information be shared among participants, especially in a conjoint model. Although it is preferable that information be shared in contexts where all parties are present, in reality, the logistics of schedules often preclude the presence of all parties at all meetings. School psychologists must, through informed consent, clarify in advance the parties they are working with and in what capacity, what information will be available to all (e.g., the results of a psychological evaluation or counseling needs assessment), and how findings from meetings or sessions will be used for planning, intervention, and evaluation. Consultees may sometimes perceive the relationship with the school psychologist as a form of personal counseling; the burden is on the school psychologist to clarify the work-focused nature of the relationship.

Limits to confidentiality must be expressly explained to the student client who may perceive the counseling relationship as private and distinct from other relationships with parents, school staff, or community providers. Even though the confidentiality right legally belongs to the consenting adult, a minor student client should be assured of the privacy of communication to the extent feasible. When providing conjoint behavioral consultation for parents and teachers in the context of individual counseling for the student, information disclosed privately by the student usually need not become content for consultation unless the student consents and the content is relevant. For example, the student may share sensitive information about a parent's job loss and subsequent financial stress; the school psychologist need not bring up this information to a parent or school staff unless the student consents or the student's welfare is at risk. Clearly, the information is relevant to the student's adjustment, but it remains private within the counseling context.

Multiple relationships, which may occur in conjoint consultation or when the school psychologist provides simultaneous consultation and counseling, can lead to triangulation. Triangulation occurs when a third person conveys information between two people who have a dysfunctional relationship. For example, when parents are estranged, their children are sometimes "put in the middle" and expected to convey information when the parents won't talk to each other. The school psychologist should avoid becoming part of triangles involving parents and teachers, parents and children, teachers and administrators, and so on. The school psychologist must be aware of this possibility and work to maintain clear boundaries, facilitate direct communication through face-to-face meetings whenever possible, and make clear what information will remain confidential (and when necessary, obtain consent or assent to disclose). Conjoint consultation provides numerous opportunities to model direct, appropriate communication to improve functioning within a system.

CASE EXAMPLE 1: CALEB

Caleb, a 6-year-old kindergartner, was referred to the student support team by the school principal in November. He had moved to a small school district from a remote rural area, where he was in a one-room school with four other students of different ages. He had received no special services. The move was precipitated by the biological mother's deciding that she could not handle Caleb's acting-out behaviors while caring for his two older brothers, ages 12 and 14. She moved to another state with her boyfriend and Caleb moved in with his biological father and paternal grandfather. The two older boys, his half brothers, moved to a nearby town, in the same school district, with their biological father. In Caleb's kindergarten class, his behaviors were severe and included throwing chairs at people, threatening the principal with a snow shovel near the front of the building, cursing at the teacher, hitting other children, and yelling, crying, and running away when disciplined. The student support team connected the biological father with a local social services agency, which assigned the family a case manager. Appointments were made for psychiatric and psychological evaluations outside the school; however, the wait lists for these services were long. In the meantime, Caleb's aggressive and threatening behaviors became so extreme that he was suspended from his kindergarten class after an unsuccessful attempt at half-day kindergarten with counseling through the general education program. Caleb's father welcomed the school and community interventions but acknowledged feeling overwhelmed. He struggled with addiction and had recently completed a prison term for a drug-related charge. He continued to work with a sobriety program but felt very much stressed by Caleb's behaviors, especially following Caleb's suspension from school, which interfered with his ability to maintain a regular work schedule.

The student support team developed a 504 plan for Caleb based on a psychiatric diagnosis of ADHD. Caleb was bused to school each morning to work with a tutor for an hour pending a comprehensive assessment to clarify cognitive and emotional functioning. Carol, the school psychologist, elected to use a collaborative consultation model. She consulted with the father, mother, tutor, kindergarten teacher, and psychiatrist before beginning the formal assessment. She was able to interview the biological mother via teleconferencing and thus obtain a fairly complete history. Consultation with the psychiatrist indicated that a family history of ADHD along with Caleb's impulsivity and poor concentration led to the ADHD diagnosis and prescription for a psychostimulant. History also revealed that the biological mother had a history of substance abuse before, during, and after her pregnancy with Caleb. Carol completed a comprehensive evaluation and learned that Caleb's cognitive functioning was above average. Academic achievement was commensurate with peers for age and grade, despite his limited educational opportunity. Severe emotional disturbance was apparent; the history indicated that the duration had been at least 2 years and included difficulties in relationships with adults and children, excessive anxiety, and inappropriate behaviors and feelings under normal circumstances. It was also apparent that adjustment difficulties related to Caleb's being moved to a new home and a new school, separate from his mother and brothers and living with his father, with whom he had not lived since age 3, contributed to the severity of his behavioral problems.

Conjoint behavioral consultation was initiated with the biological father and the self-contained special education teacher. Because Caleb attended only half days while his father was working, consultation was done separately with the parent and teacher; however, goals were shared and an informed consent to share information and intervention plans across settings ensured communication. The special education teacher, who was highly skilled and experienced with students with severe emotional and behavioral problems, benefited from time with the consultant, which allowed her to express that she was sometimes overwhelmed and uncertain about how to manage Caleb's challenging behaviors. They set up a token economy system using a behavioral contract where buttons were attached to achieved goals with Velcro; buttons could be exchanged for items in the school store. An effort was made to have consistent behavior expectations at home, with rewards contingent on reaching behavior goals, but it was difficult to assess the consistency of the intervention at home. Once behavioral goals and interventions were established across settings, consultation also centered on the teacher as the consultee, giving her support and validation and allowing her to develop new skills for handling this complex case.

Counseling goals included increasing Caleb's tolerance for the complex social milieu of school, as measured by his ability to remain in school for a half day. A correlated goal was to reduce Caleb's aggressive behaviors, initially by eliminating physical threats and then moving to reduce verbal aggression. A third goal was to increase positive self-regard, as measured by more frequent positive verbalizations rather than negative self-talk. Specific objectives to reach these goals included establishing a trusting, safe relationship with Caleb through a reliable presence and unconditional positive regard. Thirty-minute, semistructured play sessions using games, drawings, and art activities were initiated. At the same time, Carol continued conjoint behavioral consultation with the teacher and parent, monitoring Caleb's response to interventions at home and at school. She also checked in with the psychiatrist monthly to gauge Caleb's response to the medication intervention. Caleb understood that the school psychologist spoke with his father, teacher, and psychiatrist and was accustomed to seeing her in his classroom, thus establishing assent for communication with others in his world. These adult-to-adult cooperative relationships seemed to increase his sense of security at school. His medication regimen was adjusted several times in collaboration with the psychiatrist. By the end of the spring semester of kindergarten, Caleb was remaining at school for half days, had established positive relationships with his teacher and two classroom peers, and rarely showed verbal or physical aggression. He participated in some general education activities, including recess and assemblies. His home situation remained somewhat tenuous in that the biological mother and her boyfriend moved back to the vicinity, and it was unclear what the visitation arrangement would be over the summer.

Working with parents and teachers who disagree on the problem or the intervention requires that the consultant have well-developed collaborative consultation skills. Because all practitioners can have limitations, they should seek supervision or professional consultation when triangulation occurs, collaboration fails, or their objectivity becomes compromised.

CASE EXAMPLE 2: ALEX

Use the following background information to conceptualize a coordinated counseling and consultation plan.

Background

Alex is a 13-year-old transgender male. He was female gender at birth. During early childhood, records indicate psychiatric and psychological problems that resulted in several comprehensive assessments. Resulting diagnoses included, over time, pragmatic language disorder, developmental delays, autism spectrum disorder, depression, and oppositional defiant disorder. At the time of the referral to the school psychologist, Alex was living with his biological mother and 18-year-old sister. His mother had multiple medical problems and was not working. Alex had no contact with his biological father. History indicated both neglect and physical abuse in early childhood. His gender identity had been unstable throughout childhood, in that he sometimes identified as female and sometimes as male. School records sometimes used a male name and gender and sometimes a female name and gender. He was being served through special education as a student with autism. A recent comprehensive evaluation indicated superior cognitive abilities, with verbal skills better developed that visual–spatial skills. He had very high math and reading abilities, with written expression weaker but within average limits. Alex was in a self-contained classroom but had recently begun to participate in mainstream math and some social events, accompanied by a paraprofessional aide. When interviewed by the school psychologist, Alex dressed as a male and stated his identity to be male. Immediate concerns included stealing at home and school, verbal aggression toward adults and peers, and fixation on certain topics (e.g., politics, death) that dominated his conversation in social settings. He expressed being teased by classmates, especially on the school bus.

How might consultation assist the school psychologist in Alex's case? What consultation model(s) would you consider and why?

- What systems variables that are affecting Alex's school functioning might be amenable to change? Sketch an ecological systems model.
- How would you identify resources in the family, school, or community that could contribute to Alex's improved adjustment?
- What specific techniques might you use in counseling sessions to establish trust and rapport, gain more information and insight, and help Alex deal with stressors at school?
- What ethical issues must you consider in using both counseling and consultation in Alex's case?
- In what aspects of this case would you need to consult with a colleague or supervisor? How would you increase your competence?

SUMMARY

The consultation role, when integrated with the counseling role, is a powerful tool for school psychologists. Although school consultation can be perceived as a specialty area with its own research, training, and practice guidelines, in a more basic sense it also provides a framework for effective assessment and counseling in school settings. Well-developed active listening skills, combined with a degree of comfort in collaborating with parents, teachers, administrators, other school staff, and community providers, will increase the impact of the school psychologist's counseling efforts. As with counseling approaches, the school psychologist must develop working relationships by demonstrating the warmth, empathy, genuineness, and positive regard that will help to build trust and rapport. Visibility, careful attention to ethics, and thoughtful, intentional use of consultation skills will enhance the credibility of the school psychologist in the counseling role.

KEY POINTS FOR DISCUSSION

- How well trained are most school psychologists to engage in the consultation role in schools?
- What reservations do you have about your competence in specific consultation models?
- How will you balance the assessment, counseling, and consultation roles given time constraints?
- How might the work of teachers or administrators be affected by their own childhood experiences? How could consultation help increase objectivity?
- Do you see consultation as a tool for enhancing the effectiveness of counseling? Why or why not?
- What ethical issues might emerge in the case study of Alex?

REFERENCES

Bronfenbrenner, U. (1979). *The ecology of human development*. Cambridge, MA: Harvard University Press.

Caplan, G., & Caplan, R. B. (1993). *Mental health consultation and collaboration*. San Francisco, CA: Jossey-Bass.

Crothers, L. M., Hughes, T. L., & Morine, K. A. (2008). *Theory and cases in school-based consultation: A resource for school psychologists, school counselors, special educators, and other mental health professionals*. Lawrence, KY: Routledge.

Elliott, S. N. (2014). Field notes: Expectations and observations of school psychology consultation research. In W. P. Erchul & S. M. Sheridan (Eds.), *Handbook of research in school consultation* (2nd ed., pp. 13–17). New York, NY: Routledge.

Erchul, W. P., & Sheridan, S. M. (2014). *Handbook of research in school consultation* (2nd ed.). New York, NY: Routledge.

Fischer, A. J., Collier-Meek, M. A., Bloomfield, B., Erchul, W. P., & Gresham, F. M. (2017). A comparison of problem identification interviews conducted face-to-face and via videoconferencing using the consultation analysis record. *Journal of School Psychology, 63*, 63–76.

Ivey, A. E., Ivey, M. B., & Zalaquett, C. P. (2014). *Intentional interviewing and counseling: Facilitating client development in a multicultural society* (8th ed.). Belmont, CA: Brooks/Cole, Cengage Learning.

Klose, L. M., Plotts, C., & Lasser, J. (2010). Qualitative analysis of teacher and graduate student evaluations of consultation training experiences. *Trainers' Forum, 29*(1), 24–37.

Knotek, S. E., & Hylander, I. (2014). Research issues in mental health consultation and consultee-centered approaches. In W. P. Erchul & S. M. Sheridan (Eds.), *Handbook of research in school consultation* (2nd ed., pp. 359–422). New York, NY: Routledge.

Love, A. M. A., Findley, J. A., Ruble, L. A., & McGrew, J. H. (2019). Teacher self-efficacy for teaching students with autism spectrum disorder: Associations with stress, teacher engagement, and student IEP outcomes following COMPASS consultation. *Focus on Autism and Other Developmental Disabilities.* https://doi-org.libproxy.txstate.edu/10.1177/1088357619836767

Martens, B. K., DeGennaro Reed, F. D., & Magnuson, J. D. (2014). Behavioral consultation: Contemporary research and emerging challenges. In W. P. Erchul & S. M. Sheridan (Eds.), *Handbook of research in school consultation* (2nd ed., pp. 423–495). New York, NY: Routledge.

Newman, D. S., & Rosenfield, S. A. (2019). *Building competence in school consultation: A developmental approach.* New York, NY: Routledge.

Niznik, M., Poland, S., & Lieberman, R. (2019, November). Adolescent suicide prevention in the context of social media—part 1: Overview. *Communiqué, 48*(3), 1, 28–29.

Seligman, M. E. P. (2019). Positive psychology: A personal history. *Annual Review of Clinical Psychology, 15*, 1–23.

Sheridan, S. M., Clarke, B. L., & Ransom, K. A. (2014). The past, present, and future of conjoint behavioral consultation research. In W. P. Erchul & S. M. Sheridan (Eds.), *Handbook of research in school consultation* (2nd ed., pp. 496–566). New York, NY: Routledge.

Sheridan, S. M., Witte, A. L., Wheeler, L. A., Eastberg, S. R. A., Dizona, P. J., & Gormley, M. J. (2019). Conjoint behavioral consultation in rural schools: Do student effects maintain after 1 year? *School Psychology, 34*(4), 410–420.

Shernoff, E. S., Bearman, S. K., & Kratochwill, T. R. (2017). Training the next generation of school psychologists to deliver evidence-based mental health practices: Current challenges and future directions. *School Psychology Review, 46*(2), 219–231.

Warren, J. M. (2018). *School consultation for student success: A cognitive-behavioral approach.* New York, NY: Springer.

Weiss, H. B., Kreider, H., Lopez, M. E., & Chatman-Nelson, C. (2010). *Preparing educators to engage families: Case studies using an ecological systems framework* (2nd ed.). Thousand Oaks, CA: SAGE.

Chapter 5

Family Interventions

OVERVIEW

Students live within multiple systems, including families. For school psychologists, working with children in schools necessarily involves collaboration with families, but training and competence in family interventions can vary considerably. Some doctoral-level programs provide supervised training in family therapy as well as other collaborative models, while most specialist-level programs provide supervised training in family collaboration and consultation models. Although federal law requires that parents be included in school decisions and services regarding children, opportunities to practice formal interventions with families depend on sanctioned roles in employment settings. In this chapter, we briefly review family systems models the school psychologist as counselor can use for therapy and consultation. We also give an overview of family–school models, with attention to applications for special family circumstances. Specific techniques for addressing family issues in the context of counseling in schools are also discussed, with a case study provided for illustration.

OBJECTIVES

After reading this chapter, readers should be able to do the following:

- Consider the empirical support for school-based family services.
- Be familiar with the federal laws that guide school professionals for working with families.
- Identify family therapy models that inform school practice.
- Identify family interventions that may be useful for children involved in school counseling.
- Identify special issues faced by children and families that may affect school adjustment, and interventions that may be effective.
- Become familiar resources for accessing techniques that can be used in counseling to address family issues.

Introduction

In a position statement on school–family partnering, NASP (2019) stated that

> partnerships involve families and educators working together as active, equal partners who share responsibility for the learning and success of all students. Using a partnership-centered orientation, schools create equitable systems of support that all families can access where family diversity is celebrated and family culture is embedded throughout school policies and practices. (p. 2)

Empirical research cited in this position statement underscores decades of findings that partnering across homes and schools benefits all parties (Sheridan et al., 2019).

In a discussion of approaches to increasing equity in education, Hacker and Hayes (2017) focus on two themes: (a) emphasizing the resources and protective factors individuals bring to their own interventions, thus using a strengths-based approach, and (b) reconceptualizing an individual's ecological development system itself as "the client" (p. 1256). Hacker and Hayes also promote the development of partnerships across time (e.g., throughout the student's development and schooling) and across systems, including schools, families, communities, and other organizations (e.g., medical, social). Their work underscores the current perspective that dynamic systems, including families, are always operating during any interventions, and only when systems are acknowledged and engaged is meaningful, lasting change likely.

Efforts to collaborate with families are required by special education law. The Individuals with Disabilities Education Improvement Act of 2004 (IDEA Reauthorization) specifies the expectation that parents will be involved in all decision making regarding their children who are referred for or in special education. Parental involvement on the Individualized Education Program (IEP) team ensures that parents can participate in decisions regarding the education of their child, including placement decisions and development of the IEP plan. This provision includes development of the counseling IEP for students in special education. Over the several decades since the passage of Public Law 94-142 (the Education for All Handicapped Children Act of 1975), the emphasis on family involvement in school decision making has increased not only in response to federal mandates but also because of research demonstrating that home–school collaboration yields positive results for children (Sheridan et al., 2019).

The No Child Left Behind Act of 2002 (NCLB) made it clear that parents are integral to educational progress and must be partners with schools in educating children, and it provided some funding for family engagement. In December 2015, Congress passed the Every Student Succeeds Act (ESSA) to replace NCLB. ESSA mandates that school districts offer programs and activities to involve parents and family members and that schools seek meaningful consultation with parents. Specific provisions in ESSA include a requirement that the district establish its expectations and objectives for meaningful parent and family engagement and that it carry out at least one of the following strategies to engage families effectively: (a) professional development for school staff (may include parents), (b) home-based programs, (c) information dissemination, (d) collaboration with community organizations, and (e) other related activities. (An example of an education service center in Texas presents a legal framework and statewide parent involvement initiative; https://www.esc16.net.)

Together, ESSA and IDEA make it clear that the intent of federal law is to ensure that parents and families are participants in the school system, with the aid of schools that are mandated to provide encouragement and realistic opportunities. For school psychologists, these legal mandates mean that structures will likely be present in their schools that will allow them to facilitate meaningful engagement with parents and families. According to Epstein et al. (2019), effective school–family partnerships are prioritized and integrated into school routines. Further, such partnerships should not be one size fits all but rather be tailored for each school.

The stage is set through both federal law and scientific research for school psychologists to create roles for themselves in family–school partnering. Counseling presents a special opportunity because it requires parental consent, builds alliances that are known to promote positive outcomes, and it is engages family–school systems that generalize improvements and lasting change.

Besides legal requirements and research support, Heward (2009) provides several other reasons why parental involvement is desirable and beneficial: Families usually know more about certain aspects of their children's functioning than anyone else, they may be the only adults who remain involved with children throughout their school careers, they have a vested interest in the outcomes of children's education, and they have to live with the outcomes of decisions made by school-based teams.

School psychologists face practical limitations in their efforts to work with families. A recent publication (Soutullo, Sanders-Smith, & Smith-Bonahue, 2019) described a qualitative study of the experiences of five specialist-level interns as they worked to facilitate family–school partnerships with culturally diverse families. Some findings are relevant here: interns described fewer than expected opportunities to work with families, and these opportunities were typically in formal contexts like IEP meetings. Also the engagements were less like bidirectional partnerships than "one-time, insular family interactions" (p. 697). Interns were more likely to engage with families in elementary schools than in secondary schools. Soutullo et al. (2019) recommended that graduate students be offered more opportunities for direct training to work with families prior to internship.

Perhaps the most salient point for this context is that for every need or problem children may have, there is a family system (and a larger context of nested systems) in which the problem occurs and in which resources to address the problem exist. When a child is referred for counseling, it behooves the school psychologist to consider the larger picture of interdependence within the family system. For example, do the child's symptoms serve a purpose in the family that may make improvement a threat to family stability? If so, then any counseling intervention may meet resistance. Do the child's symptoms reflect issues in the family that could be addressed more effectively through consultation or referral for family therapy than through individual counseling? Have cultural, language, and other diversity factors been considered in conceptualizing the referral problem?

Service Delivery Models

In schools, supports for parents may take the form of a combination of parent education, family intervention, and parent management training (NASP, 2014). Ollendick (2005), in a commentary on evidence-based parent and family interventions in school psychology, presented several conclusions, among them the following:

- "There appears to be more support for interventions that are part of a multi-component program, that are highly focused in scope, and that entail active collaboration between parents, students, and the schools" (p. 515).
- Nearly all of the treatments deemed efficacious were cognitive or behavioral ones, including family systemic therapies that incorporated such treatments as contingency contracts and parenting management training.
- A needed direction for future research is identification of moderators and mediators, the former being the specific characteristics of participants and settings that influence response to intervention, and the latter being influences that accrue during an intervention and explain variability in outcomes.

School-Based Family Interventions

The National Center for Education Statistics (2018) reported on mental health services in K–12 public schools from a 2015–2016 School Survey on Crime and Safety, conducted with school principals. For the survey, treatment is defined as a clinical service, such as psychotherapy, medication, or counseling, intended to lessen or eliminate the symptoms of a disorder. Providers "may include" psychiatrists, psychologists, clinical social workers, psychiatric nurses, and professional counselors. Diagnostic assessment services were more common than treatment services: 74% of middle schools and 79% of high schools reported that diagnostic assessments were available, and 66% of middle schools and 69% of high schools reported that treatment services were available. A higher percentage of high schools than primary schools reported that both types of mental health services were available. The most common limiting factors to schools' providing mental health services were inadequate funding (75%) and lack of parental support (71%). The survey report did not differentiate types of mental health services by provider, so it did not shed light on provision of counseling specifically provided by school psychologists. Further, because principals were the respondents, familiarity with school psychology assessment and intervention practice may have been limited.

An example of a model using an on-site clinic is the Dallas, Texas, Independent School District (ISD), a large urban district with approximately 157,000 students. This public school district has developed the Youth and Family Center Program in partnership with the Parkland Health Hospital System, described on their website as "providing mental health care for all Dallas ISD students and their families" along with medical and physical health care to Dallas County residents ages 4 to 21 years (https://www.dallasisd.org/youthandfamilycenters). The mental health clinics, located on secondary school campuses but serving all grade levels in the neighborhood, provide evaluation and assessment, individual counseling, group counseling, family counseling, and psychiatric consultation. Staffing is provided by both school district and hospital personnel and includes licensed psychologists, psychiatrists, and therapists. Referrals can be made from a student support team or by direct contact with the neighborhood clinic. Their policy states that they accept cash and third-party payments but that no family is denied services based on inability to pay. In addition to mental and physical health services, Youth and Family Centers also provide training, parent education, case management, referrals, and refugee services.

Psychological services, distinct from special education assessment services, are in a separate department in Dallas ISD, with the philosophy, staffing, and focus described by the following:

> We believe that by addressing the physical, emotional, and social issues that a child may experience, learning will be improved. Psychologists, Licensed Specialists in School Psychology (LSSPs) and Licensed Clinical Social Workers (LCSWs) from the department work with students that may need help. We deal with issues such as anxiety, depression, inability to sleep, unfounded fears, abuse, and poor study habits. Staff also help with classroom management and school-wide issues to improve the functioning of a class or campus. (https://www.dallasisd.org/domain/3989)

Although many models exist for serving families within schools, this model provides a helpful example of partnership with the community to provide comprehensive mental health services. School psychologists in this model participate in family and counseling mental health interventions.

Family Therapy

Some of the family interventions presented below require advanced training and employer approval to practice in schools. However, school psychologists in the counseling role will encounter many students whose families need assistance for the student to make educational gains. Basic knowledge of family therapy interventions with empirical support will help the school psychologist develop perspective about systems context for problems and guide parents to seek appropriate help.

Family Systems Therapy

In the family systems approach, families are recognized as demonstrating the core features of systems, including coherence (identifiable and predictable patterns), interdependence of components (family members), and definable boundaries. In this model, the individual cannot be understood outside the context of the family. Predictable interactions within families, organized around often implicit messages and rules, work to maintain *homeostasis*, or a steady, stable state. Family systems might be more open or closed to the outside environment (*boundaries*), with the flexibility required to adapt to external influences. For example, the family that has an actively alcoholic parent may be characterized by secrecy, leading to minimal openness to outside intervention. Subsystems exist within the family; for example, there are partner subsystems, parent–child subsystems, and sibling subsystems, each with its own unique rules, boundaries, and defining characteristics. Using the example of the family with an alcoholic parent, a child may take on a parenting role, responsible for helping the younger children with basic routines such as meals and homework. A triangle is a subsystem composed of three family members, typically with two insiders and one outsider; for example, two family members might be in harmony while the third is in conflict with them, which may predict clinical problems for the outsider. The concept of triangulation is relevant when considering the child in school who becomes the identified patient, especially when traditional interventions are unsuccessful. Triangulation is also a concept in other mental health disciplines, such as consultation, where it is also viewed as the source of negative symptoms.

One feature relevant in this context is the nuclear family emotional process in which one spouse externalizes their distress onto one of more of the children, resulting in considerable anxiety focused on a child. In this pattern, the parent may have an unrealistic, overly positive or overly negative view of this child. The child targeted by this process is at greater risk for behavioral or emotional problems, with more difficulty differentiating from the family. According to Alvarez (2009), in the family projection process, three stages occur: "(a) a parent focuses his or her anxiety on a child in the family and perceives that there is something wrong with the child, (b) the parent interprets the child's reaction as a confirmation of his or her worry, and (c) the parent reacts to the child's behavior by treating the child as if something is really wrong" (p. 257). The child eventually internalizes the parent's messages, which may affect the child's marital and parenting relationships, a process that can become multigenerational.

Clearly, problems of family projection, triangulation, and poor individual differentiation can be relevant when considering a child referred for counseling in school. Discord within family systems may be contributing to the student's problems in situations where (a) new problems emerge as soon as earlier ones are resolved, (b) the child is described as sicker than observations at school would indicate, (c) inordinate time is spent in meetings or in other contact with parents, (d) parents continually shop for other professionals outside the school, and (e) interventions are not followed through at home. Triangulation within school–home relationships can become an issue, when alliances formed between two adults lead to the exclusion of a third (for example, a parent and special education teacher might form an alliance that excludes a general education teacher). Of course, all families have issues, and children's school problems may be complex for other reasons. Schools are similarly complex systems, with dynamics and issues that can interfere with objectivity and well-defined relationships. The astute school psychologist is careful to maintain appropriate boundaries while implementing interventions that have proved effective with specific referral problems across individuals and circumstances.

O'Gorman (2018), an Australian child and family therapist employed in a school system, described student problems as sometimes being best addressed by family systems therapy. She notes that a paradigm shift from the student as an individual to the family as a system has also been taking place in American schools, citing Cooper-Haber and Haber (2015). O'Gorman applies family systems work to the practice of trauma-informed therapy in schools, perhaps especially appropriate for those students who have "experienced conflicted family breakdown, displacement from homeland and significant abuse/neglect" (p. 563). Even though schools are the site for services, the model discussed in this article describes trained family therapists providing family systems work, not school psychologists.

Multidimensional Family Therapy

Multidimensional Family Therapy (MDFT) is described as a multisystemic, comprehensive family intervention program that is manualized for use in substance abuse and co-occurring disorders such as conduct disorder and juvenile delinquency (Liddle, 2009, 2010). Of the treatments for substance abuse that have been studied, MDFT, along with cognitive–behavioral therapy (CBT), appears to have a strong empirical research base (Pol et al., 2017). Analysis of moderator variables in a meta-analysis of MDFT indicated that adolescents with severe problems, including severe substance abuse and disruptive behavior disorder, benefited more from MDFT than adolescents with less severe conditions (Pol et al., 2017).

MDFT is implemented in 12–15 weekly or twice weekly 60- to 90-minute sessions, with manualized assessment and treatment modules targeting four main areas: (a) a youth's interpersonal relationships with parents and peers, (b) the parent's parenting practices and level of adult functioning independent of the parenting role, (c) parent–child interactions during therapy sessions, and (d) family communication patterns with key social systems. Assessment and intervention are closely linked, with family, parent, adolescent, and key social systems assessments conducted by the therapist. A strength of this approach is its attention to systems within which problems develop and are maintained; however, the protocol for administration is both time and skill intensive and more likely to be conducted by other mental health professionals with school support. This program may be implemented in schools, but implementation in the home or community appears more common.

Multisystemic Therapy

Multisystemic therapy (MST) is a family-focused, evidence-based intervention model with manualized assessment and intervention. According to the California Evidence-Based Clearinghouse (2018), MST is directed at antisocial behavior of youth with treatment focused on factors within the youth's social network that are contributing to the behavior problems. The stated overarching goal is to empower families to build healthier environments by mobilizing existing resources. A corollary goal is to reduce costs by avoiding out-of-home placements through hospitalization, residential treatment, or incarceration. Multiple MST manuals are commercially available, with separate manuals designed for severe emotional disturbance in children and adolescents, antisocial behavior in children and adolescents, supervision, consultation, and organization (administration). Readers can see https://www.mstservices.com for detailed information on these manuals and other resources.

Typical duration of MST is 4 months, with treatment provided through multiple weekly contacts with the therapist in natural settings, including home, school, and community. This approach employs structural and strategic family therapy, along with behavioral and cognitive–behavioral strategies. It is designed for implementation in the home setting to avoid obstacles to family involvement. According to the California Evidence-Based Clearinghouse, MST is well supported by research evidence for the purposes described above.

Henggeler and Schaeffer (2010), in a chapter on the use of MST for juveniles with serious antisocial behavior, maintain that this approach is most appropriate and cost-effective. MST is provided by full-time master's-level therapists who each carry loads of four to six families and are available 24 hours a day, 7 days a week. In the 4-month treatment duration estimate, direct contact between therapists, family members, and others in the youth's ecosystem may total 60 or more hours, which makes MST quite intensive. Providers work in teams of two to four therapists who are supervised by an advanced master's- or doctoral-level supervisor who devotes at least 50% of their time to the team.

Parent Management Training

Parent Management Training (PMT) refers to a set of programs that train parents to manage children's behavioral problems at home and at school. The focus is on parent–child interactions, and the foundation for strategies is advances in applied behavior analysis (Kazdin, 2017). PMT is not typically a school-based intervention. It is conducted primarily with parents, with the child brought in to review the program, hear concrete examples of behaviors and outcomes, and train in everyday skills and activities. Sessions cover operant conditioning techniques and environmental engineering for behavior change over about 12 weeks, with each session lasting 45–60 minutes. Teacher consultation regarding school performance and behavior is included, and home contingencies are developed. PMT is manualized (Kazdin, 2017), with accommodations for specific family circumstances. Treatment studies support the efficacy of PMT for clinically referred children with oppositional defiant disorder and compulsive disorder (Forgatch & Kjøbli, 2016; Kazdin, 2017).

Kazdin and McWhinney (2018) found that outcomes with PMT were associated with the strength of the therapeutic alliance and perceived barriers during treatment. Stronger alliances and fewer perceived barriers predicted better outcomes for referred children. Further, both the therapeutic alliance and perceived barriers were affected by parents' interpersonal relationships and quality of daily life. These findings have implications for school psychologists' efforts to form working alliances with parents when counseling their children.

Forgatch and Kjøbli (2016) describe the PMT–Oregon model (PMTO) as a merger of social interaction, social learning, and behavioral perspectives. According to Forgatch and Patterson (2010), the most proximal socializing forces for healthy or deviant adolescent adjustment are parents, and eventually peers. Interestingly, peers seem to use positive reinforcement to encourage covert (hidden) antisocial behaviors, such as lying, stealing, and substance abuse. PMTO focuses on teaching, modeling, and reinforcing positive parenting practices, including encouraging skills, setting limits, monitoring, teaching problem-solving, and being positively involved. PMTO has been delivered in homes, schools, and clinics, and more recently through telemedicine, over the past 40 years, in both group and individual formats, with research studies dating to 1970. Empirical research related to PMT, including PMTO, reinforces other sources of information that indicate that structured and intensive family therapy intervention is integral to improved outcomes for youth who have or appear to be on a trajectory for conduct disorders.

Family Engagement in Schools

Before school psychologists can form alliances with parents and families, families need to be engaged in schools. Two textbooks that provide excellent guidance for school psychologists who intend to engage families in their practice in schools are *The Power of Family–School Partnering (FSP): A Practical Guide for School Mental Health Professionals and Educators* (Lines et al., 2011) and *Preparing Educators to Engage Families: Case Studies Using an Ecological Systems Framework* (Weiss et al., 2013). These texts are school focused, practical, and case-oriented, and they consider cultural as well as systemic variables in school–family collaboration. However, they are not primarily oriented toward family therapy or student counseling; rather, they are resources for understanding diverse family systems and facilitating school engagement.

Lines et al. (2011) defines family–school partnering as "sharing responsibility for a student's school success" (p. 2). They prefer the word *partnering* over *involvement* or *engagement* because it implies equal status, joint responsibility, and close cooperation in accountability for student outcomes, consistent with the shift since the 1990s reflected in federal law (IDEIA and ESSA) and an increased focus on research-based practices. Further, they emphasize *families*, including all caregivers, rather than *parents*.

Weiss et al. (2013) focuses on families in the systems context, giving special attention to cultural issues that may affect family engagement. *Preparing Educators to Engage Families: Case Studies Using an Ecological Systems Framework* relies on Bronfenbrenner's ecological systems model to help educators understand families and children in schools within the larger developmental context. The authors use a case study approach to encourage practical application of concepts and direct their information primarily toward administrators and teachers. They maintain that better coordination among children's "executive functionaries," or adults inside and outside the family home, is needed to improve school and family collaboration.

Social–emotional learning models also offer research-supported resources for engaging families and communities in school efforts to promote students' social, emotional, and behavioral well-being (https://casel.org/homes-and-communities/). CASEL, the Collaboration for Academic, Social, and Emotional Learning, offers examples of model programs, videos, and an interactive online guide (https://schoolguide.casel.org/) for facilitating family–school–community partnerships.

Interventions to engage, or treat, families are numerous, complex, and overlapping. Commonalities in most of the evidence-based therapies include use of CBT and behavioral techniques, a systems orientation, and a specific focus. Although therapy models will most likely be implemented outside of schools or by trained family therapists within schools, several of the systems approaches address school behaviors, collaborate with school personnel, or promote generalization to school settings. Family interventions implemented in schools tend to be those that support academic growth and specific behavioral needs, and include the processes associated with assessment (informed consent, interviews, team meetings, and feedback), IEP development, IEP meetings to assess progress and plan, parent–teacher conferences, and more comprehensive family–school partnerships. Reschly (2019) identified sensitivity, trust, equality, commitment, respect, positive focus, and responsiveness as necessary elements in establishing working alliances between schools and families. These elements reflect well the ethical commitments of school psychologists.

Special Family Issues

Families are complex systems characterized by stages and transitions, as well as by structure, relationships, boundaries, and subsystems. Further, in an ecological model, families, and individuals within families, are "nested" in other contexts, adding to the complexity. Given this framework, it is not surprising that families encounter many special issues, circumstances, and challenges that will affect children's school functioning and make them vulnerable to emotional or behavioral problems that result in school referrals for counseling. Consideration of the family context will help the school psychologist identify resources for intervention. Topics that are discussed include military deployment, changes in family structure, addiction or illness, and other issues.

Military Deployment

In *School Psychology Best Practices With Military Families*, a PowerPoint presentation developed for graduate training programs and staff development, Pisano et al. (2016) provided perspective on the number of school-age children affected by parents' military deployment. He noted that over two million children have parents who are in the military, with over half in the National Guard or Reserve. After deployment, many parents experience reintegration difficulties, including marital discord and mental health struggles. Suicide rates among veterans are a major concern, with more troops dying from suicide than are killed in action. According to Pisano, children of service members are 2.5 times as likely to develop psychological problems, and 44% of these children have "moderate to difficult emotional or behavioral difficulties" (p. 11).

Deployment affects individuals differently, depending on many factors, including experience and coping skills (Meadows, Tanielian, & Karney, 2016).

Pisano (2017) reported that when spouses struggle with deployment, children are likely to struggle as well. Children struggling with deployment of a parent may present with symptoms attributed to attention deficit hyperactivity disorder (ADHD), such as distractibility, overactivity, withdrawal, daydreaming, or dropping grades. When evaluating symptoms, educators must be aware of the family member's deployment or other transition related to military service. Pexton, Farrants, and Yule (2018), in a study of children whose fathers either deployed to Afghanistan or deployed to military training, found that children exhibited clinical levels of stress and anxiety. Unexpectedly, levels of depression and behavior problems were not elevated.

Pisano (2017) provides some guidelines for schools, in addition to listing a number of resources available for families of deployed military. Pisano, who has served as a school psychologist in Fort Bragg schools for many years, recommended first that civilian school psychologists actively seek out children in their schools whose parents have been deployed, rather than waiting for referrals or for problems to emerge, and provide active collaboration with families. Other recommendations are based on the stages of deployment and include the following guidelines for school psychologists.

- First, for predeployment and anticipation of departure, encourage families to develop a plan for taking care of themselves and their household, including alleviating anxiety by providing information to children appropriate to their level of development. Such information might include finding on a map the deployed parent's location, describing duration of and activities during deployment, and planning how to communicate and stay in contact.
- Second, during deployment, have families maintain routines and consistency that help children feel informed and protected. Examples for the nondeployed parent include (a) playing a videotape at bedtime with the deployed parent reading a book aloud; (b) talking about events in the news at home that affect the nondeployed parent (in a developmentally appropriate manner); (c) putting the deployed parent's boots or shoes under the child's bed as a symbol of protection; and (d) maintaining a journal or scrapbook with photos or records of events that have occurred in the parent's absence to share when the parent returns. Suggest that parents

reassure young children that they are not responsible for the parent's absence (to counter magical thinking).
- And third, for the homecoming and adjustment period, prepare families for the dynamics of the homecoming, including having realistic plans and expectations. Help parents accept their children's feelings and provide reassurance to students when the family homecoming does not go exactly as planned.

School psychologists who have not had experience with military families will need to educate themselves regarding the stages of adjustment to deployment, the research regarding expected reactions of children to various events at each developmental level, and the resources available within the military and civilian communities for military families. The NASP website provides links to many resources, including position papers, podcasts, presentations, and links to research articles on military deployment and effects on students (www.nasponline.org).

Changes in Family Structure
Changes in family structure include, for example, divorce, remarriage, adoption, birth of siblings, removal of children because of abuse or neglect, and illness or death of a family member. Family members also may leave the home for treatment for mental health or substance abuse, college, employment, or marriage; an adult's return to or departure from the workforce may result in transition adjustments. Each of these is a complex topic for discussion and has its own body of literature. Suffice it to say, a significant portion of children and adolescents in school will be dealing with such adjustments at any given time. Some of these students will need counseling that focuses on family issues.

Divorce. Divorce is common in the United States, affecting 40–50% of all first marriages, with divorce rates in subsequent marriages even higher (https://www.apa.org/topics/divorce/). School psychologists are certain to be working with divorced parents while assessing or counseling their children. From a family systems perspective, there may be multiple caregivers, and it is not always clear who the child considers the parent based on biological parentage. For example, one child may call the stepparent mom or dad, while another may refer to a stepparent by name; it takes careful questions and listening to understand a family's structure without making assumptions. The school psychologist as counselor will need to spend time with the child and caregivers to understand the family structure, context, and history, and to determine legal access to records and legal consents required for counseling.

Collaboration with parents always benefits from rapport, a nonjudgmental stance, and openness to all involved parties to establish trust. Boundary issues, as discussed in relation to structural family therapy, may be especially salient in the context of divorced or remarried parents and their children. The school psychologist will need to keep in mind that divorced families vary as much as any other family system, with no cookie-cutter model of how they function. Variables that may affect children's adjustment include the recency of the divorce, the age of the child, predivorce individual and family issues (e.g., disabilities, medical or psychiatric disorders), level of conflict, involvement of other caregivers or parent figures, geographic or home location changes, visitation schedules, financial stressors, among many others. For these reasons, it becomes especially important for the school psychologist as counselor to use active listening and the helping interview to gain access to the family's world, so that interventions, if needed, are realistic and tailored. All parties will have prior experience as well as thoughts and feelings regarding divorce, based on personal or professional experience, and school psychologists must be alert to such effects on their objectivity and acceptance.

Blended families. Blended families represent a special case of divorce where one or more parents remarries and the child acquires one or more stepparents and possibly stepsiblings. Half-siblings are also frequently part of the family structure, and for some students, the parents may remarry more than once to individuals who have their own children. The same considerations as described above apply, along with the increased complexity in family dynamics and the need for the school psychologist as counselor to clarify caregiving roles, living and custody arrangements, legal access to school information, individuals (including stepsiblings and half-siblings) living in the family home, and the time frame for the transitions from biological parents' divorce to remarriage and blending of families. It is helpful to clarify the titles by which parents and stepparents are called so the student can communicate with the counselor without repeated explanations. Again, the transition may be more or less problematic depending upon many factors. The child's perception of and feelings about the family situation are as important as the actual structure of the family.

According to the American Psychological Association (https://www.apa.org/helpcenter/stepfamily), recent research indicates that preadolescents and younger adolescents (ages 10–14) may have the most difficulty adjusting to a stepfamily, while older adolescents typically need less parenting and may have less investment in stepfamily life. Children under age 10 tend to be more accepting of a new adult in the home, particularly when the adult is a positive influence. A parent may also live with a partner without being married. Differences in role definition and stability of the partnership will affect children's adjustment. Insight into a child's understanding of the parental relationships is key to acceptance and support in the counseling relationship.

Adoption. Adoption is a special kind of transition in which the family structure changes by choice to bring typically nonbiological children into the family. Since there are many variations in the reasons for adoption, type of adoption, age at adoption, and level of the child's information about adoption, generalizations about issues families might encounter or adoptees' reactions are not advised. Foster care is another special family arrangement with its own set of adjustments, and two relevant resources are recommended here. A 2015 special issue of *School Psychology Forum*, which was written as a guide for school psychologists, addressed foster care and international adoption. Jankowska (2015), in an introduction to the issue, notes that children in these situations are an at-risk and vulnerable school population. In 2013, the United States had 51,000 adoptions and 524,000 children in foster care. Stability of living arrangements and school enrollment will obviously influence emotional and behavioral adjustment. When there has been trauma, neglect, or abuse, risk for emotional dysfunction is heightened. The second recent addition to the literature about adoption that is specific to schools is an e-book with online downloadable resources: *Becoming an Adoption-Friendly School: A Whole-School Resource for Supporting Children Who Have Experienced Trauma or Loss* (Langton & Boy, 2017).

Death of a family member. As with other transitions that occur in families, a child's reaction to the death of a family member will be mediated by many factors that make it hard to predict the form, intensity, or duration of the reaction. Bereavement may be uncomplicated or complicated (more extreme), such as in persistent complex bereavement disorder (American Psychiatric Association, 2013). Complicated bereavement tends to occur more often when death is sudden, the circumstances are traumatic, or there are multiple losses. It is characterized by an individual's continued preoccupation with or poor adjustment to a death that occurred at least 12 months ago (6 months ago for children; Mayo Clinic, 2017). School psychologists must be sensitive to the individual differences in grieving that occur because of many variables: age, developmental level, sudden death versus long-term illness, circumstances surrounding death, age at which death occurred, child's relationship to the deceased family member, child's prior adjustment, and availability of supportive resources in the home, school, and community, to name only a few. Guidance on specific strategies for use with grieving students is covered in Chapter 9.

Addiction

When there is addiction in a family, whether it involves parents, siblings, the student, or extended family, children may experience effects of marital stress, financial distress, fear about a family member's safety or health, neglect or abuse, or legal issues. Secrecy about the addiction and its consequences is the norm, so that children in school exhibit symptoms of distress without a clear precipitant. Addiction is pervasive in U.S. culture and cuts across ethnicities, races, genders, education levels, socioeconomic groups, and family structures. Co-occurring mental health disorders are common with substance abuse and addiction (Substance Abuse and Mental Health Services Administration, 2019). In the United States in 2018, an estimated 165 million people age 12 or older had used an illicit drug in the past month. According to a Pew Survey in August 2017, 46% of U.S. adults have a close friend or family member who is or has been addicted to drugs. Drug addiction is epidemic in the United States, and addiction affects the whole family system (Gramlich, 2017).

School psychologists must be aware of the prevalence of a variety of addictive disorders and the impacts on family. Families may become distorted so that children take on pseudo-parent roles in the family system, becoming caregivers. Other family members may have responses that take the focus off the person with the addiction. For example, the student who acts out at school, with defiance of authority, aggression toward peers, and academic decline, might be identified as socially maladjusted. If there is overlooked addiction in the family system, this child may become the sole focus of intervention, or the "identified patient." The child's behavior may be a reaction to stressors and modeling of observed behaviors at home, which can bring needed attention to the family system. Both internalizing and externalizing symptoms are common in response to distress, and specific behaviors may reflect the child's role in the family system.

In counseling, and when interviewing parents for history and informed consent, unconditional positive regard and creation of a safe environment for open communication may be the counselor's most valuable tools. Concrete knowledge of resources within the community, willingness to make referrals and follow up, and focus on the resources and positive assets of the child and family may help the family system become open to help. Respect for a family's privacy is essential, with information shared only when consent is given and for legitimate educational purposes. Resilience exists in individuals and families with addictions, just as it does with other disorders and circumstances (Park & Schepp, 2015). The National Institute of Drug Abuse (https://www.drugabuse.gov/) is an excellent resource for up-to-date information, educational tools, and intervention resources.

Other Family Issues

Poverty, homelessness, abuse, and neglect clearly affect children's functioning in school, and interventions by necessity involve family. These topics cannot be fairly synopsized, since the literature is huge and crosses disciplines. The variations in reasons for and degree of poverty, and the context and type of abuse and neglect, are many and complex, and the role of the school psychologist is only one of many in the systems that may respond or intervene. Issues that are particularly salient for the school psychologist include the following:

- Awareness that these stressors will have powerful effects on school adjustment and learning.
- Knowledge of school and community resources for assisting families dealing with these issues, including shelters for homeless and abused adults and children and specific contact information for individuals who can be called upon to help.
- Consideration of the stress on families when outside agencies, including schools, become involved in family affairs, especially when there are legal implications.
- Knowledge of the legal and ethical guidelines and specific procedures for reporting known or suspected abuse and neglect, along with risks of failure to report.
- Awareness that Child Protective Services investigations may need to be carried out in the school setting, or in communication with school personnel.
- Knowledge of the distinctions between counseling for and investigation of abuse and neglect. The school psychologist is not responsible for the investigation of allegations.
- Awareness that the school may become a haven for some children who are experiencing extreme stress at home.
- Commitment to providing comprehensive school-based evaluations and careful documentation of interventions and progress so that when families seek services across agencies or geographic locations, they are not required to start from scratch to explain the complex circumstances they may have faced.

Many differences in family structures might be considered cultural and lifestyle issues. For example, families may have same-sex partners as parents, grandparents in the parenting role, single parents, foster parents, or multiple family units living in the same home. Families might be affected by rural or urban settings, ethnic and cultural communities, and so on. As with many of the other topics in this chapter, the differences and complexities among and between families, with so many mediating and moderating variables, make generalizations, especially for counseling and family interventions, challenging.

Family Interventions for Specific Childhood Disorders

This section discusses specific childhood and adolescent problems and some associated evidence-based interventions involving families. Readers can pursue these brief descriptions of the studies can be expanded on by other in the references in this chapter.

Eating Disorders

According to the National Institute of Mental Health (NIMH), anorexia nervosa, bulimia, and binge eating disorder have a lifetime prevalence rate of 2.7% among 13- to 18-year-olds, with females almost three times more likely to have eating disorders than males (NIMH, 2017). Eating disorders can be fatal if untreated and are often comorbid with other psychiatric disorders, especially anxiety. They affect all ages, ethnicities, races, body weights, and genders. Etiology is complex, involving interactions among genetics, biology, social factors, psychological factors, and behavior.

Treatment is most effective if begun early in the disease course (NIMH, 2017). Cook-Cottone et al. (2017) asserted that the three major eating disorders (anorexia nervosa, bulimia nervosa, and binge eating disorder) share the core characteristic of impaired self-regulation with the primary feature of disturbances in eating behavior, accompanied by difficulties in experiencing the embodied self. They explored a school-based yoga program aimed at preventing eating disorders in fifth-grade girls. The 14-week group intervention focused on (a) yoga practice, (b) skill building (CBT, media literacy), (c) journaling, (d) group processing, and (e) meditative relaxation. Findings showed that the program was effective in reduction of eating disorder risk factors, including dissatisfaction with the body and drive for thinness, and in development of self-care habits compared with the control group. Parental involvement included attending an information night and providing informed consent for the treatment or control condition.

Green and Venta (2018) surveyed 169 college freshmen from a public university about eating disorder prevention and education efforts in their high schools. Only 29% of respondents reported receiving any educational information and no respondents reported having experienced any prevention efforts. Differences in school characteristics were not associated with outcomes. The investigators concluded that education and prevention efforts are probably lacking across high schools.

Effective therapies typically involve families (Gorrell, Loeb, & Le Grange, 2019). Family-based treatments have been found to be effective for anorexia nervosa, bulimia nervosa, and, more recently, binge eating disorder, with comparison studies showing an advantage over CBT. Nevertheless, there is a paucity of randomized controlled studies, according to Gorrell et al., and a continued need to study moderating and mediating family variables. A major emphasis for development is the expanded dissemination of family-based therapy using telemedicine along with training for providers using web-based education and supervision.

For the school psychologist as counselor, students with eating disorders present special challenges; there is often secrecy and denial within families, and provision of intensive family therapy at school is not usually an option. Starting points for the school psychologist include becoming aware of the most effective approaches, which typically involve family therapy combined with medical treatment (NIMH, 2016); being willing to acknowledge eating disorders and encourage children and families to seek appropriate help; and knowing about available resources, including medical treatment options. Prevention should be a goal of school-based programs, because advanced eating disorders are difficult to treat and must be addressed outside the school setting.

Disruptive Behavior Disorders
Sometimes called externalizing disorders, disruptive behavior disorders tend to be manifested as undercontrolled or acting-out behavior (see Chapter 10 for more discussion). Aggressive and delinquent behaviors are often associated with eventual conduct disorder, so there is motivation to intervene as early as possible (Webber & Plotts, 2008). Evidence-based parent and family interventions include Parent Management Training, Parent–Child Interaction Therapy, and The Incredible Years (Weisz & Kazdin, 2017). Multisystemic Therapy and Multidimensional Family Therapy, discussed earlier in this chapter, are empirically supported interventions. Each of these interventions has its own protocols and research base; while school consultation may be an element of a program, interventions are typically conducted by trained professionals outside of schools.

The school psychologist has specialized knowledge and training for assessing and intervening with disruptive behavior disorders. School psychologists can contribute to reducing disruptive behaviors through functional behavioral assessments and behavior improvement plans (using techniques such as applied behavior analysis), and though consultation with parents and teachers about consistency and generalization across settings. In the counseling role, the school psychologist's approach must consider not only the specific behaviors of concern and their reduction using behavioral techniques, but also the underlying stressors, including family–school dynamics, that may be contributing to externalizing problems. Exploring underlying mechanisms is best accomplished when a trusting relationship is established and the school psychologist is aware of family systems.

A family-related issue that very frequently emerges in relation to disruptive behavior problems is the use of medication. Whether or not to medicate is clearly a parent's or guardian's decision in consultation with medical providers, but school psychologists, and other school personnel, can clearly help by providing consultation regarding changes in behavior with and without medication, and with alterations in timing or dosage (Carlson & Barterian, 2019).

Specific Counseling Techniques

Models of family therapy, the role of counseling in school-based interventions for parents and families, and special family issues that may require school-based services are all concerns of school psychologists in the counseling role. This section briefly discusses specific techniques counselors might use with children and adolescents to understand the family system and help the student develop healthy patterns of coping and adjustment.

Visual, Art, and Play Techniques
With children of any age, visual and manipulative techniques such as family and community genograms, ecological models, and kinetic family drawings can help students clarify their perceptions of themselves within the family system and larger community context. These semistructured techniques begin with a prompt followed by open-ended questions or verbal tracking, following the child's lead. The techniques are described as facilitators for communication in counseling sessions, not as diagnostic tools.

Family genograms have been widely used in counseling (Ivey, Ivey, & Zalaquett, 2016). The genogram is a diagram constructed to represent the family, typically across generations, with specific symbols and conventions used to convey information about relationships. Programs to generate genograms are available on websites (for example, www.genopro.com), or they can be constructed by hand. Elements that make up the genogram typically consist of family members for at least three generations, major events, emotional relationships, and social relationships. Figure 5.1 gives an example of a genogram developed by a school psychologist.

The approach to a genogram can be flexible, depending on the developmental level and interests of the student. For example, many older students who enjoy computers would probably like to create an online genogram. Younger children might prefer to work with miniatures in a sandtray, choosing animals or doll figures to represent family members. Others may prefer to use paper and pencil, or crayons. The medium is less important than the opportunity to develop understanding and insight and to stimulate discussion using an enjoyable activity. The role of the school psychologist is to provide the prompts and materials, unconditional acceptance, and opportunity to reflect on experiences and feelings.

FIGURE 5.1. Genogram

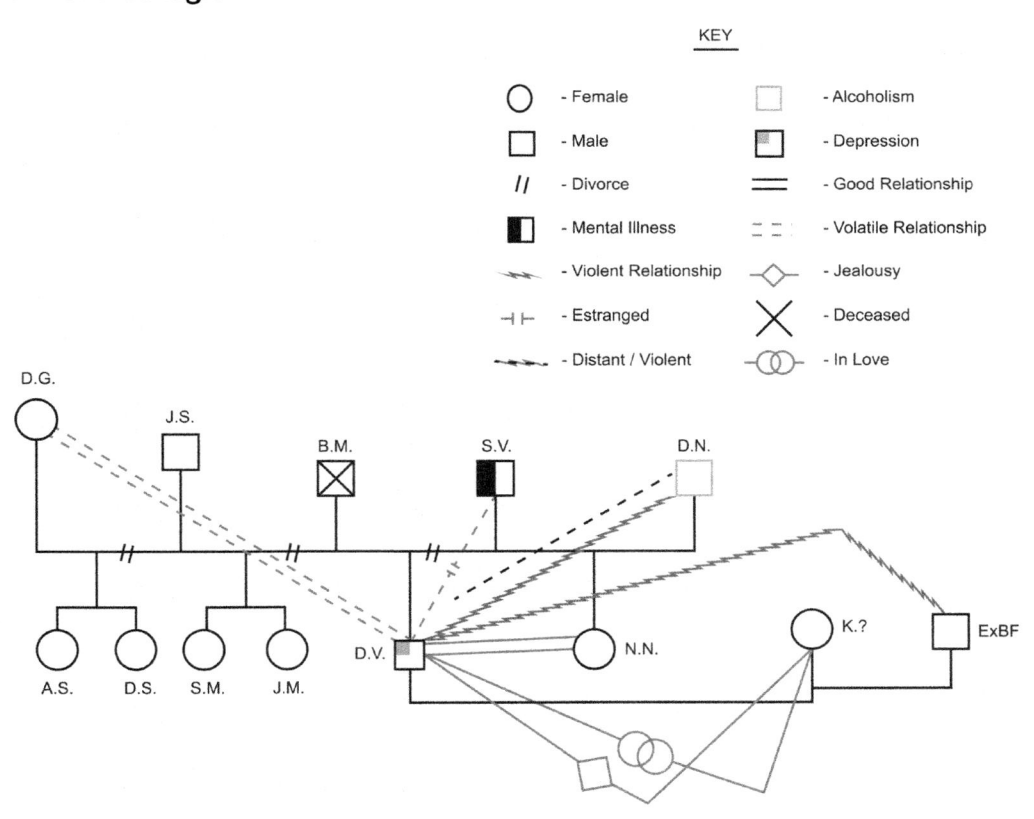

Note. From *School Psychologist as Counselor: A Practitioner's Handbook* (p. 208), by C. L. Plotts and J. Lasser, 2013, National Association of School Psychologists. Copyright 2013 by Catie Rodovsky. Reprinted with permission.

Community genograms (Ivey, Ivey, & Zalaquett, 2016) are similar to family genograms but are used to understand the child's community of origin or the community in which a child lives. They are visual representations of the individual's perception of important systems (e.g., home, school, church, best friend's home) and can be drawn as a map with proximity and distance between significant sources of support or stress. Alternatively, someone might choose to draw a flower, with the petals representing important people, places, or institutions. Some children enjoy tracing their hand and designating each finger as a significant person or system. Any variation is acceptable, with the goal being a visual representation of a client's perception of their community or the system in which they function or grew up. Discussion can explore the child's thoughts while the child draws, colors, or elaborates. Family and community genograms can clarify cultural norms and practices and identify resources for support.

Children, and even adolescents and adults, often enjoy drawings such as the kinetic family drawing, which can be used as a springboard for discussion of family roles, relationships, and boundaries. Dolls may serve the same purpose with younger children through nondirective play techniques (see Chapter 6). With both older and younger children, miniature people or animal figures or clay figures can be used in the same way as kinetic family drawings to represent different family members. These figures can be placed in a sandtray or on the floor or table and arranged and rearranged to represent roles and boundaries. The use of play, art, and symbolic materials provides some distancing for the student, which can create a sense of emotional safety, whereas talking directly about family members or issues may feel more threatening for some children. Figure 5.2 shows a child's depiction of his mother and himself. The 13-year-old foster child with intellectual disability had not talked about his incarcerated mother until prompted to create a picture of his family, which he chose to do with clay.

Timelines can be used to help children and teens identify major events in their lives and the emotional and behavioral effects of such events. Using a long piece of butcher paper laid out on the floor, the child can draw a line to represent the time from birth (beginning of line) to the present (end of line) or to project into the future. Dates and events the child identifies as important can be marked by drawings or labeling. Creative elaborations are possible, such as use of color for emotion, positive events on top, and stressful events on bottom.

Another advantage of these techniques is their use as progress evaluation tools.

School psychologists can routinely collect drawings or other visual products at intervals to gauge changes in perceptions or relationships. Though results of these tools are not necessarily empirical data, they can be used to generate hypotheses that may be validated using other techniques, such as parent consultation, direct observation, and behavior checklists.

Other Specific Techniques

The Gestalt-derived *empty chair* technique (Oaklander, 1988) can be used to encourage a verbal student who has a conflict with family to express feelings, identify thoughts, and practice perspective-taking, even if the family member of concern is no longer in the home. In this technique, the child is encouraged to talk *to* the person (imagining that person in a nearby empty chair) rather than *about* the person. To learn to gain perspective, the child can trade places (move to the empty chair) and speak from the absent person's perspective. This technique can be used

FIGURE 5.2. Clay Family Depiction

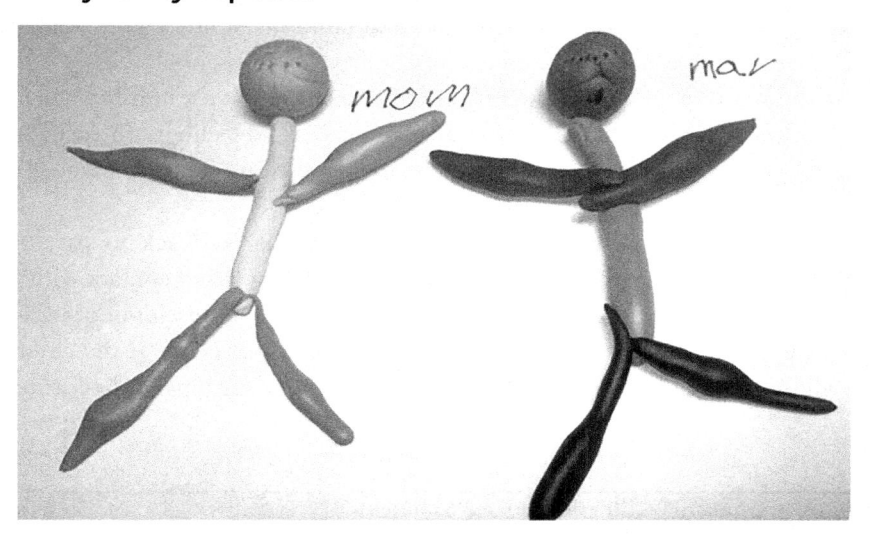

with family relationships, or any other relationships, including teacher–student or even the different voices within the student. Oaklander calls the last adaptation *topdog* and *underdog*. In this application, the student, often an adolescent, will change chairs, first playing the part of the *topdog* ("You should do this") and then the underdog ("Yes, but…" or "I can't…") to resolve the student's internally polarized perspectives (p. 152).

Role-playing, effective in many contexts, can provide the student with opportunities to practice initiating and responding to discussions with family members about topics that have created conflict, avoidance, stress, or dysfunctional communication. When appropriate, the child's homework might be to practice what they learned from role-playing to find new ways of interacting with the parent. To document the homework, the child can then write in a journal about their efforts and outcomes of using the techniques with family members. The journal can guide follow-up sessions with the counselor, who might use reinforcers (for example, games, tokens toward prizes) to encourage homework completion.

Another technique is reality therapy, which is described in Chapter 8. This approach provides a framework for brainstorming ideas for addressing problems, anticipating outcomes, implementing choices, and evaluating outcomes in the counseling sessions. Of course, there are many other specific counseling strategies that can be used to address students' family difficulties. The creative school psychologist as counselor can adapt many of the techniques presented in these chapters to encourage expression of feelings, clarify roles, and brainstorm alternatives.

All school psychologists, regardless of level of training or experience, can remember to rely on the following powerful tools to connect with children and their families:

- Parent and child interviews offer opportunities to establish credibility, reliability, and comfort that will help create an *alliance* to build on.
- Realistic counseling plans that consider system and personal resources as well as family and school concerns will foster *collaboration* and *trust*, when appropriately shared with parents and children.

- Informed consent provides a vehicle for sharing *goals, objectives,* and *techniques* and for explaining *limits of confidentiality*. Protection of the child's and family's confidential information, sharing only with consent what is needed for educational purposes, is essential.
- Counseling sessions provide a safe context for a child to talk about the family when the counselor models *nonjudgmental acceptance* of the child's experiences and feelings. The counselor who can hear and tolerate expression of traumatic experiences and strong feelings, without censoring or judging, will facilitate communication and relieve stress.
- As counseling is concluding, *follow-through* (e.g., providing feedback to parents, providing resources and contacts for ongoing help) and *follow-up* (e.g., making contact with teachers and parents about generalizing gains, coordinating with an outside counselor or other professionals) will convey that the counselor is genuinely engaged in the well-being of the child and family. Doing so will set the stage for productive family–school relationships in the future.

CASE STUDY: KALEY

Background

Kaley was enrolled as a seventh grader at her local public junior high school and received special education services as a student with an emotional disturbance (physical symptoms or fears associated with personal or school problems). Services in her IEP included positive behavioral support strategies, a cool-down space in or outside of the classroom, frequent breaks, and a daily check-in/check-out in a special education classroom by her special education monitor teacher.

Referral

School records indicated Kaley struggled with manifestations of anxiety since the third grade; however, recently she was frequently asking to leave class, reporting feeling ill to the school nurse, and being checked out early by her parents, and her absenteeism began to present as an increasing chronic pattern. An IEP meeting was requested on behalf of the school district to review Kaley's current trends and discuss changes in her educational needs.

Assessment

Information shared by the family during the IEP meeting suggested that significant changes in the home environment and family dynamics had occurred within the past 10 months. Parents reported Kaley's mother had accepted a new position within her job, which required increased travel, often for 1 to 3 weeks at a time, and her father, who previously was involved in a serious automobile accident, self-disclosed that he had entered an outpatient rehabilitation program for prescription drug abuse. Kaley's older sister had recently begun to drive and obtained employment, which often led to Kaley's sister not being at the family home after school and during the weekends. Additionally, because of the family's current situation, a relative moved into the home to help care for Kaley and her older sibling. Parents reported this school year that Kaley would often experience a panic attack in the home setting prior to the start of school, which would lead to her not attending school for the day, or when she was at school, Kaley would text her parents continually throughout the morning and plead to be checked out and picked up early. The family reported, at that time, that no outside medication or support services were in place. The IEP committee requested that additional testing in the form of a counseling evaluation and functional behavior assessment be completed by the school psychologist. Further, the family was referred to the district's social worker to help explore community-based options for the family's support needs.

Goals, Objectives, and Techniques

Results of the counseling assessment determined counseling as a related service was required to ensure FAPE (free appropriate public education). Goals were developed and techniques selected to (a) address Kaley's most pressing needs to stay in school while coping with anxiety, (b) take into account resources in her family and school systems, (c) make effective use of Kaley's existing skills and resources, and (d) promote generalization. Research and practice literature on school refusal informed interventions (see NASP resources at https://apps.nasponline.org/search-results.aspx?q=school+refusal).

Counseling goals first focused on Kaley *identifying her emotions* as assessment data revealed she was often unable to distinguish and/or articulate her feelings of anger, fear, sadness, etc. Second, Kaley was coached through *identifying her anxiety triggers*, which also included situations in the home, as these also affected her overall school attendance. To achieve this, the school psychologist worked with parents and staff on a communication log to help track the antecedents that potentially led up to Kaley's panic attacks and requests to leave class. Third, counseling goals subsequently focused on Kaley *exploring different self-soothing techniques* (such as controlled breathing, self-talk, visualization, and progressive muscle relaxation). Once Kaley was presented with several techniques, she practiced them and was guided to identify which techniques she found most effective or helpful. Finally, the proper application of *self-soothing techniques had to be transitioned into the classroom and home settings*. The school psychologist employed consultation with Kaley's general education teachers, special education teachers, and caregivers regarding Kaley's identified triggers and the positive coping strategies she identified as most effective.

Additional behavior strategies implemented also included a discreet visual (a green, yellow, orange, and red dot placed on the back of Kaley's student badge) to allow Kaley to communicate her current anxiety level to staff so they could adjust for her needs in the educational setting. Kaley was also greeted by her special education monitor teacher daily at the student drop-off location in the mornings. Then, as needed, she was allowed access to a less stimulating area than the cafeteria where the other students congregated, to cool down prior to transitioning to class at the start of the school day. The school psychologist also worked with campus staff to increase their awareness of anxiety in general and potential triggers for students, their understanding that not all manifestations of anxiety are observable, and general positive support strategies in the classroom for students with anxiety or anxiety-related disorders.

Evaluation

Outcome measures were Kaley's attendance record, self-reported anxiety level on a norm-referenced anxiety scale, and the communication log between home and school. Over the 3-month counseling/consultation intervention, absences were reduced, as were requests to leave class. Kaley's self-reported anxiety diminished from the clinically significant level to the at-risk level. Counseling sessions were gradually spaced out from weekly to biweekly. At the end of the 3-month period, the IEP team reconvened and decided to continue monthly counseling and parent–teacher consultation check-ins to maintain gains.

Case study contributed by Liz Hjort, SSP, LSSP, NCSP
Director of Psychological Services
TrinityEducational.com

SUMMARY

School psychologists can decide based on empirical support and specific case context which family-oriented interventions are likely to be efficient and effective given family, school, and community resources. This chapter included foundational information on well-established therapy models and evidence-based family interventions that have developed from these models, with attention to special family issues likely to be encountered by the school psychologist in the counseling role. These topics are far from exhaustive given the voluminous and distinct bodies of literature on family systems and issues, family therapies, and school-based interventions for parents and families.

The school psychologist must always keep in mind that no family, or individual within a family, necessarily matches the samples from which interventions are developed and empirically validated. It is always up to the mental health professional to use well-established theory (e.g., developmental stages) and intervention techniques (e.g., conjoint behavioral consultation) to address family needs in the school setting. A blend of parent and teacher consultation, reliable and valid assessment, and family–school partnering, all of which have research support, may best serve children mental health professionals see for counseling. Finally, the school psychologist must remember the need to "enter the child's world" through active listening, genuineness, positive regard, a nonjudgmental stance, respect for confidentiality and honesty about its limitations, and respect for the complexity and uniqueness of each family.

KEY POINTS FOR DISCUSSION

- How do family therapy models serve as foundations for interventions in schools?
- How much training in family systems approaches did you get in your graduate program? Do you feel your training is appropriate for selecting and implementing family-oriented interventions?
- How would you go about gaining greater competence in this area?
- How does your personal life experience affect your understanding of family situations and stressors? Consider any limitations to your objectivity.
- What existing resources does the school psychologist as counselor have available to engage families in counseling interventions for their children (consider mandated involvement, such as participation on an IEP team)?
- What roles do teachers and administrators play in the implementation of family–school partnerships?

REFERENCES

Alvarez, H. K. (2009). *Applying family systems therapy in schools*. In R.W. Christner & R. B. Mennuti (Eds.), *School-based mental health: A practitioner's guide to comparative practices* (pp. 251–271). New York, NY: Routledge/Taylor & Francis Group.

American Psychiatric Association. (2013). *Diagnostic and statistical manual of mental disorders* (5th ed.). Arlington, VA: Author.

California Evidence-Based Clearinghouse for Child Welfare. (2018, June). Multisystemic family therapy. Retrieved from https://www.cebc4cw.org/program/multisystemic-therapy/detailed

Carlson, J. S., & Barterian, J. A. (2019). *School psychopharmacology: Translating research into practice.* New York, NY: Springer.

Cook-Cottone, C., Talebkhah, K., Guyker, W., & Keddie, E. (2017). A controlled trial of a yoga-based prevention program targeting eating disorder risk factors among middle school females. *Eating Disorders, 25*(5), 392–405. https://doi.org/10.1080/10640266.2017.1365562

Cooper-Haber, K., & Haber, R. (2015). Training family therapists for working in schools. *Contemporary Family Therapy, 37,* 341–350.

Epstein, J. L. (2019). *School, family, and community partnerships: Your handbook for action.* Corwin, A SAGE Company. Retrieved from http://search.ebscohost.com/login.aspx?direct=true&db=cat00022a&AN=txi.b4744880&site=eds-live&scope=site

Every Student Succeeds Act, 20 U.S.C. § 6301 (2015).

Forgatch, M. S., & Kjøbli, J. (2016). Parent management training-Oregon model: Adapting intervention with rigorous research. *Family Process, 55*(3), 500–513. https://doi.org/10.1111/famp.12224

Forgatch, M. S., & Patterson, G. R. (2010). Parent Management Training—Oregon Model: An intervention for antisocial behavior in children and adolescents. In J. R. Weisz & A. E. Kazdin (Eds.), *Evidence-based psychotherapies for children and adolescents* (2nd ed., pp. 159–177). New York, NY: Guilford Press.

Gorrell, S., Loeb, K. L., & Le Grange, D. (2019). Family-based treatment of eating disorders: A narrative review. *Psychiatric Clinics of North America, 42*(2), 193–204. https://doi.org/10.1016/j.psc.2019.01.004

Gramlich, J. (2017). *Nearly half of Americans have a family member or close friend who's been addicted to drugs.* Pew Research Center. Retrieved from https://www.pewresearch.org/fact-tank/2017/10/26/nearly-half-of-americans-have-a-family-member-or-close-friend-whos-been-addicted-to-drugs/ft_17-10-26_drugs_manyamericans_3/

Green, E. T., & Venta, A. (2018). Lack of implementation of eating disorder education and prevention programs in high schools: Data from incoming college freshmen. *Eating Disorders, 26*(5), 430–447. https://doi.org/10.1080/10640266.2018.1453629

Hacker, A. H., & Hayes, A. (2017). Within and beyond: Some implications of developmental contexts for reframing school psychology. *Psychology in the Schools, 54*(10), 1252–1259. https://doi.org/10.1002/pits.22074

Henggeler, S. W., & Schaeffer, C. (2010). Treating serious antisocial behavior using multisystemic therapy. In J. R. Weisz & A. E. Kazdin (Eds.), *Evidence-based psychotherapies for children and adolescents* (2nd ed., pp. 259–276). New York, NY: Guilford Press.

Heward, W. L. (2009). *Exceptional children: An introduction to special education* (9th ed.). Upper Saddle River, NJ: Merrill/Prentice-Hall.

Individuals with Disabilities Education Improvement Act of 2004, 20 U.S.C. § 1400 et seq. (2004) (reauthorization of the Individuals with Disabilities Education Act of 1990).

Ivey, A. E., Ivey, M. B., & Zalaquett, C. P. (2016). *Essentials of intentional interviewing: Counseling in a multicultural world* (3rd ed.). Boston, MA: Cengage Learning.

Jankowska, A. M. (2015). Introduction to the special issue: Children in foster care and international adoption. *School Psychology Forum, 9*(1), 1–4.

Kazdin, A. E. (2017). Parent management training and problem-solving skills training for child and adolescent conduct problems. In J. R. Weisz & A. E. Kazdin (Eds.), *Evidence-based psychotherapies for children and adolescents* (3rd ed., pp. 142–158). New York, NY: Guilford Press.

Kazdin, A. E., & McWhinney, E. (2018). Therapeutic alliance, perceived treatment barriers, and therapeutic change in the treatment of children with conduct problems. *Journal of Child & Family Studies, 27*(1), 240–252. https://doi.org/10.1007/s10826-017-0869-3

Langton, E. G., & Boy, K. (2017). *Becoming an adoption-friendly school: A whole-school resource for supporting children who have experienced trauma or loss—with complementary downloadable material*. London, U.K.: Jessica Kingsley. Retrieved from http://search.ebscohost.com/login.aspx?direct=true&db=nlebk&AN=1407296&site=eds-live&scope=site

Liddle, H. A. (2009). *Multidimensional Family Therapy for Adolescent Drug Abuse: Clinician's Manual*. Center City, MN: Hazelden Publishing Co.

Liddle, H. A. (2010). Treating adolescent substance abuse using multidimensional family therapy. In J. R. Weisz & A. E. Kazdin (Eds.), *Evidence-based psychotherapies for children and adolescents* (2nd ed., pp. 416–432). New York, NY: Guilford Press.

Lines, C., Miller, G. E., & Arthur-Stanley, A. (2011). *The power of family–school partnering (FSP): A practical guide for school mental health professionals and educators*. New York, NY: Routledge.

Mayo Clinic. (2017). *Complicated grief*. Retrieved from https://www.mayoclinic.org/diseases-conditions/complicated-grief/symptoms-causes/syc-20360374

Meadows, S. O., Tanielian, T., & Karney, B. (Eds.). (2016). *The deployment life study: Longitudinal analysis of military families across the deployment cycle*. Santa Monica, CA: RAND. Retrieved from https://www.rand.org/pubs/research_reports/RR1388.html

National Association of School Psychologists. (2014). *Effective parenting: Positive support for families* [Position statement]. Bethesda, MD: Author.

National Association of School Psychologists. (2019). *School–family partnering to enhance learning: Essential elements and responsibilities* [Position statement]. Bethesda, MD: Author.

National Center for Education Statistics. (2018, May 30). Explore data on mental health services in K–12 public schools for mental health awareness month. *NCES Blog*. Retrieved from https://nces.ed.gov/blogs/nces/post/explore-data-on-mental-health-services-in-k-12-public-schools-for-mental-health-awareness-month

National Institute of Mental Health (NIMH). (2016). *Eating disorders*. Retrieved from https://www.nimh.nih.gov/health/topics/eating-disorders/index.shtml

National Institute of Mental Health (NIMH). (2017). *Eating disorders*. Retrieved from https://www.nimh.nih.gov/health/statistics/eating-disorders.shtml

No Child Left Behind Act of 2001, P.L. 107-110, 20 U.S.C. § 6319 (2002).

Oaklander, V. (1988). *Windows to our children*. Highland, NY: The Center for Gestalt Development.

O'Gorman, S. (2018). The case for integrating trauma informed family therapy clinical practice within the school context. *British Journal of Guidance & Counselling, 46*(5), 557–565.

Ollendick, T. H. (2005). Evidence-based parent and family interventions in school psychology: A commentary. *School Psychology Quarterly, 20*(4), 512–517. https://doi.org/10.1521/scpq.2005.20.4.512

Park, S., & Schepp, K. (2015). A systematic review of research on children of alcoholics: Their inherent resilience and vulnerability. *Journal of Child & Family Studies, 24*(5), 1222–1231.

Pexton, S., Farrants, J., & Yule, W. (2018). The impact of fathers' military deployment on child adjustment. The support needs of primary school children and their families separated during active military service: A pilot study. *Clinical Child Psychology & Psychiatry, 23*(1), 110–124. https://doi.org/10.1177/1359104517724494

Pisano, M. et al. (2016). *School psychology best practices with military families* [PowerPoint slides]. Bethesda, MD: National Association of School Psychologists.

Pol, T. M., Hoeve, M., Noom, M. J., Stams, G. J. J. M., Doreleijers, T. A. H., Domburgh, L., & Vermeiren, R. R. J. M. (2017). Research review: The effectiveness of multidimensional family therapy in treating adolescents with multiple behavior problems—A meta-analysis. *Journal of Child Psychology & Psychiatry, 58*(5), 532–545. https://doi.org/10.1111/jcpp.12685

Reschly, A. L. (2019). Systems theory and families. In S. A. Garbacz (Ed.), *Establishing family-school partnerships in school psychology: Critical skills* (pp. 1–17). New York, NY: Routledge.

Sheridan, S. M., Smith, T. E., Kim, E. M., Beretvas, S. N., & Park, S. (2019). A meta-analysis of family-school interventions and children's social-emotional functioning: Moderators and components of efficacy. *Review of Educational Research, 89*, 296–332. https://doi.org/10.3102/0034654318825437

Smith, T. E., Sheridan, S. M., Kim, E. M., Park, S., & Beretvas, S. N. (2020). The effects of family-school partnership interventions on academic and social-emotional functioning: A meta-analysis exploring what works for whom. *Educational Psychology Review, 32*, 511–544. https://doi.org/10.1007/s10648-019-09509-w

Soutullo, O. R., Sanders-Smith, S. C., & Smith-Bonahue, T. M. (2019). School psychology interns' characterizations of family-school partnerships. *Psychology in the Schools, 56*(5), 690–701. https://doi.org/10.1002/pits.22227

Substance Abuse and Mental Health Services Administration. (2019). Key substance use and mental health indicators in the United States: Results from the 2018 National Survey on Drug Use and Health (HHS Publication No. PEP19-5068, NSDUH Series H-54). Rockville, MD: Center for Behavioral Health Statistics and Quality, Substance Abuse and Mental Health Services Administration. Retrieved from https://www.samhsa.gov/data

Webber, J., & Plotts, C. (2008). *Emotional and behavioral disorders: Theory and practice* (5th ed.). Boston, MA: Allyn & Bacon.

Weiss, H. B., Lopez, M. E., Kreider, H., & Chatman-Nelson, C. M. (2013). *Preparing educators to engage families: Case studies using an ecological systems framework* (3rd ed.). Thousand Oaks, CA: SAGE.

Weisz, J. R., & Kazdin, A. E. (2017). *Evidence-based psychotherapies for children and adolescents* (3rd ed.). New York, NY: Guilford Press.

Chapter 6

Nondirective Approaches

OVERVIEW

Though many counseling techniques provide a structured approach to the attainment of improved social, emotional, and behavioral functioning, a nondirective orientation generally allows the child or adolescent to guide how the counseling session time is spent. Many school psychologists use play-based approaches in a nondirective format as a way of offering a child-directed approach, as well as other nondirective modalities, such as Rogerian client-centered therapy. Nondirective approaches can be used in conjunction with directive approaches, and such integration is often rewarding. This chapter introduces nondirective counseling, reviews theoretical foundations and techniques, presents the literature that provides empirical support for these approaches, and details some specific methods.

OBJECTIVES

After reading this chapter, readers should be able to do the following:

- Differentiate directive and nondirective therapy.
- Define play therapy.
- Identify the theoretical foundations of play-based therapies.
- Discuss the empirical support for play-based approaches.
- Describe the characteristics associated with effective play therapists.
- Recognize toys and materials that would facilitate therapeutic play.
- Identify play-based techniques for promoting counseling goals.
- Describe sandtray therapy methods.

Directive Versus Nondirective Approaches

For many years play therapists have disagreed as to whether play therapy should be *directive* or *nondirective* (Kenney-Noziska, Schaefer, & Homeyer, 2012), but what do these terms mean? Generally speaking, a counselor using a nondirective approach allows the child to guide the session without much influence other than basic limit setting for safety. Consequently, the purely nondirective therapist avoids leading, shaping, or eliciting specific content; the child is in control and determines how to play and with what. In this model, the counselor creates the conditions in which a child may freely explore and play to build capacities in an accepting and supportive environment. *Nondirective* does not suggest an unplanned approach to counseling; nondirective counseling should be purposeful and linked to counseling goals and objectives.

Conversely, directive methods are used by therapists to actively intervene to change thoughts and behaviors more directly (see Chapter 8). For example, the therapist may ask the child questions to elicit different ways of thinking or may reflect content to address cognitive distortions. Whereas the nondirective therapist observes the child's thinking and behavior processes unfolding, the directive therapist works more actively with the child to address social, emotional, and behavioral goals.

Though directive and nondirective approaches appear to be polar opposites, a growing consensus suggests that these two orientations need not be in opposition, and that integrating the two approaches may serve clients best (Gil, 2016; Kenney-Noziska et al., 2012). Advocates of an integrative approach suggest that the unique needs of the child are taken into consideration when developing a treatment plan, and that the intervention selected is based not only on the therapist's theoretical orientation, but also on the child's characteristics, such as developmental age, use of language, and referral concerns. This kind of integration requires some flexibility on the part of the counselor, who must use an approach that "entails a firm grounding in one system of psychotherapy, but with a willingness to actively incorporate (assimilate) practices and views from other systems" (Norcross, 2005, p. 10). With both directive and nondirective evidence-based approaches available, counselors are able to select the most appropriate interventions for each unique child, while also acknowledging that the nondirective therapist may use directive methods at times, just as the directive therapist may use nondirective techniques (Kenney-Noziska et al., 2012). Some have even argued that nondirective therapy has a directive function, as it can help the client rewrite a personal narrative (Frankel, Rachlin, & Yip-Bannicq, 2012). Even so, this book presents directive and nondirective techniques in separate chapters as a useful way of introducing these methods and organizing the content of the book.

The directive versus nondirective debate may also obscure the fact that in practice, directiveness is not dichotomous; rather it is continuous. Though some practitioners are purists who maintain strong commitments to either directive or nondirective therapy, many therapists fall somewhere on a continuum of directiveness. Therefore, it may be more appropriate to ask a therapist, "How directive are you?" rather than, "Are you directive or nondirective?" Don't be surprised if you receive a nuanced, qualified response that includes a recognition that every child and every session requires an individual approach that depends on a number of factors.

In this chapter we focus on nondirective play therapy and sandtray therapy, providing the theoretical foundations and practical, applied approaches to the methods. We encourage you to assess your interest and comfort with these nondirective techniques, while considering the populations you serve and the degree to which these therapies seem appropriate.

Empirical Support for Nondirective Counseling

The research support for nondirective counseling approaches continues to grow, though some measurement challenges exist. Many of the directive approaches, such as cognitive–behavioral therapy (CBT), have been manualized, which is to say that researchers can easily compare the work of multiple therapists working from the same treatment manual because all sessions are highly structured and contain very similar content and processes. However, nondirective sessions, such as those using a child-centered play therapy (CCPT) approach, may vary considerably because the client directs the activity. Although a nondirective stance may be consistently applied among counselors participating in an outcome study, there may be little consistency across sessions and clients because of the openness of the nondirective technique. Therefore, nondirective counseling research may be limited by the ability to isolate and control variables.

Much of the research on nondirective counseling outcomes with children has focused on CCPT, and this chapter reviews some of the data supporting the use of nondirective play therapy. But first, this section presents some of the more general findings in support of nondirective approaches. For example, King, Marston, and Bower (2014) randomized adult clients with diagnoses of depressive episode or mixed anxiety and depressive episode to three treatment conditions (CBT, nondirective Rogerian counseling, or care from a general practitioner), and found CBT and nondirective counseling to be equally effective. Jacob and Brinda (2017) found that children diagnosed with developmental delays who received nondirective play therapy demonstrated greater gains on a developmental scale than a control group. In another study, researchers trained teachers and paraprofessionals in CCPT techniques and reported improved child behavior outcomes following play sessions with the school personnel (Ewing, Monsen, & Kwoka, 2014).

Play Therapy Theory and Technique

Play therapy's theoretical foundations can be found in the child development literature and emerge from the basic idea that play is a critical activity of development. As children develop language, cognition, and social skills, "play is the child's most natural way of communicating this internal awareness of self and others" (Landreth, Ray, & Bratton, 2009, p. 281). A widely cited definition of play therapy is "the systematic use of a theoretical model to establish an interpersonal process wherein trained play therapists use the therapeutic powers of play to help clients prevent or resolve psychosocial difficulties and achieve optimal growth and development" (Association for Play Therapy, n.d.). Schaefer and Drewes (2010) note that play is universal, natural, and necessary for healthy development. They identify 25 therapeutic powers of play, among which are self-expression, access to the unconscious, direct and indirect teaching, abreaction, stress inoculation, counterconditioning of negative affect, catharsis, positive affect, sublimation, and attachment and relationship enhancement. Play in a therapeutic context may be particularly helpful because children often use it to "externalize their thoughts, picture images, feeling states, and accompanying sensations that are often impossible to put into words…" (Gil, 2014, p. 49).

Most scholars trace the history of play therapy back as far as the 1920s, citing Anna Freud and Melanie Klein as pioneers in the field (Bratton et al., 2009). Over time, other therapists came to use play and toys in a variety of ways (e.g., to trigger catharsis and promote free association). Whereas some therapists employed a nondirective approach, others used more structured, directive methods. Bratton and colleagues note that child-centered play therapy grew out of the work of Carl Rogers and one of his students, Virginia Axline. Their appreciation of an individual's propensity to self-heal and thrive in the context of unconditional positive regard suggested that a nondirective approach to play therapy would provide children the opportunity to find solutions to their problems. CCPT has been described as the approach with the greatest empirical support, longest history of use, and largest number of practitioners (Landreth et al., 2009). Today, the term CCPT is used in North America, but in Europe it is often referred to as nondirective play therapy and person-centered or client-centered play therapy (Bratton et al., 2009).

Although assessment and intervention are often regarded as distinct activities, during play therapy the counselor is gathering useful assessment data. By observing a child's play and art productions, the therapist learns about the child's thoughts, feelings, and capacities (Oaklander, 1988). Landreth (2002) regards play to be the language of children and toys to be their words. Play therapy is an opportunity for the therapist to work with children in the moment that they are acting out challenges, rather than talking about past events. Some children have a hard time expressing their thoughts and feelings verbally, and play may enhance their capacity to communicate (Porter, Hernandez-Reif, & Jessee, 2009). Play-based assessment, then, is data collection using a team approach to observing play behaviors to assess a wide range of functioning (see Linder, 2008, for more on that topic).

Play has many applications in counseling, and the past decades have seen an explosion of variations and methods, as well as applications of play therapy with specific populations. Play therapy has been used to work with children who have been sexually abused (Hill, 2006), bereaved children (Webb, 2011), children whose parents have separated (Camastral, 2008), traumatized children (Goodyear-Brown, 2010), victims of natural disasters (Dugan, Snow, & Crowe, 2010), children diagnosed with attention deficit hyperactivity disorder (ADHD; Wilkes et al., 2011), students with learning disabilities (Packman & Lebeauf, 2010), children exposed to terrorism (Cohen et al., 2010), individuals with traumatic brain injury (Plotts, Lasser, & Prater, 2008), and children with autism (Bass & Mulick, 2007).

Play therapy has been adapted for groups and families. For example, Lowenstein's (2010) edited volume includes a number of play-based activities that can be used when working with families, such as family puppet play. Similarly, Sweeney and Homeyer (1999) published an edited volume on group play therapy that provided a theoretical rationale, chapters on major approaches to group play therapy, and a section on techniques (e.g., group sandtray–worldplay, group puppetry, and group play therapy for children who are hospitalized). Both books are valuable resources for counselors who wish to work with groups and families.

The idea of teaching play therapy skills to parents and teachers to support healthy child development represents a significant outgrowth of the play therapy movement. Filial therapy (Guerney, 1964), Parent–Child Interaction Therapy (McNeil & Hembree-Kigin, 2010), Teacher–

Child Interaction Therapy and Teacher–Child Interaction Training (Gershenson, Lyon, & Budd, 2010; McIntosh, Rizza, & Bliss, 2000), and Child–Parent Relationship Therapy (Landreth & Bratton, 2006) all represent variants on the idea of providing those who spend the greatest amount of time with children the same kinds of relational skills that play therapists use. Increasingly, play therapists are recognizing that their techniques can be used by teachers and parents to help children across settings (Ewing, Monsen, & Kwoka, 2014). Landreth (2002), reflecting on the development of this approach, wrote:

> I had an intensifying belief that if what I did in the playroom was helpful to children, then parents could develop some of those same kinds of attitudes and learn to utilize those same kinds of skills with their children. Play therapists should be giving their skills away to parents and teachers. We should not hide our skills behind the door of the playroom. (p. 8)

These parent–teacher training methods are fairly structured, and a number of manualized interventions have been developed. Moreover, extensive research has been conducted using these types of interventions. The next section briefly summarizes the empirical support for these approaches.

Clinicians and scholars are becoming increasingly aware of cultural factors when developing and implementing play-based interventions (Gil, 2005), with culturally sensitive approaches described for Native American (Glover, 2005), Asian (Kao, 2005), Mexican American (Ramirez et al., 2005), and African American (Baggerly & Parker, 2005) children. Gil (2005) notes that play therapists who are sensitive to cross-cultural issues in play therapy provide children with a wide range of toys that are inclusive (e.g., pagodas, tepees). Moreover, the play therapist is aware that children may have different symbolic meanings for toys (e.g., snakes are not typically symbolic of fear in Japan, but rather represent wisdom). Therapists' behaviors and actions that reflect cross-cultural competence are better able to build trust and respect.

Another trend in play-based approaches is the blending of play therapy with other types of interventions. For example, there has been considerable work in the use of play therapy with cognitive–behavioral therapy (Drewes, 2009). Similarly, narrative therapy has been integrated with play therapy (Cattanach, 2009) and solution-focused brief therapy (Nims, 2007). Sandtray therapy also has been combined with a cognitive–behavioral approach (Sweeney & Homeyer, 2009). That play-based approaches can be tailored to work with other therapeutic modalities suggests the flexibility inherent in play therapy. At its core, play therapy is about cultivating a relationship in which a child, through developmentally appropriate means, has an opportunity for self-expression in a nonevaluative context. This quality allows play therapy to serve as the platform or foundation for a wide range of applications.

Evidence Base and Appropriate Uses

In the preface to *Child-Centered Play Therapy Research*, Baggerly (2010) reports that the empirical support for play therapy is frequently called into question, and that the impetus for publishing a book on play therapy research was "to explain the most prominent play therapy research studies in this millennium" (p. xiii). The book provides the current state of research on CCPT. It is organized around disorders (e.g., ADHD), populations (e.g., Hispanic children), symptoms (e.g., behavior problems), situations (e.g., after an earthquake), and techniques (e.g., filial therapy) and makes a very strong case for CCPT as an empirically supported intervention.

Several published reviews of scholarly work in play therapy provide a good overview for those interested in the research base. Bratton and Ray (2000) reviewed play therapy studies published from 1942 to 1999 (inclusion criteria were the words *play therapy* and an experimental design). The studies varied greatly in number of sessions (2 to 100) and the age range of subjects (3 to 17 years). The review found empirical support for play therapy as an intervention for a long list of problems, including "social maladjustment, withdrawn behavior, conduct disorder/aggression/oppositional behavior, maladaptive school behavior, emotional maladjustment, anxiety/fear, autism/schizophrenia/psychoticism" and over a dozen other concerns (p. 51).

In 2005, Bratton and colleagues published a meta-analysis of play therapy research, calculating an effect size of .80 standard deviations (regarded as strong) for the 93 studies that were reviewed. Of those 93 studies, 36 were conducted in school settings. The remaining studies were conducted in outpatient clinics ($n = 34$) or critical-incident or residential settings ($n = 18$). The average age of the children receiving the treatment across the studies was 7 years. The implications drawn by the authors were clear: "play therapy demonstrates itself to be an effective intervention for children's problems, one that is uniquely responsive to children's developmental needs. Of significant note, play therapy has a large effect on children's behavior, social adjustment, and personality" (Bratton et al., 2005, p. 385). Among their conclusions, Bratton and colleagues noted that other factors, such as parental involvement and number of sessions, also play an important role in achieving positive outcomes (in the meta-analysis conducted by Bratton and colleagues, the mean number of sessions delivered in school settings was 8.4).

As an extension of their earlier work, Ray and Bratton (2010) reviewed play therapy research from 2000 to 2009, this time differentiating experimental, quasi-experimental, and evidentiary studies (i.e., those that lack a control or comparison group but use pre- and postassessment). They concluded that the examined studies continued to support the efficacy of play therapy across a range of populations and referral concerns. The following brief discussions introduce interested school psychologists to play-based and related studies of interventions in school settings.

Another, more recent, meta-analytic study of CCPT reviewed 52 studies from 1995 to 2010 and found a moderate, statistically significant effect size (.47; Lin & Bratton, 2015). The authors found that CCPT was particularly effective for "broad-spectrum behavioral problems, children's self-esteem, and caregiver-child stress" (p. 54). They note that CCPT may be considered a treatment of choice for children because of its developmental and cultural appropriateness. Although the meta-analytic study described here looked across many CCPT studies, others have focused on the use of play therapy to treat specific referral issues.

Wilkes and colleagues (2011) reported data from a play-based social skills intervention for children with ADHD, nondiagnosed peers, and parents. Pairs of children (one with and one without ADHD) engaged in play with a therapist in a play room while parents worked with a therapist to learn more about ADHD, strategies for developing skills through play, and interventions that can be implemented at home. After seven 40-minute sessions, both groups of children showed improvements in social skills. The researchers incorporated a modeling approach (both therapist modeling and self-modeling through video recordings) and attributed much of the success to the parent and child-peer components. Although the research reported was from a pilot study, results suggest that a play-based approach to social skills development for students with ADHD may be effective.

Ray et al. (2008) conducted research to better understand the effects of CCPT on student–teacher relationship stress. The research identified 58 elementary school children with emotional and behavioral problems (based on teacher referrals) and randomly assigned each child to one of two treatment groups: short-term treatment (16 sessions over 8 weeks) and long-term treatment (16 sessions over 16 weeks). The Index of Teaching Stress was the dependent variable. Results indicated that school-based CCPT, provided either in 8-week or 16-week formats, may reduce teacher–child relationship stress, though the more intensive form of intervention may be more effective. This study is noteworthy because it was carried out in a school setting and reflects the ecosystemic nature of children's behavior (i.e., in the context of relationships).

Gershenson, Lyon, and Budd (2010) reported on the adaptation of Parent–Child Interaction Therapy (PCIT) in school settings as a universal prevention program known as Teacher–Child Interaction Training (TCIT). PCIT had previously been applied to teacher–child relationships in school settings, sometimes under the name of teacher–child interaction therapy (McIntosh et al., 2000). Gershenson and colleagues elected to use the term *training* rather than *therapy* to emphasize the indirect, consultative nature of their work. Their intervention was provided to 12 teachers in the form of workshops and in-class practice sessions over 11–13 weeks. Evaluation of the program showed increases in teachers' positive behaviors, such as praise and reflection, as well as high teacher satisfaction ratings. Gershenson and colleagues concluded that "TCIT is a promising approach for enhancing positive teacher–child interactions in a preschool setting" (p. 279).

A large body of research has been conducted with PCIT, but most of these interventions have not been in school settings. However, the evidence base is strong across a wide range of populations and situations. Hood and Eyberg (2003) reported that 6 years after children's treatment with PCIT in a clinical setting, significant improvements in child behavior were maintained. Chaffin and colleagues (2011) found that a combination of PCIT and a self-motivational orientation intervention reduced child welfare recidivism (i.e., repeated reports to child protective services). Bagner and Eyberg (2007) compared a wait-list control group with families receiving PCIT to address the disruptive behaviors of their children with intellectual disabilities and found better outcomes for the treatment group. Further research is needed in the application of PCIT in school settings.

The application of play-based approaches in school settings is clearly a developmentally appropriate and empirically supported intervention for a variety of referral concerns and populations. However, implementing these techniques in schools presents some challenges. For example, interventions that require significant time commitments from parents may not be practical during school and work hours. Ray and colleagues (2008) noted that high-stakes testing has put pressure on schools to limit time spent outside of academic settings, thereby making it difficult for counselors to gain access to students for therapy sessions. Whereas a private practice clinician may have 50-minute sessions, school-based professionals may need to have shorter sessions to accommodate school schedules and perhaps meet with children more frequently than once per week. Ray and colleagues (2008) also reviewed literature indicating that teachers' perceptions of students may remain negative, even when observable improvements in student behavior are documented. Consequently, school psychologists may need to work closely with teachers in a consultative role to support the play-based work with children.

Specific Play Therapy Techniques

The numerous variations and permutations of play-based approaches, both nondirective and directive methods, include Adlerian play therapy (based on Alfred Adler's individual psychology), sandplay therapy, group and family play therapy, and modifications for specific situations (e.g., response to trauma, blending with cognitive–behavioral therapy). This section focuses on two approaches: child-centered play therapy and sandtray therapy.

Child-Centered Play Therapy

CCPT as it is practiced today is a direct extension of Axline's eight guiding principles (as cited in Bratton et al., 2009). The play therapist does the following:

- Fosters a relationship with the child that is characterized by warmth and friendliness.
- Accepts who the child is rather than imposing expectations.
- Promotes free expression of self through permissiveness.
- Facilitates the child's capacity to gain insight through reflection of feelings.
- Recognizes that the child is capable of solving personal problems.
- Permits the child to direct the sessions.
- Does not rush the process, recognizing that change is gradual.
- Sets limits only as needed.

Ultimately, the CCPT process uses the child–therapist relationship as the means through which growth and change occur. By focusing on the child rather than the problem and creating a permissive environment with minimal limit setting, the play therapist enables the child to learn self-control and self-respect. Moreover, the child learns to make choices, take responsibility, and solve problems creatively (Landreth, 2002).

The first part of CCPT involves the therapist beginning the relationship in a way that communicates the child's importance. Upon first greeting the child, the therapist moves down to the child's level, makes eye contact, and greets the child warmly. As they enter the playroom, the therapist introduces the child to the playroom by saying something to the effect of, "This is your time to play with these toys in any way that you want." By doing so, the counselor communicates permissiveness and responsibility (Bratton et al., 2009).

Landreth (2002) has provided useful guidelines for the selection of play therapy toys and materials, favoring toys that permit the creative expression of feelings, which is the theoretical foundation of CCPT. Toys should be diverse so that they can be used to communicate a wide range of feelings and promote self-understanding. Landreth recommends the following categories of toys and materials:

- Nurturing toys, such as baby dolls, baby bottles, food and kitchen toys, and items related to medical care (e.g., stethoscope, bandages)
- Aggressive toys such as handcuffs, toy soldiers, monsters, and aggressive puppets

- Toys related to social experiences (e.g., doll house, people, cash register)
- Communication toys (e.g., telephones)
- Mastery toys (e.g., school supplies, chalkboard)

When assembling a set of toys for play therapy, one should maintain a goal of promoting the child's expression. Some toys may interfere with this goal and should be avoided. For example, toys that represent characters from movies or television programs may be counterproductive, as children sometimes use them to reenact scenes they have watched rather than express their inner thoughts and feelings. Landreth also advises against toys that are complex or mechanical, as they too may limit expression.

Ideally, the counselor has access to a room that has been designed for play therapy, with enough space and materials for a child to explore, play, and engage in self-expression freely. However, many schools have limited space, and school psychologists may be unable to secure a space that can be used exclusively as a play therapy room. Shared space with a guidance counselor may be available, and some school psychologists have developed portable play therapy kits by packing toys into rolling suitcases that can be taken from campus to campus. Arrangement of space to minimize obstacles (e.g., large desks or tables) can make small spaces more amenable to play.

As the child explores the playroom and interacts with the toys, the play therapist refrains from directing the play or entering the play unless invited by the child. Even when invited, the play therapist remains passive with respect to engagement with the child's play, instead waiting for the child's instructions and direction. This communicates that the child is in control. However, the therapist takes a very active role in tracking, reflecting, and showing interest in the child. The play therapist should lean forward, follow the child's movement in the room, and describe the child's behaviors (e.g., "You're picking up that doll and giving it a bottle"), reflect the child's language (e.g., the child says, "He's a strong tiger," and the therapist reflects back, "That's a strong tiger"), and reflect feelings (e.g., "You're really frustrated right now").

The play therapist also returns responsibility to the child. Outside of the playroom, some children do not feel competent and rely on others (parents, teachers) to do for them what they could do for themselves. In play therapy, the child is given the opportunity to experience success in a supportive environment when encouraged to try. For example, a child may ask the play therapist to open a container of markers, and the play therapist returns responsibility to the child by saying, "That's something you can do" and having the child do it. This experience builds self-esteem and decision making authentically, because the child is empowered to achieve in a concrete way as opposed to just being told that the child is capable.

Limit setting is another important part of play therapy. Many children who are referred for counseling have difficulty following rules at home and at school, so the play therapy experience provides the child with an opportunity to work with an adult who is trained in appropriate limit setting. Landreth's (2002) A-C-T model of limit setting is as follows: (a) acknowledging the child's feeling ("You would like to take that toy home with you"); (b) stating the limit ("These toys have to stay in this room"); and (c) providing an alternative ("You can play with that toy next time you come here"). Limit setting should not be arbitrary, so play therapists should decide in advance what limits will be consistently set (e.g., safety of the child and therapist, respect for the materials and toys).

Bratton and colleagues (2009) emphasize the importance of involving parents when providing play therapy. Play therapists should explain play therapy to parents, explain that play sessions are confidential (and therefore not observed by parents), and regularly consult with parents on the child's progress. Play therapists also should interact with parents with genuineness and empathy, maintaining the same unconditional positive regard that is extended toward children.

Over time, children engaging in CCPT learn how to express feelings, make choices, take responsibility, and solve problems in the context of the safe and accepting environment provided by the play therapist.

Sandtray Therapy

Another type of play therapy, sandplay or sandtray techniques have been used for decades as both assessment and counseling tools (Turner, 2005). Lowenfeld (1993) is credited with developing, in the 1920s, the technique of using miniature objects in the sand. She called it the "World Technique," and the idea was to let the child freely select and arrange the objects in the sand. The therapist was to resist making interpretations so that the child could ascribe meaning to the objects (Mitchell & Friedman, 1994).

Lowenfeld (1993) noted four aspects of the sandtray method that had therapeutic value. First, she noted that a world created in the sand could represent multiple layers of the psyche ("multidimensional nature"). Second, the narrative and dynamic aspects of sandplay have therapeutic value. Third, children's preverbal content could be accessed through sandplay. And last, children needed no specific skills to engage in the approach. Following Lowenfeld's development of the technique, others have expanded on her work to include new variations, terminology, and applications (e.g., group and family sandtray; Mitchell & Friedman, 1994). Practitioners of the technique have formed the International Society of Sandplay Therapists (ISST) and have a journal (*Journal of Sandplay Therapy*), and sandtray is now a widely used approach (Sweeney & Homeyer, 2009).

Counselors may choose sandtray therapy over other techniques for a number of reasons. Sweeney and Homeyer (2009) note that sandtray therapy can enable children to express their emotions nonverbally and provide "a necessary therapeutic distance for clients" (p. 300). In other words, some children may find it easier to represent their feelings with miniature objects when talking about their emotions would be too difficult. Similarly, the process may decrease resistance. Sand is also valued for its kinesthetic, tactile quality, which many find satisfying. The physical sandtray and miniatures can have the effect of focusing the counseling process by imposing boundaries or limits. The objects used for sandtray therapy can encourage the use of metaphor in counseling as well.

Homeyer and Sweeney (2010) note that the application of sandtray therapy varies among individuals, groups, couples, and families. For individual sandtray counseling, the client is presented with two sandtrays, one for dry sand and one for wet sand, that are about 3 inches deep, 30 inches long, and 20 inches wide. The trays are painted blue on the inside to represent water or sky. The trays are half filled with clean sand. The client is also presented with a selection of miniatures about 2 to 3 inches tall, arranged in categories:

- Buildings (houses, castles, factories, schools, churches, stores)
- People (various racial and ethnic groups, military, cowboys, sports figures, fantasy, mythological, various occupations)

- Vehicles (cars, trucks, planes, boats, emergency vehicles, farm equipment, military vehicles)
- Animals (domestic, farm, zoo, wild, marine, prehistoric)
- Vegetation (trees, shrubs, plants)
- Deities (both Western and Eastern religions)
- Structures (fences, bridges, gates, highway signs)
- Natural objects (rocks, shells, driftwood, feathers)
- Miscellaneous (jewelry, wishing well, treasure chest; Sweeney & Homeyer, 2009, p. 305)

After ensuring that the materials are organized and accessible and that the sand is smooth and free of objects from previous sessions, the therapist asks the client to make a picture, scene, or world in the sand (Sweeney & Homeyer, 2009). Some therapists may be directive and give a more specific prompt, such as "in the sand, make a scene of your life before the car accident" (Plotts et al., 2008). Others may leave the prompt open and simply ask the client to create a world in the sand.

As the client creates a scene in the sand with miniatures, the therapist neither directs nor interferes with the creation. Therapists may track, reflect, and perhaps ask questions about the emerging scene, much as a CCPT therapist would (Sweeney & Homeyer, 2009). In some cases, a therapist may decide that talking during the client's creation may interfere, in which case the therapist may communicate nonverbally that they are watching and paying attention.

After the client creates the scene or world, the therapist may ask the client to give the production a title and describe the scene. The sandtray therapist can ask questions about the scene as a whole but also may inquire about specific portions of the scene. This process is an opportunity for clients to express themselves through the explanation of the world they have created. Therapists should avoid verbalizing interpretations, as the meaning ascribed to the miniatures and the scene as a whole can be very individualized for each client. At the end of the session, the production should be photographed or sketched, and the counselor should not clean up without the client's permission (Sweeney & Homeyer, 2009).

Eberts and Homeyer (2015) note that the development of sandtray therapy skills takes time, and that those interested in developing these competencies have access to numerous resources, including book, conference workshops, graduate courses, and clinical supervision. They note that the therapist must carefully observe the client and remain attuned to the process. In this respect, the therapist is actively engaged, even if the approach skews toward the nondirective side of the directiveness continuum.

Evaluation of Outcomes

Two parallel approaches are used for evaluating outcomes in play-based therapy, both of which apply equally to CCPT and sandtray therapy. One approach can be described as a clinical process approach, in which the counselor attends to the evolution of the child's play over time, as well as to the toys and materials used and the narrative content that emerges. Progress may be seen, for example, in play that becomes better integrated with adaptive narrative themes. The second approach, and one that is more consistent with the framework of counseling as a related service, is to have observable, measurable goals and objectives for which data can be collected. In this second case, the outcomes of play therapy are measured not in the playroom but through the interpretation of data collected from parents and teachers on behavior rating scales. Both of these, the clinical process approach and the measurable objectives approach, are valuable and can be used simultaneously.

CASE EXAMPLE 1: FRANK

Background

Frank is a 5-year-old kindergarten student at Rolling Hills Elementary. He had been referred for evaluation at age 3 because of concerns about delayed language development and was subsequently placed in the preschool program for children with disabilities (PPCD) at Rolling Hills under the classification of speech impairment (expressive language disorder). Between the ages of 3 and 5, Frank made slow but steady progress in the area of expressive language, but he presented some behavioral challenges in the classroom (e.g., following directions, keeping his hands to himself, and throwing toys). His teacher and the teaching assistant in PPCD reported that although Frank's behaviors were challenging, they were able to effectively manage them with frequent monitoring and redirection. He continues to be identified as a child with a disability and receives speech therapy.

Frank's current teacher, Ms. Judson, called an Individualized Education Program (IEP) team meeting to discuss Frank's behavior. She reported that he had become increasingly oppositional over the course of the school year and had not responded to her behavior management strategies. She said she tried to praise Frank for positive behaviors and to ignore negative behaviors (unless safety was a concern, as it had been when he threw objects in the classroom). Ms. Judson also visited with Frank's parents about these concerns, and they reported that they were experiencing similar difficulties at home. The IEP team requested an evaluation to determine whether Frank was eligible for counseling as a related service.

Assessment

Mr. Sampson, the school psychologist, collected interview and behavior rating scale data from Frank's teacher and parents. He also observed Frank in the classroom and conducted a brief interview with him. Pulling together the data, Mr. Sampson came to the conclusion that Frank's behavior negatively affects his learning and the learning of others, and that although Ms. Judson had consistently applied behavior management strategies, Frank had not responded to those efforts. The evaluation concluded that Frank needed counseling as a related service to support his educational progress. Mr. Sampson proposed that the counseling goals focus on following classroom rules and responding appropriately to teachers' requests. The IEP team agreed to adopt the following goals and objectives.

Goals and Objectives

Annual Goal. Frank will make measurable progress in the area of behavioral functioning.

- Objective 1: Frank will follow the three rules posted on his classroom wall at least 80% of the time.
- Objective 2: Frank will follow his teacher's (re)directions at least 80% of the time.

Intervention

After observing and interviewing Frank, Mr. Sampson noted that Frank is a playful child who tends to express himself nonverbally. Consequently, CCPT was selected as a therapeutic modality to capitalize on Frank's strengths. After being introduced to Frank by Ms. Judson, Mr. Sampson brought Frank to the play therapy room on campus and said, "You can play with these toys any way that you want to." Frank immediately began to explore the playroom.

Mr. Sampson noted that Frank did not spend very much time with any particular toy during the first session. Rather, Frank picked up and looked at a variety of toys (e.g., plastic alligator, doll, monkey puppet, cash register) but did not spend more than a minute with any given object. Mr. Sampson tracked Frank's behavior and occasionally reflected feelings (e.g., "You seem to think that's a funny toy"). Five minutes before the session was to end, Mr. Sampson announced that time was almost up. Frank shouted "No!" and continued to play. Mr. Sampson said, "You don't want this to end, but we're out of time. You can come back another day." As Mr. Sampson stood up and approached the door, Frank put down a toy car and followed Mr. Sampson out of the room.

Over the next several sessions, Frank's play became more organized and integrated. Rather than quickly going through a series of unrelated toys, Frank began to set up the same toys on the floor each time he came into the playroom. Typically, he arranged a row of cars inside a perimeter of blocks. Also inside the perimeter were some rubber snakes. In each session, Frank moved the snakes around the cars and said, "Let's get out of here! The snakes are chasing us!" Frank then moved the cars within the perimeter and eventually crashed the cars into the blocks, creating an opening through which the cars could exit.

Following each session, Mr. Sampson took careful notes and spent time reflecting on the key elements of the sessions (e.g., content of the play, Frank's affect, changes across sessions). Mr. Sampson noted some possible interpretations of Frank's play behaviors. For example, perhaps the perimeters of blocks represent the rules and structure of school, and Frank sees himself as the cars (or drivers). Taking this line of thinking a step further, Mr. Sampson speculated that the snakes could represent teachers, and wondered whether the perimeter of blocks was somehow perceived by Frank as both an obstacle and a form of security. These interpretations were not shared with Frank but rather were used as working hypotheses toward better understanding him.

As the play therapy sessions continued, Mr. Sampson tracked Frank's behaviors, reflected feelings, and demonstrated an interest in Frank's play. Over time, Mr. Sampson wondered whether Frank's gradual transformation from unstructured to structured play was mirrored in Frank's behavior at home and in the classroom.

Evaluation

Mr. Sampson contacted Frank's parents, who reported slightly fewer battles at home over following directions. They also noted that Frank was spending more time in his room playing with his toys than he had previously. In the classroom, Ms. Judson reported that Frank was beginning to need less redirection, although he continued to have trouble keeping his hands to himself.

Mr. Sampson continued with the nondirective play therapy sessions for a total of 12 sessions. By then, the data indicated that Frank had achieved his counseling goals and objectives. The IEP team was very pleased with the outcomes and agreed that dismissal from counseling as a related service was appropriate.

CASE EXAMPLE 2: GABRIELLE

Background

Gabrielle, a 15-year-old high school sophomore, had recently transferred from another state, where she had been classified as a student with an emotional disturbance (based on her "inability to build or maintain satisfactory interpersonal relationships with peers and teachers"). Before she had left her last school, Gabrielle's IEP team had recommended counseling as a related service to assist her in forming better interpersonal relationships, but her family moved before counseling services started.

Ms. Gilbert, the school psychologist, reviewed the paperwork that the previous school district had sent and noted that members of the IEP team had expressed some concern that Gabrielle might not say much in counseling, given her history of withdrawal and difficulty establishing relationships.

Assessment

Ms. Gilbert used existing records, including the full individual evaluation and eligibility report for emotional disturbance, as part of the assessment for counseling service eligibility. Ms. Gilbert then conducted interviews with Gabrielle, her father, and two of her teachers to gather additional background information, details about present concerns, and individual perceptions of contributing factors. She also gathered data from the BASC-3 and some projective tests (Roberts-2 and sentence completion measures). The assessment indicated that Gabrielle was experiencing significant social anxiety that interfered with her peer and adult relationships and that she needed counseling services to benefit from her educational program.

Practice: Applying What You Have Learned

Complete the intervention plan for Gabrielle. Develop IEP goals and objectives, a treatment plan that uses nondirective techniques, and methods for evaluating progress.

SUMMARY AND OTHER CONSIDERATIONS

Play-based approaches can be effective in working with children and adolescents in schools. Landreth and colleagues (2009) identified a number of factors to consider when implementing play therapy in the schools. For example, they stressed the importance of gaining teacher and parent support, planning sessions that fit the school schedule, and establishing a space for play therapy and materials. If the school psychologist who is interested in using play-based techniques does not have an established play therapy room, a section of an office or workroom can be used, provided that the space is private.

A substantial body of literature supports the efficacy of CCPT, and methods are available to train parents and teachers in play therapy techniques (e.g., filial therapy, Parent–Child Interaction Therapy). Most research has been conducted in clinical settings, so more school-based play therapy research is needed. School psychologists who provide counseling as a related service will need to communicate to IEP team members how play therapy works and draw connections between the intervention and the treatment goals and objectives. In a talk therapy approach such as cognitive–behavioral therapy, the relationship between the goals and the intervention may be more explicit, so the play therapist should, in the interest of building support, become skilled at communicating how play therapy works.

Some school psychologists may have little training in play therapy but an interest in developing play therapy skills. Fortunately, they have access to many continuing education opportunities, professional organizations, books, journals, and conferences for skill development. Those who wish to gain more experience should also seek a qualified colleague who can provide supervision as needed. Many of the resources cited in this chapter will be helpful to those who wish to learn more about play therapy.

Some school psychologists may find that they are a good match for play-based therapies. Landreth (2002) identifies a number of personality characteristics that contribute to the effectiveness of play therapists. These include flexibility (with respect to acceptance of the unpredictable), objectivity (to allow for a child's individuation), and a suspension of judgment and evaluation (so that the child will experience the therapist's acceptance). These characteristics may fall under a larger umbrella of open-mindedness. The play therapist should be comfortable allowing the child to play freely without adult direction or interference.

KEY POINTS FOR DISCUSSION

- When determining whether nondirective methods would be appropriate, what child characteristics should one consider?
- When parents and teachers ask, "How does play therapy work?," how should the school psychologist respond?
- How do CCPT and sandtray therapy differ? How are they similar?
- What are the potential costs and benefits of working with parents and teachers in a school setting (e.g., using Teacher–Child Interaction Training and Parent–Child Interaction Therapy)?

REFERENCES

Association for Play Therapy. (n.d.). Play makes a difference. Retrieved from http://www.a4pt.org/ps.index.cfm?ID=1653

Baggerly, J. N. (2010). Preface. In J. N. Baggerly, D. C. Ray, & S. C. Bratton, (Eds.), *Child-centered play therapy research: The evidence base for effective practice* (pp. xiii–xviii). Hoboken, NJ: John Wiley & Sons.

Baggerly, J., & Parker, M. (2005). Child-centered group play therapy with African American boys at the elementary school level. *Journal of Counseling and Development, 83*, 387–396. https://doi.org/10.1002/j.1556-6678.2005.tb00360.x

Bagner, D. M., & Eyberg, S. M. (2007). Parent-child interaction therapy for disruptive behavior in children with mental retardation: A randomized controlled trial. *Journal of Clinical Child and Adolescent Psychology, 36*, 418–429. doi:10.1080/15374410701448448

Bass, J. D., & Mulick, J. A. (2007). Social play skill enhancement of children with autism using peers and siblings as therapists. *Psychology in the Schools, 44,* 727–735. https://doi.org/10.1002/pits.20261

Bratton, S. C., & Ray, D. C. (2000). What the research shows about play therapy. *International Journal of Play Therapy, 9,* 47–88.

Bratton, S. C., Ray, D. C., Edwards, N. A., & Landreth, G. (2009). Child-centered play therapy (CCPT): Theory, research, and practice. *Person-Centered and Experiential Psychotherapies, 8,* 266–281. https://doi.org/10.1080/14779757.2009.9688493

Bratton, S. C., Ray, D. C., Rhine, T., & Jones, L. (2005). The efficacy of play therapy with children: A meta-analytic review of treatment outcomes. *Professional Psychology: Research and Practice, 36,* 376–390. doi:10.1037/0735-7028.36.4.376

Camastral, S. (2008). No small change: Process-oriented play therapy for children of separating parents. *Australian and New Zealand Journal of Family Therapy, 29*(2), 100–106. https://doi.org/10.1375/anft.29.2.100

Cattanach, A. (2009). Narrative approaches: Helping children tell their stories. In A. A. Drewes (Ed.), *Blending play therapy with cognitive behavioral therapy: Evidence-based and other effective treatments and techniques* (pp. 423–447). Hoboken, NJ: John Wiley & Sons.

Chaffin, M., Funderbunk, B., Bard, D., Valle, L. A., & Gurwitch, R. (2011). A combined motivation and parent-child interaction therapy package reduces child welfare recidivism in a randomized dismantling field trial. *Journal of Consulting and Clinical Psychology, 79,* 84–95.

Cohen, E., Chazan, S., Lerner, M., & Maimon, E. (2010). Posttraumatic play in young children exposed to terrorism: An empirical study. *Infant Mental Health Journal, 31,* 159–181.

Drewes, A. A. (2009). *Blending play therapy with cognitive behavioral therapy.* Hoboken, NJ: John Wiley & Sons.

Dugan, E. M., Snow, M. S., & Crowe, S. R. (2010). Working with children affected by Hurricane Katrina: Two case studies in play therapy. *Child and Adolescent Mental Health, 15,* 52–55.

Eberts, S., & Homeyer, L. (2015). Processing sand trays from two theoretical perspectives: Gestalt and Adlerian. *International Journal of Play Therapy, 24*(3), 134–150. https://doi.org/10.1037/a0039392

Ewing, D. L., Monsen, J. J., & Kwoka, M. (2014). Behavioural and emotional well-being of children following non-directive play with school staff. *Educational Psychology in Practice, 30,* 192–203. https://doi.org/10.1080/02667363.2014.907128

Frankel, M., Rachlin, H., & Yip-Bannicq, M. (2012). How nondirective therapy directs: The power of empathy in the context of unconditional positive regard. *Person-Centered & Experiential Psychotherapies, 11*(3), 205–214. doi:10.1080/14779757.2012.695292

Gershenson, R. A., Lyon, A. R., & Budd, K. S. (2010). Promoting positive interactions in the classroom: Adapting parent-child interaction therapy as a universal preschool program. *Education and Treatment of Children, 33,* 261–287. doi:10.1353/etc.0.0092

Gil, E. (2005). From sensitivity to competence in working across cultures. In E. Gil & A. A. Drewes (Eds.), *Cultural issues in play therapy* (pp. 3–25). New York, NY: Guilford Press.

Gil, E. (2014). Children's self-initiated gradual exposure: The wonders of posttraumatic play and behavioral reenactments. In E. Gil (Ed.), *Working with children to heal interpersonal trauma: The power of play* (pp. 44–63). New York, NY: Guilford Press.

Gil, E. M. (2016). Using integrated directive and nondirective play interventions for abused and traumatized children. In L. A. Reddy, T. M. Files-Hall, & C. E. Schaefer, (Eds.), *Empirically based play interventions for children* (pp. 95–113). Washington, DC: American Psychological Association.

Glover, G. (2005). Musings on working with Native American children in play therapy. In E. Gil & A. A. Drewes (Eds.), *Cultural issues in play therapy* (pp. 168–179). New York, NY: Guilford Press.

Goodyear-Brown, P. (2010). *Play therapy with traumatized children: A prescriptive approach.* Hoboken, NJ: John Wiley & Sons.

Guerney, B. (1964). Filial therapy: Description and rationale. *Journal of Consulting Psychology, 28,* 303–310.

Hill, A. (2006). Play therapy with sexually abused children: Including parents in therapeutic play. *Child and Family Social Work, 11,* 316–324.

Homeyer, L. E., & Sweeney, D. S. (2010). *Sandtray therapy: A practical manual* (2nd ed.). New York, NY: Routledge.

Hood, K. H., & Eyberg, S. M. (2003). Outcomes of parent-child interaction therapy: Mothers' reports of maintenance three to six years after treatment. *Journal of Clinical Child and Adolescent Psychology, 32,* 419–429. doi:10.1207/S15374424JCCP3203_10

Jacob, S., & Brinda, V. (2017). Effect of non-directive play therapy on development among mentally challenged children in selected institutions of Coimbatore. *Asian Journal of Nursing Education and Research, 7,* 482–490.

Kao, S.-C. (2005). Play therapy with Asian children. In E. Gil & A. A. Drewes (Eds.), *Cultural issues in play therapy* (pp. 180–193). New York, NY: Guilford Press.

Kenney-Noziska, S. G., Schaefer, C. E., & Homeyer, L. E. (2012). Beyond directive or nondirective: Moving the conversation forward. *International journal of play therapy, 21,* 244–252.

King, M., Marston, L., & Bower, P. (2014). Comparison of non-directive counselling and cognitive behaviour therapy for patients presenting in general practice with an ICD-10 depressive episode: A randomized control trial. *Psychological Medicine, 44,* 1835–1844.

Landreth, G. L. (2002). *Play therapy: The art of the relationship* (2nd ed.). New York, NY: Brunner-Routledge.

Landreth, G. L., & Bratton, S. C. (2006). *Child–Parent Relationship Therapy (CPRT): A 10-session filial therapy model.* New York, NY: Routledge.

Landreth, G. L., Ray, D. C., & Bratton, S. C. (2009). Play therapy in elementary schools. *Psychology in the Schools, 46,* 281–289.

Lin, Y., & Bratton, S. C. (2015). A meta-analysis of play therapy outcomes. *Counseling Psychology Quarterly, 14,* 149–163. https://doi.org/10.1080/09515070110059142

Linder, T. W. (2008). *Transdisciplinary play-based assessment.* Baltimore, MD: Brookes.

Lowenfeld, M. (1993). *Understanding children's sandplay.* London, UK: George Allen & Unwin.

Lowenstein, L. (2010). *Creative family therapy techniques: Play, art, and expressive activities to engage children in family sessions.* Toronto, ON: Champion Press.

McIntosh, D. E., Rizza, M. G., & Bliss, L. (2000). Implementing empirically supported interventions: Teacher-child interaction therapy. *Psychology in the Schools, 37,* 453–462. https://doi.org/10.1002/1520-6807(200009)37:5<453::AID-PITS5>3.0.CO;2-2

McNeil, C. B., & Hembree-Kigin, T. L. (2010). *Parent–Child Interaction Therapy* (2nd ed.). New York, NY: Springer.

Mitchell, R. R., & Friedman, H. S. (1994). *Sandplay: Past, present, and future.* New York, NY: Routledge.

Nims, D. R. (2007). Integrating play therapy techniques into solution-focused brief therapy. *International Journal of Play Therapy, 16,* 54–68.

Norcross, J. (2005). A primer on psychotherapy integration. In J. C. Norcross & M. R. Goldfried (Eds.), *Handbook of psychotherapy integration* (2nd ed., pp. 3–23). New York, NY: Oxford University Press.

Oaklander, V. (1988). *Windows to our children.* Highland, NY: Gestalt Journal Press.

Packman, J., & Lebeauf, I. (2010). A school-based group activity therapy intervention with learning-disabled preadolescents exhibiting behavior problems. In J. N. Baggerly, D. C. Ray, & S. C. Bratton, (Eds.), *Child-centered play therapy research: The evidence base for effective practice* (pp. 163–176). Hoboken, NJ: John Wiley & Sons.

Plotts, C., Lasser, J., & Prater, S. (2008). Exploring sandplay therapy: Application to individuals with traumatic brain injury. *International Journal of Play Therapy, 17,* 138–153. https://doi.org/10.1037/1555-6824.17.2.138

Porter, M. L., Hernandez-Reif, M., & Jessee, P. (2009). Play therapy: A review. *Early Child Development and Care, 179,* 1025–1040.

Ramirez, S. Z., Flores-Torres, L. L., Kranz, P. L., & Lund, N. L. (2005). Using Axline's eight principles of play therapy with Mexican-American children. *Journal of Instructional Psychology, 32,* 329–337.

Ray, D. C., & Bratton, S. C. (2010). What the research shows about play therapy: Twenty-first century update. In J. N. Baggerly, D. C. Ray, & S. C. Bratton, (Eds.), *Child-centered play therapy research: The evidence base for effective practice* (pp. 3–33). Hoboken, NJ: John Wiley & Sons.

Ray, D. C., Henson, R. K., Schottelkorb, A. A., Brown, A. G., & Muro, J. (2008). Effects of short- and long-term play therapy services on teacher-child relationship stress. *Psychology in the Schools, 45,* 994–1009.

Schaefer, C. E., & Drewes, A. A. (2010). The therapeutic powers of play and play therapy. In A. A. Drewes & C. E. Schaefer (Eds.), *School-based play therapy* (pp. 15–26). Hoboken, NJ: John Wiley & Sons.

Sweeney, D. S., & Homeyer, L. E. (1999). *Group play therapy: How to do it, how it works, whom it's best for.* San Francisco, CA: Jossey-Bass.

Sweeney, D. S., & Homeyer, L. E. (2009). Sandtray therapy. In A. A. Drewes (Ed.), *Blending play therapy with cognitive behavioral therapy: Evidence-based and other effective treatments and techniques* (pp. 297–318). Hoboken, NJ: John Wiley & Sons.

Turner, B. A. (2005). *The handbook of sandplay therapy.* Cloverdale, CA: Tenemos Press.

Webb, N. B. (2011). Play therapy for bereaved children: Adapting strategies to community, school, and home settings. *School Psychology International, 32,* 132–143. https://doi.org/10.1177/0143034311400832

Wilkes, S., Cordier, R., Bundy, A., Docking, K., & Munro, N. (2011). A play-based intervention for children with ADHD: A pilot study. *Australian Occupational Therapy Journal, 58,* 231–240. doi:10.1111/j.1440-1630.2011.00928.x

Chapter 7

Mindfulness

OVERVIEW

Mindfulness has become a popular approach in counseling both to prevent and to address a wide range of concerns, including depression, anxiety, inattention, and anger management. This chapter provides an introduction to mindfulness and its application to counseling services in schools. Though not a panacea, mindfulness practice may be a helpful technique for school psychologists to add to their repertoire of counseling skills, either as a standalone intervention or as a complementary approach used with other methods. This chapter defines and describes mindfulness, reviews the research supporting mindful practices, and provides some examples of the ways the approach can be applied with children and adolescents. The chapter concludes with a case example illustrating the use of mindfulness to help a group of students challenged by emotional regulation difficulties.

OBJECTIVES

After reading this chapter, readers should be able to do the following:

- Define mindfulness.
- Explain the term *equanimity*.
- Articulate the benefits of mindfulness practice.
- Discuss the empirical support for mindfulness interventions.
- Develop a mindfulness activity for an individual or group counseling session.
- Link IEP goals to mindfulness interventions.
- Provide a rationale for the use of mindfulness in school settings.

An Introduction to Mindfulness

After reading this paragraph, place one hand on your belly and notice how it rises and falls with each breath you take. Count five inhalations and five exhalations and notice how it feels to be aware of your breathing. Set the book down now and give this a try. When you're ready, pick up the book and continue reading.

Pause for breathing exercise.

Paying attention to breathing may be one of the most commonly used techniques in mindfulness, which has been defined as "one's ability to orient attention toward immediate experience in a purposeful and positive way" (Renshaw & Cook, 2017, p. 6). The breathing exercise above is an example of an activity that draws your attention to the present sensory experience, where the focus isn't on the past or future, but on the here and now. Attending to breathing is a great starting point because we all breathe, but we typically fail to notice our respiration. Of course, there are other ways that we can focus on our experiences, and we'll share some of those later in the chapter.

Mindfulness also involves maintaining an open, nonjudgmental stance of curiosity and acceptance (Wisner & Starzec, 2016). When practicing mindfulness, we notice and acknowledge thoughts and feelings without evaluating or judging. Rather than overreacting to experienced events, the mindful practice of *equanimity* involves noticing what is happening and how we feel. The following folk tale illustrates this approach.

A farmer had six horses that were essential to his livelihood, for they pulled his plows, brought his crops to market, and provided fertilizer for his fields. One day he awoke to find that his six horses were gone. The villagers gathered and expressed dismay.

"This is terrible! Your horses are gone!"

"I do not know if this is good or bad," said the farmer. "All I know is that my horses are gone."

The next day the horses returned, and with them was a new, seventh horse. The villagers expressed great enthusiasm.

"How fortunate you are! Your horses have returned and brought with them another! You are a very lucky farmer."

"I do not know if this is good or bad," said the farmer. "All I know is that my horses have returned, and with them is a new horse."

The farmer's son was eager to ride the new horse, but it threw him to the ground and broke his leg.

"How terrible," cried the villagers. "Your son has broken his leg!"

"I do not know if this is good or bad," said the farmer. "All I know is that my son has a broken leg."

The next day, some soldiers came to the village to recruit young men for the battlefield, but they did not take the farmer's son because of his injury.

This story illustrates the concept of *equanimity*, in which the mindful farmer observes and notices but does not judge the events, recognizing that evaluation may result in overreaction. Many children and adolescents experience challenging social, emotional, and behavioral concerns when they overreact to situations at home and school, so mindfulness practice can help them adjust by allowing them to attend to their experiences with openness and acceptance. The goal of mindfulness is not to repress our feelings or to distract ourselves from subjective experience. Rather, the aim is to improve our awareness of our experiences without excessive judgment. Kabat-Zinn's (2003) definition of mindfulness integrates the elements of awareness of the present and equanimity, calling mindful practice "the awareness that emerges through paying attention on purpose, in the present moment, and nonjudgmentally" (p. 145). Mindfulness may be conceptualized as a set of approaches that fall under the larger context of positive psychology, which is a strengths-based approach.

Benefits of Mindfulness and Empirical Support

A growing body of research has documented the benefits of mindfulness, including applications in school settings (Sheinman et al., 2018; Suárez-García et al., 2020; Tobin et al., 2020). Given the well-established relationship between social and emotional functioning, self-regulation, and academic success, it should come as no surprise that mindfulness interventions targeting one area (e.g., stress reduction) might also demonstrate gains in other areas (e.g., academic engagement; Seligman, 2011). For example, mindfulness interventions with children have been shown to improve academic engagement, self-regulation, and focused attention (Singh et al., 2016). In a review of the literature, Lyons and DeLange (2016) noted that although the vast majority of studies on mindfulness have been conducted with adults, the findings, which showed a positive effect in the areas of attention, working memory, and the regulation of emotions, should also extend to children. In fact, in one innovative study that looked at brain images of children, researchers were able to observe functional neural changes linked to decreased anxiety in children ages 6–17 as a result of mindfulness (Marusak et al., 2018).

A meta-analysis of 76 studies on mindfulness interventions with youth found "a small positive average treatment effect for controlled and pre–post designs," and after a follow-up period, "a slightly larger average treatment effect relative to post-treatment" (Klingbeil et al., 2017, p. 96). The meta-analysis supported the idea of conceptualizing mindfulness intervention as the development of social–emotional learning (SEL) skills, with consistently small, positive effects across a range of outcomes. This particular meta-analysis confirmed the findings of prior meta-analyses, lending greater support to the belief that mindfulness interventions yield positive outcomes.

Given that mindfulness-based interventions have been shown to be effective, both as a positive psychology prevention program and as an evidence-based treatment for identified concerns (e.g., ADHD, anxiety, depression), school psychologists may find these approaches to be useful in promoting psychosocial wellness in students in school settings. In their review of the mindfulness literature, Roodenrys and colleagues (2017) noted:

> Student learning takes place within a system involving peers, teachers, and family… Mindfulness-based programmes that are specifically designed for school settings may therefore be of benefit in mitigating risk for psychopathology and helping students thrive. (pp. 38–39)

Increasingly, school psychologists are recognizing that mindfulness interventions may help students build important competencies that confer protective resiliency against life's adversities.

Although this is an emerging area of research, initial findings are promising (Kraayenbrink, Skaar, & Clopton, 2018). Mindfulness-based programs offered to all children as a means of preventing social, emotional, and behavioral concerns may be a valuable component of a multitiered system of support (MTSS) at Tier 1 (Felver et al., 2013). For example, following the implementation of a 5-week mindfulness curriculum called Mindful Schools, teachers reported that students displayed improved attention, kindness, self-control, and participation in learning activities (Black & Fernando, 2014).

Mindfulness researchers have also looked at how these interventions may be helpful in reducing intrusive thoughts and rumination (Mendelson et al., 2010), improving emotional regulation (Metz et al., 2013), and treating depression (Raes et al., 2014). When applied to small groups of students who display concerns in spite of evidence-based prevention efforts, mindfulness-based interventions to address or ameliorate these problems may be appropriate Tier 2 approaches (Felver et al., 2013). By extension, at Tier 3, school psychologists may use more targeted, individual mindfulness-based interventions for concerns that were not resolved by efforts at Tier 2.

As mindfulness research with children and adolescents continues to develop, a wide range of effects and benefits have been explored. Salmoirago-Blotcher and colleagues (2018) examined the effects of mindfulness training on health behaviors (diet and exercise) among high school students and found that, among males, mindfulness training was associated with greater physical activity. Others have examined the delivery of mindfulness-based practices with yoga activities, generating lessons learned from qualitative data; for example, success may be enhanced when there is good communication among teachers and administrators about the intervention (e.g., Dariotis et al., 2017). Mindfulness-based interventions have been studied in alternative schools as well (Wisner & Starzec, 2016).

Increasingly, investigators have focused on randomized controlled trials of published mindfulness curricula. For example, Schonert-Reichl and colleagues (2015) randomly assigned students to either the MindUP curriculum (a social responsibility program) or business as usual to compare outcomes across a wide range of indicators, including executive functioning, salivary cortisol, self-reported well-being, prosocial skills, and academic outcomes. Although some of these studies are promising, more research is needed in this area.

Some caution that, although a growing body of research supports the implementation of mindfulness-based practices in the schools, more studies are needed to develop a stronger evidence base (Kraayenbrink et al., 2018). For example, some published reports are promising, but they are classified as pilot studies and were conducted with relatively small samples (e.g., Liehr & Diaz, 2010; Nadler et al., 2017). Other studies comparing students who receive a mindfulness curriculum compared with a control group show no group differences (e.g., Johnson et al., 2017). Researchers are examining not only the intervention outcomes but also treatment feasibility and acceptability (e.g., Kuyken et al., 2013). School psychologists interested in implementing mindfulness should always consider both the empirical support for the interventions as well as practical considerations when working with children and adolescents.

Applying Mindfulness to IEP Counseling

As discussed in Chapter 2, school psychologists work with families and educators to develop IEP goals and objectives that are informed by assessment data and are individualized to meet the unique needs of each child. Similarly, the interventions that are selected to help reach the goals also should be thoughtfully designed for each child, taking into consideration individual characteristics such as motivation, cognitive and language development, and interests. School psychologists should also consider the evidence base that supports the intervention. Though mindfulness interventions have been used effectively with elementary school students, most of the empirical evidence has come from studies with older students and adults (Kraayenbrink et al., 2018). In many cases, mindfulness-based programs may be appropriate and helpful for children and adolescents who present a range of concerns.

In the example of Amanda, the fifth-grade student introduced in Chapter 2, the school psychologist documented her present level of performance as follows:

> *Amanda's frequent angry outbursts and difficulty getting along with peers have a significant negative effect on her academic progress and development of socialization skills. She has a strong desire to please adults and is motivated to improve her social, emotional, and behavioral functioning.*

Following 3 years of documented efforts to manage her behaviors through Tier 2 group counseling interventions, her IEP team recommended related psychological services, and the school psychologist developed, in consultation with the IEP team, the following goals and objectives:

Annual Goal. Amanda will make measurable progress in the area of emotional functioning.

- Objective 1: Amanda will accurately identify signs that she is getting angry before she has an outburst (effective at identifying signs four out of five times).
- Objective 2: Amanda will employ appropriate ways of expressing her anger (expresses anger in appropriate ways three out of five times).

How might mindfulness be helpful in addressing this goal and these objectives? One of the key benefits of mindfulness as an intervention to address social, emotional, and behavioral concerns is the increased focus on internal thoughts and feelings. According to Kraayenbrink and colleagues (2018), "when people feel basic emotions such as sadness or anger, they may not take time to determine the function of these emotions. Left unchecked, the source giving rise to the emotion may get worse or more pronounced" (p. 32). In the case of Amanda, using mindfulness to help her become more aware of her emotions may improve her capacity to regulate them. This may be accomplished through controlled breathing, guided meditation, or a series of activities designed to practice stress reduction. Assuming that Amanda is willing and able to engage with the school psychologist in some mindfulness exercises, she may be able to develop a better awareness of her feelings and the physiological signs associated with those emotions. Like any other skill, mindfulness skills can be taught, practiced, and incorporated into routines (Renshaw & Cook, 2017).

While mindfulness may be well aligned with Amanda's first objective, with its focus on improving self-awareness, it may not be as directly related to the second objective, which is focused on expressing feelings appropriately. In such cases, school psychologists may use more than one approach. For example, Objective 1 may be attained through mindfulness-based interventions, while Objective 2 may be achieved with social skills training.

Following are two examples of mindfulness activities that could be used in school settings with individuals or groups. As you read them, you might imagine how they could be applied to Amanda's concerns above, or you may think about some of the students you serve and how these activities could be used or adapted to meet other needs.

Mindfulness Activities

There are many mindfulness activities that school psychologists can use in individual and group counseling sessions to help students attain their counseling goals. Most of the activities included here require no materials, though in some cases it may be helpful to have some free or inexpensive props for the exercises. School psychologists are encouraged to try these suggestions on their own before applying them to counseling sessions. Although some manualized treatment protocols are available—for example, *A Still Quiet Place: A Mindfulness Program for Teaching Children and Adolescents to Ease Stress and Difficult Emotions* (Saltzman, 2014)—school psychologists new to mindfulness may want to start by trying to incorporate a few mindful practices as an adjunct to other modalities (i.e., cognitive–behavioral therapy with some mindfulness). For younger children, school psychologists may use bibliotherapy with a mindfulness component (e.g., Sileo, 2017). For the exercises listed in this chapter, readers should feel free to modify as needed for their settings and students. Resources at the end of this chapter contain additional ideas and suggestions.

NATURE BASKET

This activity helps children and adolescents practice directing their attention to their immediate sensory experiences. By tuning into breathing and other sensations, students develop mindfulness skills.

Bring a basket to the counseling session with objects found in nature. For example, you may provide pine cones, seashells, acorns, leaves, twigs, etc. Ask the students to select an object and hold it. The following script is suggested.

1. Take a moment to hold your object and take a few breaths, paying attention to the air moving in and out of your lungs. (Allow time for noticing the breathing.)
2. Now, using your fingertips, feel the object in your hand. Pay attention to the way it feels as you rub your fingers across it. Is it rough or smooth? Do parts of it feel different from other parts? (Allow time for noticing the feelings.)
3. Bring the object to your nose. Does it have a smell? If so, what does it smell like? (Allow time for noticing the smell.)
4. Sometimes objects have sounds. Gently shake your object near your ear, or you rub your fingers on your object near your ear. Pay attention to the sound, or to the silence. (Allow time for noticing the sounds.)
5. Gently squeeze the object in your hands. How does it feel to have it pressed in your palm? (Allow time for noticing the pressure sensation.)
6. Now let your object rest gently in your hand again and focus on your breaths. Take a deep breath and a slow exhalation. Do this two more times.

CONTROLLED BREATHING

By working with children and adolescents on controlled breathing, school psychologists can increase students' awareness of respiration while building self-regulation through breathing management. To begin this activity, start by making sure that everyone is seated comfortably and minimize any distractions in the room. This exercise was adapted from the Greater Good in Action website (https://ggia.berkeley.edu/). The following instructions can be modified to meet the needs of the group.

1. Let's take a few moments to focus on our breathing. Usually we don't pay attention to our breathing, but we're going to think about it now.
2. We'll start by just noticing that we're breathing. This is something our bodies do all the time, even when we're not paying attention to it. Notice the natural rhythm of your breathing and where you feel the air in your body. (Allow a few moments for this.)
3. Now we will breathe in through our noses and out through our mouths. How about three breaths like that, in through the nose and out through the mouth. (Allow time for three of these breaths.)
4. Next, breathe in through your nose for 2 seconds, and exhale through your mouth for 4 seconds. We'll do three breaths like this. (Allow time for three of these breaths.)
5. Let's try that again, inhaling through your nose for 2 seconds, but stretching out the exhalation for 5 seconds. We'll do three breaths like this. (Allow time for three of these breaths.)
6. Continue to control your breathing, paying attention to the deeper relaxation that comes with it.
7. As you relax into your breathing, your mind may wander. There's nothing wrong with that, and it's good to notice it. If you start thinking about something else, notice that, and then return your focus to your breathing.

SUMMARY AND RATIONALE FOR MINDFULNESS IN THE SCHOOLS

This chapter has defined mindfulness, reviewed the benefits and empirical support of mindful practices, and provided some examples of mindfulness activities that school psychologists may use in a counseling context. Given the research support linking these interventions to positive outcomes across social, emotional, behavioral, and academic domains, school psychologists should be able to make a good case for implementing these types of activities. Even so, they may find themselves in the position of having to justify or explain why mindfulness is appropriate in the schools.

In some cases, advocates of mindful practices may be met with concerns that mindfulness is aligned with a religious practice, just as some may believe that yoga instruction has a religious component. When promoting mindfulness in school settings, it may be helpful to emphasize that it is a secular activity that is available to all students regardless of their religious affiliation. When talking about mindfulness to teachers, administrators, parents, and students, school psychologists should focus on the defining characteristics outlined earlier in this chapter: deliberately paying attention to immediate experiences without judgment, as a way of improving self-awareness and self-regulation.

Aside from the demonstrated positive benefits of mindfulness on a number of outcomes relevant to school (e.g., focused attention, decreased anxiety), mindfulness may also be an appropriate school-based intervention because it aligns so well with social–emotional learning (SEL), multitiered systems of support (MTSS), and response to intervention (RTI). Some of the core SEL competencies identified by the Collaborative for Academic, Social, and Emotional Learning (CASEL) are self-awareness and self-management, both of which are improved through mindfulness activities (CASEL, 2018). As mentioned earlier, mindfulness can also be applied at all three tiers to meet students' needs (Felver et al., 2013). In this respect, mindfulness can easily be integrated into existing structures to advance shared goals.

Finally, mindfulness interventions can be tailored to meet the unique goals and objectives of diverse students (Fung et al., 2019; Kang et al., 2018). Mindfulness can target inattention, anxiety, depression, and a number of other concerns seen in the schools. Though mindfulness is not a panacea and may not be appropriate for some students, it has been used effectively across a wide range of ages in school settings to prevent or mitigate a number of social, emotional, and behavioral concerns. It may also be used in conjunction with other methods and techniques, making it a flexible tool.

KEY POINTS FOR DISCUSSION

- How would you describe mindfulness to a parent or to a middle school student?
- What does mindfulness have in common with cognitive–behavioral therapy? How is it different?
- For which students would mindfulness be appropriate? For which students would mindfulness be inappropriate?
- Search online for a mindfulness activity that could be used with elementary school students and describe it.

ADDITIONAL RESOURCES

Mindfulness Awareness Center at UCLA, http://marc.ucla.edu/
Mindful Schools, www.mindfulschools.org
Mindfulness in Schools Project, www.mindfulnessinschools.org
Mindfulness for Children, https://annakaharris.com/mindfulness-for-children/
MindUP, https://mindup.org/

REFERENCES

Black, D. S., & Fernando, R. (2014). Mindfulness training and classroom behavior among lower-income and ethnic minority elementary school children. *Journal of Child and Family Studies*, 23, 1242–1246.
Collaborative for Academic, Social, and Emotional Learning. (2018). Core SEL competencies. Retrieved from https://casel.org/core-competencies/
Dariotis, J. K., Mirabal-Beltran, R., Cluxton-Keller, F., Gould, L. F., Greenberg, M. T., & Mendelson, T. (2017). A qualitative exploration of implementation factors in a school-based mindfulness and yoga program: Lessons learned from students and teachers. *Psychology in the Schools*, 54, 53–69.

Felver, J. C., Doerner, E., Jones, J., Kaye, N. C., & Merrell, K. W. (2013). Mindfulness in school psychology: Applications for intervention and professional practice. *Psychology in the Schools, 50*, 531–547.

Fung, J., Kim, J. J., Jin, J., Chen, G., Bear, L., & Lau, A. S. (2019). A randomized trial evaluating school-based mindfulness intervention for ethnic minority youth: Exploring mediators and moderators of intervention effects. *Journal of Abnormal Child Psychology, 47*(1), 1–19. doi:10.1007/s10802-018-0425-7

Johnson, C., Burke, C., Brinkman, S., & Wade, T. (2017). A randomized controlled evaluation of a secondary school mindfulness program for early adolescents: Do we have the recipe right yet? *Behaviour Research and Therapy, 99*, 37–46.

Kabat-Zinn, J. (2003). Mindfulness-based intervention in context: Past, present, and future. *Clinical Psychology: Science and Practice, 10*, 144–156.

Kang, Y., Rahrig, H., Eichel, K., Niles, H. F., Rocha, T., Lepp, N. E., Gold, J., & Britton, W. B. (2018). Gender differences in response to a school-based mindfulness training intervention for early adolescents. *Journal of School Psychology, 68*, 163–176. doi:10.1016/j.jsp.2018.03.004

Klingbeil, D. K., Renshaw, T. L., Willenbrink, J. B., Copek, R. A., Chan, K. T., Haddock, A., … Clifton, J. (2017). Mindfulness-based interventions with youth: A comprehensive meta-analysis of group-design studies. *Journal of School Psychology, 63*, 77–103.

Kraayenbrink, A., Skaar, N., & Clopton, K. (2018). Using mindfulness to promote resilience. *Communiqué, 46*(8), 1, 31–33.

Kuyken, W., Weare, K., Ukoumunne, O. C., Vicary, R., Motton, N., Burnett, R., Cullen, C., Hennelly, S., & Huppert, F. (2013). Effectiveness of the Mindfulness in Schools Programme: Non-randomised controlled feasibility study. *British Journal of Psychiatry, 203*, 126–131.

Liehr, P., & Diaz, N. (2010). A pilot study examining the effect of mindfulness on depression and anxiety for minority children. *Archives of Psychiatric Nursing, 24*, 69–71.

Lyons, K. E., & DeLange, J. (2016). *Mindfulness matters in the classroom: The effects of mindfulness training on brain development and behavior in children and adolescents.* In K. A. Schonert-Reichl, & R. W. Roeser, (Eds.), *Handbook of mindfulness in education* (pp. 271–283). New York, NY: Springer.

Marusak, H. A., Elrahal, F., Peters, C. A., Kundu, P., Lombardo, M. V., Calhoun, V. D., … Rabinak, C. A. (2018). Mindfulness and dynamic functional neural connectivity in children and adolescents. *Behavioural Brain Research, 336*, 211–218. doi:10.1016/j.bbr.2017.09.010

Mendelson, T., Greenberg, M. T., Dariotis, J. K., Gould, L. F., Rhoades, B. L., & Leaf, P. J. (2010). Feasibility and preliminary outcomes of a school-based mindfulness intervention for urban youth. *Journal of Abnormal Child Psychology, 38*, 985–994.

Metz, S. M., Frank, J. L., Reibel, D., Cantrell, T., Sanders, R., & Broderick, P. C. (2013). The effectiveness of the learning to BREATHE program on adolescent emotion regulation. *Research in Human Development, 10*, 252–272.

Nadler, R., Cordy, M., Stengel, J., Segal, Z. V., & Hayden, E. P. (2017). A brief mindfulness practice increases self-reported calmness in young children: A pilot study. *Mindfulness, 8*, 1088–1095.

Raes, F., Griffith, J. W., Van der Gucht, K., & Williams, J. M. G. (2014). School-based prevention and reduction of depression in adolescents: A cluster-randomized controlled trial of a mindfulness group program. *Mindfulness, 5*, 477–486.

Renshaw, T. L., & Cook, C. R. (2017). Introduction to the special issue: Mindfulness in the schools—Historical roots, current status, and future directions. *Psychology in the Schools, 54,* 5–12.

Roodenrys, S., Badawi, A., & Lovegrove, W. (2017). *How strong is the evidence that mindfulness produces healthy psychological change in children?* In T. Ditrich, R. Wiles, & B. Lovegrove, (Eds.), *Mindfulness and education: Research and practice* (pp. 33–54). Newcastle upon Tyne, U.K.: Cambridge Scholars.

Salmoirago-Blotcher, E., Druker, S., Frisard, C., Dunsiger, S. I., Crawford, S., Meleo-Meyer, F., … Pbert, L. (2018). Integrating mindfulness training in school health education to promote healthy behaviors in adolescents: Feasibility and preliminary effects on exercise and dietary habits. *Preventive Medicine Reports, 9,* 92–95.

Saltzman, A. (2014). *A still quiet place: A mindfulness program for teaching children and adolescents to ease stress and difficult emotions.* Oakland, CA: New Harbinger.

Schonert-Reichl, K. A., Oberle, E., Lawlor, M. S., Thompson, K., Oberlander, T. F., & Diamond, A. (2015). Enhancing cognitive and social-emotional development through a simple-to-administer mindfulness-based school program for elementary school children: A randomized controlled trial. *Developmental Psychology, 51,* 52–66.

Seligman, M. (2011). *Flourish.* New York, NY: Simon & Schuster.

Sheinman, N., Hadar, L. L., Gafni, D., & Milman, M. (2018). Preliminary investigation of whole-school mindfulness in education programs and children's mindfulness-based coping strategies. *Journal of Child and Family Studies, 27*(10), 3316–3328. doi:10.1007/s10826-018-1156-7

Sileo, F. (2017). *A world of pausabilites: An exercise in mindfulness.* Washington, DC: Magination Press.

Singh, N. N., Lancioni, G. E., Karazsia, B. T., Felver, J. C., Myers, R. E., & Nugent, K. (2016). Effects of Samatha meditation on active academic engagement and math performance of students with attention deficit/hyperactivity disorder. *Mindfulness, 7,* 68–75.

Suárez-García, Z., Álvarez-García, D., García-Redondo, P., & Rodríguez, C. (2020). The effect of a mindfulness-based intervention on attention, self-control, and aggressiveness in primary school pupils. *International Journal of Environmental Research and Public Health, 17*(7), 2447. doi:10.3390/ijerph17072447

Tobin, J., Hardy, J. A., Calanche, M. L., Gonzalez, K. D., Baezconde-Garbanati, L., Contreras, R., & Bluthenthal, R. N. (2020). A community-based mindfulness intervention among Latino adolescents and their parents: A qualitative feasibility and acceptability study. Retrieved from https://www.ncbi.nlm.nih.gov/pubmed/32078725

Wisner, B. L., & Starzec, J. J. (2016). The process of personal transformation for adolescents practicing mindfulness skills in an alternative school setting. *Child and Adolescent Social Work Journal, 33,* 245–257.

Chapter 8

Directive Approaches

OVERVIEW

This chapter on directive approaches, those that are structured by the counselor rather than being student-directed, addresses techniques school psychologists are likely to use, including cognitive–behavioral therapy (CBT) and related approaches of behavioral, rational–emotional, dialectical behavioral, reality, trauma-focused CBT, motivational interviewing, and solution-focused counseling. Cognitive–behavioral techniques focus on altering maladaptive patterns of thought and the distorted beliefs that underlie such thinking. Related approaches are typically goal oriented and problem (or solution) focused. We also discuss the populations and problems for which CBT and related approaches are effective and describe specific techniques that may be used in school settings.

OBJECTIVES

After reading this chapter, readers should be able to do the following:

- Describe the shared foundations of nondirective and directive approaches.
- Recognize the distinct features of CBT and related counseling applications.
- Identify the problems and populations for which directive approaches have demonstrated efficacy.
- Describe specific techniques appropriate with different ages, presenting behaviors, and other individual differences.
- Identify the variables in school settings that facilitate and limit the effectiveness of directive counseling approaches.
- Develop a counseling plan that uses a CBT or related approach and includes evaluation of outcomes.

Introduction of Theory and Technique

All counseling efforts should have as their shared foundation the therapeutic alliance, or relationship, between the counselor and the client. School psychologists foster therapeutic relationships by being reliable and genuine, establishing and maintaining trust and boundaries, incorporating humor and fun, initiating unique interactions distinct from other adult–child relationships, and using a personalized approach. The job of the school psychologist as counselor is to figure out how best to communicate with each client, with the goal of facilitating and unblocking communication so that it is productive and healing. The basic premises of this philosophy are that all people have problems, that they have a cultural background and personal history, that those experiences will affect the school psychologist's interpretation of an individual's behavior and the choice of intervention, and that the means to develop communication is to use the powerful tool of active listening.

School psychologists work to provide a place of trust and safety, support other school missions, and build students' capacity for self-help, self-direction, and cognitive and emotional self-regulation. Helping students develop their executive functions furthers their capacity for empathy and social relating (Aliakbari et al., 2013).

Executive functions are developmental, so that over time, individuals' cognitive, emotional, and behavioral self-regulation are gradually achieved through cognitive mediation, or the mind's assessment of a situation and of the meaning of that situation (Fiske & Holmboe, n.d.). Thus, counseling approaches associated with cognition, such as CBT methods, are closely associated with the development of executive functions, including self-reflection and self-monitoring. In contrast, strict behavioral interventions, such as applied behavior analysis, may place lesser demands on cognitive mediation on the part of the client. Of course, humans are whole organisms, with thoughts, feelings, behaviors, and biological functions operating simultaneously, not easily carved into components for intervention.

Although the approaches and techniques discussed in this chapter tend to be structured, the counselor may choose an eclectic model (see Figure 8.1), using techniques from different approaches to address referral problems in the context of individual and systems differences.

The counselor can decide to be more or less directive, depending on the student's level of cognitive development, verbal skill and preference, executive function capacity, and willingness to disclose. The degree to which a counseling approach is directive (or nondirective) exists on a continuum, and the counselor can shift strategies depending on the response. The selection of techniques is based on the client's characteristics, such as cognitive development, verbal abilities, and interpersonal style (discussed in Chapter 1). A student's executive functions, such as working memory, attention, organization, planning, and self-regulation, will also enter into decisions about the counseling approach.

Behavioral Approaches

Behavioral approaches (a) have documented efficacy for targeted behavior change, (b) are often familiar to teachers, and (c) can be incorporated into counseling to achieve desired outcomes. In some instances, targeted behavior change through consultation with teachers and parents (Chapter 4) may be more effective in school settings than cognitive approaches that require greater time commitment and adequate verbal abilities and insights on the part of the client. A further

FIGURE 8.1. Eclectic Model

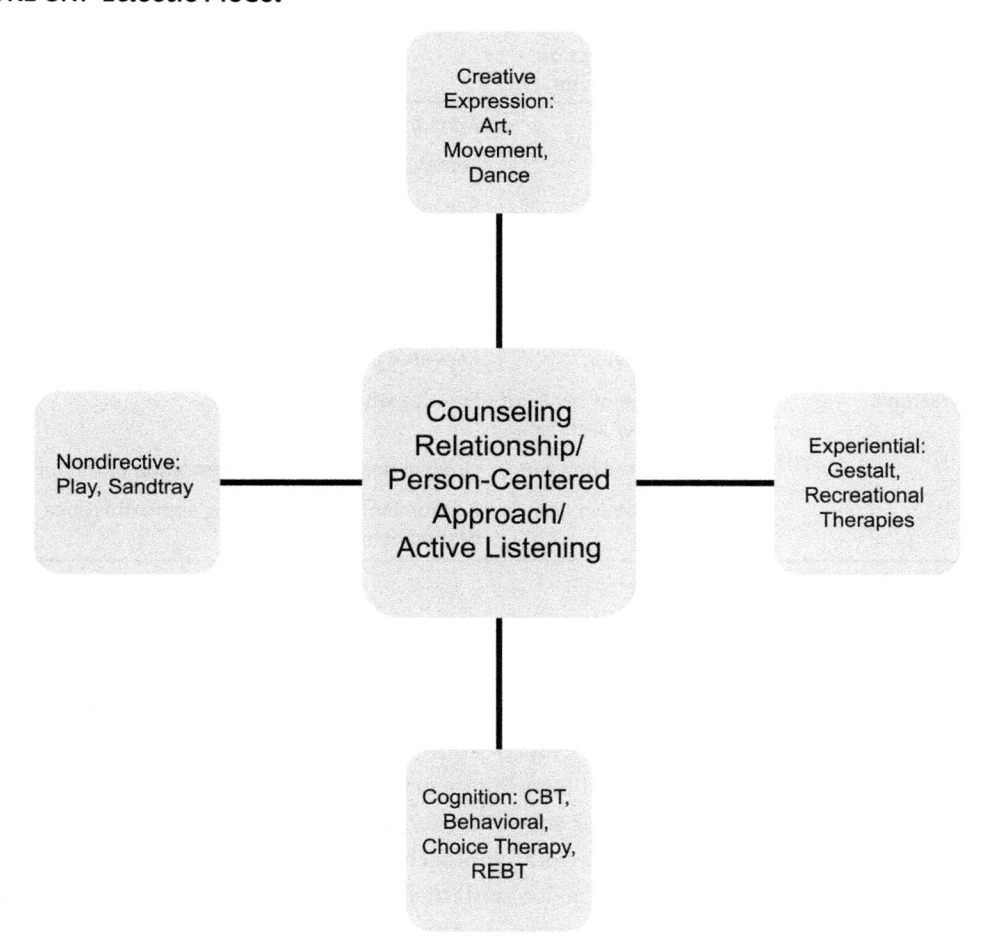

```
                    Creative Expression:
                    Art, Movement, Dance
                            |
                            |
Nondirective:      Counseling Relationship/       Experiential:
Play, Sandtray ——  Person-Centered Approach/  ——  Gestalt,
                   Active Listening                Recreational Therapies
                            |
                            |
                    Cognition: CBT,
                    Behavioral,
                    Choice Therapy,
                    REBT
```

Note. From *School Psychologist as Counselor: A Practitioner's Handbook* (p. 111), by C. A. Plotts and J. Lasser, 2013, National Association of School Psychologists. Copyright 2013 by National Association of School Psychologists. Reprinted with permission.

advantage of behavioral approaches may be enhanced credibility with teachers and parents who are eager for more rapid behavior change for specific issues. For example, shaping specific behaviors, such as raising one's hand, taking turns, or using words instead of hitting, are amenable to a behavioral approach.

Behavioral approaches to counseling focus on objective analysis of student behavior, which may include behaviors to be reduced, eliminated, acquired, or increased, depending on the goals of counseling. The emphasis on observable behavior is primary, while relationship variables are important but theoretically secondary. For the behavioral therapist, the setting in which the behavior occurs is of the utmost importance (Webber & Plotts, 2008). The setting variables, antecedents, and consequences are considered in any intervention. The therapist obtains the client history specifically with respect to how behaviors of concern were acquired and what efforts have

TABLE 8.1 Basic Behavioral Techniques and Intended Effects

Technique	Intended Effect on Target Behavior	Mechanism of Action
Positive reinforcement	Increase behavior	Administration of reward
Negative reinforcement	Increase behavior	Removal of unpleasant consequence
Overcorrection	Increase behavior	Repeated practice of alternative acceptable behavior immediately following unacceptable behavior
Punishment	Decrease behavior	Administration of undesirable consequence
Extinction	Decrease behavior	Removal of reinforcement
Satiation	Decrease behavior	Repeated practice until aversive
Generalization	Demonstration of behavior change in other settings	Practice with reinforcement
Fading	Establish desired behavior	Gradual decrease in administration of reinforcement
Shaping	Gradually establish desired behavior	Reinforcement of increasing approximations of desired behavior

been made to change it. Well-defined and integral counseling goals must have identified observable and carefully defined behaviors and reflect analysis of the functions of behavior to be altered (target behavior).

Behavioral approaches have been developed from well-established theories of learning (e.g., operant and classical conditioning, social learning theory); thus, they use very specific techniques such as behavior contracts, reinforcement schedules, social modeling, systematic desensitization, and assertiveness training. Further, behavioral approaches lend themselves to empirical analysis because they emphasize observable behavior and tracking of change in response to specific interventions. Table 8.1 provides a summary of these behavioral techniques with respect to intended effects.

Cognitive–behavioral and other directive approaches are often viewed as an extension and elaboration of behavioral approaches. A basic premise of cognitive–behavioral theory is that people acquire and maintain thought patterns through the same learning mechanisms by which they acquire and maintain behavior patterns. Therefore, cognitions can be modified to improve adjustment.

Cognitive–Behavioral Approaches

Aaron Beck pioneered what is now known as CBT in the 1960s, having first developed cognitive therapy in the 1950s. CBT methods focus on the interactions of cognitions, emotions, and behaviors, in other words, opening up the world of thoughts and feelings (the black box). In comparison with other therapy approaches, CBT is considered short term; treatment usually lasts between six and 20 sessions. Homework is a central aspect of CBT and supports the need for fewer sessions; clients are asked to practice what they learn between sessions. Clients are taught that their thoughts are hypotheses that can be evaluated and tested for validity.

Distortions in thinking can negatively affect emotions and behaviors, so CBT techniques involve actively monitoring and evaluating thoughts. Such distortions include, for example, filtering (magnifying the negative), polarizing (black and white, all or none thinking), overgeneralizing, catastrophizing (expecting disaster to strike), thinking in "shoulds" ("I should be energetic"), using emotional thinking ("If I feel that way, it must be true"), and personalizing ("Everything others do is a reaction to me"), among others (Grohol, 2019).

CBT and its variants continue to be heavily researched. When searching for relevant publications since 2012, a search engine returned over 47,000 articles and books. Narrowing the search to peer-reviewed publications on CBT and schools yielded over 7,000 publications. Clearly, we are not able to comprehensively review the CBT literature in this text. For each of the subtypes of CBT presented in this chapter, we attempt to provide a relevant sample of recent empirical literature. We provide some examples of specific techniques later in this chapter.

Kirk and colleagues (2019) maintained that school interventions must be expeditious and potent because of the time limitations caused by school summer and holiday breaks, along with the primary educational focus of schools. They explored dose–response effects of CBT in a school mental health program. Their sample consisted of 133 adolescents across 14 sessions of CBT. They found a meaningful decrease in symptoms on the Youth Outcome Questionnaire-30 (YOQ-30) after 14 sessions. Further, a reliable change in the YOQ score was found to occur with an average of 3 sessions. Response to treatment was predicted by baseline scores on the depression and hyperactivity subscales of the BASC-2 and YOQ-30. These findings support consideration of CBT techniques as potentially effective and efficient approaches in schools and underscore the need to assess baseline symptoms before intervention.

Use of CBT with ethnic and racial minorities has been explored in the literature (Benuto & O'Donohue, 2015; Kataoka, Novins, & DeCarlo Santiago, 2015). In their review of the literature on culturally sensitive CBT for Hispanics, Benuto and O'Donohue concluded that there is a paucity of empirically sound research on this topic. However, they came to several conclusions, including that there is evidence that Hispanics may be effectively treated using conventional CBT and that there is little evidence that cultural adaptations of the therapy consistently improve effect sizes. Kataoka, Novins, and DeCarlo Santiago (2015), in a discussion of CBT for ethnic minority youth, distinguish between evidence-based treatments and evidence-based practice, with the latter considering the client's characteristics, preferences, and culture as well as relevant research. Kataoka and others conclude that very few evidence-based treatments for ethnic minorities have been specifically studied, and that consensus exists to guide researchers regarding operationalization of cultural competence. For guidance on incorporating multicultural awareness into counseling in schools, see *The Psychology of Multiculturalism in Schools*, edited by Janine Jones (2009).

For the reader who would like to explore CBT interventions in schools in greater depth, the comprehensive text, *Clinical Practice of Cognitive Therapy with Children and Adolescents: The Nuts and Bolts* (2nd ed.) by Friedberg and McClure (2015) has been positively reviewed as valuable for school psychologists in the NASP *Communiqué* (Slonaker, 2019). Several specific CBT approaches are briefly discussed below; each model has its own research base and instructional content. In this context, we provide an overview and direct the reader to other resources for more detail.

Rational Emotive Behavior Therapy

Rational Emotive Behavior Therapy (REBT) is often considered a subtype of CBT; whereas CBT focuses on cognitions as a source of maladaptive behaviors, REBT concentrates on extreme emotions that interfere with healthy, adaptive functioning. Albert Ellis, the founder of REBT, began development of the approach in the 1950s. Originally the approach was described as rational therapy; it was later changed to rational emotive therapy because of the emphasis on emotional outcomes. In the 1990s Ellis changed the name to rational emotive behavior therapy to acknowledge the centrality of behavioral methods to this approach (David et al., 2018). According to David et al., CBT actually emerged from REBT.

Ellis suggested that REBT should address the activating event that preceded the emotional or behavioral consequence (A), the belief system, sometimes described as automatic thoughts that occur after the activating event (B), the emotional and behavioral consequences (C), and disputation (D). Disputation, at its most basic, refers to the questioning of thoughts and beliefs that contribute to undesirable emotions and behaviors, replacing them with alternative, more rational and functional beliefs. Together these elements are known as the ABCD model (Banks & Ziontz, 2009). The ABCD model sometimes includes an additional element E, for evaluation of the effectiveness of the behavior choice. Ellis theorized that consequences are affected not only by the activating event but also by an individual's beliefs about the event.

David et al. (2018) describe REBT as focusing on altering irrational beliefs so that they become more rational, thus changing maladaptive behaviors into more functional and adaptive ones. They emphasize that REBT differs from other CBT approaches in that it focuses specifically on evaluative beliefs and how they affect emotions and behaviors. For example, a teenager might attribute not making the cheerleading squad as "I'm not good at anything and I'll never be able to compete," eventually leading to diminished self-confidence, unwillingness to try new things, and eventual depression. In REBT, the counselor would help the client to develop arguments to dispute this irrational belief, thus allowing for other behavior choices. In this example, the student might decide to take gymnastics and try again the following year or to choose another activity.

REBT also offers the advantage of flexibility within structure. The basic steps in REBT (activating events, beliefs and attitudes, consequences, disputations, and evaluation) apply to many problems and situations encountered by children in school and can be incorporated into numerous methodologies, including talking, and activities such as games, art, and play. Students can be taught to monitor events in their environment, their own reactions to the events (thoughts and feelings), and the consequences of their reactions. Teaching children to acknowledge, name, and appropriately express feelings is a goal shared by many therapeutic approaches. In REBT, this goal is furthered and expanded upon by teaching children to systematically and repeatedly connect thoughts, feelings, and behaviors and thus develop habits that lead to more choice and greater control.

David et al. (2018) presented a meta-analysis of 84 published articles, concluding that REBT shows medium effect sizes for both irrational beliefs and outcomes and is "a sound psychological intervention" (p. 305). Interventions that were reviewed included counseling (nonclinical populations), psychotherapy (clinical populations), and educational (classroom) delivery formats. They asserted that REBT interventions are effective for a range of conditions, independent of the mode of delivery.

Dialectical Behavior Therapy

Originally, dialectical behavior therapy (DBT) was developed for highly suicidal individuals (Linehan & Wilks, 2015). With this population, randomized controlled trials supported DBT, with improvements in problem behaviors, including suicidal ideation and behavior and nonsuicidal self-injury. The term DBT refers to the integration of elements from behaviorism, mindfulness, and dialectics. *Dialectics* refers to the notion that two different ideas can be true at the same time; when considered together, they can open new ways of thinking about situations. Recently, DBT has been extended to counseling with adolescents exhibiting a broad range of emotion regulation difficulties that typically result in behavioral excess (e.g., suicidal behaviors, eating disorders, externalizing disorders, mood disorders, and borderline personality disorder).

Hanson (2016) has presented and written about the use of DBT in schools, describing implementation of a school-wide, multitiered curriculum in Oregon, among other regions across the United States. The emphasis of this school-based DBT approach is on self-regulation, particularly coping skills and decision making in emotionally challenging situations. Elements of the adaptation of DBT to schools include emotional regulation, behavioral regulation, cognitive regulation, interpersonal regulation, and self-regulation. The approach focuses on initially decreasing maladaptive behaviors (life threatening, self-harming) and moving toward increasing adaptive behaviors (coping skills, enjoyment of life). For the interested reader, Hanson described implementation of a school-based DBT approach within MTSS and RTI frameworks (Hanson, 2016). This approach requires specialized training, parental involvement, and adherence to structured treatment elements.

Perepletchikova and colleagues (2017) reported on the use of DBT with children ages 7 to 12 years (DBT-C) who had a diagnosis of disruptive mood dysregulation disorder (DMDD). The authors selected DBT because of the focus on emotional regulation because DMDD is characterized by severe emotional and behavioral dysregulation. Treatment duration was up to 32 weeks in the control condition and 32 weeks for DBT-C. The DBT-C intervention included a parent training component, along with individual therapy, skills training, phone coaching, and therapist team consultation. This wraparound approach is the more traditional application of DBT than the school adaptation discussed above. The study used a randomized control methodology, with 21 students in the DBT-C sample and 22 students in the treatment as usual (TAU) sample. Results were quite remarkable: None of the participants in the DBT-C condition dropped out, compared with eight students in the TAU condition. The rate of positive response was over 90.4% in DBT-C and only 45.5% in TAU, even though three times as many children in TAU received psychiatric medications. Remission rates were 52.4% for DBT-C compared with 27.3% for TAU. Gains were maintained at a 3-month follow-up. Finally, parents and children expressed significantly higher treatment satisfaction in DBT-C than in TAU. Even though the sample size was small, these results support the efficacy of DBT for children with severe emotional and behavioral regulation problems. For school psychologists, limitations on implementation include the parent training component and the need to be specifically trained to adhere to DBT methods, both of which are time- and resource-intensive.

Choice Theory and Reality Therapy

Choice theory and its application, reality therapy, were developed by William Glasser, who in the 1960s became critical of the conventional approaches to psychiatry and clinical psychology

(Glasser, 1965). He argued that mental illness could best be explained as the expression of unfulfilled needs. Choice theory assumes that behavior is purposeful and driven by needs (Walter, Lambie, & Ngazimbi, 2008). Stutey and colleagues (2019) describe reality therapy as helping clients to evaluate their choices and to plan for future ways to get more of what they want to meet their basic needs. Glasser's formulation postulates five universal human needs: survival and reproduction, love and belonging, power, freedom, and fun. Behavior addresses unfulfilled needs, with the assumption that present behaviors are an attempt to meet the most unsatisfied need (Glasser, 1986).

Survival and reproduction needs are met by behaviors that help us acquire food, air, water, and so on. Sexual behaviors meet what Glasser calls the reproductive need, though it is acknowledged that not all sexual behaviors are reproductive. Individuals may ignore higher-level needs in order to meet basic survival needs; in this sense there is some hierarchy to the needs (Wubbolding, 2017).

Humans are inherently social creatures with a strong need to belong and to love. When this need is unmet, individuals often report feeling depressed or anxious. So fundamental is the need for love and belonging that prisons use solitary confinement as a severe punishment. Schools might impose time out from reinforcement. Much of human behavior is directed at satisfying this need for *love and belonging*.

The need for *power* can be understood in terms of humans' psychological need to feel important, recognized, and valued. Humans work hard to meet this need so they can reap the emotional benefits that come with goal attainment.

Everyone has a basic need to move around freely, make independent choices about how to spend time, and choose activities and companions. Restrictions on *freedom* are felt as a significant loss, and individuals go to great lengths to acquire freedom when it is lacking. Finally, the need for *fun* includes play, laughter, and entertainment. Fun is integral to learning and is related to socialization and belonging.

In addition to the basic needs, the other foundational concepts in choice theory and reality therapy are the quality world and total behavior. The *quality world* consists of individuals' ideal fulfillment of the basic needs and is represented by the images they have in mind of this ideal. The *quality world* is highly individualized and is shaped by experiences. Glasser's theory is based on the idea that all humans do is behave, and that their behavior is chosen. Total behavior consists of acting, thinking, and feeling, and physiological responses. Acting and thinking are under our direct control, whereas we have indirect control over feelings and physiological responses. For example, we can choose what to eat (acting), which results in digestive processes (physiological response). Total behavior is chosen as a means of reducing the perceived gap between what we have and what we want and value (the quality world; Wubbolding, 2017). When we are dissatisfied with our circumstances and choices, alternative (and superior) choices can be made.

Glasser's application of choice theory to school settings meshes well with tiered systems of support and the indirect service model of consultation (see Chapter 4). Just as positive behavioral interventions and supports (PBIS) seeks to address the reasons for problem behaviors, applied choice theory seeks to identify (and satisfy) student needs so that problem behaviors do not emerge as an attempt to meet such needs. In this respect, both approaches are prevention oriented, as is multitiered systems of support (MTSS). Glasser aims to address behavior and learning at the universal level by changing the school's culture and environment. Much like consultation, the focus in Glasser's application of choice theory to schools is through changes of the school's managers (e.g., teachers and administrators; Glasser, 1998).

Studies on the efficacy of reality therapy have been conducted in the United States and abroad (Wubbolding, 2017). Choice theory and reality therapy have been used widely in a variety of applications, including counseling groups for students displaying emotional and behavioral problems (Walter, Lambie, & Ngazimbi, 2008), working with children of prisoners (Edwards, 2009), managing behaviors of children with autism (Renna, 2004), coaching athletes (Klug, 2006), promoting social skills and appropriate behaviors in the classroom (Donato, 2004), crisis counseling (Palmatier, 1998), and preventing bullying (Kim, 2006).

Interestingly, a search for peer-reviewed publications since 2014 on the efficacy of reality therapy yielded minimal findings, most of which were conducted outside the United States with adult populations. Olver (2017) noted that "Dr. Glasser was never big on research. He was too busy doing the work, as were his followers" (p. 14). Olver reported that the number of professionals trained in reality therapy has diminished in the United States as it has risen in Europe, Japan, and Korea. Wubbolding (2017) noted that the European Association for Psychotherapy has recognized reality therapy as a scientifically validated psychotherapy. This approach is included in this chapter because of the supportive research outside the United States, the application to play techniques, and the practicality of the related tools and techniques for school psychologists.

Recent research relevant to practice with school-age populations (Stutey et al., 2019) describes an approach that melds reality therapy with play therapy. Their study investigated therapists' perceptions of the model, confidence in using the techniques, and likelihood of implementing the approach with children and young adolescents. In general, their findings showed positive perceptions. A later section of this chapter, on reality therapy techniques, includes a reality play therapy model described by Stutey et al. (2019).

Trauma-Focused CBT

One outcome of trauma is difficulty with emotional regulation, a term for the processes that enable individuals to monitor, evaluate, and modify their emotional reactions. Such emotional dysregulation is also a predictor of psychopathology (Thornback & Muller, 2015). Vigilance, which is an adaptation to an abusive or traumatic situation and is the anticipation of further trauma, is maladaptive in other settings. To address this response, Trauma-Focused CBT (TF-CBT) offers an evidence-based intervention for children and their parents that has been reported as effective for depressive and hyperactive symptoms caused by a range of traumas, including sexual abuse, traumatic grief, and posttraumatic stress (Thornback & Muller, 2015).

Two phases are described in the implementation of TF-CBT. In the first phase, children are taught to recognize a wide range of emotions, practice arousal reduction techniques (e.g., deep breathing, progressive muscle relaxation), and learn cognitive strategies for hurtful or unhelpful thoughts. Skills taught to parents include recognition of emotions, selective attention, praise, and use of contingency reinforcement to encourage children to manage emotional reactions. The second phase involves helping children develop a trauma narrative to serve as a vehicle for gradual exposure to the trauma. As the narrative becomes progressively more detailed, the child is helped to use the strategies learned in phase one to regulate difficult emotions. Parents are coached on how to respond to their child's sharing of the narrative.

Reduction of parent and child-reported posttraumatic stress symptoms after TF-CBT is established in the empirical literature (Konanur et al., 2015; Thornback & Muller, 2015). Thornback and Muller, in a study of children ages 7–12 years, investigated whether TF-CBT can improve emotional regulation, and whether improvements in emotional regulation predict symptom improvement. Their findings showed that TF-CBT can result in improvements in emotional regulation. They concluded that the extent of improvement in maladaptive emotional regulation strategies is associated with the degree of symptom improvement.

Moving beyond specific counseling applications, Berger (2019) addressed the application of multitiered trauma-informed care to school settings by reviewing 13 published and unpublished studies. She described her study as the first systematic review of evidence on the growing field of multitiered, trauma-informed approaches to address trauma in schools. She concluded that further research, guided by empirical evidence of the effectiveness of multitiered and trauma-sensitive approaches in schools, is required. Specifically, greater consistency in interventions and research methods is needed for empirical validation. Berger advocated for more studies incorporating teacher training and improved alignment with Tier 1 positive behavioral supports.

Other Approaches

This section describes two approaches—motivational interviewing, including school-based motivational interviewing, and solution-focused brief therapy—that have a broad empirical research base as shown through meta-analyses and literature reviews.

Motivational Interviewing

Motivational interviewing (MI) is an approach that uses therapist–client conversations to help individuals resolve their ambivalence about making behavior changes by highlighting discrepancies in their values and behaviors (Miller & Rollnick, 2013). MI, originally developed to motivate adults to reduce alcohol and drug abuse, is considered a brief, client-centered approach that assumes people are much more likely to do things they say they will do instead of what they are told to do. Because multiple meta-analyses have indicated MI to be effective in this arena (Strait et al., 2019), the model has broadened to include work with children and teens around school issues.

Four elements of MI are described as integral: engagement, focusing, evoking change talk, and planning for change. Of these, change talk has emerged as the best supported mechanism in the MI research. Change talks refers to "any verbal expression of a need, reason, ability, desire, plan, or commitment for change" (Strait et al., 2019, p. 2).

Although a detailed presentation of MI is beyond the scope of this chapter, *School-Based Motivational Interviewing: Strategies for Engaging Parents, Teachers, and Students* provides an in-depth discussion of MI and its application to schools (Herman et al., 2014). It is written for school professionals, including school psychologists. User-friendly websites include *Motivational Interviewing for Schools* (https://miforschools.org/) and the *Student Checkup: School Based Motivational Interviewing and More* (https://studentcheckup.org).

In school-based motivational interviewing (SBMI), partnership, client autonomy, compassion, and guidance around talk of change are essential elements (Strait et al., 2019). Reduction of maladaptive behaviors, such as substance abuse, is a primary goal, and a corollary is adoption of adaptive behaviors, for example, exercise and good diet. Both are accomplished through motivation of adolescents and adults to change their own behavior to be more consistent with their goals and values. SBMI focuses on improving students' academic and behavioral outcomes by motivating change behaviors among the adults around them (i.e., through consultation with teachers and parents) or by directly motivating students to adopt adaptive behaviors and reduce disabling behaviors. Counselors use open-ended questions, affirmations, reflections, and summaries. During the change evocation phase, more directive questioning is typically used to evoke and reinforce change talk (Strait et al., 2019). Herman and colleagues (2014) explain how the acronym FRAMES applies to MI by describing each principle:

- Feedback is individualized and personal (i.e., regarding progress toward a targeted goal).
- Responsibility to make change is ultimately left with the client.
- Advice is given selectively and only with the permission of the client.
- A menu of options for new behaviors is made available as requested.
- Empathy maintains a collaborative relationship and increases likelihood of change.
- Self-efficacy (i.e., the belief that individuals have the capacity to change if they choose to do so) is promoted.

The empirical research base for MI is broad and includes studies involving numerous populations and mental health problems. Although applications to substance abuse are prominently featured, "MI has been extended to address a seemingly limitless array of problems in health care settings, the corrections system, and education . . . The common thread of applications has been to any problem where compliance or adherence is an issue; in other words, virtually any situation that requires human change" (Herman et al., 2014, p. 8).

Solution-Focused Brief Therapy

Solution-focused brief therapy (SFBT) has received considerable attention in school-based literature. Positive psychology, reviewed earlier in this book, shares features with solution-focused therapy in that both approaches acknowledge that individuals' strengths and resources play an integral part in recovery of emotional health and behavioral improvement. As described by the Institute for Solution-Focused Therapy (n.d.), SFBT is "future-focused, goal-directed, and focuses on solutions, rather than on the problems that brought clients to seek therapy" (https://solutionfocused.net/what-is-solution-focused-therapy/). Kim and colleagues (2019) provide a review of studies over the past decade that support the use of SFBT for emotional, behavioral, and interpersonal problems in school settings.

An assumption of the SFBT approach is that all clients have knowledge about what will improve their lives. The therapeutic interchange is directed toward eliciting and achieving the client's vision of solutions by doing the following:

- Looking for previous solutions by asking questions about times when this was less of a problem or was successfully addressed (e.g., "What did you or someone else do that was helpful?").
- Looking for exceptions, or times when the problem could have occurred but didn't (e.g., "What was different?").
- Using present- and future-focused questions versus past-focused questions (e.g., "What will you do this week about joining a social activity?").
- Complimenting and validating what the client is doing well by using an appreciative tone to encourage self-compliments (e.g., "How did you accomplish that?").
- Inviting clients to try doing more of what is working or to try an experiment based on actions they've indicated they'd like to try.
- Exploring miracle questions, scaling questions, and coping questions. In general, questions are designed to (a) open up the client's awareness that small changes can result in relief and be building blocks toward more major change, (b) help to track progress, and (c) promote awareness of personal resiliency and strength in the face of challenges and stressors.

In a review of SFBT research, Franklin (2015) noted that rigorous research has been conducted over the past 10 years using randomized controlled trials and quasi-experiments. Thus, SFBT is considered an evidence-based practice, although further randomized controlled trials with larger samples are needed. Franklin and Bolton (2015) described the application of SFBT in schools, including strategies for assessment and intervention, supportive research, specific solution-focused techniques in a case study, and application in a multitiered program such as RTI.

Research-Supported Applications of CBT

Research supports the use of CBT with children diagnosed with a variety of mental health concerns. According to the Effective Child Therapies website (https://effectivechildtherapy.org), CBT has empirical research support for treating many psychological disorders, including depression, anxiety, substance use, behavior problems, eating disorders, and posttraumatic stress disorder (PTSD).

This section briefly summarizes current findings on effectiveness of these approaches for selected problems likely to be encountered in schools. More about the evidence base for specific approaches with school-age populations can be found in *Evidence-Based Psychotherapies for Children and Adolescents* (Weisz & Kazdin, 2018).

David and colleagues (2018) completed a meta-analysis of 84 articles investigating the effectiveness of REBT. The samples were heterogeneous and included youth as well as adults. They found medium effect size compared with other interventions both on outcomes and on irrational beliefs (the cornerstone of REBT theory) for a variety of conditions, regardless of subjects' age and clinical status and of the delivery format (educational/classroom, psychotherapy/clinical, or counseling/nonclinical). In a study evaluating the use of REBT in a school-based group counseling program for adolescent boys with emotional disturbance, Banks and Zionts (2009) suggest that REBT can be used to address teasing, academic failure, criticism, parental rejection, unfair treatment by peers, and difficult tasks.

Battagliese and colleagues (2015) conducted a meta-analysis (21 studies) to evaluate the effectiveness of cognitive–behavioral therapy (CBT) to reduce externalizing symptoms in attention deficit hyperactivity disorder (ADHD) and oppositional defiant disorder (ODD). They found improvements in ODD and ADHD symptoms, including externalizing behaviors, in the studies implementing CBT. Additionally, they reported that reductions in parental stress and maternal depression were associated with CBT. These authors recommended that multimodal treatments targeting both children's and parents' symptoms are optimal.

A review of the literature conducted by Stark, Arora, and Funk (2011a) indicated that CBT has a solid foundation of research to support efficacy with children and adolescents experiencing depression. Likewise, it supports the efficacy of CBT use in preventing the development of suicidal ideation in individuals with depressive symptoms (TADS Team, 2007, as cited in Stark et al., 2011). Arora and colleagues (2019) investigated the effects of component parts of CBT on depressive symptoms in 40 females ages 9–14 years. Interestingly, these researchers found that age moderated the effects of the behavioral, cognitive, and relational (therapeutic relationship and group cohesion) factors. Younger females benefited more from high-quality behavioral and relational components (determined by rating scales). For the overall sample, behavioral and relational intervention components were associated with positive effect on posttreatment depressive symptoms, while cognitive components were marginally associated with worsening depressive symptoms. This study emphasizes the importance of developmental level on response to specific elements of CBT.

CBT also is effective for children experiencing anxiety (Weeks, Hill, & Owen, 2017). Students with anxiety problems are at risk for several negative outcomes at school, including impaired school performance, reduced attendance (school refusal), and difficulties socializing with peers and developing peer relationships. Sanchez et al. (2019) explored the effectiveness of CBT, medication (sertraline), and a combination CBT/sertraline compared with placebo on anxiety-related school impairment in youth. They found that all treatment conditions produced superior outcomes to the placebo, with combination therapy most effective. Chiu et al. (2013) examined the effectiveness of CBT delivered in a school setting to children ages 5–12 with diagnosed anxiety disorders. They found that 95.0% of the children who received the intervention showed a positive treatment response, compared with only 16.7% of children on the 3-month wait list.

Kircanski, Peris, and Piacentini (2011) maintain that a growing body of research demonstrates the efficacy of CBT for childhood obsessive–compulsive disorder (OCD), both alone and in combination with psychopharmacological interventions. Based on a review of the literature and expert consensus, they describe CBT "as the initial treatment of choice for OCD in children and adolescents in terms of efficacy, safety, and durability of response" (p. 239). OCD appears to negatively affect students across domains, including social abilities, executive functioning, and organizational skills (Dyches et al., 2010). A review of case examples and research studies conducted by Dyches and colleagues revealed that CBT and the component techniques of cognitive restructuring, psychoeducation, and exposure and response prevention were effective with children. They noted, however, that few studies exist to support the efficacy of CBT with very young school-age children. Young students may have not yet developed the metacognitive abilities to evaluate their own cognitive distortions.

PTSD results from exposure to events involving stressors such as death or serious injury to individuals or others. Children and adolescents suffering from PTSD experience persistent fear, feelings of helplessness, or horror related to the event. Students exposed to traumatic events may have difficulties socializing with others and exhibit aggressive behaviors (American Psychiatric Association, 2013). In addition, studies indicate that students may be affected academically by deficits in attention and concentration, executive functioning, and abstract reasoning abilities (Beers & De Bellis, 2002). Trauma-focused cognitive–behavioral therapy (TF-CBT) is considered to be a well-established psychosocial treatment for children and adolescents (Silverman, Ortiz, & Viswervaran, 2008). Thornback and Muller (2015) recommend TF-CBT as a brief and effective intervention for treating different types of trauma, including sexual abuse, traumatic grief, PTSD symptoms, and sexually inappropriate behavior. The results of their study with traumatized children ages 7–12 years (107 preassessment, 58 at posttreatment, and 44 at 6-month follow-up) indicated that TF-CBT decreases maladaptive forms of emotional regulation, which predicts a reduction in symptoms.

Eating disorders in children and adolescents are highly concerning, potentially causing long-term physical health issues as well as difficulty with social relationships, emotional competence, and cognitive development. Removing students from school to obtain treatment may further exacerbate the negative impact of the disorder on their education. In the classroom, difficulties may appear as mood instability, inability to concentrate, reduced work ethic, and decreased work performance (Hellings & Bowles, 2007). Craig and colleagues (2019) reported on a study of 54 adolescents (age 13–18) with anorexia nervosa or atypical anorexia nervosa. Either subjects had received family-based treatment prior to CBT, or family-based treatment had been determined to be inappropriate. Whether or not they had received family-based treatment, the patients showed positive outcomes on all measures, with moderate to large effect sizes. Outcomes were not influenced by severity and duration of the eating disorder. Craig and colleagues (2019) concluded that their results were comparable with those from other efficacy studies of the effectiveness of family-based therapy and CBT for adolescents with anorexia nervosa and bulimia nervosa.

Fischer and Peterson (2015) implemented a 6-month dialectical behavior therapy (DBT) outpatient intervention for bulimia nervosa accompanied by symptoms of mood disorder and nonsuicidal self-injury in adolescents. Seven of 10 original participants completed the intervention and a 6-month follow-up. Results indicated significant improvements in frequency of self-harm, binge episodes, purge episodes, and rating scale scores. Although this was a small sample with no control group, the authors concluded that DBT to address multiple forms of psychopathology appeared effective. Geller and Dunn (2011) report on the use of CBT combined with motivational interviewing for the treatment of eating disorders. Motivational interviewing adds to the CBT techniques the elements of attention to the therapist's style (warmth, empathy, genuine curiosity about the client's experience) and attention to the client's readiness and motivation for change. This article is helpful to practitioners in that it provides sample therapist–client dialogue for four different scenarios.

Wood and colleagues (2017) reviewed studies investigating CBT for autism spectrum disorders (ASD). They concluded that although no CBT program is well established for use with ASD, CBT for anxiety and core ASD symptoms, along with the Stepping Stone program for parents, is probably efficacious. A study with students diagnosed with ASD who received a school-based CBT intervention for symptoms of anxiety showed improvement in anxiety symptoms compared with a wait-list group (Luxford, Hadwin, & Kovshoff, 2017). In a review of five studies using CBT with school-age children with ASD, Rotheram-Fuller and MacMullen (2011) concluded that CBT shows efficacy with high-functioning ASD in the areas of anxiety and social skills.

Specific Techniques

The major elements of cognitive–behavioral approaches allow for flexibility in use of techniques and strategies. Whether the school psychologist chooses to begin by focusing on thoughts, behaviors, or feelings will depend upon the student's verbal abilities, willingness to talk, degree of insight, and immediate concerns.

Common elements in all CBT approaches include (a) deliberate attention to the effects of thoughts on emotions and behavior, (b) interventions designed to help learners mediate cognitions to achieve goals, (c) self-talk to guide cognition, and (d) practice and review to solidify and generalize skills. This section first describes basic self-regulation techniques, followed by a review of selected, research-supported CBT intervention programs appropriate for school-age children.

Self-Regulation Techniques

Self-regulation techniques are integral to cognitive–behavioral therapy (Webber & Plotts, 2008). Examples of self-regulation include self-instruction, self-monitoring, and self-evaluation. Self-instruction, sometimes called private speech, self-mediation, or verbal mediation, can be described as the process of talking to oneself to regulate one's own behavior (Meichenbaum & Goodman, 1971). Arguably, this technique is done automatically and frequently by most people; however, therapeutic use would involve purposeful, goal-directed use of self-instruction to modify behavior. Children who don't learn these skills automatically would be at risk for learning and behavioral problems in school. For example, the sixth grader who reliably reacts with aggression to every verbal taunt from peers and gets punished while his peers do not has probably not learned to tell himself he has options that may have better outcomes. Meichenbaum and Goodman (1971) recommended five steps for teaching children self-mediation that can be adapted for counseling purposes:

- The counselor talks aloud while performing a task while the student observes.
- The student performs the same task while the counselor verbalizes instructions.
- The student performs the task while verbalizing aloud the instructions.
- The student performs the task while whispering instructions.
- The student performs the task with covert (internalized) verbalizations.

This sequence could be used in role-playing to address the response to taunting described earlier; the victim in this case might be taught self-talk to develop alternatives to hitting ("I can turn away"; "I'll take five deep breaths"; "I can ask my teacher to stand near her").

Self-monitoring teaches individuals to record data regarding their own behavior, with the goal of changing the rate of the target behavior (Webber & Plotts, 2008). Students' recordings develop awareness of the behavior and establish external cues (the act of recording and the document that results from recording become external cues that generate self-directed change), both of which can lead to greater self-regulation through repeated practice. Students might be taught to tally the number of actual behaviors (completion of a reading assignment), or to mark time intervals during which target behaviors occur (e.g., duration of staying seated). A student might place a marble in a jar for each instance of complimenting another student if positive social engagement is a goal. When self-monitoring skills are being learned, the counselor (or teacher, through consultation) may reinforce appropriate recording to establish the behavior.

Self-evaluation is used to observe one's own behavior, as described above, but also to evaluate it against a predetermined goal or standard (Webber & Plotts, 2008). For the school psychologist using a CBT approach, it would be necessary to determine if self-evaluation is negatively distorted and to correct faulty self-talk so that this strategy can be effective. Students will be taught to accurately record data about their performance, then to evaluate it according to criteria set with the counselor. For example, a teenager who is highly argumentative with teachers might record each instance of compliance with a teacher's directive (e.g., putting cell phone away). A synchronous brief report from the teachers would validate the frequency of the student's compliance. The school psychologist would be charged with observing and reflecting the cognitions and emotions associated with the self-evaluation to challenge distortions; in counseling work, these are considered advanced counseling skills that must build from a foundation of rapport, trust, and active listening (Ivey, Ivey, & Zalaquett, 2016).

Several well-established CBT interventions are detailed in the research and practice literature, with implementation materials available for purchase or download. Some of these are reviewed in the following section.

Techniques for Anxiety and Depression

This section describes several well-researched manualized programs that use directive techniques to target children and adolescents with anxiety and depression. The programs include Coping Cat, ACTION treatment programs, EMOTION, and Super Skills for Life.

Coping Cat was developed at the Child and Adolescent Anxiety Disorders Clinic (CAADC) at Temple University and is targeted to children ages 7–13 with anxiety disorders (Kendall, Furr, & Podell, 2010). This program includes a treatment manual for the therapist, a workbook for each child participant, and a parent companion resource. The treatment program is considered appropriate for children with secondary comorbid conditions (e.g., depression, ADHD). The CBT components include psychoeducation, somatic management skills, cognitive restructuring, gradual exposure to anxiety-provoking situations, and relapse prevention plans. The typical individual treatment program consists of 16 weekly sessions with the child and two parent sessions. There is also a brief format (eight sessions).

Coping Cat is divided into two phases: the first focuses on skills training (sessions 1–9) and the second on skills practice (sessions 10–16). Kendall and others use the acronym FEAR as a framework for developing the treatment plan:

- **F**eeling frightened? Awareness and relaxation training use modeling, role-play, and practice.
- **E**xpecting bad things to happen? Faulty expectations are identified and eventually challenged. Cartoons in the *Coping Cat Workbook* are used to provide children with some distance and practice in identifying thoughts before being expected to share their own thoughts.
- **A**ttitudes and **A**ctions that might help. A problem-solving approach is used to develop the child's confidence in taking action to meet daily challenges, with the focus on generating and evaluating alternative solutions. Children are guided in the session and expected to record in their workbooks results of problem-solving efforts outside the session.
- **R**esults and **R**ewards. Self-monitoring and contingent reinforcement are used to shape approach behavior and reduce avoidance and fear behaviors. The counselor rewards partial successes, models coping strategies, and uses role-playing to demonstrate self-monitoring, self-rating, and self-reward. "Perfection is not an option and is never expected" (p. 50).

The second phase of the program (sessions 10–16) is devoted to application and practice of the FEAR plan through exposure to situations that are increasingly anxiety-provoking for the child. A later, and unique, step in this sequence is the creating of a product (booklet, video) in which the child summarizes personal experiences to help other children master their anxiety. Coping Cat allows and encourages therapists' flexibility in addressing specific needs within the overall structure of the sequential program.

A modification of Coping Cat for group intervention has also been developed with its own therapist manual. Additional adaptations are the computerized CBT approach titled Camp Cope-A-Lot, a 12-module program for children ages 7–13, and the online parenting program Child Anxiety Tales (CAT). Khanna and colleagues (2017) evaluated CAT with a sample of 73 parents who reported anxiety concerns about their 7- to 14-year-old children. The study included a bibliotherapy condition and a wait-list control group. On the basis of pre- and posttest data on parent knowledge, treatment acceptability, and child anxiety symptoms, these researchers concluded that CAT is feasible, acceptable, and beneficial for parents whose children have impairment from anxiety. Materials for Coping Cat as well as a 16-week adaptation of Coping Cat for adolescents ages 12–18 are available at http://www.workbookpublishing.com/anxiety.html).

A highly organized and researched CBT program for depression, the ACTION treatment program for girls, has been commercially available since 2007 (Stark et al., 2007), and in 2011, ACTION intervention materials for boys were made commercially available (Stark et al., 2011b). The program is designed for use by therapists with extensive training in case conceptualization for depressed youth and in CBT approaches. Although the program is designed to be implemented in a group format for ages 9–13, the authors maintain that it can be effectively adapted for individual implementation.

Core therapeutic components of the ACTION program include teaching coping skills, problem-solving skills, and cognitive restructuring. An integral subgoal is behavior activation through pleasant events scheduling. Another component is parent training, which includes creating a supportive environment characterized by increased positive reinforcement and sending of positive messages (Stark et al., 2010). Therapist manuals provide the structure and content for parent and child therapy components; accompanying parent and child workbooks are also available and can be purchased from the following website: http://www.workbookpublishing.com/depression.html.

Martinsen and colleagues (2016) describe a transdiagnostic (symptoms of more than one diagnostic category) treatment program. EMOTION: "Coping Kids," for managing anxiety and depression, incorporates elements from both Coping Cat and Taking ACTION. This group counseling program for children ages 8–13 with anxiety, depression, or both was piloted in Norway to explore its acceptability and feasibility for treating co-occurring anxiety and depression. EMOTION involves 20 twice-weekly sessions designed for implementation in schools. Sessions incorporate play and experiential activities, along with workbooks and homework. Parent group meetings are included. Martinsen and colleagues (2016) provide a detailed description of the format and some of the activities included in EMOTION. Their analysis of findings indicated that EMOTION is both acceptable and feasible for implementation in schools, with high user-friendliness. Both the group leaders and the children said they would recommend the program to others. The authors recommend that a future study have a larger sample (only 11 students completed the pilot), a comparison condition, and a randomized design to examine intervention effects on anxiety and depression problems.

A school-based manualized CBT intervention, Super Skills for Life (Essau & Ollendick, 2013) was developed for children ages 6–18 evidencing transdiagnostic emotional problems, hoping to demonstrate effectiveness even with the real-life constraints of schools compared to controlled clinical settings. The program incorporates behavioral activation and video feedback. Essau and colleagues (2019) found that emotional symptoms were significantly reduced according to self, parent, and teacher reports following the manual-guided eight-session program implemented by school professionals. The program, supportive research, and opportunities for training are described on the website https://www.superskillsforlife.com/. This program is based in the United Kingdom but according to the website has been globally implemented, though not in the United States.

Reality Therapy Techniques

Reality therapy provides specific counseling techniques. First, the counselor establishes a warm and trusting relationship with the student, followed by teaching the student about the approach using developmentally appropriate language. Students learn that the focus of the therapy is on the present and future, that individuals make choices to satisfy their needs, and that sometimes those choices may be ineffective. They also learn that the emphasis of the approach is on choices rather than on excuses.

Wubbolding (2017) describes a system for organizing the key components of reality therapy, which he calls WDEP, or wants, doing, evaluation, and planning:

- *Wants* may include what the client wants to happen as a result of counseling, the client's hopes for change in a relationship, or the client's goals for the future. In school settings, clients may want more friends, better grades, fewer restrictions, and so on.
- *Doing* concerns the client's behavior or choices. The counselor asks the student to describe what they do to address wants or needs. If the student says, "I wish other kids wanted to talk to me,'

then the reality therapist could ask the student to describe actions being taken to make this happen.
- *Evaluation* requires the client to self-evaluate. The counselor may facilitate this self-evaluation by asking the client, "If you continue to make the same choices and don't change anything, will things get better?" (Wubbolding et al., 2004). In self-evaluation, students must acknowledge the role of their choices with respect to the presenting problem. Ideally, the evaluation leads to a plan for change.
- *Planning* consists of determining a new set of behaviors and choices to better address unmet needs. The counselor can serve as a sounding board for the client's planning and provide objective feedback with respect to the client's proposed choices (e.g., is the plan realistic and achievable?). After making the plan, clients may come for another session and report that they did not execute the plan.

The counselor discourages excuses and encourages the client to focus on the four components in the WDEP system. Corey (2017) stated, "Clients are helped by the therapist who does not easily give up believing in their ability to make better choices, even if they are not always successful in completing their plans" (p. 326).

When working through the four components, the creative counselor can develop visual or manipulative aids for illustrating the WDEP system, such as charts and signs on walls. One good example is to simply reword the four steps into questions: What do I want? What am I doing? Is it helping or hurting? What is my plan?

A reality play therapy model is described by Stutey et al. (2019). Reality play therapy integrates elements of reality therapy with play therapy, integrating nondirective activities with more directive activities. It is designed as a brief intervention (6-week model, 60-minute sessions) for children ages 7–14. The model has not been studied in school settings that have been published in peer-reviewed publications; however, it fits well with the eclectic, flexible approach.

Wubbolding, Casstevens, and Fulkerson (2017) further describe the WDEP system as lending itself to treatment planning. Although this discussion is not in the context of children in schools, WDEP provides a useful structure for specifying goals, listing objectives, creating intervention plans, and evaluating outcomes.

Evaluation of Outcomes

Cognitive–behavioral counseling in its recommended implementation uses pre- and postintervention measures to evaluate outcomes. Without this component, the interventions cannot be supported as effective in addressing a student's educational needs. For example, the ACTION model for depression uses Beck depression inventories for pre- and posttesting, and the Coping Cat program includes a final product that exemplifies the learning that took place across the treatment sessions.

Because specific programs have often been designed for and researched with target populations, when selecting programs or techniques, school psychologists should understand how these constraints may affect outcomes. They must be prepared to select or develop their own pretest and posttest measures to assess the effectiveness of counseling in achieving IEP goals and objectives. Numerous norm-referenced measures are familiar to the school psychologist, including anxiety and depression inventories and parent and teacher rating scales, tools that might be employed along with the results of observations and interviews with students, teachers, and parents. School psychologists may want to consider getting pretest and posttest data from school professionals and from family members to gauge whether changes have been generalized.

The creative school psychologist might also develop outcome measures specific to the student and the intervention. For example, with appropriate parental consent, sequential photos of sandtrays produced during the course of counseling can document progress. Similarly, children's family and school drawings may demonstrate change over time. If a mood rating scale (such as a simple thermometer diagram) is used at the beginning of each session, they become measurement tools to assess change over time. The California Evidence-Based Clearinghouse for Child Welfare maintains a list of screening and assessment tools that have empirical validity, reliability, and guidelines for use (https://www.cebc4cw.org/assessment-tools/). Do2Learn—A Resource for Individuals with Special Needs (https://do2learn.com/) provides many free interventions and simple evaluation tools.

CASE EXAMPLE 1: GINGER

Background

Ginger is a 15-year-old high school sophomore. During elementary school, she was classified as a student with emotional disturbance, with chronic, severe depression being the most prominent feature. Ginger received individual counseling outside of school and in-school counseling as a related service through sixth grade. After sixth grade, her IEP team, including Ginger's mother, determined that she had made great progress on goals for emotional and behavioral functioning. Her academics were at grade level. At that time, Ginger was dismissed from special education. During seventh through ninth grades, Ginger continued to function adequately compared with peers, both academically and behaviorally. Outside counseling was discontinued. During the summer after ninth grade, Ginger experienced several major stressors. Her parents divorced and Ginger's parents argued over custody arrangements for her and her younger brother. When school began for her sophomore year, Ginger was dividing her time equally between her parents' homes. Late in the summer, one of Ginger's close friends was killed in an automobile accident.

Presenting Problems

Ginger's mother approached Henry, the school psychologist, because he had completed the full evaluation at the end of sixth grade. She expressed her worry about Ginger's recurring depression. Symptoms she noted were withdrawal, sleep difficulties, sadness, and tearfulness. Henry learned that the parents had joint custody and that consent from both parents was required for any psychological intervention. The family had already sought outside family counseling. Henry recommended to the parents that the school convene a family–school meeting. Both parents agreed.

Assessment

The family–school team concluded that Ginger was showing signs of depression. Given the major stressors she had recently suffered, Henry expressed his opinion that at this time Ginger's symptoms likely reflected an adjustment disorder that could resolve in the next several months with appropriate intervention and support. Henry was aware from his training that adjustment disorders often resolve within 6 months of a triggering event if appropriate intervention is provided, without the need for referral to the 504 or IEP teams. Because of Ginger's depression history, he explained that intervention should begin soon and remain in place for at least 6 months, after which time he would reevaluate her status. Henry obtained consent from Ginger's mother and father to contact the family therapist, to interview Ginger, and to obtain rating scale information from parents and teachers. Self, parent, and teacher ratings on a norm-referenced rating scale for internalizing and externalizing disorders were consistent in indicating significant elevations on scales related to depression. He concluded that counseling through general education, coordinated with the private therapist, was necessary to support Ginger's educational progress, and he obtained consent from both parents to conduct counseling. Henry recommended 16 weeks of individual counseling followed by evaluation; if appropriate, counseling would be gradually phased out over the following 8 weeks.

Goals and Objectives

Goal. Ginger will make measurable progress in the area of emotional functioning during the 16-week period.

- Objective 1: Ginger's self-reported symptoms of depression will be reduced to the "average" level for her age on the Reynolds Adolescent Depression Scale-2.
- Objective 3: Parent and teacher ratings on the depression and withdrawal scales of the Behavior Rating System for Children-3 will yield "average" range scores.
- Objective 2: Ginger will engage in academic and extracurricular activities at a level similar to involvement during her ninth-grade year.

Intervention: Ginger's private therapist was meeting with the family weekly to process feelings and do problem-solving of logistical issues related to the divorce and custody. She and Henry concurred that individual counseling for Ginger around depression related to grief and loss would be appropriate. Henry selected individual counseling because Ginger had benefited from counseling in the past, presented problems that research has shown are responsive to cognitive–behavioral techniques, and had outside support for associated family issues.

During the first few sessions, Henry and Ginger talked while walking around the track to establish rapport, develop a trusting relationship, and encourage physical activity. Henry initially used primarily active listening techniques, reflecting and summarizing Ginger's verbalizations and attending closely to and reflecting her expression of emotion. He also acknowledged the skills and strengths she had demonstrated in overcoming depression in the past, using validation statements typical of solution-focused therapy. During this phase, Henry observed frequent statements about responsibility for and guilt about her parents' divorce. He reflected this back to her. As trust increased, Henry disputed associated thoughts by exploring the decisions made by her parents that were their responsibility. Distorted thinking also emerged about her difficulty adjusting to her friend's death, with Ginger stating, "All the other kids got over it so fast and just got back to normal. I'm just weird. I'll never get better." She expressed some guilt that she was still alive. Henry empathized with the major losses and stressors she had endured over the summer and the shared experience of grief that others have in similar circumstances, noting that everyone grieves differently and that her feelings were normal. He also reassured her that while grief can't be rushed, it tends to lessen over time.

As part of a CBT approach, Ginger developed a plan for engaging in activities she'd enjoyed in the past. She agreed to try staying in the family room to watch a movie with her brother once a week and to accept one invitation each week to do something outside of home or school (a meal with a parent or friends, a movie or sports event). This aspect of her intervention was gradually increased to include participation in the school drama club and working as an office assistant. At each weekly meeting, Ginger evaluated her adherence to her plan and described her thoughts and feelings about her efforts and their outcomes.

Henry routinely assigned homework, including engaging in one or more enjoyable activities and journaling about thoughts and feelings. In sessions, he and Ginger processed these experiences and actively discussed thoughts and feelings, challenging thoughts that were distorted and caused negative self-evaluation, helplessness, or hopelessness. Through this process, Ginger developed awareness of her tendency to "awfulize" about the future and assign herself disproportionate responsibility for others' behaviors, resulting in unwarranted guilt.

Evaluation

Henry checked in with Ginger's parents and teachers throughout the intervention to gauge progress or concerns. Changes were gradual but in a positive direction. At the end of the 16-week period, he asked that Ginger, her parents, and her teachers repeat the behavior rating scales they had done at pretest. He provided feedback to Ginger, observing that she had improved in the areas of social engagement and decreased sadness. He also reviewed with Ginger the records they had created of thoughts and feelings about her experiences and efforts, pointing out the reduced frequency of having distorted thoughts result in negative self-evaluation. They agreed to meet every other week for the next month. When gains were seen after that month, with Ginger involved in school and social activities at about the same level as in ninth grade and continued improvement in mood, they agreed to meet once monthly, with more frequent check-ins if needed.

CASE EXAMPLE 2: BRIAN

Background

Brian is an 8-year-old student diagnosed 1 year ago with high-functioning autism. Because he achieves at an above-average level in all academic areas, he has not been served through special education for ASD. He does, however, receive speech therapy as a student with a speech impairment, diagnosed during early childhood. The IEP team referred Brian for consideration for counseling for social anxiety. In reviewing school records, Adam, the school psychologist, observed that Brian has not had a full individual evaluation through the school. He received the ASD diagnosis from a pediatric neurologist. Speech evaluation conducted through the school revealed above-average receptive and expressive vocabulary, with a mild to moderate articulation impairment and low average pragmatic language. Referral concerns include Brian's avoidance of group activities at school, including outdoor games, classroom group projects, and singing in music class. When expected to participate, Brian often says he has a stomachache and asks to sit separately and watch the group instead of participating. His social anxiety has gradually increased during elementary school. His speech therapist noted that he has made good progress on speech goals but tends to speak infrequently when therapy is provided in a group setting.

Assignment

Let the following questions guide your decisions in Brian's case:

- What would be your first steps in conceptualizing this case? What further information do you need? What areas of functioning should be assessed?
- In the assessment phase, how would you propose to work with the speech therapist? Teachers? Pediatric neurologist? Parents?
- If you obtain sufficient assessment information that supports counseling for social anxiety, consider the following questions
    - What counseling approach, or approaches, would be most likely to benefit Brian?
    - How do his language skills affect choice of the counseling approach?
    - What research, if any, supports this approach?
    - What tools might you use for pretest and posttest?
    - Describe realistic goals, objectives, and the time frame or number of sessions you would recommend for Brian.

SUMMARY

In this chapter we reviewed directive techniques that generally fall under the umbrella of CBT, acknowledging that nondirective and directive techniques exist on a continuum. Although the many approaches we presented overlap, each has its own proponents and supportive literature. The common core is attention to the client's inner world of thoughts and feelings and how they relate to behavior. Deliberate efforts to access the student's inner world distinguishes CBT from strictly behavioral interventions. Change can be accomplished through different approaches. For example, the school psychologist might choose to first address behaviors using a reality therapy approach. Alternatively, a student's current primary target behavior (e.g., marijuana abuse) may lead first to the student's world of feelings or thoughts, making motivational interviewing an appropriate choice. However, for a student who has had significant trauma and is self-medicating with marijuana, a different approach might be needed, such as trauma-focused CBT or REBT. The student with severe emotional regulation problems might benefit from DBT. Individuals are both unique and complex, and the levels of students' language proficiency and executive functions (e.g., capacities to self-reflect, plan, and evaluate potential outcomes), as well as the nature and severity of referral problems, will have a bearing on what approaches are most effective.

Schools are dynamic environments in which multiple systems affect each student's academic and social functioning. Counseling interventions to improve functioning require well-organized communication among systems. Schools may be ideal settings in which to deliver counseling services if systems support and communication are at least adequate; however, professionals must be prepared for the challenges of implementing counseling interventions with fidelity when so many other demands compete for time and resources. The review of the literature reveals that the research base for CBT involves studies that involve careful definition and selection of participants, control of extraneous variables, adherence to manualized techniques over specific periods, formal evaluation with reference to control groups, and replication. This degree of precision in intervention is challenging in school settings. Nevertheless, recent research seems to be moving in the direction of portability—translating interventions developed and studied in controlled, usually clinical, settings into real-life contexts such as schools. How can school psychologists overcome this? Because school professionals have many other mandates that take most of their time, school psychologists as counselors might model the use of CBT techniques for teachers, nurses, administrators, parents, and other related services personnel. The multitiered approach to trauma-informed care in schools advocates that more staff be trained in this model to maximize its value. For example, the basic self-regulation steps described in this chapter could be effectively used by a teacher, an aide, or a school counselor. The WDEP framework in reality therapy could be implemented by an administrator, in consultation with a school psychologist, or when dealing with a discipline problem.

This chapter has emphasized the importance of a having a trusting, stable relationship between the student and the school psychologist. CBT involves significant self-disclosure of internal processes (thoughts and feelings), with the expectation that target problems result at least in part from, or are maintained by, faulty thinking. To successfully challenge such distortions, the student must be able to acknowledge and verbalize them, and to accept and consider evaluation from the counselor. Techniques for establishing self-regulation of thoughts and behaviors require that the counselor and student be able to agree on goals. The use of a highly structured curriculum for CBT that is implemented without taking time to build rapport and trust might lead to poor adherence to treatment.

Some of the advantages of having schools provide CBT counseling services include the accessibility of students, ample opportunities for generalization from one setting to another, and the likelihood that challenges and opportunities will occur at school, giving the counselor immediate and salient content for counseling sessions. Opportunities to discuss such situations in CBT sessions and complete CBT homework within the context of school are abundant. The naturalistic setting in which CBT occurs in the schools can also reduce the stigma associated with mental health issues.

KEY POINTS FOR DISCUSSION

- Why do you think the empirical support in recent literature is stronger for CBT than for many other counseling approaches?
- Do you find yourself drawn to a particular approach covered in this chapter? How would you gain proficiency in practicing this approach?
- Would you advocate for your school district to provide training in one or more of these approaches? How would you approach administrators about this?
- In a typical school setting, would the school psychologist be able to implement manualized CBT interventions like Coping Cat for anxious children and the ACTION treatment program for depressed girls? What constraints should be considered?

- When deciding to use cognitive–behavioral approaches, what developmental issues must be considered?
- Is it necessary or desirable for a school psychologist to select a specific evidence-based counseling approach during intervention planning? Why or why not?

REFERENCES

Aliakbari, M., Juibari, A. K., Amirabadi, F., Shaghaghi, F., Zare, N., & Khalegi, F. (2013). The role of theory of mind and executive function in predicting empathy. *Advances in Cognitive Science, 15*(2), 1–10.

American Psychiatric Association. (2013). *Diagnostic and statistical manual of mental disorders* (5th ed.). Washington, DC: Author.

Arora, P. G., Baker, C. N., Marchette, L. K., & Stark, K. D. (2019). Components analyses of a school-based cognitive behavioral treatment for youth depression. *Journal of Clinical Child and Adolescent Psychology, 48*(Suppl 1), S180–S193.

Banks, T., & Zionts, P. (2009). REBT used with children and adolescents who have emotional and behavioral disorders in educational settings: A review of the literature. *Journal of Rational-Emotive & Cognitive Behavior Therapy, 27*(1), 51–65.

Battagliese, G., Caccetta, M., Luppino, O. I., Baglioni, C., Cardi, V., Mancini, F., & Buonanno, C. (2015). Cognitive-behavioral therapy for externalizing disorders: A meta-analysis of treatment effectiveness. *Behaviour Research and Therapy, 75*, 60–71.

Beers, S. R., & De Bellis, M. D. (2002). Neuropsychological function in children with maltreatment-related posttraumatic stress disorder. *American Journal of Psychiatry, 159*(3), 483–486. https://doi.org/10.1176/appi.ajp.159.3.483

Benuto, L. C., & O'Donohue, W. (2015). Is culturally sensitive cognitive behavioral therapy an empirically supported treatment?: The case for Hispanics. *International Journal of Psychology and Psychological Therapy, 15*(3), 405–421.

Berger, E. (2019). Multi-tiered approaches to trauma-informed care in schools: A systematic review. *School Mental Health, 11*(4), 650–664.

Chiu, A. W., Langer, D. A., McLeod, B. D., Har, K., Drahota, A., Galla, B. M., … Wood, J. J. (2013). Effectiveness of modular CBT for child anxiety in elementary schools. *School Psychology Quarterly, 28*(2), 141–153.

Corey, G. (2017). *Theory and practice of counseling and psychotherapy* (10th ed.). Boston, MA: Cengage Learning.

Craig, M., Waine, J., Wilson, S., & Waller, G. (2019). Optimizing treatment outcomes in adolescents with eating disorders: The potential role of cognitive behavioral therapy. *International Journal of Eating Disorders, 52*(5), 538–542.

David, D., Cotet, C., Matu, S., Mogoase, C., & Stefan, S. (2018). 50 years of rational–emotive and cognitive–behavioral therapy: A systematic review and meta-analysis. *Journal of Clinical Psychology, 74*(3), 304–318.

Donato, T. (2004). Maintenance for the CT/RT student in the classroom. *International Journal of Reality Therapy, 24*(1), 38–42.

Dyches, T. T., Leininger, M., Heath, M. A., Prater, M. A. (2010). Understanding obsessive-compulsive disorder in students: Symptoms and school-based interventions. *School Social Work Journal, 34*(2), 35–55.

Edwards, O. W. (2009). A choice theory teaching and learning model for working with children of prisoners. *Educational Psychology in Practice, 25*(3), 259–270.

Essau, C. A., & Ollendick, T. H. (2013). *The Super Skills for Life program.* London, U.K.: University of Roehampton.

Essau, C. A., Sasagawa, S., Jones, G., Fernandes, B., & Ollendick, T. H. (2019). Evaluating the real-world effectiveness of a cognitive behavior therapy-based transdiagnostic program for emotional problems in children in a regular school setting. *Journal of Affective Disorders, 253,* 357–365.

Fischer, S., & Peterson, C. (2015). Dialectical behavior therapy for adolescent binge eating, purging, suicidal behavior, and non-suicidal self-injury: A pilot study. *Psychotherapy, 52*(1), 78–92.

Fiske, A., & Holmboe, K. (n.d.). Neural substrates of early executive function development. *Developmental Review, 52,* 42–62. https://doi-org.libproxy.txstate.edu/10.1016/j.dr.2019.100866

Franklin, C. (2015). An update on strengths-based, solution-focused brief therapy. *Health & Social Work, 40*(2), 73.

Franklin, C., & Bolton, K. W. (2015). Solution-focused brief therapy. In R. H. Witte & G. S. Mosley-Howard (Eds.), *Mental health practice in today's schools: Issues and interventions* (pp. 145–167). New York, NY: Springer Publishing Company.

Friedberg, R. D., & McClure, J. M. (2015). *Clinical practice of cognitive therapy with children and adolescents: The nuts and bolts* (2nd ed.). New York, NY: Guilford Press.

Geller, J., & Dunn, E. C. (2011). Integrating motivational interviewing and cognitive behavioral therapy in the treatment of eating disorders: Tailoring interventions to patient readiness for change. *Cognitive and Behavioral Practice, 18*(1), 5–15.

Glasser, W. (1965). *Reality therapy: A new approach to psychiatry.* New York, NY: Harper & Row.

Glasser, W. (1986). *Control theory in the classroom.* New York, NY: Harper & Row.

Glasser, W. (1998). *Choice theory in the classroom.* New York, NY: Harper Collins.

Grohol, J. M. (2019, June 24). 15 common cognitive distortions. *PsychCentral.* https://psychcentral.com/lib/15-common-cognitive-distortions

Hanson, J. B. (2016, September 29). *Dialectical behavior therapy in the public schools.* Presentation to Community High School District 218 INSPiRE, Grand Rounds, Chicago, Ill.

Hellings, B., & Bowles, T. (2007). Understanding and managing eating disorders in the school setting. *Australian Journal of Guidance & Counselling, 17*(1), 60–67.

Herman, K. C., Shepard, S., Frey, A., & Reinke, W. M. (2014). *Motivational interviewing in schools: Strategies for engaging parents, teachers, and students.* New York, NY: Springer. Retrieved from http://search.ebscohost.com.libproxy.txstate.edu/login.aspx?direct=true&db=nlebk&AN=673607&site=eds-live&scope=site

Institute for Solution-Focused Therapy. (n.d.). What is solution-focused therapy? https://solutionfocused.net/what-is-solution-focused-therapy/

Ivey, A. E., Ivey, M. B., & Zalaquett, C. P. (2016). *Essentials of intentional interviewing: Counseling in a multicultural world* (3rd ed.). Boston, MA: Cengage Learning.

Jones, J. M. (Ed.). (2009). *The psychology of multiculturalism in schools: A primer for practice, training, and research*. Bethesda, MD: National Association of School Psychologists.

Kataoka, S., Novins, D. K., & DeCarlo Santiago, C. (2010). The practice of evidence-based treatments in ethnic minority youth. *Child and Adolescent Psychiatric Clinics of North America*, *19*(4), 775–789. https://doi.org/10.1016/j.chc.2010.07.008

Khanna, M. S., Carper, M. M., Harris, M. S., & Kendall, P. C. (2017). Web-based parent-training for parents of youth with impairment from anxiety. *Evidence-Based Practice in Child and Adolescent Mental Health*, *2*(1), 43. https://doi.org/10.1080/23794925.2017.1283548

Kim, J. (2006). The effect of a bullying prevention program on responsibility and victimization of bullied children in Korea. *International Journal of Reality Therapy*, *26*(1), 4–8.

Kim, J., Jordan, S. S., Franklin, C., & Froerer, A. (2019). Is solution-focused brief therapy evidence-based? An update 10 years later. *Families in Society—Journal of Contemporary Social Services*, *100*(2), 127–138. https://doi.org/10.1177/1044389419841688

Kircanski, K., Peris, T. S., & Piacentini, J. C. (2011). Cognitive-behavioral therapy for obsessive-compulsive disorder in children and adolescents. *Child and Adolescent Psychiatric Clinics of North America*, *20*(2), 239–254. https://doi.org/doi:10.1016/j.chc.2011.01.014

Kirk, A., Michael, K., Bergman, S., Schorr, M., & Jameson, J. P. (2019). Dose response effects of cognitive-behavioral therapy in a school mental health program. *Cognitive Behaviour Therapy*, *48*(6), 497–516. https://doi.org/10.1080/16506073.2018.1550527

Klug, K. (2006). Applying choice theory and reality therapy to coaching athletes. *International Journal of Reality Therapy*, *25*(2), 36–39.

Konanur, S., Muller, R. T., Cinamon, J. S., Thornback, K., & Zorzella, K. P. M. (2015). Effectiveness of Trauma-Focused Cognitive Behavioral Therapy in a community-based program. *Child Abuse & Neglect*, *50*, 159–170. https://doi.org/10.1016/j.chiabu.2015.07.013

Linehan, M. M., & Wilks, C. R. (2015). The course and evolution of dialectical behavior therapy. *American Journal of Psychotherapy*, *69*(2), 97–110. https://doi.org/10.1176/appi.psychotherapy.2015.69.2.97

Luxford, S., Hadwin, J., & Kovshoff, H. (2017). Evaluating the effectiveness of a school-based cognitive behavioural therapy intervention for anxiety in adolescents diagnosed with autism spectrum disorder. *Journal of Autism and Developmental Disorders*, *47*(12), 3896–3908.

Martinsen, K. D., Kendall, P. C., Stark, K., & Neumer, S.-P. (2016). Prevention of anxiety and depression in children: Acceptability and feasibility of the transdiagnostic EMOTION program. *Cognitive and Behavioral Practice*, *23*(1), 1–13. https://doi.org/10.1016/j.cbpra.2014.06.005

Meichenbaum, D. H., & Goodman, J. (1971). Training impulsive children to talk to themselves: A means of developing self-control. *Journal of Abnormal Psychology*, *77*(2), 115–126.

Miller, W. R., & Rollnick, S. (2013). *Motivational interviewing: Helping people change*. New York, NY: Guilford Press.

Olver, K. M. (2017). That was then . . . A message from the William Glasser international executive director. *International Journal of Choice Theory & Reality Therapy*, *36*(2), 13–17.

Palmatier, L. L. (1998). *Crisis counseling for a quality school community: Applying William Glasser's choice theory*. Washington, DC: Accelerated Development.

Perepletchikova, F., Nathanson, D., Axelrod, S. R., Merrill, C., Walker, A., Grossman, M., ... Walkup, J. (2017). Randomized clinical trial of dialectical behavior therapy for preadolescent children with disruptive mood dysregulation disorder: Feasibility and outcomes. *Journal of the American Academy of Child and Adolescent Psychiatry, 56*(10), 832–840.

Renna, R. (2004). Autism spectrum disorders: Learning to listen as we shape behaviors blending choice theory with applied behavior analysis. *International Journal of Reality Theory, 23*(2), 17–22.

Rotheram-Fuller, E., & MacMullen, L. (2011). Cognitive-behavioral therapy for children with autism spectrum disorders. *Psychology in the Schools, 48*(3), 263–271. https://doi.org/10.1002/pits.20552

Sanchez, A. L., Comer, J. S., Coxe, S., Albano, A. M., Piacentini, J., Compton, S. N., ... Kendall, P. C. (2019). The effects of youth anxiety treatment on school impairment: Differential outcomes across CBT, sertraline, and their combination. *Child Psychiatry and Human Development, 50*(6), 940–949.

Silverman, W. K., Ortiz, C. D., Viswesvaran, C., Burns, B. J., Kolko, D. J., Putnam, F. W., & Amaya-Jackson, L. (2008). Evidence-based psychosocial treatments for children and adolescents exposed to traumatic events. *Journal of Clinical Child and Adolescent Psychology, 37*(1), 156–183.

Slonaker, A. R. (2019). CBT interventions in schools. *Communiqué, 47*(6), 38.

Stark, K. D., Arora, P., & Funk, C. L. (2011a). Training school psychologists to conduct evidence-based treatments for depression. *Psychology in the Schools, 48*(3), 272–282.

Stark, K. D., Schnoebelen, S., Simpson, J., Hargrave, J., Molnar, J., & Glen, R. (2011b). *'ACTION' workbook: Cognitive-behavioral therapy for treating depressed boys*.

Stark, K. D., Streusand, W., Krumholz, L. S., & Patel, P. (2010). Cognitive-behavioral therapy for depression: The ACTION treatment program for girls. In J. R. Weisz & A. E. Kazdin (Eds.), *Evidence-based psychotherapies for children and adolescents* (2nd ed.; 93–109). New York, NY: Guilford Press.

Strait, G. G., Strait, J. E., Schanding, T., Anderson, J. R., Stinson, D., Schmidt, S., & Kim, S. Y. (2019). Ethical considerations for using school-based motivational interviewing with parents, teacher, and students. *Journal of Applied School Psychology*. https://doi-org.libproxy.txstate.edu/10.1080/15377903.2019.1665606

Stutey, D. M., Klein, D. E., Wubbolding, R. E., & Dunnigan, N. (2019). Therapists' perceptions of the reality play therapy model. *International Journal of Play Therapy, 28*(2), 69–78. https://doi.org/10.1037/pla0000092

Thornback, K., & Muller, R. T. (2015). Relationships among emotion regulation and symptoms during trauma-focused CBT for school-aged children. *Child Abuse & Neglect, 50*, 182–192.

Walter, S. M., Lambie, G. W., & Ngazimbi, E. E. (2008). A choice theory counseling group succeeds with middle school students who displayed disciplinary problems. *Middle School Journal, 40*(2), 4–12.

Webber, J., & Plotts, C. (2008). *Emotional and behavioral disorders: Theory and practice* (5th ed.). Boston, MA: Allyn & Bacon.

Weeks, C., Hill, V., & Owen, C. (2017). Changing thoughts, changing practice: Examining the delivery of a group CBT-based intervention in a school setting. *Educational Psychology in Practice, 33*(1), 1–15. https://doi.org/10.1080/02667363.2016.1217400

Weisz, J. R., & Kazdin, A. E. (2018). *Evidence-based psychotherapies for children and adolescents* (3rd ed.). New York, NY: Guilford Press.

Wood, J., Klebanoff, S., Renno, P., Fujii, C., & Danial, J. (2017). Individual CBT for anxiety and related symptoms in children with autism spectrum disorders. In C. M. Kerns, P. Renno, E. A. Storch, P. C. Kendall, & J. J. Woods, (Eds.), *Anxiety in children and adolescents with autism spectrum disorder: Evidence-based assessment and treatment* (pp. 123–141). London, U.K.: Academic Press.

Wubbolding, R. E. (2017). *Reality therapy and self-evaluation: The key to client change*. Alexandria, VA: American Counseling Association.

Wubbolding, R. E., Casstevens, W. J., & Fulkerson, M. H. (2017). Using the WDEP system of reality therapy to support person-centered treatment planning. *Journal of Counseling & Development, 95*, 472–477. https://doi.org/10.1002/jcad.12162

Chapter 9

Therapeutic Responses to Trauma, Loss, and Crisis

OVERVIEW

At some point, every school psychologist will be working with students who have experienced trauma, loss, or crises. This chapter provides information for school psychologists regarding trauma-informed care in schools, crisis prevention and intervention, crisis counseling, suicide prevention, and interventions for students experiencing grief and loss. The goals of crisis counseling are distinct from the counseling goals described in much of this book. These goals include helping individuals cope in the short term and helping them return to normalcy while reducing the probability of long-term trauma. Given school systems' varying levels of crisis prevention and preparedness, organization, and student supports, school psychologists will be called on to expand their skills beyond the traditional foci of assessment, intervention, and consultation to include coordinating and providing counseling during trauma and crisis responses to effectively meet students' needs.

Given the importance of these topics and the space limitations of this book, this chapter is only an introduction to some of the evidence-based practices essential for preventing and responding to serious crisis, trauma, and grief issues that may affect students. The references introduce important resources for readers to learn more.

OBJECTIVES

After reading this chapter, readers should be able to do the following:

- Define trauma and trauma-informed care.
- Define crisis.
- Articulate strategies to prevent crises in schools.
- Articulate methods of school-based crisis preparation.

- Describe the levels of crisis intervention.
- Recognize developmental factors that affect individual responses to crises.
- Define grief and loss.
- Describe effective approaches to working with grief and loss in school settings.
- Name the components of a suicide risk assessment.

Introduction

Schools have shown great potential in meeting the needs of students affected by trauma and crisis (Reinbergs & Fefer, 2018). Much of the general skill set that school psychologists use can be applied in situations involving trauma and crisis. For example, understanding individuals' developmental and cultural differences is critical not only for performing assessments and consultations but also for responding to a disaster (Heath et al., 2009; Ortiz & Voutsinas, 2012; Pollio & Deblinger, 2017). Similarly, the capacities to make data-based decisions, demonstrate empathy, and work effectively with systems serve school psychologists well in times of crisis. Even so, school psychologists need specialized training in coordinating and providing counseling to victims of trauma and crisis to effectively meet students' needs.

School systems have different crisis response organization, levels of preparedness, and student supports, so it follows that the counseling roles of school psychologists in crisis situations will depend on the crisis prevention and intervention efforts that are already in place. The next sections define trauma and crises; introduce crisis prevention and response, including trauma-informed care; and discuss suicide prevention and grief counseling to assist school psychologists as counselors when they are faced with these challenges.

Trauma

The concepts of *trauma* and *crisis* have many definitions, and the terms used to explain and describe these phenomena overlap considerably. The Substance Abuse and Mental Health Services Administration (SAMHSA) developed a definition of trauma that not only has been informed by the literature but also incorporates the voices of those who have experienced trauma in their lives. SAMHSA (2014) conceptualizes trauma around the "Three E's":

> Individual trauma results from an **event**, series of events, or set of circumstances that is **experienced** by an individual as physically or emotionally harmful or life threatening and that has lasting adverse **effects** on the individual's functioning and mental, physical, social, emotional, or spiritual well-being. (p. 7)

This definition is broad enough to encompass a wide range of traumatic events, experiences, and effects. Events may include violence, natural disasters, or the threat of adversity. Individuals experience such events and threats differently, and their perceptions determine whether an event is traumatizing. The same event may be experienced as traumatic by one individual but not by another. Traumatic effects may be experienced immediately, or onset may be delayed. Nevertheless, the symptoms can be disruptive to daily functioning and adversely affect a range of thoughts, feelings, and behaviors. For example, individuals who have experienced trauma may have traumatic stress reactions such as difficulty with concentration, sleep, emotional regulation, relationships, and memory (SAMHSA, 2014).

Increasingly, school psychologists and other educators have come to understand that trauma-informed approaches can help to support the needs of students (Overstreet & Chafouleas, 2016). Trauma-informed care arose from the awareness that adverse experiences could increase an individual's potential for engaging in risky behaviors and having serious health problems over their lifetime (SAMHSA, 2014). Trauma-informed practices are designed to permeate all aspects of schools' administration and culture, including prevention, implementation of positive behavior supports, development of safe learning environments, and the provision of mental health services. A trauma-informed approach considers the ways in which trauma affects individuals and tailors practices to meet the needs of those affected by trauma.

What does a trauma-informed school look like? Although there are many definitions of trauma and many contributions to practice from multiple disciplines (e.g., counseling, social work, educational leadership), a useful and integrative approach developed by Chafouleas and colleagues (2016) applies trauma-informed practices to school-wide positive behavioral interventions and supports (SWPBIS). Their "blueprint for trauma-informed service delivery in schools" includes details not only for implementation, but also for professional development and evaluation. By implementing trauma-informed practices in a multitiered service delivery model, the blueprint demonstrates the importance of prevention, screening, and interventions that are matched to the severity of concerns.

In terms of direct counseling approaches for children who have experienced trauma, a number of techniques and models are available to school psychologists. One of the approaches often cited in the literature is the well-researched Trauma-Focused Cognitive–Behavior Therapy (TF-CBT; Salloum et al., 2017). TF-CBT was first developed to help children who had been sexually abused, but the method is now used and supported for individuals who have experienced all kinds of trauma (NREPP, 2016). Treatment may be for individuals or groups and typically occurs over 12–16 sessions (longer for complex trauma). TF-CBT combines relationship building with cognitive, behavioral, and family therapy to help address traumatic experiences. Specialized training in TF-CBT is required (certification information can be found at www.tfcbt.org).

For young children, the capacity to engage in counseling methods that rely heavily on talking and thinking may be limited. Consequently, play-based techniques have been developed to assist children affected by trauma. For example, trauma-focused integrative play therapy (TF-IPT) applies the principles of play-based or expressive therapies in situations in which children have experienced trauma (Gil, 2012). In many ways, TF-IPT has the same goals as TF-CBT, though the methods are distinct. TF-IPT is delivered across three phases: (a) establishment of safety and relationship building, (b) trauma processing, and (c) social reconnection (Gil, 2012). These phases are marked by structured, play-based activities to help children safely process their trauma in a developmentally appropriate way. (See Chapter 6 for a review of play-based approaches and Chapter 8 for a discussion of cognitive–behavioral therapy.)

Given the prevalence of traumatic experiences in childhood and adolescence, school psychologists are likely to encounter students who will benefit from interventions for traumatic stress reactions. Schools may be the ideal setting for serving children who have experienced trauma; however, school professionals need training, support, and other resources (Reinbergs & Fefer, 2018). Talking to a student about traumatic experiences may be challenging for all parties.

Crisis

Steeves and colleagues (2017) define a school crisis as "a sudden, uncontrollable, and extremely negative event that has the potential to impact the entire school community" (p. 563). Like trauma, a crisis starts with an event, such as a tornado, but is also formed by individuals' perceptions of or responses to the event. Any number of events or situations can precipitate a crisis, including violent acts, natural disasters, accidents, and so forth, along with the stressors related to individuals' life changes. Some dangerous and stressful events do not necessarily lead to a crisis, because they may not result in adverse psychosocial impacts (Brock, 2012). The following conditions must be present to meet the criteria of a crisis: "(a) the individual's perception that the stressful event will lead to considerable upset and/or disruption; and (b) the individual's inability to resolve the disruption by previously used coping methods" (Roberts, 2005, p. 13). School shootings meet the definition of a crisis, but it has been found that schools' preparation and drills for these increasingly common tragedies are also known stressors and have been controversial.

Because a crisis encompasses a wide range of situations and experiences, school psychologists, administrators, and other staff must have the necessary skills and knowledge to be fully prepared for all contingencies (e.g., tornado, bomb threat, suicide, or school intruder) and to put in place practices for crisis prevention, preparation, intervention, and follow-up. School psychologists who are aware of different types of crises and understand some of the commonalities that extend across all crises also will be more capable of responding successfully.

Some programs and curricula, such as NASP's PREPaRE and school-based threat assessment programs, can systematically improve schools' ability to anticipate, prepare for, and respond to crisis situations. The PREPaRE School Crisis Prevention and Intervention Training Curriculum, developed by the National Association of School Psychologists (NASP), is an evidence-based resource for improving school readiness and response (Brock et al., 2016). The acronym stands for the following:

Prevent and **P**repare for psychological trauma
Reaffirm physical health and perceptions of security and safety
Evaluate psychological trauma risk
Provide interventions
and
Respond to psychological needs
Examine the effectiveness of crisis prevention and intervention

The curriculum is divided into two parts: Workshop 1 is Comprehensive School Safety Planning: Prevention Through Recovery; Workshop 2 is Mental Health Crisis Interventions: Responding to an Acute Traumatic Stressor in Schools. In the United States, over 9,000 individuals have completed Workshop 1 and over 11,000 individuals have completed Workshop 2. Information about the workshops, available training opportunities, and trainers can be found on the NASP (2019) website.

Crisis Prevention and Preparation

Although many crises cannot be prevented, schools can take steps to minimize the chance that a crisis will occur. Prevention efforts may take many forms, including training, education, and security enhancements. For example, by making changes to the physical environment, crisis teams can identify and eliminate or reduce spaces where individuals who wish to do harm to others could remain undetected. Other steps include restricting access, managing visitors, and training faculty and staff to maintain a consistent visitor screening policy. Good crisis prevention activities also can minimize the degree to which individuals experience and perceive a crisis. Although sometimes a school community will experience a crisis regardless of the amount of preparation and planning, schools and districts that prepare for a crisis can make the adjustment and coping easier for the school community. Also, by developing the capacity to respond to significant events, schools are creating a more resilient school climate and culture (Reeves et al., 2012).

For example, School A and School B are both in the path of a tornado. The crisis team at School A has prepared faculty, staff, and students for tornados by developing and practicing a detailed response plan. School B is unprepared. Though the tornado caused only superficial damage to both schools and resulted in no injuries, School B experienced a crisis and School A did not. Why? In School A, everyone knew what to expect and what to do, so they were able to effectively cope with the natural disaster. Because School B was unprepared, chaos and panic ensued. Thus, School A did not prevent the tornado, but it did avert a crisis.

In addition to growth in prevention and preparation efforts, the past decade has also witnessed greater interest in threat assessment methods as a means of preventing violence. Cornell and colleagues (2018) studied a state-mandated threat assessment program in Virginia public schools to better understand the impact of such efforts. Using a multidisciplinary team, the Virginia model collects data to assess the seriousness of a threat so that appropriate actions may be taken. Such student threat assessments are systematic ways of identifying threats, evaluating the seriousness of them, and intervening appropriately (NASP, 2015). Ideally, schools that apply high-quality threat assessment will not overreact to nonserious threats and will not miss opportunities to prevent serious threats from becoming crises. The review of Virginia's program of threat assessment in public schools yielded some important findings. For example, threats made by elementary school students were not as likely to be deemed serious when compared with threats made by older students. Threats made by students receiving special education services were significantly more likely to be rated as serious, perhaps because of implicit bias. Cornell and colleagues concluded that sound threat assessment practices have the potential to better identify serious threats and to direct students toward appropriate mental health supports or law enforcement to prevent violence.

Crisis Teams

One of the best ways that school psychologists can involve themselves in crisis prevention and preparation is by participating in a crisis team (or by forming a team if one does not exist). Kerr

(2009) provides a set of characteristics and qualifications for crisis team members. Those include the ability to perform multiple tasks under pressure, awareness of developmental differences in the students they serve, commitment to continuing educational efforts in the area of crisis, effective communication skills in stressful situations, and an understanding and application of rules regarding confidentiality. Moreover, practical factors must be taken into consideration; for example, classroom teachers should not be given a role that would require removing them from their students in a crisis. Jaksec (2007) notes that crisis team members must also have a willingness to learn, patience, and courage.

The composition of a crisis team will vary based on the unique characteristics of each school. Kerr (2009) recommends the following membership:

- School principal or another administrator to take on a leadership role
- Someone who can act as a leader if the principal or administrator is absent
- Off-site manager without direct responsibility for students (perhaps from a centralized district office)
- Security team member (e.g., student resource officer or security guard)
- Medical responder (often the school nurse, or a faculty or staff member who has specialized training in this area)
- Communications coordinator (an individual who may need to work with interpreters to ensure that communications are accessible to all)
- Mental health specialist
- Facilities manager (e.g., custodian or building superintendent)
- Other (to be determined based on the unique needs of the setting)

The composition of the suggested crisis team provides a division of labor with clear roles for members. The crisis team's policies and procedures can provide specific details regarding the roles and functions of the various members. For example, in the U.S. Department of Homeland Security model, an Incident Command System (ICS) with an incident commander can be helpful for organizing the response (Reeves et al., 2012). The team's capacity to respond effectively and efficiently to a crisis will depend largely on the degree to which roles and responsibilities are clear. Crisis teams must also be culturally competent, representative of the school's diversity, and aware of cultural biases (Ortiz & Voutsinas, 2012).

Schools exist in communities and frequently interface with community resources when preparing for and responding to crises. For example, police and fire departments often respond to school crises, and the juvenile justice system plays a role in addressing the criminal activity of youth. Community agencies can help schools with training, collaboration, and coordination of services (Kerr, 2009). Schools in turn can provide community resource personnel with valuable information, such as building layouts and floor plans, as part of the crisis preparation process. Metzgar (2002) recommends that a parent or Parent–Teacher Association member serve on the crisis committee as well.

Given the roles described above, the school psychologist would be a good candidate for the mental health specialist role. However, school psychologists may also be able to use their role as family, school, and community collaborator on a crisis team. Any individual member of the team should have a clearly defined role; the school psychologist should consider personal strengths and potential contributions but also set some realistic limits and share responsibilities. Each school psychologist comes to the crisis team with a unique set of skills and interests that should also be considered in the context of the crisis team. School counselors are often in key roles as well, given their training in mental health skills, on-site location, and familiarity with administrators, teachers, students, and other staff. When school psychologists are itinerant, the school counselor may be in a key mental health role, with the school psychologist being available for counseling, collaboration, or community liaison as needed. In some cases, school psychologists may also feel less visible or overlooked when crisis teams are formed. Therefore they may need to step up so that others are aware of the mental health resources that are available. Any individual counselor could become overwhelmed and require mental health support and backup if in the key mental health role.

When developing crisis prevention and preparation plans, the crisis team should consider the school's and community's history, geography, and culture. The team should answer the following questions:

- What crises have been experienced at this school or in this community in the past?
- Are we at risk for any natural disasters based on past experiences?
- Has there been a history of violence at the school or in the community?
- How have the school and community responded to stressful situations in the past?

Kern, Benson, and Clemens (2010) recommend a community assessment to consider factors such as "institutionalized poverty, gang and drug activity, or lack of activities or resources to positively engage young people" (p. 467). These variables may contribute to a climate of stress and have the effect of normalizing violence. It is especially important to educate crisis team members who are new to the region and may be unaware of these historical and community-specific factors.

The future cannot be predicted, but anticipating potential crises can help a school be better prepared and also plan for novel situations. Whereas reviewing the past involves taking an inventory of what has happened, thinking about the future requires speculating about possibilities and answering questions like the following:

- What are the most likely crises our school and community may experience in the future?
- What changes (in demographics, technology, culture, or climate) might lead to new crisis situations?
- Based on trends in other schools and communities, what might we anticipate in the coming years?

Assessment of community variables can lead directly to school–community partnering to prevent violence, such as the development of greater opportunities for supervised activities for children and adolescents when they are not in school (Kern et al., 2010). In some cases, school facilities may be used in the afternoons by organizations that provide opportunities for youth involvement (e.g., scouting groups, Big Brothers Big Sisters). Though crisis teams tend to focus on preparing for crises, they have an opportunity to play a role in prevention as well.

Crisis teams should develop clear policies and procedures that are published and can be accessed by faculty, staff, and community support organizations (e.g., police, fire, EMS). Should a traumatic or unexpected event occur, teachers might not recall the different procedures for fires, bomb threats, tornadoes, and so forth. Therefore, the printed crisis plan can quickly put the information in the hands of those who need it. Kerr (2009) recommends that these procedures be included in "go kits" for teachers and staff that also contain essentials such as class rosters, a flashlight, a first aid kit, and other items needed for effective crisis management. (More information can be found at the U.S. Department of Education Readiness and Emergency Management Technical Assistance Center website.)

Procedures for emergencies should be specific to each building or campus, as generic instructions for evacuations and other crisis responses would likely lack the specificity necessary for practical applications. Consequently, changes to buildings or personnel should be reflected in revisions to crisis policies and procedures. Moreover, new faculty and staff, as well as substitute teachers, should receive orientations in the crisis policies and procedures.

The school psychologist must know how to quickly access and apply the crisis intervention plan for a given event. All too often, school staff may not know the exact location of a campus plan, the plan may not have been updated, or the staff may not have been trained recently. When entering a new school position, the school psychologist is obligated to make certain that crisis intervention procedures are current, readily available, and regularly shared through staff training, even if this responsibility technically belongs to another individual or group, such as school administrators.

Communication is a critical function of a crisis response team. In the event of a crisis, information needs to be shared with students, parents, community support systems (e.g., police, fire, and EMS personnel), and in most cases the media. When communication is unclear or inconsistent, rumors and misinformation may spread, resulting in increased confusion, stress, and harm. To ensure that individuals have access to accurate information, schools should consider disseminating information through a consistent script, delivered to students and parents by teachers or administrators. One member of the crisis team should be designated as a media contact, and staff should direct all media inquiries to that individual. When communicating to parents, the school representatives should explain the basic details of the event, what actions are being taken, how students are likely to respond, and where to go for help (Metzgar, 2002).

Crisis Response and Counseling

One of the ways school psychologists can be most helpful in a school crisis is through the coordination and provision of crisis counseling services. Rather than addressing social, emotional, and behavioral goals to promote success in school, home, and community, crisis counseling specifically focuses on the short-term goals of helping individuals cope and return to normalcy while minimizing the probability of long-term trauma. Crisis counseling also includes a psychoeducational component that provides individuals with information that will help them cope in the long term (e.g., teach them that sounds or smells may trigger memories of the traumatic incident). In this respect, crisis counseling is sometimes considered to be a form of psychological assistance rather than psychotherapy. Those who do not benefit from the psychological assistance may be referred for more targeted psychotherapy.

When a large number of people have been affected by a crisis, one school psychologist cannot possibly provide crisis counseling to everyone affected. Recognizing the need for indirect service delivery models in such cases, Caplan (1970) developed his model of consultation as an indirect service based on the belief that mental health improves when support systems improve. To meet students' needs, faculty and staff need to function well, so mental health specialists such as school psychologists and counselors indirectly serve students by enhancing teachers' effectiveness through consultation. In this respect, consultants (school psychologists, school counselors, social workers, etc.) empower those who work directly with children on a daily basis to meet their needs. Those not trained in crisis counseling can help students by reassuring them, answering questions honestly with factual information, and listening (Kerr, 2009).

The school psychologist may also coordinate with mental health specialists outside of the school setting, particularly when a large-scale crisis affects a community and external crisis counselors are sent for support (Metzgar, 2002). Coordination of services prevents redundancies, maintains consistency, and ensures that there are not gaps in services. Trained responders to a traumatic event will provide "*psychological first aid*: emotional support, psychoeducation about our experience and what to expect, information about what we can do or how our routines change, safety, medical care, shelter, and food" (note that there is an evidence-based model developed by the National Child Traumatic Stress Network called Psychological First Aid; Kerr, 2009, pp. 143–147). For coordination of services from outside the school to be effective, campus personnel need to be informed that unfamiliar people will be working on their campus. Advance preparation may minimize confusion, resentment, and fear when unfamiliar individuals are in the building following a crisis situation.

Sandoval, Scott, and Padilla (2009) emphasize the importance of preventing posttraumatic stress disorder (PTSD) in children following a crisis, noting that the school can serve as "an important environment where prevention and healing can take place" (p. 251). By offering support and promoting adaptive coping, school psychologists can help facilitate a healthy transition from crisis to normalcy. Two empirically validated approaches, Trauma-Focused Cognitive–Behavior Therapy (TF-CBT) and Cognitive–Behavioral Intervention for Trauma in Schools (CBITS), became important components of Project Fleur-de-lis, which was developed to assist children affected by Hurricane Katrina in 2005. Based on a three-tier model and response to intervention, Project Fleur-de-lis provides treatments at the intensity level needed for each individual (e.g., group psychosocial support, or referral for CBITS or Tier 3 TF-CBT, as indicated). Research has shown that these interventions are helping to reduce symptoms of PTSD and depression (Jaycox et al., 2010).

School psychologists and other mental health specialists must also be aware of their own experience of grief and trauma (Burns, 2010). A survey of school psychologists regarding crisis response work indicated that the vast majority of those who had participated in crisis intervention experienced one or more negative reactions (Bolnik & Brock, 2005). Self-care is important for professionals helping with a crisis response and should not be neglected (Pearrow & Jacob, 2012). Moreover, the school psychologist should be aware of the needs of other helping adults (e.g., counselors, teachers, staff) and make appropriate referrals as needed. Even if those adults have not dealt directly with loss during the crisis, working with grieving children can take a toll even on mental health specialists, so self-care must be prioritized (self-care is addressed in Chapter 12). Sufficient personnel should be available so that frontline responders can take needed breaks for rest, food, and support.

Debriefing following a crisis has been recommended as a critical process for all affected parties (Metzgar, 2002). Researchers have been unable to demonstrate that debriefing is an evidence-based activity, perhaps because there is not a uniform protocol for postcrisis debriefing. Anecdotal evidence suggests that debriefing is helpful to crisis victims as well as responders. Reported benefits of debriefing include the opportunity for responders to share factual information, answer questions, and normalize reactions (Kerr, 2009). Staff debriefing also reportedly helps assess the degree to which the crisis intervention was successful so that improvements can be made in the future. However, Wei, Szumilas, and Kutcher (2010) summarized the research on debriefing in the schools and concluded that the interventions were ineffective and possibly even harmful. Potentially harmful effects of debriefing have been attributed to increasing distress without allowing sufficient time to manage symptoms (Bisson, McFarlane, & Rose, 2000). Others have argued that because debriefing is not empirically supported, it may be, at best, a waste of resources (McNally, Bryant, & Ehlers, 2003). Recommended alternatives include protocols such as psychological first aid and cognitive–behavioral interventions for trauma in schools. Others have suggested that in cases of war or terrorism, psychological debriefing may be expected and should be provided carefully by a trained mental health professional (Castro-Olivio, Albeg, & Begum, 2012). School psychologists should exercise caution in this area and collect data to determine whether such actions are efficacious.

Related Topics

School psychologists may find themselves working with students who experience thoughts of suicide and assisting school communities in the aftermath of a completed suicide. They also work with students experiencing grief and loss. These important roles extend to helping school personnel recognize and respond to students experiencing such difficulties.

Suicide

According to the Centers for Disease Control and Prevention (CDC, 2016), suicide is the second leading cause of death (after accidents and homicides) for individuals between the ages of 10 and 23. Suicide and self-harm are attempted and completed by individuals of various ages, races, socioeconomic levels, and religions, though some cultural groups have higher rates than others (Goldston et al., 2008; Jobes, Berman, & Martin, 2005). For example, the highest youth suicide rates are found among Native American/Alaskan Native and Hispanic youth (CDC, 2019). Working with suicidal clients and responding to the aftermath of a suicide are among the most challenging tasks that mental health professionals perform. This section provides some background information on suicide and intervention; some structured, concrete strategies that can be used to help stabilize students who are suicidal; and an overview of effective school responses to completed suicides.

School psychologists and other school-based mental health specialists must be prepared to work with students who show signs of suicidal ideation, but a 2008 American Association of Suicidology study found that 78% of National Association of School Psychologist (NASP) members surveyed reported that their graduate training did not adequately prepare them to work with suicidal youth (as cited in Berman, 2009, p. 234). In contrast, a more recent survey of graduate directors from NASP-approved programs indicated that overall, adequate training in suicide prevention and intervention is provided (Liebling-Boccio & Jennings, 2013). Given these differing results, graduate educators are encouraged to ensure that training in this area establishes a foundational knowledge base on suicide.

In 2012, the U.S. Department of Health and Human Services published a national strategy for suicide prevention that detailed specific goals and objectives: develop community-based prevention programs, implement training to improve the identification of at-risk behaviors, promote prevention research, and others. The report specifically identifies schools as an integral site for suicide prevention and makes multiple references to schools in the document. For example, the authors note that suicide prevention can be enhanced by expanding existing health education curricula in schools to encompass mental health and suicide awareness and prevention components. The report recognizes the need to reduce risk factors and bolster protective factors, and it cites a three-tier model of prevention (universal, selected or targeted, and indicated or intensive) as appropriate for settings such as schools. Miller and Mazza (2017) provide evidence-based interventions for suicidal behavior and also use a tiered prevention model.

Though more research is needed regarding suicide prevention, some useful findings can be applied to school settings (Miller & Mazza, 2017). For example, sharing information with students and staff about suicide tends to produce more mental health referrals and does not inadvertently increase risk. Unfortunately, universal prevention programs have yet to demonstrate that they work, largely because of the superficial nature of such programs (Berman, 2009). However, comprehensive programs such as the Miami-Dade Youth Suicide Prevention and Intervention Program (Zenere & Lazarus, 2009) have demonstrated efficacy over time, but they need to be studied further before experts in suicidology will fully endorse them (Berman, 2009). More recently, research has shown some preliminary support for a suicide prevention and depression awareness program called Surviving the Teens (King, Strunk, & Sorter, 2011; Strunk et al., 2014).

Kerr (2009) provides a detailed example of a suicide policy and procedures document that could be adapted for a school or district using local details. The components of the policy and procedure example include prevention, preparation, response, and recovery. Prevention efforts include developmentally appropriate guidance on healthy choices, safety, and the importance of reporting concerns about peers. Preparation requires training staff to detect warning signs and make appropriate referrals (see Gibbons & Studer, 2008, for a teacher training model). The bulk of the policy and procedures document, which outlines how a school responds to suicidal threats and suicidal acts (both on and off school property), is reserved for the response. Recovery refers to the postvention activities of the crisis support team. A suicide policy and procedures document should be regularly updated and revised to reflect changes in staff, community resources, and local needs. It is the responsibility of the school crisis team to develop and maintain the suicide policy and procedures document.

School psychologists must be aware of risk factors and indicators of suicidal ideation so that they can intervene when needed, and they should promote prevention and early intervention in schools and communities. Most suicidal individuals display signs of or clues about their feelings (Jobes et al., 2005). The CDC lists the following risk factors:

- History of previous suicide attempts
- Family history of suicide

- History of depression or other mental illness
- Alcohol or drug abuse
- Stressful life event or loss
- Easy access to lethal methods
- Exposure to the suicidal behavior of others
- Incarceration

When working with an individual, school psychologists should look closely for indications of hopelessness, verbal and nonverbal indications of suicidal ideation (both direct and indirect), and artifacts such as drawings or journal entries that suggest self-harm. Comments from students, such as "Things would be so much better if I were gone," should be regarded as possible indicators and should be addressed with further probing (Jobes et al., 2005).

Many clinicians are uncomfortable with speaking directly to clients about suicide, in part because of social mores and perhaps because they fear that talking about suicide may make the client more likely to follow through with it. However, talking specifically about suicidal thoughts and plans is the most responsible and effective course of action (Jobes et al., 2005).

Designed as a general approach to crisis response, the seven-stage crisis intervention model developed by Roberts (1991) has been applied to suicide by Jobes and colleagues (2005). Although the components of the model are presented sequentially, application of the model does not necessary follow a linear sequence. For example, parts of the action plan (Stage 6) may be put into place immediately using information gathered in the initial assessment (Stage 1). Roberts's seven-stage model is as follows:

- Stage 1: Assessing lethality or risk
- Stage 2: Establishing rapport and communication
- Stage 3: Identifying major problems
- Stage 4: Providing support
- Stage 5: Exploring alternatives
- Stage 6: Developing an action plan
- Stage 7: Providing follow-up

As applied to suicide, Stage 1 (assessing lethality) is essentially risk assessment. When a student has directly or indirectly communicated thoughts of suicide or self-harm, the school psychologist or another trained mental health specialist must assess the danger. The assessment of lethality typically results in one of three courses of action: (a) emergency psychiatric treatment for imminent threats; (b) counseling or psychotherapy for significant concerns that do not pose an imminent threat; and (c) education, validation, and emotional support for concerns that, based on assessment, do not indicate the potential for self-harm.

Professionals should not be afraid to ask, "Have you been thinking about suicide?" Asking such questions can help identify risk and inform treatment decisions, and it may provide some feelings of relief for the student. If the student discloses suicidal ideation, then the counselor attempts to assess the level of risk by directly inquiring about "(a) psychological intent, (b) the suicide plan, (c) the history of previous suicidal behavior, and (d) clinical risk variables" (Jobes et al., 2005, p. 403).

Psychological intent refers to the individual's motivation, which may be an attempt to eliminate painful or hopeless feelings. Alternatively, some youth report that their intent is to gain more attention (Berman & Jobes, 1991). Having an understanding of the student's goal helps paint a clearer clinical picture and informs the focus of the intervention.

Students who show signs of hopelessness or suicidal ideation should be asked whether they have a suicide plan. Those who have a detailed plan are at greater risk than those who have a vague plan or no plan at all. Specificity (location, time, and method) is considered to be high risk. Access to guns, pills, or other methods should be determined and, if present, should be removed; here collaboration with families may be instrumental. Of particularly high risk are plans that involve an irreversible method (e.g., gun, as opposed to pill overdose) with minimal chance of rescue (e.g., an isolated location; Jobes et al., 2005).

School psychologists have an ethical and legal responsibility to notify parents or guardians of their child's suicidal ideation (Berman, 2009). Though the school psychologist has made a commitment to maintain confidentiality with the student, the agreement should always include limits of confidentiality that include risk of self-harm (see Chapter 1 for a discussion of confidentiality). An exception is made when the student discloses parental abuse, in which case a report must be filed with child protective services (Lieberman, Poland, & Cowan, 2006). Also, families should always be an integral component of the school's intervention (Goldston et al., 2008).

Stage 2 (establishing rapport and communication) is critical when the risk of suicide is present. The focus of this stage is building a strong therapeutic relationship, which may be challenging when the student did not self-refer. Establishing a relationship is important in all counseling, but given the potential risk of suicide, the counselor must work more quickly to build trust and rapport when students are suicidal. Because these students are likely to feel hopeless and powerless, the counselor must be more involved and directive so that the student feels more stability (Jobes et al., 2005). At this stage, the likelihood of the student accepting intervention is enhanced by the perception that the school psychologist is empathetic, is able to tolerate intense feelings, and has some degree of familiarity and comfort with effective interventions. Such a reassuring stance can help to build hope.

Stage 3 (identifying major problems) is, like the first stage, an assessment process. However, whereas the first stage's focus is risk assessment, the aim of the third stage is to gather information with more breadth and depth. Through a detailed clinical interview, the counselor should gather information about the student's history (health, developmental, social, educational, etc.), current status, risk variables, and resources (internal and external). A comprehensive assessment will also collect data from other sources (e.g., parents and teachers) and use other methods, such as norm-referenced behavior rating scales and measures of suicidality (e.g., the Modified Scale for Suicidal Ideation). Just as the risk assessment is important for psychiatric triage (determining whether the student needs hospitalization or other safety measures), the assessment at the third stage is valuable for informing and guiding the intervention.

Stage 4 (providing support) involves connecting emotionally with the student with empathy. Students who are suicidal experience pain, so it is essential that the counselor communicate an understanding of the student's subjective experience of pain (Jobes et al., 2005). This aim can be achieved in several ways, but the fundamental listening and counseling skills are the basis of this stage. Jobes and colleagues also recommend a subjective rating scale of emotional pain (e.g., ranging from 0 to 10) to help the counselor understand the level of pain, reduce some abstraction, and provide an ongoing measure of progress.

Regarding treatment modalities, evidence has not shown whether some therapeutic approaches are better than others. A study that compared a skills-based, cognitive–behavioral treatment protocol with a supportive relationship treatment protocol for adolescents who had attempted suicide found significant improvement in both groups (e.g., decreases in suicidal ideation and depressed mood), but no significant difference between the groups (Donaldson, Spirito, & Esposito-Smythers, 2005). An Australian study of adults found that specialized, structured therapeutic approaches (e.g., cognitive–behavioral therapy and problem-solving therapy) were more effective than case management (Stewart et al., 2009).

Stage 5 of Roberts's (1991) seven-stage model (exploring alternatives) involves working with the student to inventory stressors and strengths so that alternatives to suicide can be established (Jobes et al., 2005). This may be particularly challenging when cognitive distortions mask the assets and place too much emphasis on the perceived deficits. In such cases, the therapist may find that a cognitive–behavioral approach is indicated so that negative thinking can be replaced with more adaptive cognitions.

Stage 6 (developing an action plan) for a suicidal student primarily involves taking steps to maximize the immediate safety of the student and to make the transition from crisis to resolution (Hoff, 1995). When a student is determined to be at risk for suicide, the school and family must collaborate to eliminate the student's access to lethal means (e.g., guns, pills). The action plan begins the process of moving from the present crisis to a future with a resolution. This process helps the student visualize "a different and hopefully better future, creating distance from the immediate crisis" (Jobes et al., 2005). Students who are at risk should also be monitored closely and never left alone; hospitalization may be necessary for safety. Although it is often recommended that the counselor negotiate a no-harm contract with the student (basically, the student agrees to not engage in harmful behaviors between counseling sessions, and the contract is renewed each session), this practice is not universally supported. Hyldahl and Richardson (2009) note that such contracts depend largely on the quality of the counselor–client relationship, and that in the absence of a strong relationship, the contract may be ineffective. In their review of the literature regarding no-suicide contracts, Rudd, Mandrusiak, and Joiner (2006) concluded that such contracts lack empirical support, and they suggest using "commitment to treatment" as an alternative. Rather than asking the client to sign a contract, the counselor asks the client to attend counseling sessions and commit to working with the counselor on reducing symptoms to maintain safety.

Finally, Stage 7 (providing follow-up) involves the counseling that occurs after the immediate crisis has resolved, as well as additional risk assessment. The history of a suicide attempt places an individual at a greater risk for future attempts, so the counselor should not assume that resolution of the present crisis means that another crisis will not emerge (Jobes et al., 2005).

Smith noted that schools should be sensitive to transitional needs of students who are returning to school after hospitalization (as cited in Ryerson & Kalafat, 2002, p. 104). In the interest of providing ongoing support, school staff may visit the student prior to discharge, collaborate with hospital staff regarding continuity of care, and assist with missed academic work. Schools may also provide mentoring, monitoring, individual and/or group counseling, and coordination with outside providers.

Numerous postvention school procedures for a completed suicide have been published in a variety of sources and are summarized by Ryerson & Kalafat (2002). First, a faculty or staff meeting should be called before the next school day during which everyone has an opportunity to communicate reactions and offer and receive support. To ensure that students receive accurate information, faculty and staff should agree upon a standard account that will be shared. The school should also prepare to identify any other students who may be at risk, including family, close friends, and those who appear to have strong reactions to the suicide. Schools must be aware of the potential risk of contagion, or "the process by which suicidal behavior or a suicide influences an increase in the suicidal behaviors of others" (Zenere, 2009, p. 12).

The next steps are as follows:

- Share a prepared statement with students.
- Set up crisis counseling spaces on campus for 2 to 3 days for individual or group support and allow students to leave class to access these resources. Continue to offer support as needed following the initial postvention period.
- Maintain contact, support, and monitoring of at-risk students.
- Hold a meeting for concerned parents, but exclude the media from the meeting. Provide parents with details of the school's postvention activities and resources. Media inquiries can be addressed with a statement that includes referral sources and risk indicators. Only one school official should be in contact with the media.
- Have the crisis team continue to engage in frequent debriefing sessions and have a follow-up faculty meeting.

Grief and Loss

Most children and adolescents experience loss at some point in their lives, so school psychologists must be prepared to assist students in such situations (Barrett & Nichols, 2017). Loss can potentially affect a child socially, emotionally, and academically (Burns, 2010). Ultimately, the form of support most needed by grieving students is empathic listening.

Burns (2010) provides a set of definitions for key terms related to grief and loss that are useful for differentiating concepts:

- *Loss* refers to the end of a relationship with a person or thing.
- *Bereavement* is the state of having suffered a loss.
- *Grief* is an individual's response to loss.
- *Mourning* refers to the process (public and private) of coping with loss.

A variety of events can bring about loss, and though it is often associated with death, loss may also be unrelated to death. Children may experience loss when parents divorce or when a friend moves away. A student who dreams of being on an athletic team but is not selected may experience loss, just as parents who learn that their child has been diagnosed with a disability may feel the loss of their idealized future for their child. Such non-death-related losses are collectively known as *nonfinite loss* (Burns, 2010).

When providing support to someone who is mourning following a death, the counselor should seek to understand the loss from the student's perspective—how the individual died, whether the loss was anticipated, and the context of the loss—to better inform treatment. For example, a case study of the school-based response to Hurricanes Katrina and Rita noted that the stressors associated with multiple losses in a natural disaster (e.g., loss of loved ones, loss of home, loss of personal belongings) necessitate a "persistent, compassionate and attentive engagement process" (Clettenberg et al., 2011).

The counselor should always consider developmental factors when supporting a student who knows someone who has died (Comerchero, 2017). Webb (2011) provides an overview of developmental patterns, noting that children do not develop a "mature" understanding of death (e.g., that it is permanent) until age 8 or 9. Preschool children may feel responsible or guilty and fail to understand that the person who died is not coming back (particularly when euphemisms such as passed away are used). Preschool children may also demonstrate anxiety and regression, such as a return to behaviors that had previously been discontinued, such as bed-wetting and thumb sucking (Graydon, Jimerson, & Fisher, 2010). Adults are encouraged to be patient with children and to explain death accurately to avoid confusion, but they also should recognize that although young children may not fully understand death, they are likely aware of others' emotions (Mauk & Sharpnack, 2006).

Older school-age children come to understand death better but may assume that only old people die. The idea of culpability may continue to be a concern, particularly if a child believes that they could have done something to prevent someone's death. Some have argued that the rapid developmental changes occurring in early adolescence (ages 11–14) may make adjustment to loss even more challenging for this population (O'Halloran, Ingala, & Copeland, 2005). Individual factors may also affect a child's grief following a death, such as the child's relationship with the deceased, whether the child participated in rituals (e.g., viewing, funeral), and the nature of the death (e.g., anticipated or unexpected, traumatic; Mauk & Sharpnack, 2006; Webb, 2011). High school students may appear depressed or withdrawn and sometimes display academic or peer problems (Graydon et al., 2010). Adolescents are capable of increased abstract reasoning and may think philosophically about death and dying (Busch & Kimble, 2001).

Understanding context may also assist mental health professionals in determining whether childhood traumatic grief has occurred (Cohen & Mannarino, 2011). Cohen and Mannarino (2004) define childhood traumatic grief as "a condition in which a child or adolescent has lost a loved one in circumstances that are objectively or subjectively traumatic and in which trauma symptoms impinge on the child's ability to negotiate the normal grieving process" (p. 819). If a child experiences a death as traumatic (even if adults do not experience it as such), then traumatic grief may occur. Whereas most crisis counseling is geared toward quickly restoring normalcy and coping, children experiencing childhood traumatic grief may need more focused counseling, such as trauma-focused cognitive–behavioral therapy over a longer period of time (Cohen & Mannarino, 2011).

Burns (2010) developed a conceptual framework for understanding grief responses that takes into account "the physical, psychological, social, emotional, cultural, and environmental issues that variably affect each griever and draws from multiple perspectives" (p. 18). The framework's acronym, PRECEDENT, stands for the following elements:

Personality traits of the individual
Relationship with the person being grieved
Experience with loss
Culture and values with respect to grief and emotional expression
Environmental factors (e.g., socioeconomic status, social support, community)
Development (cognitive, linguistic, emotional, social)
Equilibrium or balance between grief and moving forward with life
Nature of the loss (e.g., anticipated or not, traumatic or not, finite or not)
Transcendence, or one's capacity to find meaningful ways of coping

The PRECEDENT framework may be most useful for understanding the diverse ways in which individuals express grief and some of the contributing factors. Counselors should not expect all students to grieve the same way and may find the model helpful for understanding the experiences of grieving children and adolescents. Families have diverse perspectives on death, and the school psychologist should make every effort to respect a wide range of cultural responses to loss. School psychologists who train faculty and staff about grief responses should include acceptance of cultural differences with respect to death.

Children with developmental disabilities face unique challenges associated with grief (Comerchero, 2017; Sormanti & Ballan, 2011). For example, adults may erroneously assume that children with developmental disabilities are unable to grieve as a result of their disability, and signs of grief may be misinterpreted as unrelated mental health concerns. School psychologists can play an important role in identifying grief reactions among children with developmental disabilities and support their adaptive adjustments to loss.

Graydon and colleagues (2010) note that support for grieving students can be provided at multiple levels in school settings, much like a tiered intervention model. At the first level, support comes naturally from parents, friends, teachers, and community members. School personnel should identify healthy and unhealthy grieving. This type of support is not considered therapeutic and comes from existing relationships. At the second level, teachers may provide psychoeducational interventions, and mental health specialists, including school psychologists, social workers, and school counselors, may provide individual and group counseling. The third level is for those students who are significantly impaired by their grief experience, and counseling interventions are provided by professionals with specialized skills in grief treatment. These interventions may include play therapy, bibliotherapy, cognitive–behavioral methods, or other techniques that are appropriate for the student and circumstances (Brown & Jimerson, 2017).

Though grieving one's loss is a normal process, school personnel should be aware of behaviors that may require intervention or referral to a specialist such as the school psychologist. Signs of depression (including a loss of interest in activities that were previously a source of pleasure), sleep disturbance, suicidal ideation, fear of being left alone, hallucinations unrelated to the deceased, a decline in psychomotor functioning, or a sudden decline in academic performance should be brought to the attention of the school psychologist or another mental health specialist (Graydon et al., 2010; Mauk & Sharpnack, 2006).

A number of protective factors have been identified that may contribute to healthy outcomes for individuals faced with loss. For example, secure attachment style, high self-efficacy, an internal locus of control, and adaptability are among the individual characteristics that may predict positive outcomes. Other factors, such as the circumstances surrounding the death (e.g., anticipated or nontraumatic), also play a role in the grieving experience (Hagan & Morford, 2017). Sahler (2000) reported that children cope better with the death of a loved one when they are allowed to ask questions and express their feelings.

Grief counseling requires patience and time, and children and adolescents tend to grieve intermittently and in highly individualized ways (Mauk & Sharpnack, 2006). As students develop over time, they may deal with grief repeatedly as they transition through developmental tasks (Barrett & Nichols, 2017). Because students are likely to benefit from peer support, school-based bereavement groups may be particularly helpful (Garcia, 2017). Adults working with children who have experienced death should provide honest information that is developmentally appropriate. Children need opportunities to talk about their loss and express their feelings (Mauk & Sharpnack, 2006). School psychologists may also support children by enhancing coping strategies (Mullen & Storie, 2012).

OTHER CONSIDERATIONS

Because numerous situations may occur that can result in crisis and loss for students and school personnel, this chapter could not possibly cover every contingency. However, by focusing on crises, suicide, and grief, it has addressed many of the key points that can be generalized to other concerns. The following considerations will be useful for school psychologists facing difficult and unique challenges:

- Always consider cultural variables, including family. Coping, communication, and expression of emotions vary considerably across cultures and families, and school psychologists must be sensitive to diversity (López, 2017).
- Partnering with families and other members of the community is critical for effective crisis intervention.
- The need for prevention and preparation cannot be understated, and school psychologists have an opportunity to play a pivotal role in these activities.
- Ultimately, crisis intervention is about being an empathic listener and helping individuals cope as they go through the transition from crisis to normalcy.

Effective crisis preparation and intervention requires core sets of knowledge and skills that may be introduced in graduate school but continue to develop throughout the career of the school psychologist. Those interested in this area may consider focusing their training on these content and skill domains. Starling, Elias, and Coleman (2019) have suggested that concentrations or specialties in school psychology may be appropriate to meet the diverse needs of children and schools, and a crisis specialization may be one such avenue.

SUMMARY

In this chapter we defined trauma and crisis and discussed the ways that school psychologists can help prepare for crisis situations that affect schools. We also described the unique nature of crisis counseling, as well as counseling skills to help students cope with grief and loss. We identified the skills and techniques that must be employed when a student discloses suicidal ideation for effective intervention. The school psychologist must have a broad repertoire of knowledge and skills to address the challenging situations that may arise in schools.

KEY POINTS FOR DISCUSSION

- Consider the ways in which school psychologists should prepare to effectively respond to crises.
- Identify the personal characteristics that would be helpful for crisis response and intervention.
- Discuss the ways in which school psychologists and families can collaborate to address a teen's suicidal ideation.

REFERENCES

Barrett, T., & Nichols, L. M. (2017). Defining loss: Preparing to support bereaved students. In J. A. Brown & S. R. Jimerson (Eds.), *Supporting bereaved students at school* (pp. 10–24). New York, NY: Oxford University Press.

Berman, A. L. (2009). School-based suicide prevention: Research advances and practice implications. *School Psychology Review, 38*, 233–238.

Berman, A. L., & Jobes, D. A. (1991). *Adolescent suicide: Assessment and intervention*. Washington, DC: American Psychological Association.

Bisson, J. I., McFarlane, A. C., & Rose, S. (2000). Psychological debriefing. In E. B. Foa, T. M. Keane, & M. J. Friedman (Eds.), *Effective treatments for PTSD* (pp. 53–105). New York, NY: Guilford Press.

Bolnik, L., & Brock, S. E. (2005). The self-reported effects of crisis intervention work on school psychologists. *California School Psychologist, 10*, 117–124.

Brock, S. E. (2012). Preparing for school crisis intervention. In S. E. Brock & S. R. Jimerson (Eds.), *Best practices in school crisis prevention and intervention* (2nd ed., pp. 265–283). Bethesda, MD: National Association of School Psychologists.

Brock, S. E., Nickerson, A. B., Reeves, M. A. L., Conolly, C. N., Jimerson, S. R., Pesce, R. C., & Lazarro, B. R. (2016). *School crisis prevention and intervention: The PREPaRE model* (2nd ed.). Bethesda, MD: National Association of School Psychologists.

Brown, J. A., & Jimerson, S. R. (2017). *Supporting bereaved students at school*. New York, NY: Oxford University Press.

Burns, D. M. (2010). *When kids are grieving: Addressing grief and loss in school*. Thousand Oaks, CA: Corwin.

Busch, T., & Kimble, C. S. (2001). Grieving children: Are we meeting the challenge? *Pediatric Nursing, 27*, 414–418.

Caplan, G. (1970). *Theory and practice of mental health consultation*. New York, NY: Basic Books.

Castro-Olivio, S., Albeg, L., & Begum, G. (2012). War and terrorism. In S. E. Brock & S. R. Jimerson (Eds.), *Best practices in school crisis prevention and intervention* (2nd ed., pp. 437–454). Bethesda, MD: National Association of School Psychologists.

Centers for Disease Control and Prevention (CDC). (2016). 10 leading causes of death by age group 2016. Retrieved from https://www.cdc.gov/injury/wisqars/pdf/leading_causes_of_death_by_age_group_2016-508.pdf

Centers for Disease Control and Prevention (CDC). (2019). National Vital Statistics Report https://www.cdc.gov/nchs/data/nvsr/nvsr68/nvsr68_06-508.pdf

Center for Homeland Defense and Security. (n.d.). K-12 School Shooting Database. Retrieved from https://www.chds.us/ssdb/

Chafouleas, S. M., Johnson, A. H., Overstreet, S., & Santos, N. M. (2016). Toward a blueprint for trauma-informed service delivery in schools. *School Mental Health, 8*, 144–162. https://doi.org/10.1007/s12310-015-9166-8

Clettenberg, S., Gentry, J., Held, M., & Mock, L. A. (2011). Traumatic loss and natural disaster: A case study of a school-based response to Hurricanes Katrina and Rita. *School Psychology International, 32*, 553–566. https://doi.org/10.1177/0143034311402928

Cohen, J. A., & Mannarino, A. P. (2004). Treatment of child traumatic grief. *Journal of Clinical Child and Adolescent Psychiatry, 33*, 819–831.

Cohen, J. A., & Mannarino, A. P. (2011). Supporting children with traumatic grief: What educators need to know. *School Psychology International, 32*, 117–131. doi:10.1207/s15374424jccp3304_17

Comerchero, V. A. (2017). Cognitive developmental considerations in supporting bereaved students. In J. A. Brown & S. R. Jimerson (Eds.), *Supporting bereaved students at school* (pp. 25–37). New York, NY: Oxford University Press.

Cornell, D., Maeng, J. L., Burnett, A. G., Jia, Y., Huang, F., Konold, T., . . . Meyer, P. (2018). Student threat assessment as a standard school safety practice: Results from a statewide implementation study. *School Psychology Quarterly, 33*, 213–222. https://doi.org/10.1037/spq0000220

Cox, J. W., & Rich, S. (2018). No, there haven't been 18 school shootings in 2018. That number is flat wrong. *The Washington Post*. Retrieved from https://www.washingtonpost.com/local/no-there-havent-been-18-school-shooting-in-2018-that-number-is-flat-wrong/2018/02/15/65b6cf72-1264-11e8-8ea1-c1d91fcec3fe_story.html

Donaldson, D., Spirito, A., & Esposito-Smythers, C. (2005). Treatment for adolescents following a suicide attempt: Results of a pilot trial. *Journal of the American Academy of Child and Adolescent Psychiatry, 44*, 113–120. doi:10.1097/00004583-200502000-00003

Garcia, R. B. (2017). Using grief support groups to support bereaved students. In J. A. Brown & S. R. Jimerson (Eds.) *Supporting bereaved students at school* (pp. 115–129). New York, NY: Oxford University Press.

Gibbons, M. M., & Studer, J. R. (2008). Suicide awareness training for faculty and staff: A training model for school counselors. *Professional School Counseling, 11*, 272–276.

Gil, E. (2012). Trauma-focused Integrated Play Therapy. In P. G. Brown (Ed.), *Handbook of child sexual abuse: Identification, assessment, and treatment* (pp. 251–278). New York, NY: Wiley & Sons.

Goldston, D. B., Molock, S. D., Whitbeck, L. B., Murakami, J. L., Zayas, L. H., & Hall, G. C. N. (2008). Cultural considerations in adolescent suicide prevention and psychosocial treatment. *American Psychologist, 63*, 14–31. doi:10.1037/0003-066X.63.1.14

Graydon, K. S., Jimerson, S. R., & Fisher, E. S. (2010). Death and grief in the family: Providing support at school. In A. Canter, L. Z. Paige, & S. Shaw (Eds.), *Helping children at home and school III: Handouts for families and educators* (pp. S9H6-1–S9H6-3). Bethesda, MD: National Association for School Psychologists.

Hagan, M. J., & Morford, A. (2017). Family considerations in supporting bereaved students. In J. A. Brown & S. R. Jimerson (Eds.), *Supporting bereaved students at school* (pp. 82–95). New York, NY: Oxford University Press.

Heath, M. A., Nickerson, A. B., Annandale, N., Kemple, A., & Dean, B. (2009). Strengthening cultural sensitivity in children's disaster mental health services. *School Psychology International, 30*, 347–373. https://doi.org/10.1177/0143034309106944

Hoff, L. A. (1995). *People in crisis*. Menlo Park, CA: Addison-Wesley.

Hyldahl, R. S., & Richardson, B. (2009). Key considerations for using no-harm contracts with clients who self-injure. *Journal of Counseling and Development, 89*, 121–127.

Jaksec, C. M. (2007). *Toward successful school crisis intervention: 9 key issues*. Thousand Oaks, CA: Corwin.

Jaycox, L. H., Cohen, J. A., Mannarino, A. P., Walker, D. W., Langley, A. K., Gegenheimer, K. L., Scott, M., & Schonlau, M. (2010). Children's mental health care following Hurricane Katrina: A field trial of trauma-focused psychotherapies. *Journal of Traumatic Stress, 23*, 223–231.

Jobes, D. A., Berman, A. L., & Martin, C. E. (2005). Adolescent suicidality and crisis intervention. In A. R. Roberts (Ed.), *Crisis intervention handbook: Assessment, treatment, and research* (3rd ed., pp. 395–415). New York, NY: Oxford University Press.

Kern, L., Benson, J. L., & Clemens, N. H. (2010). Strategies for working with severe challenging and violent behavior. In G. G. Peacock, R. A. Ervin, E. J. Daly, & K. W. Merrell (Eds.), *Practical handbook of school psychology: Effective practices for the 21st century* (pp. 459–474). New York, NY: Guilford Press.

Kerr, M. M. (2009). *School crisis prevention and intervention*. Upper Saddle River, NJ: Pearson.

King, K. A., Strunk, C. M., & Sorter, M. T. (2011). Preliminary effectiveness of Surviving the Teens Suicide Prevention and Depression Awareness Program on adolescents' suicidality and self-efficacy in performing help-seeking behaviors. *Journal of School Health, 81*, 581–590.

Lieberman, R., Poland, S., & Cowan, K. (2006). Suicide prevention and intervention. *Principal Leadership, 7*(2), 11–15.

Liebling-Boccio, D. E., & Jennings, H. R. (2013). The current status of graduate training in suicide risk assessment. *Psychology in the Schools, 50*, 72–86. https://doi.org/10.1002/pits.21661

López, S. A. (2017). Cross-cultural considerations in supporting bereaved students. In J. A. Brown & S. R. Jimerson (Eds.), *Supporting bereaved students at school* (pp. 70–81). New York, NY: Oxford University Press.

Mauk, G. W., & Sharpnack, J. D. (2006). Grief. In G. G. Bear & K. M. Minke (Eds.), *Children's needs III: Development, problems, and alternatives* (pp. 239–254). Bethesda, MD: National Association of School Psychologists.

McNally, R. J., Bryant, R. A., & Ehlers, A. (2003). Does early psychological intervention promote recovery from posttraumatic stress? *Psychological Science in the Public Interest, 4*(2), 45–79. https://doi.org/10.1111/1529-1006.01421

Metzgar, M. (2002). Preparing schools for crisis management. In R. G. Stevenson (Ed.), *What will we do? Preparing a school community to cope with crises* (2nd ed., pp. 25–43). Amityville, NY: Baywood.

Miller, D. N., & Mazza, J. J. (2017). Evidence-based interventions for suicidal behavior in children and adolescents. In L. A. Theodore (Ed.), *Handbook of evidence-based interventions for children and adolescents* (pp. 55–66). New York, NY: Springer.

Mullen, J. A., & Storie, M. S. (2012). Treating complicated grief. In S. E. Brock & S. R. Jimerson (Eds.), *Best practices in school crisis prevention and intervention* (2nd ed., pp. 671–679). Bethesda, MD: National Association of School Psychologists.

National Association of School Psychologists. (2015). Threat assessment for school administrators and crisis teams. Retrieved from https://www.nasponline.org/resources-and-publications/resources-and-podcasts/school-climate-safety-and-crisis/systems-level-prevention/threat-assessment-at-school/threat-assessment-for-school-administrators-and-crisis-teams

National Association of School Psychologists. (2019). PREPaRE training curriculum. https://www.nasponline.org/professional-development/prepare-training-curriculum

National Registry of Evidence-Based Programs and Practices (NREPP). (2016). Trauma-focused cognitive behavioral therapy. Retrieved from https://nrepp.samhsa.gov/ProgramProfile.aspx?id=96

O'Halloran, M. S., Ingala, A. M., & Copeland, E. P. (2005). Crisis intervention with early adolescents who have suffered a significant loss. In A. R. Roberts (Ed.), *Crisis intervention handbook: Assessment, treatment, and research* (3rd ed., pp. 362–394). New York, NY: Oxford University Press.

Ortiz, S. O., & Voutsinas, M. (2012). Cultural considerations in crisis intervention. In S. E. Brock & S. R. Jimerson (Eds.), *Best practices in school crisis prevention and intervention* (2nd ed., pp. 337–357). Bethesda, MD: National Association of School Psychologists.

Overstreet, S., & Chafouleas, S. M. (2016). Trauma-informed schools: Introduction to special issue. *School Mental Health, 8,* 1–6. https://doi.org/10.1007/s12310-016-9184-1

Pearrow, M. M., & Jacob, S. (2012). Legal and ethical considerations in crisis prevention and response in schools. In S. E. Brock & S. R. Jimerson (Eds.), *Best practices in school crisis prevention and intervention* (2nd ed., pp. 359–375). Bethesda, MD: National Association of School Psychologists.

Pollio, E., & Deblinger, E. (2017). Trauma-focused cognitive behavior therapy for young children: Clinical considerations. *European Journal of Psychotraumatology, 8*(Suppl 7), https://doi.org/10.1080/20008198.2018.1433929

Reeves, M. A. L., Connolly-Wilson, C. N., Pesce, R. C., Lazzaro, B. R., & Brock, S. E. (2012). In S. E. Brock & S. R. Jimerson (Eds.), *Best practices in school crisis prevention and intervention* (2nd ed., pp. 245–264). Bethesda, MD: National Association of School Psychologists.

Reinbergs, E. J., & Fefer, S. A. (2018). Addressing trauma in schools: Multitiered service delivery options for practitioners. *Psychology in the Schools, 55,* 250–263.

Roberts, A. R. (1991). *Contemporary perspectives on crisis intervention and prevention*. Englewood Cliffs, NJ: Prentice Hall.

Roberts, A. R. (2005). Bridging the past and present to the future of crisis intervention and crisis management. In A. R. Roberts (Ed.), *Crisis intervention handbook: Assessment, treatment, and research* (3rd ed., pp. 3–34). New York, NY: Oxford University Press.

Rudd, D. M., Mandrusiak, M., & Joiner, T. E. (2006). The case against no-suicide contracts: The commitment to treatment statement as a practice alternative. *Journal of Clinical Psychology: In Session, 62*, 243–251. doi:10.1002/jclp.20227

Ryerson, D., & Kalafat, J. (2002). The crisis of youth suicide. In R. G. Stevenson (Ed.), *What will we do? Preparing a school community to cope with crises* (2nd ed., pp. 91–107). Amityville, NY: Baywood.

Sahler, O. J. (2000). The child and death. *Pediatrics in Review, 21*, 350–353.

Salloum, A., Small, B. J., Robst, J., Scheeringa, M. S., Cohen, J. A., & Storch, E. A. (2017). Stepped and standard care for childhood trauma: A pilot randomized clinical trial. *Research on Social Work Practices, 27*, 653–663. https://doi.org/10.1177/1049731515601898

Sandoval, J., Scott, A. N., & Padilla, I. (2009). Crisis counseling: An overview. *Psychology in the Schools, 46*, 246–256. https://doi.org/10.1002/pits.20370

Sormanti, M., & Ballan, M. S. (2011). Strengthening grief support for children with developmental disabilities. *School Psychology International, 32*, 179–193. https://doi.org/10.1177/0143034311400831

Starling, N. R., Elias, E. M., & Coleman, M. S. (2019). Concentrations in school psychology: Can specialization empower the evolution of the profession? *Contemporary School Psychology*. Retrieved from https://doi.org/10.1007/s40688-019-00264-x

Steeves, R. M. O., Metallo, S. A., Byrd, S. M., Erickson, M. R., & Gresham, F. M. (2017). Crisis preparedness in schools: Evaluating staff perspectives and providing recommendations for best practice. *Psychology in the Schools, 54*, 563–580. https://doi.org/10.1002/pits.22017

Stewart, C. D., Quinn, A., Plever, S., & Emmerson, B. (2009). Comparing cognitive behavior therapy, problem solving therapy, and treatment as usual in a high risk population. *Suicide and Life-Threatening Behavior, 39*, 538–547. https://doi.org/10.1521/suli.2009.39.5.538

Strunk, C. M., King, K. A., Vidourek, R. A., & Sorter, M. T. (2014). Effectiveness of the Surviving the Teens suicide prevention and depression awareness program: An impact evaluation using a comparison group. *Health Education and Behavior, 41*, 605–613. https://doi.org/10.1177/1090198114531774

Substance Abuse and Mental Health Services Administration. (2014, October). *SAMHSA's concept of trauma and guidance for a trauma-informed approach*. HHS Publication No. (SMA) 14-4884. Retrieved from https://store.samhsa.gov/sites/default/files/d7/priv/sma14-4884.pdf

U.S. Department of Health and Human Services. (2012). National strategy for suicide prevention: Goals and objectives for action. Retrieved from https://www.ncbi.nlm.nih.gov/pubmed/23136686

Webb, N. B. (2011). Play therapy for bereaved children: Adapting strategies to community, school, and home settings. *School Psychology International, 32*, 132–143. https://doi.org/10.1177/0143034311400832

Wei, Y., Szumilas, M., & Kutcher, S. (2010). Effectiveness on mental health of psychological debriefing for crisis intervention in schools. *Educational Psychology Review, 22,* 339–347. https://doi.org/10.1007/s10648-010-9139-2

Zenere, F. J. (2009). Suicide clusters and contagion. *Principal Leadership, 10*(2), 12–16.

Zenere, F. J., & Lazarus, P. J. (2009). The sustained reduction of youth suicidal behavior in an urban, multicultural school district. *School Psychology Review, 38,* 189–199.

Chapter 10

Substance Abuse, Delinquency, and Psychopharmacology

OVERVIEW

This chapter addresses topics that may go beyond the scope of typical counseling theory and practice. When students engage in substance abuse or delinquent behavior, the responsibility for intervention often falls to administrators, law enforcement personnel, parents, and community providers. Similarly, when students are prescribed (or misuse) psychotropic medications, responsibility to intervene and monitor may be assigned solely to medical providers working with parents or guardians. School psychologists, however, work with students for whom these issues are relevant to their intervention. Substance use and abuse considerations include the scope of the problem, risk factors and warning signs, and consideration of comorbid disorders and developmental factors. Juvenile delinquency, which involves illegal behavior by minors, is discussed in relation to trauma history, comorbid disorders, school disciplinary practices, and outcomes, with attention to discriminatory practices. Because psychopharmacology is an increasingly common intervention for emotional and behavioral problems in school-age children, and some psychotropic drugs are subject to abuse, this chapter includes only basic information about drug classes, typical uses in pediatric populations, risks and benefits, roles of the school psychologist in medication monitoring, and resources for further information. Effective interventions for students with substance abuse and delinquency require attention not only to individual variables, such as trauma history and comorbid disorders, but also to family, school, and community systems and resources.

OBJECTIVES

After reading this chapter, readers should be able to do the following:
- Recognize the scope of the problem with respect to students affected by problems of substance abuse and delinquency.
- Identify risk factors for these problems.

- Recognize symptoms of substance abuse in the behaviors of students at school.
- Describe effective interventions for these problems.
- Describe psychotropic drug classifications and their typical appropriate uses in school-age populations.
- Consider ethical issues around pediatric psychopharmacology for school psychologists.
- Recognize the problem of abuse of psychotropic drugs.

Introduction

Many children and adolescents encounter situations of substance use, abuse, and dependency, whether these situations involve personal use, family-related use, peer use, or use by other involved persons. Gramlich (2017) reported that nearly half of Americans have a family member or close friend who has been addicted to drugs. Substance use disorder cuts across ethnicities, races, genders, education levels, socioeconomic groups, and family structures (SAMHSA, 2019). According to the *Diagnostic and Statistical Manual of Mental Disorders* (5th ed.; DSM-5), a substance use disorder is characterized by a problematic pattern of substance use that results in impairment in daily life or noticeable distress (American Psychiatric Association, 2013). The term *substance abuse* has been removed from the DSM-5 because of pejorative connotations; the term *substance use disorder* combines characteristics of substance dependence and substance abuse. Lipari and Van Horn (2017) add that substance use disorders result in problems such as inability to control use of the substance, failure to meet obligations at work, home, or school, poor health, and increased time obtaining, using, or recovering from the effects of using the substance. The terms *substance abuse* and *addiction* continue to be commonly encountered in the popular and research literature.

Behavioral and interpersonal dynamics that develop around substance use disorder tend to be complex, affecting the user and individuals within the user's realm emotionally and, in some cases, legally and financially. Children who live in families with substance abuse are at higher risk for depression, anxiety, cognitive difficulties, and parental abuse and neglect. These children are four times as likely as other children to develop substance abuse problems themselves, with increased risk for delinquency (Lipari & Van Horn, 2017). Rosenberg (2011), in advocating for trauma-informed treatment for substance abuse and mental health, pointed out that greater trauma results in greater risk for alcoholism and alcohol abuse, depression, illicit drug use, suicide attempts, and other negative outcomes.

Juvenile delinquency is defined as unlawful conduct by minors, meaning those under the age of 18 in most states. Some children and youth become involved with the juvenile justice system because they are accused of committing a criminal act, including drug-related crimes. Other youth encounter the juvenile justice system for behaviors that are illegal only because of their age, such as truancy, underage drinking, and running away from home (youth.gov, n.d.). Juvenile delinquency disrupts family, school, and social life and may leave youth with legal burdens. If incarceration follows, it multiplies developmental, emotional, behavioral, and educational issues. Substance abuse and juvenile delinquency frequently co-occur (Mulvey, 2011).

School psychologists must recognize warning signs that require intervention when substance abuse is present and worsening. Consider the following example of a student who manifested warning signs throughout his school years.

Andrew was diagnosed with severe attention deficit hyperactivity disorder (ADHD) in early childhood. He was extremely distractible, hyperactive, and impulsive, and was often disciplined at home and school for rule infractions. Socially, he became marginalized by his peers because of his excessive talking, clowning, and poor social judgment. He was prescribed psychostimulant medication in elementary school and continued to be prescribed psychostimulants through high school. Because academic grades and test scores remained above average despite frequent absences from school, Andrew was never referred for special education or 504 services. By age 12, Andrew was experimenting with alcohol and skipping school and had multiple school removals for disciplinary infractions, including marijuana possession on campus and drug intoxication during school. His parents sought outside counseling and Andrew was moved to a different school. He began bringing his prescription Adderall and other medications (opiates such as hydrocodone, benzodiazepines such as Xanax, and sedative-hypnotics such as Ambien) found in his family's and others' homes to school and sharing them with peers. Andrew was arrested multiple times for drug infractions and theft related to drug use during high school and college, ultimately completing a short prison term. He entered several drug rehabilitation programs, completing one program while incarcerated. Andrew overdosed on heroin but survived when a friend called emergency services. He had multiple vehicle infractions (evading arrest, speeding) and sustained a severe orthopedic injury in a rollover accident. At age 25, Andrew was the driver in a head-on collision that killed him and a passenger in the other vehicle.

In the K–12 school setting, what might have been done to help Andrew and his family? Should the school psychologist have been involved? The reader might consider these questions while reading this chapter.

School psychologists provide services to students who are affected by substance abuse and delinquency, sometimes in conjunction with co-occurring academic and emotional problems. Students who are referred for counseling may also be receiving psychopharmacological intervention for emotional and behavioral problems. It is imperative that school psychologists consider the context of these students' presenting issues, including the probability that coordination will be needed across multiple systems (such as medical, legal, and educational). Families may be overwhelmed, and the well-informed, compassionate school psychologist can be a supportive resource.

Substance Abuse

According to SAMHSA (2019), the 2018 National Survey on Drug Use and Health revealed that over 60% of Americans age 12 and older were substance users during the past month, taking into account use of alcohol, tobacco, and illicit (illegal) drugs. Specific to the school-age population, the survey indicated that over 2 million adolescents ages 12–17 drank alcohol, and more than 1 million of these teens binge drank during the period covered by the survey. According to the Office of Juvenile Justice and Delinquency Prevention (OJJDP, 2019), more than one of every five high school seniors used marijuana in the past month, and three of every 10 seniors used alcohol. Approximately 1 in 10 eighth graders vaped nicotine, according to the Monitoring the Future 2019 Survey Results report (NIDA, 2019). The National Institute on Drug Abuse (NIDA; https://www.drugabuse.gov) provides many current and updated articles and reports on substance abuse, along with handouts for providers, parents, and students.

NIDA (2019) described commonly abused classes of drugs, which include alcohol, tobacco, cannabinoids (marijuana/hashish), opioids (heroin, opium), stimulants (cocaine, amphetamine, methamphetamine), club drugs (MDMA/Ecstasy), dissociative drugs (ketamine, PCP, dextromethorphan, salvia), hallucinogens (LSD, mescaline, psilocybin), and other drugs (anabolic steroids, inhalants). Some of these categories are *scheduled drugs*, meaning their availability is regulated by the U.S. Food and Drug Administration (FDA). For example, amphetamines are Schedule II drugs that are available only by prescription, cannot be automatically refilled, and require a form for ordering. Heroin is a Schedule I drug, with no approved medical use. Dextromethorphan is not a scheduled drug and is commonly available in some over-the-counter cough and cold medicines. A detailed chart describing common drugs of abuse, their commercial and street names, FDA schedule status, mode of administration, acute effects, and health risks is available from NIDA (n.d.). NIDA (2020b) reported that the most commonly abused drugs by high school seniors, in order of frequency of abuse, were alcohol, tobacco, marijuana, amphetamines (with Adderall most often abused), synthetic marijuana ("K2" or "Spice"), prescription painkillers (primarily Vicodin and OxyContin), cough medicines, sedatives, tranquilizers, hallucinogens, MDMA (Ecstasy), and salvia (a type of sage plant, not currently a scheduled drug).

The following are possible warning signs of specific substance abuse in teens:

- Tobacco products: frequent smell of tobacco; irritability; discolored fingertips, lips, or teeth; cigarette butts at curbside
- Cannabinoids: reddened whites of eyes, sleepiness, excessive hunger, lack of motivation, excessive happiness, paranoia
- Cold medications: sleepiness, rapid or slowed heart rate
- Inhalants: runny nose, smell of gasoline or other solvent, confusion, irritability
- Depressants (such as alcohol or benzodiazepines that depress the central nervous system): sleepiness, decreased inhibition, poor coordination, slowed heart rate or blood pressure, dizziness
- Stimulants: rapid heart rate or blood pressure, irritability, euphoria, less need for sleep, paranoia, seizures, psychotic behavior
- Narcotics (such as opioids): higher pain threshold, excessive happiness, sleepiness, slowed or stopped breathing, presence of needles
- Hallucinogens: trouble sleeping, blurred perceptions, paranoia
- Dissociative anesthetics: higher blood pressure and heart rate, memory loss, nausea and vomiting, irritability, aggressiveness
- Club drugs (e.g., Ecstasy): feverish without sweating, presence of multiple lollipops or other hard candies, euphoria
- Others (e.g., anabolic steroids): increased irritability or aggressiveness, rapid increase in muscle definition, thinning or loss of head hair, marked increase in acne over a short period of time, presence of needles (Dryden-Edwards, n.d.)

Medical intervention is often necessary for substance intoxication, given that many drugs of abuse affect heart rate, blood pressure, and breathing. Further, intoxication may be associated with impaired judgment, severe aggression, and suicidal behavior that requires psychiatric evaluation. Common indicators of drug use and abuse that may be observed by families include lying, stealing, changes in peers, mood swings, sleeplessness, presence of paraphernalia such as rolling papers, syringes, items that may be used as tourniquets, unmarked or unfamiliar pill bottles, and pipes (Dryden-Edwards, n.d.).

Beyond these indicators and warning signs for substance abuse, school psychologists must attend to risk factors and comorbid disorders, addressed in the following discussion.

Comorbidity and Developmental Issues

When two medical or mental health disorders occur in the same person, simultaneously or sequentially, they are described as comorbid. Comorbid disorders are presumed to interact, thus affecting the course and prognosis of both disorders. Among individuals who abuse substances, about half have a comorbid mental illness. In community-based substance abuse treatment programs, over 60% of teens meet diagnostic criteria for another mental disorder (NIDA, 2020a).

Although few studies have been done on comorbidity in children, those that have been completed suggest that youth with substance use disorders also have high rates of comorbid disorders such as depression and anxiety, including generalized anxiety disorder, panic disorder, and posttraumatic stress disorder (PTSD). Bipolar disorder, ADHD, borderline personality disorder, and antisocial personality disorder also frequently co-occur with substance use disorder. Further, individuals with schizophrenia have higher rates of alcohol, tobacco, and drug use disorders than the general population. Adolescents with major depression were more likely than those without major depression to binge drink and to use an illicit drug (SAMHSA, 2019). Youth appear to develop internalizing disorders such as depression and anxiety prior to developing substance use disorders. Evidence also suggests that untreated ADHD, particularly when conduct disorder is also present, may present a higher risk for substance use disorder (NIDA, 2020a).

It is not clear that mental illness causes substance use disorder or vice versa. Early drug use can change the brain so that it becomes more vulnerable to mental illness. Further, early symptoms of a mental disorder may increase vulnerability to drug abuse. Shared risk factors for substance abuse and mental illness may include genetic vulnerability, psychosocial experiences, and general environmental influences. Epigenetic influences are also the subject of research. Epigenetics refers to genetic changes that result from environmental factors, such as stress or trauma, that can be passed down through generations and may contribute to the development of mental illnesses or a substance use disorder (Compton et al., 2019; NIDA, 2020a).

Because the adolescent brain is not fully mature, it is more vulnerable to long-term effects of substance use, including increased risk of addiction. Adolescence is a period of high risk for the initiation of substance use and abuse. Limbic structures of the brain are involved in emotional responsivity and reward. These structures mature earlier than cortical areas involved in executive functions such as judgment, anticipation of outcomes, decision making, and impulse control. In fact, the prefrontal cortex, associated with the executive functions, continues to mature through at least the mid-20s, corresponding to a propensity for risk taking in adolescence (Compton et al.,

2019). Familial risk factors include low level of parental supervision or communication, family conflicts, inconsistent or severe parental discipline, and family history of alcohol or drug abuse (Dryden-Edwards, n.d.).

Higher levels of stress have been shown to reduce activity in the prefrontal cortex and increase responsivity in the limbic system, which leads to decreased behavioral control and increased impulsivity. Individuals who have been physically or emotionally traumatized are at much higher risk for substance abuse, which may reflect an attempt to reduce anxiety and avoid dealing with trauma and its aftermath (NIDA, 2020a).

A shared effect of drugs of abuse is the release of the neurotransmitter dopamine in the brain. While other neurotransmitters are also involved, much of the research has examined the role of dopamine in chronic drug abuse. The "high" produced by drugs results from a flooding of the brain's reward circuits with much more dopamine than natural rewards (e.g., eating, social connection, exercise) generate. This intense pleasure creates an especially strong drive to repeat the experience. Methamphetamine, for example, can cause a surge in dopamine about 1,000% above basal levels. It not only increases dopamine release but blocks reuptake and remains in the synapse much longer than other stimulants (Allerton & Blake, 2008). The immature brain, still developing the executive function capacity to balance impulse and self-control, is more likely to seek drugs again without adequately considering the consequences (NIDA, 2020a).

Murrie and colleagues (2019) conducted a literature review and meta-analysis of 50 studies, involving 40,783 people, that examined the transition from substance-induced, brief, or atypical psychoses to schizophrenia. They concluded that 25% of people who experienced substance-induced psychosis were eventually diagnosed with schizophrenia; the highest rate of transition to schizophrenia, 34%, was associated with cannabis-induced psychosis, followed by psychoses precipitated by hallucinogens (26%) and amphetamines (22%). These findings suggest that substance abuse accompanied by substance-induced psychotic states is associated with later diagnosis of schizophrenia in a significant percentage of individuals. NIDA (2020a) also reported that frequent marijuana use during adolescence can heighten the risk of psychosis in adulthood, specifically in individuals with a particular gene variant.

Adding to problems associated with drug abuse in youth is the increased risk for other destructive behaviors, including suicide, health complications, and juvenile delinquency (Rosenberg, 2011). Individuals who have both a drug use disorder and another mental disorder often exhibit symptoms that are more persistent, severe, and resistant to treatment. Assessment and integrated intervention for comorbid disorders is essential, particularly in the criminal justice system (NIDA, 2020a). The scope of the problem of juvenile delinquency is addressed below.

Juvenile Delinquency

According to Ford (2016), as many as two thirds of teens face traumatic events such as life-threatening accidents, injuries, illnesses, disasters, violence, or threats of sexual or emotional abuse and exploitation. Ford further asserted that all teens who live in families or communities where violence, poverty, neglect, racism, or discrimination are prevalent must cope with such traumatic events. In advocating for a trauma-informed approach to intervention for juvenile delinquency, Ford (2016) stated that over 90% of youth involved in the juvenile justice system have experienced one or more traumatic stressors, with one quarter to one third developing PTSD. Even so, research suggests that the path from the educational system to the criminal justice system has expanded over time, as described in the following study.

McCarter (2017) described the school-to-prison pipeline as referring to "a path from the education system to the juvenile or adult criminal justice system" (p. 53). According to McCarter, this path has grown considerably since the 1990s and begins with school-related offenses. Six primary effects of the school-to-prison pipeline can be gleaned from available research:

- The majority of school disciplinary action is discretionary (in contrast with mandatory) for actions such as defiance, cell phone use, clothing, petty theft, and insubordination. Students of color are overrepresented in discretionary discipline.
- Consequences often do not fit the offense and are not administered impartially, without regard to race, ethnicity, or national origin.
- Discipline is disproportionately applied to minority students, students with disabilities (particularly those with emotional disturbance), and students identifying as LGBTQ.
- Suspension rates vary across schools, with rates significantly affected by school climate (climate refers to organizational factors, such as school leadership, discipline, academics, and family–school community interactions).
- Suspension and expulsion negatively affect both students and schools. Students who are suspended or expelled are significantly more likely to repeat a grade or drop out of school. Schools with high suspension and expulsion rates tend to have less high-quality instructional time, lower academics, and lower graduation rates.
- Exclusionary discipline increases the likelihood of students' involvement with the justice system, with students who are suspended or expelled for discretionary offenses being three times as likely to enter the juvenile justice system within a year after the offense.

For those hoping to prevent juvenile delinquency, or to intervene when the pattern has developed, a central question is how to predict outcomes. Why do some juveniles become desisters (time-limited delinquency with eventual remission) while others become chronic offenders, or persisters? Mulvey (2011) addresses this issue in a report on the Pathways to Desistance Study, a multidisciplinary longitudinal study that followed 1,354 serious juvenile offenders (1,170 males 184 females ages 14–18) for 7 years after their convictions. The study examined the factors that lead serious juvenile offenders to continue or desist from serious offending. The report made the following key points:

- Most youth who commit felonies greatly reduce offending over time, regardless of the intervention.
- Longer stays in juvenile detention facilities do not decrease recidivism. In fact, for youth with lower offending levels, incarceration may increase the likelihood of committing more crimes.
- Community-based supervision is effective for youth after incarceration.
- Substance abuse treatment reduces both substance use and criminal offending for a limited period. For youth whose substance abuse treatment lasted at least 90 days and included significant family involvement, there was a significant decrease in both drug use and criminal offending over the next 6 months.

The rate of substance use was very high among the population in this study, with clear links between substance abuse and criminal offending. Two factors that appear to distinguish desisters from persisters, based on results of Mulvey's findings, are (a) lower levels of substance use, and (b) greater stability and structure in daily routine, measured by stability in living arrangements, daily work, and school attendance. Another major finding, with implications for the discussion on incarceration, was that even for serious juvenile offenders, incarceration may not be the most effective or appropriate option (Mulvey, 2011).

The relationship between juvenile delinquency, substance abuse, and mental health is demonstrated in many studies. Underwood and Washington (2016) cite research showing that approximately 50–75% of youth in the juvenile justice system meet criteria for a mental health disorder; of those incarcerated, from 40% to 80% have at least one diagnosable mental health disorder. Disorders frequently found in youth offenders include affective disorders, bipolar disorders, psychotic disorders, anxiety disorders, obsessive–compulsive disorder, PTSD, disruptive behavior disorders (conduct, oppositional defiant disorder, and ADHD), and substance use disorders (Ford, 2016; Underwood & Washington, 2016). Scheuermann and Nelson (2019) included learning disorders as frequently occurring in this population as well.

Conduct disorder is the most frequently identified comorbid disorder, probably because of the overlap in diagnostic criteria and offenses that result in criminal charges; in other words, delinquent behaviors are symptoms of conduct disorder. In some studies mood disorders have been found to be more common than conduct disorders in the delinquent population, and this may be especially true for females in the juvenile justice system (Goldstein et al., 2005).

Across several studies cited by Goldstein and colleagues (2005), drug use or dependence was found in 40–63% of juvenile delinquents. Although the direction of causality is unclear (substance abuse causing delinquent behaviors or delinquent behaviors predicting substance abuse), it is well established that substance abuse and delinquency are interrelated. Mind-altering substances can lower inhibition, leading to the propensity toward criminal behavior; drug dependence also requires money or other means of purchasing drugs, which can lead to criminal behaviors. Substances may also be used to self-medicate for depression, for example. Females in the juvenile justice system are known to have high rates of co-occurring childhood abuse, trauma, and substance abuse and are at high risk for drug dependence and abuse (Smith & Saldana, 2013).

The OJJDP (2019) reported that in most delinquency cases, juveniles are not detained (jailed or incarcerated). Detention, when it does occur, may be at any time between an arrest for an offense and a court-ordered sanction or legal penalty. Regarding case disposition, racial disparities exist. The referral rate to juvenile court (versus dismissal of charges) for delinquency cases involving Black youth was about three times higher than the rates for White and Hispanic youth. Once adjudicated, cases involving Black or Hispanic youth were more likely to result in residential placement than cases involving White youth (U.S. Department of Justice, 2019).

Incarceration can be thought of as an intervention, though not necessarily an effective one. As noted earlier, the Pathways to Desistance Study findings suggest that longer periods of incarceration for juveniles are not associated with better outcomes and may in fact increase the likelihood of subsequent crimes (Mulvey, 2011).

Having established the scope of the problem of substance abuse in youth, with overlapping problems of juvenile delinquency and risk of involvement in the juvenile justice system, the discussion now turns to intervention.

Effective Interventions

Teachers, principals, school psychologists, and other school personnel, because of their daily contact with students, are ideally placed to observe warning signs of adolescent behaviors that may be linked to substance use and delinquency, often termed social maladjustment in school settings, and to intervene. Such signs may include chronic misbehavior and rule violations, truancy, declining academic performance, change in peer group, and disciplinary referrals. Such signs, of course, are not exclusive to substance abuse, and students engaging in such behaviors may not exhibit illegal behaviors associated with delinquency.

Certainly, primary prevention is ideal and secondary prevention is desirable; however, data from multiple studies (Underwood & Washington, 2016) clearly reveal that much of the intervention provided to students with substance abuse and social maladjustment is tertiary and often occurs when they are in the criminal justice system. Inpatient and outpatient treatment can be very costly, even with insurance. Response to intervention (RTI), multitiered systems of support (MTSS), and positive behavioral intervention and support (PBIS) models can provide protection from the development of problems such as substance abuse and delinquency. Tiered approaches, in which prevention and early intervention are emphasized, could address the early onset of emotional and behavioral disorders that often precede or become comorbid with substance use disorders (NIDA, 2020a). Even for minors already in custody, PBIS has been evaluated as effective. Scheuermann and Nelson (2019) describe the increasing implementation of PBIS in juvenile detention facilities across the United States as an effort to change the punitive focus of confinement, which they say has failed to support the developmental needs of adolescents. They assert, citing supportive research, that improved secure care conditions result in reduced rates of major and minor behavior infractions, increased academic engaged time, lower rates of exclusionary discipline, greater sense of safety, and improved rates of program completion.

Schools have existing interventions, some of which are punishers that are intended to extinguish behavior, including in-school suspension and expulsion. Zero tolerance policies are often the foundation for disciplinary sanctions, such as suspension or expulsion, for drugs, violence, or weapons in public schools (Burrow-Sanchez, Jenson, & Clark, 2009). Although safety is of primary concern, too often the underlying mental health issues are not addressed in punitive disciplinary responses. According to the American Psychological Association Zero Tolerance Task Force (2008), zero tolerance policies have not proved to be an effective solution to school discipline, appear to conflict with knowledge concerning adolescent development, and may negatively affect the relationship of education with juvenile justice. Because most school-based discipline is discretionary (not requiring suspension or expulsion), school psychologists may have some leverage in how discipline is handled. Having system-wide positive behavior supports in place will, according to substantial research, reduce the need for punitive discipline and more intensive interventions.

For the special education student, protections are in place to ensure that the student continues to receive a free and appropriate public education, with the IEP maintained during any period of removal from the educational setting. The school psychologist will be involved in manifestation determination meetings to help figure out whether a violation of a school behavior code is linked to a disability. Manifestation determination is a complex process that becomes particularly difficult when dealing with social maladjustment, which is described in the Individuals with Disabilities Education Improvement Act (2004 IDEA Reauthorization) as a potentially exclusionary consideration in the definition of emotional disturbance. As discussed earlier in this chapter, even when social maladjustment is present, such as in chronic juvenile delinquency, comorbid substance use, academic, and emotional disorders are common. During manifestation determination deliberations, school personnel may consider options, including a functional behavioral assessment or behavioral intervention plan if these are not already in place. The school psychologist may also be expected to complete additional psychological assessment to ensure that special education classification is up-to-date and reflects the student's current needs and resources. Additionally, students who have not been identified for special education may need such assessment based on history and patterns of behavior. These school psychology roles allow for entry into the student's world, including family and community systems, and thus may constitute a form of intervention, including advocacy for appropriate assessment, intervention, and referral for treatment, if warranted.

Referrals for treatment for substance abuse must take into account community resources, parental resources (insurance, financial means), and student characteristics, including prior interventions. If a family has insurance benefits, the insurance representative will often have knowledge of resources in the area that accept the insurance for substance abuse treatment. Substance abuse treatment, whether through private payer, insurance, or public agencies, can occur on several levels of increasing intensity, such as outpatient support groups and individual therapy as well as intensive outpatient programs with multiple components. Residential programs can include partial hospitalization or full hospitalization and may take place across 30, 60, or 90 days.

Within communities, state or county organizations may coordinate resources for outpatient and inpatient treatment. State departments of health will often have online information about resources for indigent or uninsured individuals who need treatment. Some medical doctors and mental health professionals specialize in issues of substance abuse; if so, they may be on a referral list for local agencies. Dual diagnosis treatment programs, which take into account comorbidity of substance use disorder and other mental health diagnoses, are usually designated as such on their own and referring organizations' websites.

SAMHSA maintains a national helpline for treatment referral and information (in English and Spanish) for individuals and families dealing with substance use and disorders (1-800-662-HELP). SAMHSA also provides a treatment locator for behavioral health services (https://findtreatment.samhsa.gov/). This locator service is described on the website as confidential and anonymous for those seeking treatment facilities for substance use or addiction and mental health problems. School psychologists are encouraged to develop referral resources to share with students, families, and colleagues.

Systems and Family Interventions

The *Model Programs Guide* from the Office of Juvenile Justice and Delinquency Prevention (n.d.) includes 353 researched programs that cover the continuum from prevention to sanctions for offenses to reentry into the school and community. Of these programs, 18% were determined to be effective, 58% were promising, and 24% had no effects. This chapter focuses on those interventions that are most likely to be accessible to school psychologists who work with students in the context of the school system. The Model Programs Guide identifies 27 school-based programs as effective. These include system-wide positive behavioral supports (SWPBS), which is a general framework that is consistent with PBIS, along with specific programs for implementation in schools. Family intervention models are prominent in the youth-relevant literature (Weisz & Kazdin, 2017). Several of these models were discussed in Chapter 5 and are briefly reviewed here.

Of the family interventions, Multidimensional Family Therapy (MDFT) appears promising. MDFT follows a systems model, in which personal issues, interpersonal relationships, overall family functioning, and social forces must all be addressed to accomplish lasting change. Some MDFT sessions are joint; others are individual with teens or with parents separately. In joint sessions the therapist leads parents and their teens to discuss family problems and build family strengths, including improving communication and reducing conflict. Counselors using this model also help families negotiate school, work, justice systems, and community service agencies (NIDA, 2014). For school practitioners, this model may involve training and time commitments in the areas of family and community interventions that are beyond their typically available time. However, school psychologists should be knowledgeable about MDFT so they can inform families and help them locate resources.

Multisystemic therapy (MST) has also received empirical research support as an effective intervention (NIDA, 2014). MST is a comprehensive family and community-based intervention that targets juveniles ages 12–17 who are at high risk (chronic, violent, or substance abusing) for out-of-home placement. Intervention strategies include structural and strategic family therapy, behavioral family therapy, and cognitive–behavioral strategies in a social–ecological context. As with MDFT, the school psychologist's role may vary depending on how the family therapist decides to intervene. In some cases, the school psychologist may act as a consultant or referral source. In other cases, the therapist may actually provide some therapy in the school setting, if it is more accessible than the home or clinic settings, because the focus is on the nested systems in which the student's development is taking place.

Specific Counseling Techniques

Regarding counseling interventions for students who are already abusing or dependent on substances, or who have been engaging in serious delinquent behavior, the most promising appear to be variations of cognitive–behavioral therapy (CBT) incorporated into a systems approach (OJJDP, 2019). The interventions described here adhere to CBT models incorporating psychoeducation, modeling, and supervised practice to modify thoughts, behaviors, and feelings.

Childhood aggression and early hostile behavior have been linked to delinquency, substance abuse, and conduct disorders (Lindsey et al., 2019). Such behaviors may include bullying, threatening, and physical attacks. If such behaviors persist throughout a child's development, the child may experience increasingly negative interactions with teachers and peers, resulting in increased alienation from school and increased susceptibility to deviant peer influences.

The Coping Power program (Lindsey et al., 2019) is based on the contextual social–cognitive prevention model. This program focuses on two potential mediators of adolescent antisocial behavior: (a) child-level factors, which include poor social–cognitive skills and lack of social competence, and (b) parent-level contextual factors, such as poor discipline and involvement. This program was created to prevent the development of adolescent antisocial behavior by addressing maladaptive parenting strategies and children's problems with processing social information.

NIDA (2014) lists cognitive–behavioral therapy as an effective treatment during and following treatment for substance abuse to help students maintain recovery from substance use disorder (see Chapter 8). A core element of CBT is teaching participants how to anticipate problems and helping them develop effective coping strategies. In CBT, teens are encouraged to honestly explore the positive and negative consequences of using drugs. By learning to monitor feelings and thoughts, recognize distorted thinking patterns and cues that trigger substance abuse, and identify and anticipate high-risk situations, teens can then apply self-control skills, including emotion regulation and anger management, practical problem solving, and substance refusal. As with all CBT approaches, the student must be engaged and able and willing to explore thoughts, feelings, and new behaviors. Caution is needed when using group CBT because of the tendency of former substance abusing peers to glorify drugs or drug-related experiences in group settings, thereby undermining recovery goals.

For more than a decade, there has been a movement toward incorporating trauma-informed intervention in the juvenile justice system (Ford, 2016). Interventions that are trauma informed aim to identify and provide traumatized youth with services that aid recovery from chronic posttraumatic stress. Instead of treating these youth as either antisocial (warranting restrictive programs or confinement) or mentally impaired (requiring psychiatric behavior management and treatment), Ford advocates for an evidence-based treatment designed to help them overcome traumatic stress reactions. One such program is TARGET (Trauma Affect Regulation: Guide for Education and Therapy), a trauma-informed CBT approach. TARGET is described as an intervention for traumatized youth that can be done in one-to-one, group, family, or milieu modalities. It is directed toward individuals with PTSD in juvenile justice settings and those with co-occurring substance use disorders. TARGET can also be used for training juvenile justice staff on emotion regulation skills. It was reviewed in the OJJDP (n.d.) Model Programs Guide as an effective evidence-based intervention, with supportive research cited. Training and materials for this manualized program are available only through the group that developed the curriculum, Advanced Trauma Solutions (advancedtrauma.com). This intervention model, though not readily accessible to school psychologists, is notable in that it represents a shift toward recognizing the role of trauma in the development of substance abuse and delinquency in youth. Further, it emphasizes the effectiveness of trauma-informed CBT for these youth.

Solution-focused brief therapy, which is directed toward eliciting and achieving the client's vision of solutions, and motivational interviewing, which has demonstrated empirical support for reduction of maladaptive behaviors such as substance abuse, were reviewed in Chapter 8 (NIDA, 2014). Contingency therapy is a form of behavioral therapy in which immediate and tangible reinforcers are provided for engaging in behaviors to maintain sobriety (e.g., staying in treatment, attending therapy, staying sober in high-risk situations). Rewards might include cash vouchers, movie tickets, gift cards for restaurants, access to technology, tickets to sports events and so on.

NIDA (2014) considers 12-step facilitation therapy to be an evidence-based counseling approach. This approach is designed to increase the likelihood that an adolescent with a substance abuse problem will become actively involved in a 12-step program like Alcoholics Anonymous (AA) or Narcotics Anonymous (NA). These programs are available in most communities at no cost, meet in accessible spaces (churches, community centers), are anonymous, and are offered at multiple times and locations during the day and night, including weekends, when professional care is not typically available. These meetings are not led by professionals but are facilitated by peers in recovery. Such 12-step programs stress acceptance that life has become unmanageable, that abstinence from alcohol or drug use is needed, and that willpower alone cannot overcome the problem. Participation in 12-step groups extends the benefits of addiction treatment, according to recent research (Kelly & Urbanoski, 2012). Information on 12-step programs, including meeting locations and times across the world, is available online (Alcoholics Anonymous, https://www.aa.org/; Narcotics Anonymous, https://www.na.org/). For families of persons with substance use disorders who are seeking no-cost support, Al-Anon is another 12-step program, with Alateen meetings also available (https://al-anon.org/).

Because 12-step programs are anonymous and report no data for accountability or research, empirical data are limited. To assess effectiveness of 12-step AA meetings for youth, Kelly and Urbanoski (2012) recruited 127 adolescent outpatients with substance use disorder and conducted follow-up at 3, 6, and 12 months. The proportion of subjects attending regularly was low across the follow-ups (24–29%); however, more frequent attendance at 12-step meetings was independently associated with greater abstinence. Over and above the effects of attendance, contact with a 12-step sponsor (peer in recovery) outside of meetings, and more verbal participation during meetings were associated with improved outcomes (abstinence).

Another peer-supported recovery model, the SMART (Self-Management and Recovery Training) approach, also emphasizes abstinence, and group facilitators are volunteers who receive training (https://www.smartrecovery.org/). Similar to 12-step models, SMART Recovery provides free and anonymous mutual support meetings. It differs from 12-step programs in that it does not use labels such as "addict" or "alcoholic." SMART embodies four basic points: (a) developing and maintaining motivation to change; (b) learning to cope with urges to engage in addictive behaviors; (c) effectively regulating thoughts, behaviors, and feelings without addictive behaviors; and (d) living a balanced, positive, and healthy life. The SMART model emphasizes self-efficacy and incorporates elements of CBT and motivational therapy approaches (Beck et al., 2017). It has been applied to addictive behaviors including substance use disorders, overeating, and gambling (SMART Recovery, n.d.). Beck and colleagues (2017) reviewed 12 studies related to SMART Recovery. While positive effects were reported, small sample sizes and diverse methods precluded conclusive findings about efficacy or variables contributing to positive outcomes.

Beyond the school-based multitiered prevention and intervention and individual or family counseling, psychopharmacology has grown in use. Psychopharmacological approaches do not directly target addictions, substance abuse, or conduct disorders; rather, they are aimed at the underlying or comorbid psychiatric disorders that may predispose individuals to later substance abuse and its complications, or to chronic psychopathology that interferes with life adjustment. Because the majority of youth with substance use disorders are diagnosed with one or more comorbid psychiatric disorders, many of these youth will be prescribed psychotropic drugs (Kaminer, Goldberg, & Connor, 2010).

Psychopharmacology

School psychologists do not prescribe psychotropic medications. However, they work with many students who take prescribed medications intended to improve emotional and behavioral functioning. Medication regimens may be concurrently implemented with other interventions, such as psychological assessment, behavioral interventions, and counseling. Therefore, school psychologists must have foundational knowledge of psychotropic medications and their use with school-age populations. A recently published book, *School Psychopharmacology: Translating Research Into Practice* (Carlson & Barterian, 2019), testifies to the growing recognition of the importance of school professionals being well informed about psychopharmacology and school practice.

Psychopharmacology refers to the study of drug-induced changes in mood, thinking, and behavior (https://www.sciencedaily.com/terms/psychopharmacology.htm). The following are some terms that will be encountered in the literature on psychopharmacology:

- Psychotropic (psychoactive) drug—a naturally derived or synthetic drug capable of affecting the mind, emotions, and behavior, usually in the treatment of mental illness. The term can also be applied to illicit drugs.
- Polypharmacy—concurrent use of multiple medications.
- FDA approved—FDA has determined that benefits outweigh risks for planned use of a drug, specific to age and planned use.
- Off-label use—drugs prescribed for uses other than what the FDA has approved. The term doesn't equate to unsafe use.

Psychotropic Medications

Psychotropic medications are prescribed by medical professionals to treat emotional and behavioral problems. The three psychotropic drug classes most often prescribed for pediatric populations, with selected examples of medications in that drug class and their targeted symptoms, include the following:

- Antidepressants—used for depressive, obsessive, compulsive, and anxiety symptoms
  - Selective serotonin reuptake inhibitors (SSRIs), such as fluoxetine (Prozac), sertraline (Zoloft), and citalopram (Celexa)
  - Selective serotonin and norepinephrine reuptake inhibitors (SNRIs), such as duloxetine (Cymbalta) and venlafaxine (Effexor)
- Antipsychotics—used for psychotic symptoms, irritability (e.g., in autism), and mood regulation
  - Second generation (atypical), such as aripiprazole (Abilify), olanzapine (Zyprexa), quetiapine (Seroquel), and risperidone (Risperdal)
  - First generation (typical), such as haloperidol (Haldol)

- Stimulants and other ADHD medications—used for inattention, distractibility, and hyperactivity
  - Stimulants, such as methylphenidate (Ritalin, Concerta, Daytrana, Quillivant), dexmethylphenidate (Focalin), lisdexamphetamine (Vyvanse), and d- and l-amphetamine (Adderall)
  - Other, such as atomoxetine (Straterra, antidepressant class) and guanfacine (Intuniv, Tenex, alpha2 adrenergic agonist class; Carlson, 2019; Scahill & Rojas, 2019)

Drug classification descriptions vary by source and may use different terms depending on the age group and typical use. *Mood stabilizers* are often considered a drug class and typically include lithium carbonate/citrate (Eskalith, Lithobid, approved for bipolar mania in age 12 and older) and antiseizure drugs (anticonvulsants), such as divalproex (Depakote), lamotrigine (Lamictal), and oxcarbazepine (Trileptal). Although most anticonvulsants are FDA approved only for seizure disorders below age 18, these drugs may be prescribed off label for mood stabilization. Olanzapine/fluoxetine (Symbyax, a combination of Zyprexa and Prozac) is approved for bipolar depression for ages 10 and older. Also, some antianxiety medications (anxiolytics) are FDA approved for pediatric use, such as buspirone (Buspar) for generalized anxiety disorder ages 6 to 17, lorazepam (Ativan) for anxiety ages 12 and older, and diazepam (Valium) for anxiety ages 6 months and older. The reader can glean from these examples the complexity of FDA approval and prescribing considerations for pediatric populations.

A regularly updated reference to psychotropic medications can be downloaded from http://psyd-fx.com/quick-reference-chart/quick-reference-direct/ (Preston, 2020). This reference guide, last updated in 2019, classifies the psychotropic drugs as antidepressants, bipolar disorder medications, psychostimulants, antipsychotics, antianxiety agents, hypnotics, and over-the-counter medications. Generic and brand names, along with adult dosage ranges and targeted neurotransmitter systems, are included in this reference guide. Some of the medications included in the guide are not typically prescribed for pediatric populations (e.g., benzodiazepines, hypnotics), but it is not unusual for teens to gain access to these drugs (e.g., Xanax, Ambien) for illicit recreational use or self-medication.

For current FDA approval information is available at https://www.ncbi.nlm.nih.gov/pmc/articles/PMC5875361/. Hirsch (2018) observed that prescribing medications off label for childhood psychiatric disorders (without FDA approval for that age or intended purpose) has been the rule rather than the exception, often without adequate dosing guidelines, because of limited research in the context of the pressing need for help with emotional and behavioral problems. As an example of the complexity of the approval process, Abilify (an atypical antipsychotic) is approved for irritability associated with autism for ages 6 and older, with schizophrenia for ages 13 and older, and with bipolar I disorder (mixed or manic phases) for ages 10 and older. The past two decades have seen a dramatic increase in the number of studies looking specifically at pediatric psychopharmacology, although more research is needed.

Scope of Use

The number of peer-reviewed publications that use the term *pediatric psychopharmacology* has reached more than 1,300 since 2016. When the web search is narrowed to include the term *schools*, the result is 508 publications. Clearly this area of research and study is of growing importance for school psychologists, especially given that schools are often the primary or only source of mental health services provided to pediatric populations, typically students up to age 18 (Carlson, 2019).

In 2008, information from a national database indicated that more than 7 million children ages 18 and under were prescribed psychotropic medications (Sultan et al., 2018, cited in Carlson, 2019). Since that time, increased rates of prescribing indicate that more than 8 million children, or about 16% of the U.S. population, likely were prescribed psychotropic medications. In outpatient mental health care for children and adolescents, psychotherapy alone or in combination with psychotropic medication is declining, while treatment relying exclusively on psychotropic medication appears to be increasing across time (Carlson, 2019).

During a longitudinal study of 9,230 adolescents with disabilities (Sullivan & Sadeh, 2015), over 18% received pharmacotherapy. Of that group, almost 12% received monopharmacy (single medication), over 6% received polypharmacy (multiple medications), and almost 6% simultaneously received multiple classes of medications.

In a study of students attending a self-contained middle school for special education students with emotional and/or behavioral problems, psychotropic medication was used in almost 80% of participants, with 52% receiving more than one medication (Mattison, Rundberg-Rivera, & Michel, 2014). In this study, the most commonly prescribed medications were found to be atypical antipsychotics and ADHD medications. Atypical antipsychotics were most often prescribed for irritability and aggression in ADHD in pediatric populations, an off-label use. Serious psychopathology was reported to still occur in many students who were prescribed psychotropic medication.

Addiction medicine has emerged as a specialty field in which medications are prescribed specifically for substance use disorders, typically to help individuals maintain sobriety by relieving symptoms of craving and withdrawal. For example, buprenorphine reduces symptoms of withdrawal from opioids, including cravings, by acting as a *partial opioid agonist*, meaning that it both blocks and activates opioid receptors in the central nervous system. When buprenorphine is combined with another drug, naloxone, in a formulation marketed as Suboxone, the intention is to deter abuse by triggering a withdrawal reaction if the drug is intravenously injected (NIDA, 2020c). Although several medications have been found to be effective in treating addiction to opioids, alcohol, or nicotine in adults, *none* are FDA approved to treat adolescents. Further, no evidence is available on the neurobiological impact of these medications on the developing brain. However, some healthcare providers do use medications off label when treating adolescents (especially older adolescents) who are addicted to opioids, nicotine, or alcohol. Not infrequently, individuals treated for substance use disorders may also be treated with psychotropic drugs for comorbid disorders, such as depression, anxiety, or psychosis. Some drugs may be used for more than one purpose; for example, buproprion (Wellbutrin) is an antidepressant that has also been found to be effective in reducing nicotine withdrawal in adult smokers (American Addiction Centers, 2020; NIDA, 2020c; Volkow, 2020). Psychopharmacology in general, and polypharmacy for comorbid psychiatric disorders, including substance use disorders, involve both benefits and risks, as discussed in the following section.

Benefits and Risks

The general target of psychotropic drugs is the central nervous system, which, in children and adolescents, is continuously undergoing maturational changes (Kubiszyn, Mire, & Meinert, 2019; Preston, O'Neal, & Talaga, 2015). Differences in body size and maturation make determining optimal dose challenging for many drugs. Because actions of the body on the drug (pharmacokinetics) and actions of the drug on the body (pharmacodynamics) are complex, drug effects are not necessarily generalizable across people, even those within the same demographic, such as age, gender, and ethnicity. Effects of the drugs on the body and effects of the body on the drugs vary as a function of maturation, fat distribution, body size, genotype, health, and other drugs in the system, among other variables.

Neurotransmitter systems are complex; specific neurotransmitters may have different modes of action at different receptor sites. Other factors, such as the activity of the second messengers (which convey the chemical message of a neurotransmitter from the cell membrane to the cell's internal biochemical structures) and tolerance, may mediate the effects of drugs on target neurotransmitter systems (Preston et al., 2015). DuPaul and Franklin (2019) assert that, in general, medication treatment standards are less comprehensive for younger children, leading to greater risk. So although most psychotropic medication prescriptions are not FDA approved for children, some psychiatric disorders are subject to progressive neurobiological dysfunction if left untreated (e.g., bipolar disorder, ADHD, schizophrenia, some cases of PTSD, and unipolar depression), and psychopharmacology may be neuroprotective (Preston et al., 2015).

Given these cautions, current research supports the effectiveness of psychotropic drugs when supported by research and used as prescribed. Scahill and Rojas (2019), in their review of commonly used medications in children, report that stimulants have extensive empirical support for the short- to intermediate-term treatment of ADHD in school-age children (there is less empirical support for children under age 5). Those children who exhibit a positive response to stimulants in the short and intermediate term may continue to do well when stimulant medication is discontinued. Scahill and Rojas recommend deliberate discontinuation of stimulant medication to reassess the value of continued treatment, possibly annually. SSRIs are effective for major depression and are generally well tolerated, and medication in combination with CBT for depression is more effective than medication alone. SSRIs have also been found effective for anxiety and obsessive–compulsive symptoms, especially when combined with CBT. Regarding atypical antipsychotics, Scahill and Rojas conclude that their use in pediatric populations should be reserved for the most severe behavioral problems (e.g., mania, psychosis, severe behavior problems in autism spectrum disorders, and severe tics in Tourette's) because of the serious potential metabolic side effects, including rapid weight gain.

Kubiszyn and colleagues (2019) present a comprehensive discussion of risk–benefit analysis for use of psychotropic medications with pediatric populations. They cover adverse side effects for four major drug classes using only FDA sources of information generated from empirical studies: antidepressants, ADHD drugs (stimulants and nonstimulants), atypical (second generation) antipsychotics, and mood stabilizers (including lithium and anticonvulsants). The following is a very brief synopsis of possible unwanted side effects that may affect school functioning (excluding rare and severe adverse events):

- Somnolence/sedation (antidepressants and atypical antipsychotics)
- Insomnia (ADHD drugs)
- Blurred vision (atypical antipsychotics)
- Extrapyramidal symptoms (atypical antipsychotics): involuntary movements, grimacing, posturing, tremoring
- Nausea and dyspepsia (ADHD drugs and antidepressants)
- Dizziness (ADHD drugs and atypical antipsychotics)

In addition to some of the points made above, Kubiszyn and colleagues (2019) note that harm may result from not providing drug treatment when there are serious safety risks for the child and others, such as self-destructive behavior or aggression, and when other effective interventions are unavailable, such as psychosocial interventions, family systems therapy, or hospitalization. Even though there may be insufficient research data on safety and efficacy of drug treatment, and unwanted side effects may occur, the risk of not providing this intervention may be unacceptably high in some cases.

Ethical Considerations

Carlson and Barterian (2019) make the point that "siloed approaches to promoting children's developmental functioning and care for when mental health challenges are present are not best practice. Schools, hospitals, physician offices, and community-based mental health centers often work in isolation around a child's mental health needs" (p. vii). Carlson and Barterian advocate for collaboration, including with schools, to integrate mental health treatment for children.

DuPaul and Franklin (2019) address legal, ethical, and professional issues around the use of psychoactive drugs in school-age populations. Regarding the law, both IDEA and Section 504 state that schools are legally required to dispense psychoactive medications during the school day if students require such medication to access a free and appropriate public education (FAPE). Conversely, schools with federal funding cannot require parents to obtain medication prescriptions as a condition for gaining access to educational services. Additionally, under Section 504, the determination of impairment must be made without regard to the positive effects on symptoms from measures such as medication. Ethical considerations include rights to privacy of information and restrictions on sharing of confidential information across settings, with appropriate informed consent when collaboration across settings is undertaken (DuPaul & Franklin, 2019). Also, parents may choose not to disclose their child's medication status.

Another ethical issue is the preparation of school psychologists to collaborate with other professionals, families, and caregivers when students are prescribed psychotropic medication. School psychologists are well-positioned to identify and implement evidence-based interventions, consult and collaborate with others, and monitor effectiveness of intervention. They should have at least a basic grasp of how psychotropic medications fit into a comprehensive psychological service delivery model (Carlson, 2019). However, even the most basic education related to psychotropic medication is missing from many university school psychology training programs (DuPaul & Franklin, 2019), bringing into question the competence of most school psychologists to collaborate within an integrated care model. Currently, neither the National Association of School Psychologists nor the American Psychological Association has formal standards for training on medication issues for school psychologists.

DuPaul and Franklin (2019) present five potential roles for school psychologists, all of which would need appropriate graduate training and supervision to achieve competence: "(a) diagnostic decision-making and determining need for medication; (b) consulting with physicians and families to assess medication effects; (c) assisting physicians and families to determine the optimal dosage of medication: (d) assessing and supporting adherence with prescribed regimens; and (e) facilitating integration of interventions" (p. 20). These roles are only possible if formal training in school psychology programs is expanded to include education on medication-based interventions.

A related ethical issue is the overlap between psychotropic drugs as a prescribed intervention and misuse or abuse of prescribed medications, often by others who obtained the drug illegally. In an online article, SAMHSA (2020) described the fastest growing drug problem in the United States as prescription drug abuse, with opioids, stimulants (such as Adderall), and central nervous system depressants (such as sedatives, benzodiazepines, and hypnotics) the most frequently abused prescription drugs. Education for students and parents regarding safe storage and disposal, the impact of psychotropic drugs on the developing brain, and monitoring of adherence to prescribed use can help reduce abuse of these drugs. Graduate training programs, when addressing training on psychotropic medication issues, should include attention to illicit use of medications.

School psychologists who see students for assessment or counseling must be aware that psychotropic medications, when taken as prescribed, are designed to positively affect cognition, emotion, and behavior. These intended effects and any side effects should be closely monitored and considered in evaluating behavior, with feedback provided to parents and prescribing physicians. On the other hand, illicit use of substances, whether prescription or nonprescription drugs, may negatively affect behavioral, emotional, and physical health. The astute school psychologist will be aware of warning signs for drug abuse, will be alert to the possibility of a trauma history and comorbid mental health disorders, and will have resources available for referral and intervention.

PRACTICE CASE: VALENTINO

Background

Valentino, a 10th grader registered at his local public high school, was referred for an initial special education evaluation by the student support team. Valentino was described as a highly intelligent child, and he is enrolled in all advanced placement or honors courses this school year. School records indicated that Valentino was recently hospitalized when he was experiencing hallucinations and suicidal thoughts. Further, records available at the time of the referral indicated that Valentino was previously diagnosed with major depressive disorder with psychosis, and he has undergone inpatient treatment for illicit drug use (marijuana and cocaine) as well. School staff documented a significant decline in Valentino's educational performance resulting from frequent absenteeism and failure to complete or turn in assignments.

At the time of the referral, discharge paperwork from his recent hospitalization was limited, but indicated that his medication was recently changed to Lexapro (5 mg) and Latuda (20 mg), daily. Records noted that Valentino has also been prescribed Prozac (5 mg) in the past, although no additional data regarding psychopharmacological information were shared.

After informed consent to assess was obtained, an initial interview with the student was conducted by the school psychologist. Valentino reported his hallucinations began shortly after his father's sudden death, approximately 16 months ago. Valentino indicated that he missed his father greatly and was very shocked and "numbed" by his sudden passing. The student also shared with the school psychologist drawings of the items/shapes he frequently sees during the hallucinations. Valentino stated he typically enjoys staring off at the hallucinations, but prescription medication does cause them to be less frequent. However, Valentino also reported, at times, he will purposely not take his medication as he initially enjoys how he feels without his prescriptions. Valentino stated he finds pleasure in the variations of feelings and experiences when he engages in illicit drug use as well, and that he may not always be honest with adults about his choices to engage in recreational drug use or to not take his medication, because he does not believe he has issues controlling his use. Further, Valentino self-disclosed that he suffers from anxiety and depression, which make him not want to come to school. He was open about previously experiencing suicidal thoughts but reported he does not currently feel impulses to self-harm. Valentino expressed he feels school-based counseling will be helpful and indicated a desire to work with a professional in that capacity.

Questions for the School Psychologist

- Considering the limited data included within the referral packet, coupled with the student's level of self-disclosure during an initial interview, what questions do you feel are most important to investigate first? Examples include length of time on his new medication regimen, FDA approval status, actual frequency of illicit drug use, potential prescription drug and illicit drug interactions, and potential ramifications of inconsistent prescription drug use.
- What resources can you use to find out about drug effects and interactions?
- What other possible contributing factors do you feel require additional follow-up? How will you obtain needed information?
- Given the limited information at this time, what do you feel school-based counseling services should address? What would be your initial goals?
- What type of consultation or collaborative services do you feel a school psychologist will need to enact in this case?
- How could you help monitor medication compliance?
- What steps would you take next? How would you prioritize them, and how did you arrive at your plan of action?

Contributed by Liz Hjort, SSP, LSSP, NCSP
Director of Psychological Services
TrinityEducational.com

SUMMARY

From a practical perspective, the school psychologist in the counseling role must be willing to recognize the early warning signs of substance abuse and delinquency and to intervene with children and their families with sensitivity and respect, knowing that these problems affect many families. Research has taught us that mental health issues, systems dysfunction, and trauma are often precursors to substance abuse and the physical, educational, social, and legal complications that may ensue. The school psychologist's role may be primarily as a consultant, to provide perspective and connect the family to community resources, when the substance abuse or delinquent behavior has become a set pattern. If a student has risk factors, school counseling interventions in individual or group formats can be effective in reducing the likelihood that the student will develop a behavior or substance use disorder that results in personal, social, and legal consequences. CBT approaches appear to have the most empirical support, whether provided individually, in groups, or in family systems approaches, with trauma-informed approaches gaining traction.

School psychologists, by virtue of their roles in positive behavioral supports, response to intervention, comprehensive individual assessments, IEP development, consultation, and intervention, have many points of entry to help the student who is struggling with family, social, and emotional problems. Whether substance use progresses to abuse or involvement in delinquent activities may hinge on connections with empathic and supportive adults at school. Even though problems covered in this chapter tend to involve multiple, complex systems and often require specialized intervention, schools may be the starting point for positive change.

Psychopharmacology was addressed in this chapter because of (a) its increasing relevance to the practice of school psychology and (b) the potential overlap among mental health disorders, substance abuse, and psychopharmacology. For some students, more than one of these factors will affect both assessment and intervention decisions. Students will usually return to school after treatment for substance abuse; after being suspended, expelled, or jailed; and after crises within their families. Students will be prescribed psychoactive drugs to ameliorate feelings and behaviors that are interfering with life adjustment; some students may self-medicate by using illicit drugs. How can you help? School psychologists need to seek continuing education in issues of substance abuse, delinquency prevention and intervention, and psychopharmacology through professional organizations, reading, and consultation. They also can advocate for training programs to incorporate related content into their curriculum to prepare them to collaborate with other professionals in prevention and intervention efforts.

As we have stressed throughout this book, a key component of effective intervention is the establishment of effective working relationships with clients, including students, teachers, families, and other professionals. By using active listening skills, respecting confidentiality and clearly describing its limits, establishing reliability, and building optimism, school psychologists can help facilitate positive change. When school psychologists are able to enter the world of a student and family, the system has been opened to change. This accomplishment in and of itself is an intervention.

KEY POINTS FOR DISCUSSION

- How commonly are children and teens affected by substance abuse? Does this match your experience?
- What is meant by dual diagnosis, or comorbidity?
- What interventions have the most empirical support for established patterns of substance abuse and juvenile delinquency?

- What specific counseling strategies appear to be effective with students who are at risk for entering or in early stages of drug use?
- How effective is incarceration for drug or alcohol infractions or other forms of delinquency?
- How can school psychologists be prepared for assessing, referring, or counseling students with substance abuse issues or delinquency problems?
- How do you feel about the need for school psychologists to obtain training in psychopharmacology? What have your experiences been so far?

REFERENCES

Allerton, M., & Blake, W. (2008). The "party drug" crystal methamphetamine: Risk factor for the acquisition of HIV. *The Permanente Journal, 12*(1), 56–58. doi:10.7812/tpp/07-127

American Addiction Centers. (2020, March 9). *What drugs are used in addiction rehabilitation treatment?* American Addiction Centers. Retrieved from https://americanaddictioncenters.org/addiction-medications

American Psychiatric Association. (2013). *Diagnostic and statistical manual of mental disorders* (5th ed.). Washington, DC: Author.

American Psychological Association Zero Tolerance Task Force. (2008). Are zero tolerance policies effective in the schools? An evidentiary review and recommendations. *American Psychologist, 63*(9), 852–862. doi:10.1037/0003-066X.63.9.852

Beck, A. K., Forbes, E., Baker, A. L., Kelly, P. J., Deane, F. P., Shakeshaft, A., Hunt, D., & Kelly, J. F. (2017). Systematic review of SMART Recovery: Outcomes, process variables, and implications for research. *Psychology of Addictive Behaviors, 31*(1), 1–20. doi:10.1037/adb0000237

Burrow-Sanchez, J. J., Jenson, W. R., & Clark, E. (2009). School-based interventions for students with substance abuse. *Psychology in the Schools, 46*(3), 238–245. https://doi.org/10.1002/pits.20368

Carlson, J. S. (2019). Introduction to school psychopharmacology. In J. S. Carlson & J. A. Barterian (Eds.), *School psychopharmacology: Translating research into practice* (pp. 1–11). Cham, Switzerland: Springer.

Carlson, J. S., & Barterian, J. A. (Eds.). (2019). *School psychopharmacology: Translating research into practice.* Cham, Switzerland: Springer.

Compton, W. M., Jones, C. M., Baldwin, G. T., Harding, F. M., Blanco, C., & Wargo, E. M. (2019). Targeting youth to prevent later substance use disorder: An underutilized response to the US opioid crisis. *American Journal of Public Health, 109*, S185. doi:10.2105/AJPH.2019.305020

Dryden-Edwards, R. (n.d.). *Teen drug abuse.* MedicineNet. Retrieved from http://www.medicinenet.com/teen_drug_abuse/page4.htm#what_are_the_symptoms_and_warning_signs_of_drug_abuse

DuPaul, G. J., & Franklin, M. K. (2019). Legal, ethical, and professional issues related to use of psychotropic medications in school-aged populations. In J. S. Carlson & J. A. Barterian (Eds.), *School psychopharmacology: Translating research into practice* (pp. 13–28). Cham, Switzerland: Springer.

Ford, J. (2016). *What is a "trauma-informed" juvenile justice system? A TARGETed approach.* Juvenile Justice Information Exchange. Retrieved from https://jjie.org/2016/06/20/what-is-a-trauma-informed-juvenile-justice-system-a-targeted-approach/

Goldstein, N. E. S., Olubadewo, O., Redding, R. E., & Lexcen, F. J. (2005). Mental health disorders: The neglected risk factor in juvenile delinquency. In K. Heilbrun, N. E. S. Goldstein, & R. E. Redding (Eds.), *Juvenile delinquency: Prevention, assessment, and intervention* (pp. 85–110). New York, NY: Oxford University Press.

Gramlich, J. (2017). *Nearly half of Americans have a family member or close friend who's been addicted to drugs.* Pew Research Center. Retrieved from https://www.pewresearch.org/fact-tank/2017/10/26/nearly-half-of-americans-have-a-family-member-or-close-friend-whos-been-addicted-to-drugs/ft_17-10-26_drugs_manyamericans_3/

Hirsch, G. S. (2018). Dosing and monitoring: Children and adolescents. *Psychopharmacology Bulletin, 48*(2), 34–92.

Individuals with Disabilities Education Improvement Act of 2004, 20 U.S.C. § 1400 et seq. (2004).

Kaminer, Y., Goldberg, P., & Connor, D. F. (2010). Psychotropic medications and substances of abuse interactions in youth. *Substance Abuse, 31*(1), 53–57. doi:10.1080/08897070903442665

Kelly, J. F., & Urbanoski, K. (2012). Youth recovery contexts: The incremental effects of 12-step attendance and involvement on adolescent outpatient outcomes. *Alcoholism, Clinical and Experimental Research, 36*(7), 1219–1229. doi:10.1111/j.1530-0277.2011.01727.x

Kubiszyn, T., Mire, S. S., & Meinert, A. (2019). *Psychotropic medication side effects in school-aged populations.* In J. S. Carlson & J. A. Barterian (Eds.), *School psychopharmacology: Translating research into practice* (pp. 137–158). Cham, Switzerland: Springer. https://doi.org/10.1007/978-3-030-15541-4_9

Lipari, R. N., & Van Horn, S. L. (2017, August 24). *Children living with parents who have a substance use disorder.* In *The CBHSQ Report.* Rockville (MD): Substance Abuse and Mental Health Services Administration. https://www.ncbi.nlm.nih.gov/books/NBK464590/

Lindsey, M. A., Romanelli, M., Ellis, M. L., Barker, E. D., Boxmeyer, C. L., & Lochman, J. E. (2019). The influence of treatment engagement on positive outcomes in the context of a school-based intervention for students with externalizing behavior problems. *Journal of Abnormal Child Psychology, 47*(9), 1437–1454. doi:10.1007/s10802-019-00525-6

Mattison, R. E., Rundberg-Rivera, V., & Michel, C. (2014). Psychotropic medication characteristics for special education students with emotional and/or behavioral disorders. *Journal of Child and Adolescent Psychopharmacology, 24*(6), 347–353. doi:10.1089/cap.2013.0073

McCarter, S. (2017). The school-to-prison pipeline: A primer for social workers. *Social Work, 62*(1), 53–61. doi:10.1093/sw/sww078

Mulvey, E. P. (2011). *Highlights from Pathways to Desistance: A longitudinal study of serious adolescent offenders.* OJJDP Fact Sheet. Retrieved from http://www.ojjdp.gov/index.html

Murrie, B., Lappin, J., Large, M., & Sara, G. (2019). Transition of substance-induced, brief, and atypical psychoses to schizophrenia: A systematic review and meta-analysis. *Schizophrenia Bulletin, 46*(3), 505–516. https://doi.org/10.1093/schbul/sbz102

National Institute on Drug Abuse (NIDA). (n.d.). *Commonly used drug charts.* Rockville, MD: Author. Retrieved from https://www.drugabuse.gov/drug-topics/commonly-used-drugs-charts

National Institute on Drug Abuse (NIDA). (2014, January). *Principles of adolescent substance use disorder treatment: A research-based guide.* Rockville, MD: Author. Retrieved from https://

www.drugabuse.gov/publications/principles-adolescent-substance-use-disorder-treatment-research-based-guide

National Institute on Drug Abuse (NIDA). (2019, December 18). *Monitoring the Future 2019 survey results: Overall findings*. Rockville, MD: Author. Retrieved from https://www.drugabuse.gov/drug-topics/trends-statistics/infographics/monitoring-future-2019-survey-results-overall-findings

National Institute on Drug Abuse (NIDA). (2020a, April). *Common comorbidities with substance use disorders research report*. Retrieved from https://www.drugabuse.gov/publications/research-reports/common-comorbidities-substance-use-disorders/

National Institute on Drug Abuse (NIDA). (2020b, June 2). What drugs are most frequently used by adolescents? Rockville, MD: Author. Retrieved from https://www.drugabuse.gov/publications/principles-adolescent-substance-use-disorder-treatment-research-based-guide/frequently-asked-questions/what-drugs-are-most-frequently-used-by-adolescents

National Institute on Drug Abuse (NIDA). (2020c, June 2). Addiction medications. Retrieved from https://www.drugabuse.gov/publications/principles-adolescent-substance-use-disorder-treatment-research-based-guide/evidence-based-approaches-to-treating-adolescent-substance-use-disorders/addiction-medications

Office of Juvenile Justice and Delinquency Prevention (OJJDP). (n.d.). *Model programs guide*. Washington, DC: U.S. Department of Justice. Retrieved from https://www.ojjdp.gov/MPG/Topic/Details/107

Office of Juvenile Justice and Delinquency Prevention (OJJDP). (2019, October 31). *OJJDP statistical briefing book*. Washington, DC: U.S. Department of Justice. Retrieved from https://www.ojjdp.gov/ojstatbb/population/qa01401.asp?qaDate=2018

Preston, J. D. (2020). *Quick reference to psychiatric medications*. psyd-fx.com. Retrieved from http://psyd-fx.com/quick-reference-chart/quick-reference-direct/

Preston, J. D., O'Neal, J. H., & Talaga, M. (2015). *Child and adolescent clinical psychopharmacology made simple* (3rd ed.). Oakland, CA: New Harbinger.

Rosenberg, L. (2011). Addressing trauma in mental health and substance use treatment. *Journal of Behavioral Health Services Research, 38*, 428. doi:10.1007/s11414-011-9256-9

Scahill, L., & Rojas, J. (2019). Pediatric psychopharmacology: Commonly used medications in children. In T. Ollendick, S. White, & B. White (Eds.), *The Oxford handbook of clinical child and adolescent psychology* (pp. 1–26). New York, NY: Oxford University Press.

Scheuermann, B. K., & Nelson, C. M. (2019). Sustaining PBIS in secure care for juveniles. *Education and Treatment of Children, 42*(4), 537–556. doi:10.1353/etc.2019.0025

SMART Recovery. (n.d.). Self-management and recovery training. Retrieved from https://www.smartrecovery.org/

Smith, D. K., & Saldana, L. (2013). Trauma, delinquency, and substance use: Co-occurring problems for adolescent girls in the juvenile justice system. *Journal of Child and Adolescent Substance Abuse, 22*(5), 450–465. doi:10.1080/1067828X.2013.788895

Substance Abuse and Mental Health Services Administration (SAMHSA). (2019). Key substance use and mental health indicators in the United States: Results from the 2018 National Survey on Drug Use and Health (HHS Publication No. PEP19-5068, NSDUH Series H-54).

Rockville, MD: Center for Behavioral Health Statistics and Quality, Substance Abuse and Mental Health Services Administration. Retrieved from https://www.samhsa.gov/data/

Substance Abuse and Mental Health Services Administration (SAMHSA). (2020, May 4). *Rise in prescription drug misuse and abuse impacting teens*. Rockville, MD: Author. Retrieved from https://www.samhsa.gov/homelessness-programs-resources/hpr-resources/teen-prescription-drug-misuse-abuse

Sullivan, A. L., & Sadeh, S. (2015). Psychopharmacological treatment among adolescents with disabilities: Prevalence and predictors in a nationally representative sample. *School Psychology Quarterly, 30*(3), 443–455. doi:10.1037/spq0000105

Sultan, R. S., Correll, C. U., Schoenbaum, M., King, M., Walkup, J. T., & Olfson, M. (2018). National patterns of commonly prescribed psychotropic medications to young people. *Journal of Child and Adolescent Psychopharmacology, 28*(3), 158–165. doi:10.1089/cap.2017.0077

Underwood, L. A., & Washington, A. (2016). Mental illness and juvenile offenders. *International Journal of Environmental Research and Public Health, 13*(2), 228. doi:10.3390/ijerph13020228

U.S. Department of Justice. (2019, October). Delinquency cases in juvenile court, 2017. *Juvenile Justice Statistics: National Report Series Fact Sheet*. Washington, DC: U.S. Department of Justice.

Volkow, N. D. (2020). Stigma and the toll of addiction. *New England Journal of Medicine, 382*, 1289–1290. doi:10.1056/NEJMp1917360

Youth.gov. (n.d.). *Youth involved with the juvenile justice system*. Retrieved from https://youth.gov/youth-topics/juvenile-justice/youth-involved-juvenile-justice-system

Weisz, J. R., & Kazdin, A. E. (2017). *Evidence-based psychotherapies for children and adolescents* (3rd ed.). New York, NY: Guilford Press.

Chapter 11

Practical Applications and Resources

OVERVIEW

Although school psychologists apply many counseling theories and principles in their work with children and adolescents, each case presents unique contextual variables and challenges. This chapter describes how some of the theories described in the previous chapters can be applied to counseling sessions in the schools. Specifically, we provide recommended materials and resources that school psychologists may use to engage students and help them understand and change their emotions and behaviors. The chapter then presents three case examples to illustrate the application of these counseling approaches and to show ways in which school psychologists creatively adapt methods to meet the individual needs of each client.

Some psychologists have trained in a particular therapeutic modality such as cognitive–behavior therapy (CBT) and have successfully used the method with many clients, but then they discover that for a new client the approach is completely inappropriate. Rather than persisting with their use of CBT, which will be counterproductive, the school psychologist must draw on other skills and resources to select a different intervention. That process should be informed by a number of factors, including a child's cognitive and language abilities, capacity for insight, and motivation to change, among others.

Some children and adolescents may benefit greatly from counseling but may not engage verbally in counseling sessions (perhaps because of an expressive language disorder, shyness, or apprehension). The school psychologist who typically engages in talk therapy with students in counseling may need to adapt their method to quiet students by using counseling activities that place few verbal demands on the child (e.g., reading bibliotherapy books to a student, using art materials, using sandtray therapy).

The school psychologist who embraces a solution-focused orientation may be motivated to identify and address concerns directly and to work toward solving problems efficiently. When faced with a child or adolescent who doesn't feel particularly prepared or motivated to face challenges directly, the school psychologist may have to consider other ways of connecting with the student, building a relationship, and adjusting the pace of therapy to align better with the student's needs. It may be possible to move toward a solution-focused approach over time as the student gains comfort and confidence, but it may also be helpful to consider other approaches that may better meet the needs of this particular student.

Effective school psychologists use evidence-based practices whenever possible to ensure that they provide the highest quality of services and achieve the best outcomes (Jordanova, Gerlach, & Faulkner, 2015). Selecting interventions that are supported by data constitutes a component of ethical practice (Blease, Kelley, & Trachsel, 2018). Selection of evidence-based interventions should be deliberate and systematic, following a standard protocol (see the steps provided by Jordanova et al., 2015). Hundreds of evidence-based practices have been organized on clearinghouse websites, some of which are listed in the resources section at the end of this chapter. School psychologists should be able to differentiate between interventions that are considered well supported (the highest rating), supported, and promising (California Evidence-Based Clearinghouse for Child Welfare, n.d.).

In short, when making decisions about therapeutic modalities or techniques, school psychologists must consider students' characteristics to ensure that the methods chosen are a good fit. In particular, they should ensure that interventions are culturally relevant and appropriate for diverse students, including those who identify as LGBTQIA+ (lesbian, gay, bisexual, trans, queer or questioning, intersexual, asexual, plus any not named). Counseling approaches that are selected without use of a culturally sensitive lens may be less effective, at best, and at worst feed feelings of alienation and isolation (National Resource Center for Mental Health Promotion and Youth Violence Prevention, n.d.). Resources for culturally sensitive practices can be found at the end of this chapter.

Although this process may seem obvious to some, therapists can sometimes adhere to a particular counseling approach and try to impose it on all clients, regardless of the suitability. Such misalignments may be likened to forcing square pegs into round holes and rarely result in productive therapy. In fact, pressing a student into a method or technique that doesn't feel right may very well reduce the likelihood that the student will want to come to counseling. An ongoing process of data-based decision making and progress monitoring will also yield valuable information about the appropriateness of an intervention.

This is not to suggest that discomfort should be avoided in counseling. Many clients benefit greatly from the experience of discomfort and use that unpleasant state as a springboard for growth. For example, students who face the fact that their behavior has alienated others and decreased their social opportunities may take corrective action by exhibiting greater kindness in the interest of making more friends. That being said, the skilled counselor is sensitive to clients' needs and works hard during each session to help the client in the ways that seem most effective for that person.

OBJECTIVES

School psychologists will achieve greater success and satisfaction in the counseling role when they are well prepared with a variety of techniques, methods, and tools to draw out and address students' social, emotional, and behavioral concerns. As such, there are many benefits to developing an eclectic repertoire of tools to meet a variety of student needs. The counselor who is limited to play-based approaches may have a difficult time supporting a child who verbalizes and intellectualizes difficulties. Similarly, those who steadfastly adhere to a cognitive approach may struggle when trying to assist children who are less verbal and express their inner experiences through play. Because school psychology training programs must prepare future practitioners broadly in the areas of assessment, consultation, and intervention, graduate training in counseling approaches may be limited. School psychologists may need additional professional development to learn about and develop skills in a variety of counseling methods (though finding the time and financial resources for training may be challenging). The next section reviews some of the suggested techniques and materials that can be useful for working with children and adolescents. The case examples and the discussions then demonstrate the use of these methods and others.

Selection of Techniques, Methods, and Tools

School psychologists may find that having a variety of materials that can be used creatively is particularly helpful and rewarding when working with students on their Individualized Education Program (IEP) counseling goals. An office or counseling space that is stocked with a variety of materials that can be used to provide diversion, focus, or individual expression can be a worthwhile investment. The space could include a supply of paints (acrylic, tempera, watercolor), markers, crayons, oil pastels, chalk, and charcoal, along with a variety of surfaces for painting (e.g., watercolor paper, canvas, large rolls of butcher paper, etc.). Clay provides a tactile, kinesthetic experience that many kids enjoy, and working with clay can relieve stress, allow the child to express feelings through a different medium, and provide an alternative to drawing that may be more forgiving than markers or paint (mistakes are easily reshaped and forms need not be perfect). Art materials may be used by students of all ages, either as a tool for expression or for something to occupy their hands while talking.

The school psychologist's office may also be filled with carefully selected books that help advance therapeutic goals. Some books have been written specifically to help children cope with challenges (e.g., picture books about depression, attention deficit hyperactivity disorder, or anxiety), and others that are written for a more general audience can be used to address a particular goal. *Bibliotherapy*, or the use of books as a psychotherapeutic tool, may work well for a variety of reasons:

- Books are a familiar and comfortable medium through which adults and children communicate.
- School psychologists can send books home with children to be read with family members to reinforce progress across home and school settings.

- Children may identify with characters in books and apply components of the narrative to their own lives.
- Reading and talking about a story may be less threatening or difficult for the child than talking about their own challenges.

A list of bibliotherapy resources is provided at the end of this chapter.

A number of therapeutic games are commercially available and may be used in counseling sessions as a fun way to address IEP goals. Some of these games are better than others, and school psychologists are encouraged to try the games with adult volunteers to assess the suitability for use in counseling. Many of the games contain cards that prompt students to talk about a particular issue or concern (e.g., "Talk about a time that you got really angry. How did you feel in your body as your anger was building?"). Any cards that are determined to be inappropriate or distract from the focus of the work to be done can be removed in advance. Groups of students also can develop their own games, collaboratively designing a board, instructions, rules, and the various components such as cards and moving tokens. Just as with books, some games that were not designed for therapy may also be used, but counselors should avoid spending counseling time playing games without a clear rationale or connection to the IEP goals. A game like Monopoly may be fun, but it may not be therapeutic. On the other hand, if the school psychologist is working on social skills like turn taking, perspective taking, and listening, a game of Monopoly could be used effectively to address those goals, particularly if the school psychologist is actively monitoring and facilitating the students' play. A list of recommended games can be found at the end of this chapter.

Using toys in play therapy will require having a collection of toys to stimulate a child's expression. Chapter 6 identified categories of toys that may be included in a well-stocked play therapy room, and some school psychologists who travel to more than one campus have assembled portable sets of toys that can be easily transported. The key is to start somewhere—starting with some puppets, a furnished dollhouse with people, some vehicles, and dress-up items (hats, cape, uniform, etc.)—and add items over time to expand the collection.

For students who like structure and are task oriented, a number of good-quality therapy workbooks and worksheets are available. School psychologists should carefully review and screen materials to ensure that they are supported by research, culturally appropriate, and aligned with counseling goals and avoid commercially available products that are of poor quality. Some forms, such as dysfunctional thought records, can be found in CBT books, including some that were specifically designed for CBT with children and adolescents. Some therapy worksheets also can be found on websites such as Do2Learn.com (e.g., social skills worksheets to promote reciprocal conversation skills). Workbook and worksheet resources are listed at the end of this chapter.

Another type of materials to have on hand are those that can simply be held or manipulated during counseling sessions. Like clay, these objects provide some stimulation, resistance, and kinesthetic experience. Most children feel more comfortable talking in a session if they have something to occupy their hands. Objects like stress balls, Koosh balls, or therapy putty can be available for kids to hold, squeeze, and look at while they're engaged in therapy. These objects also provide the opportunity to break eye contact, which may help build the level of comfort. Similarly, if school policy allows, going for a walk with a student may be productive during a session.

Case Examples

This section presents some examples of how school psychologists select interventions, from gathering information about their students to selecting and tailoring interventions that help the students make progress toward completing their goals. Although the goals may be similar across the cases, the techniques selected to meet those goals may be very different. The case examples are inspired by actual cases but are composites that have no identifying information.

The first example involves an elementary school student who has emotional–behavioral concerns. The school psychologist selects a play-based approach to counseling. As discussed in Chapter 6, nondirective approaches may be chosen for children who express themselves better nonverbally or who are less likely to benefit from techniques that place too much of a cognitive demand on the child. Child-centered play therapy allows the school psychologist to support a child's development by creating the conditions through which the child can grow and learn self-regulation skills.

CASE EXAMPLE 1: MIRANDA

In the middle of October, Lincoln Elementary School received a new 5-year-old student named Miranda who had just transferred in from a rural district about 75 miles away. Though Miranda's father made no mention of behavioral concerns, it became immediately apparent to her teacher that there were significant challenges, including elopement (running out of class), noncompliance, aggression, and inappropriate language. When Miranda was asked to comply with teacher requests, she became defiant, climbed on top of furniture, cursed at her teacher, and threw a tantrum when removed from class.

When Miranda's father was contacted, he reported that there had been behavioral concerns in the previous district, as well as some family issues, but he insisted that Miranda has not had behavioral problems at home. The school psychologist scheduled a meeting with the teacher, father, and school counselor to discuss these concerns and develop a plan. Meanwhile, the principal approved some additional support for the classroom, in the form of a teacher aid, and consultation with one of the district's behavior specialists.

The meeting with Miranda's father yielded some helpful information and some clear plans moving forward. The school psychologist facilitated the meeting and, using a semistructured interview, asked Miranda's father some questions about the family history. The team learned that Miranda's parents divorced when she was 3, and that there was a traumatic event in the home following the divorce. After custody was granted to Miranda's father, Miranda's mother attempted to take Miranda from the house outside of the terms of the custody agreement. Miranda's uncle tried to prevent Miranda from leaving and inadvertently injured her mother. Miranda witnessed this and has reported having nightmares about it. Miranda's father also suggested that there are indeed behavioral concerns at home, though he had previously denied this.

The team came up with a short-term plan to ensure Miranda's and other students' safety at school, to support Miranda's behavioral needs, and to provide the teacher with additional resources to be successful. Consent was obtained from Miranda's father to assess for a possible emotional behavior disorder. The school counselor agreed to visit the classroom and have some sessions with Miranda as well. Over the next 30 days, the evaluation was completed and it was determined that Miranda met the eligibility criteria for emotional disturbance (inappropriate types of behavior or feelings under normal circumstances) and that Miranda was eligible for counseling as a related service. The following counseling goals and objectives were approved by the IEP team:

Goal 1. Miranda will make measurable progress in the area of behavioral functioning.
- Objective 1: Miranda will comply with teacher requests with no more than one reminder three out of five times.
- Objective 2: Miranda will use her words rather than her hands to express her frustration three out of five times.

Goal 2. Miranda will make measurable progress in the area of emotional functioning.
- Objective 1: Miranda will employ calming techniques (e.g., focused breathing) when she begins to get angry three out of five times.
- Objective 2: Miranda will communicate her feelings to her teacher at least twice each day when prompted.

When considering potential methods or techniques to help Miranda make progress on her counseling IEP goals, the school psychologist considered Miranda's presenting problems, cognitive and language capacities, and strengths (including her eagerness to seek out novel stimuli and engage in imaginative play). These factors, coupled with Miranda's limited ability to have explicit insight regarding her challenges, suggested that a nondirective, child-centered play therapy (CCPT) approach would be an appropriate starting point. The school psychologist had been trained in this method, was familiar with the research supporting CCPT, and felt confident that Miranda would be responsive.

Session 1

The school psychologist brought Miranda to her office and showed her a variety of toys and other play materials, including art supplies, dress-up clothes, and a sandtray. "You can play with these things any way you like," the school psychologist told her. Miranda appeared to be excited at the start of her first session and explored the toys freely. She took joy in trying on wigs and clothing accessories and seemed particularly interested in the set of human figures. She spent most of the session with the "two dads, two moms, kid, and baby." She put the baby in a castle and said that the other human figures didn't know where the baby was. The baby emerged and they all went to sleep. This was repeated a few times. The school psychologist adhered closely to the nondirective approach by tracking, reflecting, and permitting Miranda to explore and play freely.

Twice Miranda left the play area and explored an area of the office that had a desk and file cabinet. The school psychologist set a gentle limit and asked her to return. She initially ignored the school psychologist but eventually returned. Because the school psychologist did not feel that Miranda was being unsafe, she was able to wait for her to return without being punitive. She noted to herself that ignoring adults' directives in the classroom had escalated to tantrums.

Miranda returned to the human figures and managed frustration well when one of the human figures fell over repeatedly. She expressed some disappointment when the session ended but transitioned well back to class.

Session 2

When the school psychologist went to Miranda's classroom to get her for the session she was watching a cartoon with her class. The school psychologist thought it might be hard for her to stop watching and leave the room, but she transitioned easily and seemed excited about starting the session.

Miranda smiled throughout and seemed delighted by the opportunity to play with the toys again. Though she briefly explored all of the toys and seemed to remember them, she only fully engaged with the people, animal puppets, play dough, and motorcycle.

Some of her play clearly challenged her fine motor skills: opening containers of play dough, dressing and undressing a doll, etc. Even so, she did not show frustration and persisted at tasks. The people she stood on the table frequently fell down, but she picked them up and started over without incident. She seemed delighted to stand the baby on her feet. The school psychologist noted to herself that Miranda appeared to have more patience than others may have thought possible.

Miranda enjoyed putting play dough on the human figures, standing them in containers of play dough, etc. She separated the adult figures from the children. At one point Miranda said the baby was playing hide and seek.

When time was up, Miranda put away the play dough and transitioned back to class easily. She invited the school psychologist to play with a toy in the classroom, but the school psychologist politely declined and said that she would see Miranda next week.

Session 3

With very little advance notice, the school psychologist was informed that her office was needed for some testing, so she gathered her play therapy toys and materials and moved them to a room that is used to store books. Miranda adjusted well to the change and happily left her class activity with the school psychologist. She reached out to hold the school psychologist's hand as they went to the new room.

Once there, Miranda continued to play primarily with the human figures and puppets (though she did put on a wig for a brief period of time, and put one on the school psychologist as well). Miranda continued the "hiding" of the human figures that she had started in previous sessions.

The school psychologist noted today that Miranda made more eye contact with her and was more verbally expressive than she had been previously. She also used some of the toys to show affection (e.g., the owl puppet hugged a person and a baby owl puppet). She seemed to enjoy stroking the soft puppets and seemed very relaxed. When time was up she transitioned well out of the session, again holding the school psychologist's hand and smiling. The school psychologist begins to hypothesize about the themes in Miranda's play and considers the behaviors in the sessions as a form of communication.

Session 4

This was Miranda's first session in a couple of weeks because of a holiday and her absence from school the week after. She was excited to return and continued to play with her favorite toys. The school psychologist noted that Miranda's play is becoming a little bit more integrated, with simple narratives emerging (e.g., a group of people playing hide and seek). She is starting to engage with the school psychologist a little bit more over time. For example, Miranda picked up a monkey puppet and told the school psychologist that it was biting her nose as she put it in front of the school psychologist's face. Miranda also asked the school psychologist to look for the person hiding in the game of hide and seek.

Some of her play shows characters being warm and affectionate with each other (cuddles, hugs). Miranda played a lot with the owl puppet (but called it a "white eagle") and put small human figures in the puppet and said she was laying eggs.

Miranda also undressed and dressed a small doll again and said that the doll was going swimming. She worked hard, using her fine motor skills, to manipulate the clothes. At the end of the session she transitioned well on the way back to class and gave the school psychologist a hug before leaving.

In this case example, although the school psychologist was keeping the counseling IEP goals in mind, these goals were not explicitly discussed during the counseling sessions. Rather, the technique of creating a supportive environment in which she could freely play advances Miranda toward the goals indirectly. Absent the power struggles and an adult–child interaction defined by control, Miranda has the opportunity to express herself through play, build her confidence and competencies, and, by extension, become better prepared to meet challenges outside of her counseling sessions.

Over the course of these counseling sessions, the relationship between Miranda and the school psychologist developed and supported Miranda's development of social–emotional competencies (e.g., communication skills, reciprocity) that she could use with other people in her life. The weekly sessions also provided Miranda with some routine and regular opportunities to express herself in a nurturing environment.

Miranda was seen for five more sessions. The school psychologist collected data from Miranda's teacher and father in the form of behavior rating scales and counselor-made scales regarding progress on her IEP goals, and supplemented their reports with observations of Miranda in her classroom, on the playground, and in the cafeteria. Using Goal Attainment Scaling (a criterion-referenced progress-monitoring tool; see Coffee & Ray-Subramanian, 2009), the school psychologist was able to determine that Miranda had made progress on both of her goals, but additional sessions were recommended to make further gains.

The following are discussion questions for Case Example 1:

1. What other approaches could the school psychologist have selected other than child-centered play therapy?
2. What are some advantages of working with a child on counseling goals without explicitly talking about those goals during sessions? What are some disadvantages?
3. The school psychologist used Goal Attainment Scaling to measure progress on the counseling goals. What are some other ways that Miranda's progress could be measured?
4. Counseling services are most effective when they are coordinated with other social–emotional–behavioral supports. What could the school psychologist do outside of sessions to maximize the impact of the counseling?

The second case example demonstrates a school psychologist's process for assessing a child's record of behaviors and performance in school to design a plan. Although nondirective, play-based approaches may be effective for many children, school psychologists may choose more directive talk therapy approaches to meet the needs of other students. As shown in this second example, the use of cognitive techniques is particularly helpful for students who have high cognitive and verbal abilities and show some motivation to reflect on past behaviors and work toward the completion of one or more goals. Chapter 8 reviewed many of these therapeutic modalities, including cognitive–behavioral therapy (CBT), reality therapy, and dialectical behavior therapy (DBT). In this case, the school psychologist assesses Nathan's needs and carefully selects interventions that match his characteristics.

CASE EXAMPLE 2: NATHAN

Nathan, a 17-year-old high school junior, has been classified as a student with an emotional disturbance since he was in the fifth grade. Though he has had a history of depression and anxiety for several years, he had not received counseling services until recently. Perhaps because he was primarily internalizing, his behaviors did not draw the kind of attention from teachers and administrators that externalizing students generate. Even so, his parents and teachers noted an increase in absences and called an IEP meeting to share concerns and develop a plan to assist Nathan.

To prepare for the meeting, the school psychologist gathered some information from Nathan's parents and teachers about current functioning to develop some preliminary hypotheses. Over the past year Nathan had become increasingly isolated at home and at school. He had stopped participating in the chess club and his Boy Scout troop and was spending a lot of time in his room. Teachers noted some irritability, and his parents had expressed concern that Nathan had an irregular sleeping schedule. The school psychologist also reviewed existing records, including grades and attendance, to prepare for the IEP meeting.

The IEP meeting proved to be challenging, as team members voiced a variety of explanations and attributions regarding Nathan. One of the teachers suggested that Nathan be placed in an alternative school because, "he seems to do better when he doesn't have to interact with a lot of people." Nathan's mother wondered whether he needed his medications adjusted and reported that she would schedule a psychiatry consultation. The school principal noted that Nathan's attendance record was "alarming" and indicated that absences would need to be addressed, perhaps by making up some time in the summer.

The school psychologist listened carefully to each member of the IEP team and acknowledged all of the contributions. Because of the limited amount of available data, the IEP team agreed to an assessment to determine whether Nathan may be eligible for counseling as a related service. More specifically, the IEP team hoped that the assessment would provide useful information about Nathan's current social, emotional, and behavioral functioning; possible sources of Nathan's current difficulties; and recommendations for addressing concerns. The school psychologist obtained informed consent from Nathan's parents and started planning for the assessment.

Over the next 3 weeks, the school psychologist collected data, both quantitative and qualitative, from a variety of sources and integrated the findings in an effort to directly address the assessment referral questions. The assessment data, which included an interview with Nathan, indicated that behaviors associated with depression (e.g., withdrawal, hypersomnia, and inactivity) had exacerbated Nathan's depression over time. The recommendations from the report included counseling to help Nathan become more active, replace negative thought patterns with more adaptive thinking, and improve school attendance. The school psychologist recommended to the IEP team that Nathan receive weekly counseling as a related service and suggested some goals and objectives. The IEP team unanimously supported the recommendation.

When selecting a counseling method or technique for working with Nathan, the school psychologist carefully considered Nathan's needs. Nathan has demonstrated strong cognitive and verbal abilities and wants to feel better, though he acknowledges that he has been plagued by low motivation and feelings of hopelessness. When asked how he felt about working with the school psychologist for weekly counseling sessions, Nathan indicated that he wasn't opposed to the idea. These considerations pointed to an approach that would leverage Nathan's strengths while allowing him to progress toward his goals. Would a cognitive–behavioral therapy (CBT) be most appropriate, or would reality therapy align best with Nathan's constellation of skills and needs?

The school psychologist understood that reality therapy is sometimes selected over CBT because of a belief that acting one's way into thinking differently is easier than thinking one's way into acting differently. Even if that is the case for most people, the school psychologist had an obligation to determine what was most appropriate for Nathan, and decided that using CBT would be a good way to begin, at least initially. If some progress was made with CBT, it would then be possible to introduce some behavioral activation techniques (e.g., scheduling activities that generate positive feelings), which could potentially introduce elements of reality therapy to their work together.

Session 1

The first session was designed to build rapport and introduce Nathan to the goals and therapeutic approach. The school psychologist and Nathan spent the first 15 minutes of the session getting to know one another better and talked about sports, music, and other shared interests. Noting that Nathan seemed to feel comfortable and at ease, the school psychologist reviewed the IEP counseling goals with Nathan and asked him whether he had any other goals. Nathan said that the goals looked fine, and that the only thing he wanted to add was that he wanted to "feel better." The school psychologist assured him that feeling better was a good addition and that they could certainly work on that, spending some time elaborating on what feeling better might look like. He then proceeded to tell Nathan about the therapy approach.

"You can think of this counseling as a team that you and I are on, and we're working together to accomplish the same thing. Each time we meet we'll be focused on helping you feel better, and we'll do that by helping you learn how to replace negative thoughts with thoughts that help you stay more positive. How does that sound?"

Nathan seemed to like the approach and said that he was a bit relieved that counseling wouldn't look like the Freudian psychoanalysis he had seen in movies. He also liked the approach because "it's logical, like me." Next, the school psychologist explained the relationship between thoughts and feelings, using an example of a hypothetical student who consistently makes negative attributions. Nathan demonstrated that he understood the concept and even provided an example from his own experience of thinking negatively. As the session came to a close, the school psychologist gave Nathan the homework assignment of trying to notice his thinking and pay attention to specific thoughts so that they could talk about them at the next session.

Session 2

The school psychologist greeted Nathan and thanked him for remembering his appointment. He told Nathan that they would start each session with an agenda so that they could make the most of their time and maintain a focus on the goals. "Today I'd like to start with what we call a *mood check* to see how you're feeling, take a closer look at our goals, and introduce you to CBT in more detail. I'll also ask you about your counseling homework. Is there anything you would like to add to the agenda?" Nathan said he didn't have anything to add, and that the agenda seemed fine.

For the mood check, the school psychologist asked Nathan how he had been feeling over the last week. Nathan reported that he had not really felt like doing much, other than sleeping. The school psychologist reflected this back and emphasized the importance of paying attention to those feelings, as that is an important part of getting better. They then spent some time looking at the goals again and confirmed that they were appropriate. Looking at the goals periodically can help the school psychologist and student maintain an awareness of the purpose of counseling and keep the focus on the targets.

For the remainder of the session, the school psychologist explained how CBT works, keeping Nathan engaged as an active learner. They talked about how we sometimes have automatic thoughts in response to the events in our lives, and that those automatic thoughts directly affect how we feel. When we feel bad, we tend to withdraw, which may in turn lead to more negative thoughts. Nathan confirmed that he understood this. They ended with a review of the homework, and Nathan said that he had forgotten to track his feelings. The school psychologist encouraged him to think about one moment in the last few days during which he was aware of his feelings, and Nathan said that when he was getting ready for school today he felt like staying home. The school psychologist told him that's just the kind of awareness that he can build and maintain and encouraged him to keep doing that, but to begin noting these moments, either in a journal or on his phone. By keeping a record of these events and feelings, Nathan will be able to bring them to future sessions.

Session 3

Nathan arrived at his third session in what appeared to be an improved mood compared with previous sessions. The school psychologist noted this to himself and recalled that he had seen others on his counseling caseload show some demonstrable increase in outward happiness after a few sessions, though he maintained an awareness that this should not be misinterpreted as a quick fix, nor should the focused work on changing thoughts and feelings cease.

Together they reviewed the agenda, and again Nathan noted his approval of the agenda and had nothing to add, though he did report that he had tracked his feelings over the past week and brought in some examples to share. The school psychologist thanked him and said that completion of this work was very helpful for their work together. They did a mood check (Nathan reported that he was indeed feeling better than he had last week, though he didn't know why), and then the school psychologist showed Nathan a list of common dysfunctional thoughts (e.g., all-or-nothing thinking, labeling, mind reading) and explained how these patterns of thinking can lead to negative thinking. Nathan observed that he's aware of his habit of thinking in terms of *should* statements and *mental filters*. The school psychologist explained to Nathan that his comprehension of this would help him as he identifies and replaces these thoughts with more adaptive patterns.

They used the last part of the session to learn about how automatic thoughts come from core beliefs about ourselves. The school psychologist provided Nathan with some examples to illustrate this point. For example, someone who has the automatic thought, "I just can't get my work done" may have a core belief such as "I'm hopeless" or "I'm not capable." The school psychologist explained to Nathan that in the next few sessions they would spend some time identifying thoughts, feelings, and core beliefs. The emphasis of the work would be on looking for evidence that erodes the strength of the core belief. For example, someone who holds the core belief of "I'm not capable" may be encouraged to think about the degree to which he believes the core belief is true, and to identify data points that go against that core belief (e.g., "I did build my own computer, so I'm not entirely without capabilities"). Nathan played an active role in the session, asking questions, providing examples, and showing interest. He told the school psychologist that he liked coming to counseling and was glad that he was able to work on changing the way he thinks and feels.

Sessions 4–8

Over the next several sessions the school psychologist and Nathan worked collaboratively through the structured process of completing dysfunctional thought records and challenging irrational thoughts and core beliefs. Over time, Nathan came to see that he had been endorsing a negative view of himself and the world around him (and denying himself the opportunity to see the positive aspects of his personhood and life). Weekly mood checks suggested that Nathan was also slowly starting to feel better. In an effort to build on this momentum, the school psychologist introduced some behavioral activation (encouraging Nathan to get out and engage more with others in an active way). Nathan was receptive and they developed a realistic plan for him to join an after-school hiking club.

The school psychologist measured progress on Nathan's goals using a variety of data sources, including Nathan's self-report, his attendance records, and parents' and teachers' perceptions of his mastery on each counseling IEP objective. By all accounts, Nathan was making great progress and was showing fewer symptoms. He was sleeping on a more regular schedule, attending school consistently, and spending more time socializing with others.

Nathan's parents were pleased with the progress and asked the school psychologist about the counseling intervention. The school psychologist explained the collaborative nature of CBT and emphasized the active role that Nathan played in achieving his goals. The school psychologist reported that Nathan's change in mood over time was due to a combination of factors, including his ability to recognize how his thoughts were interfering with his feelings, his motivation to address these negative thought patterns, and a willingness to try new ways of thinking.

The following discussion questions can be used for Case Example 2:

1. Suppose Nathan had been resistant to the idea of talking to someone about his problems? What could the school psychologist do to enlist Nathan's participation?
2. How would the counseling sessions with Nathan have been different had the school psychologist started with reality therapy?
3. Suppose that after a few sessions it became apparent that Nathan was not a good match for a CBT or reality therapy approach. What other techniques might be appropriate?
4. After Nathan made sufficient progress to discontinue counseling, what might be put in place to maintain the progress made?

The third case example illustrates that, although in many cases the school psychologist will find a clear fit between a student's needs and a counseling modality, some referrals will have no obvious method or technique. The lives and presenting problems of children are often complicated, and an individual's needs may not direct the school psychologist to a discrete course of treatment. In such situations, school psychologists must rely on flexibility, creativity, and careful attention to how a child responds to the counseling environment and interventions. There must be a willingness to adapt and change in response to the student's evolving needs. The next case example demonstrates how an experienced school psychologist who has trained on a variety of counseling techniques takes an eclectic approach to a multifaceted client profile.

CASE EXAMPLE 3: ARLO

School records cataloged years of academic and behavioral difficulties for Arlo, but not until the fifth grade did the concerns lead to a formal problem-solving process. A team of teachers, administrators, and school-based mental health professionals met to better understand Arlo's challenges and develop a plan to address them. As it turned out, the problem identification process proved to be complicated. The team noted the following strengths:

- Motivated to please
- Friendly
- Creative

Several concerns were also noted:

- Easily angered
- Unusual thoughts and behaviors
- Poor handwriting
- Reading difficulties

The problem-solving team reviewed interventions that had previously been tried, including small-group instruction with a reading specialist, many office referrals for behavioral incidents in the classroom, and participation in an anger management group facilitated by the school counselor. Unfortunately, over time Arlo's behavior and learning difficulties only worsened. Because Arlo had attended three different schools, the team was unable to determine whether any of the prior interventions had been implemented with fidelity, and very little data were collected to measure intervention outcomes. Arlo was referred for an assessment to better understand his difficulties and to consider whether special education services were needed. Results of the evaluation indicated that Arlo met the criteria for emotional disturbance (inappropriate behaviors and feelings under normal circumstances) and needed counseling as a related service to be successful.

Arlo's counseling goals focused on his social–emotional development and included objectives related to increasing his awareness of his feelings, developing more appropriate ways to express anger, and improving his awareness of others' thoughts and feelings. The IEP team approved the goals and objectives and supported the school psychologist's recommendation that Arlo receive a combination of individual and group counseling to address these goals.

Session 1 (Individual)

The school psychologist decided to start meeting with Arlo individually before starting group sessions so that there would be an opportunity to build rapport and ensure that Arlo was a good fit for an established anger management group at his school. During the first session the school psychologists introduced a simple game in which the two of them threw a ball back and forth, taking turns answering questions on the ball (e.g., What is your favorite food?). Arlo seemed to enjoy the game and the school psychologist noted that Arlo made good eye contact and engaged in reciprocal turn taking. After the game, the school psychologist reviewed the goals with Arlo, but noted that Arlo quickly lost interest when the focus turned to his social–emotional needs. The school psychologist also asked Arlo how he felt about being in a weekly group with other kids his age and Arlo said that he would like that. For the remainder of the session the school psychologist and Arlo worked with some clay and talked about things that Arlo liked and did not like about school.

Session 1 (Group)

Arlo joined an anger management group that had been meeting weekly for 3 weeks, and the group members welcomed him. In this session the school psychologist was encouraging group members to share about some of the physical sensations that they experience as their anger starts building. One boy said that he can feel his face getting hot, and another shared that his fists clench. Arlo said that he gets so angry that he can't even remember what happened before. The school psychologist handed out paper and markers and asked each student to draw a picture of their anger. Students socialized while drawing and the school psychologists monitored the group while they worked. They ended by taking turns showing their drawings to the group and talking about them. The school psychologist gave group members the following homework assignment: pay attention to how you feel before you get angry over the next week and be prepared to share that with the group.

Session 2 (Individual)

Arlo arrived at his second session and began to explore the office. He asked the school psychologist whether he could open the bag of clay that was in the corner of the room.
　　He was told, "When you come here, you get to make choices about what you want to do."
　　Arlo opened the bag, pulled out some clay, and invited the school psychologist to join him. The two worked with the clay side by side as the school psychologist observed, tracked, and reflected. Arlo has had years of academic and behavioral difficulties, but in his counseling sessions, he was having the experience of being accepted. As Arlo tried to make an airplane out of the clay, he became frustrated as the long wings of the plane began to sag and fall off. Arlo yelled, "Stupid clay!" and threw a piece across the room. Patiently, the school psychologist identified the feeling and encouraged Arlo to talk to the clay about his feelings.
　　"Take a deep breath and tell the clay what you want. Tell the clay what you need."
　　Arlo told the clay that he needed the clay to stick on tightly and not fall off. He told the clay that it was very important that the wings stay on the plane.
　　The school psychologist suggested that maybe the clay needed some help, so they looked for some materials together to help the wings stay put. Arlo used some Popsicle sticks and appeared to be very satisfied with his solution. The school psychologist noticed that Arlo had calmed down considerably and was ready to return to class.

Session 2 (Group)

The session started with a quick go-around in which each member checked in and said a few words about how they were feeling. The school psychologist then asked them to take turns sharing their homework assignments, reminding them that they were to notice how they were feeling just before they got angry over the past week. To his surprise, the first response came from Arlo, who shared that he had been feeling very good, working with clay, when all of the sudden he became very angry when the clay wings fell off of his plane. Another group member asked, "What did you do?" Arlo gave a fairly accurate response to the question and encouraged other group members to breathe and problem-solve. He received a lot of social support for participating.

Session 3 (Individual)

In an effort to build on the experience of the group session, the school psychologist invited Arlo to return to the clay, but this time to make some human figures of people at school. Arlo made clay figures of his English language arts teacher and of some peers. The school psychologist then asked Arlo to show, with the clay figures, a recent event in which there was some anger or conflict. Arlo demonstrated a scene in which another student threw a paper airplane across the room, but Arlo was scolded (for a crime he didn't commit). The school psychologist then facilitated some perspective taking by asking Arlo to talk about what each of the clay figures was thinking and feeling before, during, and after the event. Notably, Arlo initially had some difficulty distinguishing thoughts and feelings, but with some support and encouragement from the school psychologist, he was able to get better at this. Moreover, Arlo stated that seeing things from the perspective of others helped him feel less angry about getting in trouble for something that he didn't do, though he still had some angry feelings about it. The school psychologist recorded in the session notes that this activity aligned with the IEP goal of improving awareness of the thoughts and feeling of others.

Session 3 (Group)

Following the weekly go-around, the school psychologist told group members that when we find ourselves in an argument with someone else, it's often because of a misunderstanding. For example, a teacher didn't realize that a student had turned in his homework, so she told him he had to stay in during recess to complete the work. The student was very upset and kicked a chair, yelling, "That's not fair! I turned it in this morning!" How could that angry outburst have been avoided? One group member said that it would have been helpful for the teacher and student to talk about the misunderstanding. The school psychologist then introduced the students to a board game (Dixit) that involves taking the perspective of others. It also requires turn-taking, reciprocal social behavior, and other skills that are related to the students' IEP goals. The students enjoyed the game and the school psychologist intervene minimally, only to support students when they struggled.

Over the next several weeks Arlo made steady progress through the individual and group sessions, which were bolstered by consultations between the school psychologist and Arlo's parents and teachers. There were times at which the progress felt uneven (one step forward, two steps back), but the general trend, as measured by the data collected by the school psychologist, was in the right direction.

At the annual IEP meeting, the school psychologist reported progress on the counseling IEP goals, noting that the data collected demonstrated significant progress, though Arlo still exhibits some challenges. The IEP team supported the school psychologist's recommendation that counseling services continue, as the support appears to be helpful. Overall, Arlo developed improved anger management and perspective-taking skills.

The following are discussion questions for Case Example 3:

1. To what extent was the group counseling a significant component of Arlo's counseling services? What was gained from the group experience?
2. Some counseling, such as child-centered play therapy, is decidedly nondirective, whereas other approaches, such as CBT, are fairly directive by design. How would you characterize the approach the school psychologist took with Arlo?

3. If progress has not been made after several weeks of these interventions, what would you recommend?
4. Suppose that Arlo had been very resistant to going to counseling. What other ways could his goals be supported?

RESOURCES

Evidence-Based Practices

The California Evidence-Based Clearinghouse for Child Welfare, https://www.cebc4cw.org/registry/

Substance Abuse and Mental Health Services Administration, https://www.samhsa.gov/ebp-resource-center

What Works Clearinghouse: Behavior, https://ies.ed.gov/ncee/wwc/FWW/Results?filters=,Behavior

Culturally Relevant Practices

Trainers of School Psychologists Anti-Racism Resources, https://tinyurl.com/yawchj24

School Psychology in a Global Society: Roles and Functions, by S. Y. Song, A. H. Miranda, K. M. Radliff, & D. Shriberg (Bethesda, MD: National Association of School Psychologists), 2019.

The Psychology of Multiculturalism in the Schools: A Primer for Practice, Training, and Research, by J. M. Jones (Bethesda, MD: National Association of School Psychologists), 2009.

Therapy Games and Websites

The following resources are recommended as potential tools to support your counseling work with children and adolescents. Items in this list may be appropriate for some kids but not for others, so always think carefully matching client needs to techniques and tools.

Games
  Royal Rage: The Fun Anger Management Game for Kids
  Totika Therapy Game
  Dixit
  Thumball
  Pocket Ungame (kids version)
  Family Pastimes Co-operative Games, https://familypastimes.com/

Websites
  Do2Learn, www.do2learn.com
  The Beck Institute, https://beckinstitute.org/
  Bibliotherapy & Play Therapy, http://guides.library.txstate.edu/bibliotherapy-play-therapy
  Association for Play Therapy, https://www.a4pt.org/
  Association for Child and Adolescent Counseling, http://acachild.org/

REFERENCES

Blease, C. R., Kelley, J. M., & Trachsel, M. (2018). Evidence-based practice and psychological treatments: The imperatives of informed consent. *Journal of Contemporary Psychotherapy, 48,* 69–78. doi: 10.3389/fpsyg.2016.01170

California Evidence-Based Clearinghouse for Child Welfare. (n.d.). Understanding evidence-based practices. Retrieved from https://www.cebc4cw.org/files/CEBCUnderstandingEvidence-BasedPractices.pdf

Coffee, G., & Ray-Subramanian, C. E. (2009). Goal attainment scaling: A progress-monitoring tool for behavioral interventions. *School Psychology Forum, 3*(1), 1–12.

Jordanova, T., Gerlach, B., & Faulkner, M. (2015, September). *Developing strategies for child maltreatment prevention: A guide for selecting evidence-based practices.* Austin, TX: University of Texas at Austin.

National Resource Center for Mental Health Promotion and Youth Violence Prevention. (n.d.). Selecting evidence-based programs. Retrieved from https://healthysafechildren.org/sites/default/files/Selecting_EBPs_Website_508.pdf

Chapter 12

Self-Knowledge and Self-Care

OVERVIEW

The work of a school psychologist is difficult. All mental health professionals encounter challenges related to clients' complex emotional and behavioral needs as they are expressed within their classrooms, homes, or communities. In school settings, educational progress is the metric by which success of interventions is measured, yet the myriad social, emotional, and situational stressors students experience in their family, school, and community systems may not be most evident in the academic domain. Further, the counseling role is one of several for most school psychologists and may not be the primary role. The current cultural climate in the United States—with school safety concerns, high suicide rates, epidemic rates of substance abuse and addiction, immigration conflicts, and global threats such as climate change—influences students' adjustment in ways that are not fully understood. Students are not the only ones affected by these stressors—so are their families, friends, and the professionals who work with them. School psychologists must work with many individuals within these systems, including teachers, administrators, other school staff, families, and peers, adding to the demands of understanding needs and problems and facilitating change. Large caseloads and limited time and resources contribute to work-related stress. In this chapter, we address issues of self-knowledge and self-care as necessary prerequisites for developing and sustaining productive and satisfying careers in school psychology.

OBJECTIVES

After reading this chapter, the readers should be able to do the following:

- Identify stressors inherent in the practice of school psychology, specifically in the counseling role.
- Acknowledge that personal history, current experiences, and known and unknown biases may affect the school psychologist's reactions to specific individuals and situations.

- Discuss indicators that personal problems may be impairing the work of the school psychologist.
- Explore opportunities for self-care that enhance effectiveness and career success and sustainability.
- Consider ways in which the school psychologist can contribute to a healthy school environment for both the individual student and the larger system.

School Psychology and Stress

Self-care is important given that school psychologists must be able to manage stress and remain healthy and motivated within the system. Just how much of a problem is stress for school psychologists? Of course, school psychologists are different from each other, not only in how they experience stress, but also in their work settings, interpersonal adjustment, years of experience in the field, life outside of work, and general mental and physical health. General research findings don't always apply to the individual; however, the research around stress and the work of the school psychologist is informative. Every individual, as a helping professional, works with those who have emotional, behavioral, learning, and environmental problems, and they may at times carry the weight of others' burdens as well as their own. They also work in systems that experience the stressors of high demand for services in the context of limited resources.

Bearse and colleagues (2013) observed that among professional psychologists, several factors are associated with burnout: a tendency to place the needs of others above one's own, a need to control one's own emotions when encountering clients' experiences of trauma and intense emotion, increased sensitivity to people and the environment, and a sense of isolation. Further, negative client behaviors, lack of success in therapy, and administrative duties and paperwork can also contribute to burnout. Although their research was not specific to school psychologists, some of these factors certainly appear relevant.

Shortages of school psychologists are well documented (National Association of School Psychologists [NASP], 2017b), which means that caseloads are high for most practitioners. Walcott and Hyson (2018) report that the average national ratio of school psychologists to students is 1 to 1,381. NASP recommends one school psychologist to 500–700 students (Griffith, 2018). Schilling, Randolph, and Boan-Lenzo (2018) commented that, according to recent research, not only do particular school resources best predict feelings of burnout; practitioners' level of satisfaction with their settings also do. It follows that feelings of dissatisfaction with one's work, for example, related to caseload, salary, or perceived support, may account for differences among practitioners in similar settings with respect to burnout.

To assess burnout and job satisfaction, Schilling and colleagues (2018) surveyed school psychologists working in four Southeastern states, obtaining a response rate of 45% (122 respondents). Most respondents were female (84.6%), with 98.3% working in public school settings. A range of experience characterized respondents, from less than 5 years to more than 20 years. They found that 90% of the respondents reported experiencing burnout at some point in their school psychology careers, a higher rate than expressed in earlier studies, according to Schilling and colleagues (2018). These authors also reported that a significant number of study participants had considered leaving the field because of these feelings.

What is burnout? Recent research and commentaries often use the Mayo Clinic (2018) definition that burnout is a state of feeling exhausted, physically, mentally, or emotionally, within the context of work. Maslach and Jackson (1986) described three elements of burnout that are still cited in recent literature: emotional exhaustion, depersonalization, and a lowered sense of personal accomplishment. Gill Lopez (2016) writes that emotional exhaustion happens when work demands outpace personal resources; depersonalization occurs when people become problems to fix; and a lowered sense of personal accomplishment emerges as a kind of learned helplessness, the perception that no matter how hard one tries, nothing makes a difference. Decreased energy and motivation, cynicism, and mental health difficulties can be signs of burnout. Gill Lopez (2016) points out that the burnout rate among school psychologists is likely exacerbated by the fact that psychologists employed in schools have less control over aspects of service delivery than those in private practice. Schilling and colleagues (2018) note that factors identified as contributing to burnout among school psychologists include perception of one's worth within the school system, lack of opportunities for advancement, lack of perceived support from administrators and supervisors, and pressure to act unethically.

The Counseling Role

In the counseling role, school psychologists may encounter unique stressors. For some, counseling is seen as an extra role that can be taken on only when the assessment caseload is under control. In such cases, school psychologists may feel some pressure to turn away referrals or get rapid results. Increased collateral work may be necessary to coordinate interventions, thus requiring more time; for example, they might have ongoing consultations with providers outside the school (psychiatrists, therapists, pediatricians) and with parents. Another factor in stress is the bounds of competence: ethical school psychologists recognize that they are not able to treat all types of disorders or problems that occur in the student population. For example, a high school student who has been receiving counseling may disclose having been sexually assaulted while under the influence of alcohol. Graduate training programs and experience in the field cannot prepare the school psychologist for the entire range and diversity of problems that can occur across the spectrum of students' age, circumstances, and individual characteristics. Limits of a school psychologist's competence bring into play other demands, for example, limits of confidentiality, knowledge of appropriate resources, duty to increase skills through professional development, and consultation.

Bearse and colleagues (2013), when discussing burnout among psychologists, describe *vicarious traumatization* as an effect of the severe and graphic traumatic material that may be presented by clients. Although counseling in schools might be viewed by some as less intensive than clinical psychotherapy, the fact is that human experience does not conform itself to the characteristics of the provider or setting. Students may be subjected to extreme trauma and need to feel safe expressing their experiences even when the school psychologist feels underprepared for this role. *Compassion fatigue* may occur as a response to cumulative exposure to clients' emotional suffering, and it can compromise empathic ability and motivation to respond. In *countertransference*, the school psychologist who has experienced stressors, traumas, relationship problems, or mental health issues similar to those of a client may have a heightened emotional reaction and reduced objectivity, resulting in their unknowingly transferring their emotions to a client. Countertransference needs to be recognized and addressed. It also may occur in reaction to transference, in which clients transfer feelings for others in their life onto the mental health professional.

In the assessment-only role, the school psychologist's active involvement may end or be limited after the final report and team meetings are completed, with minimal accountability for outcomes of intervention. In contrast, when providing counseling, the school psychologist's role will be ongoing for the duration of counseling, with accountability for outcomes related to counseling goals and objectives. Although accountability is considered to be appropriate and desirable, it may add extra stress for the time-challenged school psychologist. A related time management challenge involves simply finding counseling slots that are acceptable to parents and teachers, given the emphasis on academic instructional time in the school day. Students also need special classes such as physical education, art, and music; they should be able to attend field trips, assemblies, holiday parties, and so on; and they must be present for benchmarks and other group testing. The counseling IEP will have a designated number of sessions or minutes across a specified time period; as a legal document, the IEP must be followed or, if necessary, adjusted with IEP team consensus.

The Personal Side

The same range of problems seen in clients occurs among school psychologists—family stressors like divorce, child care, and loss; financial crises; alcoholism and substance abuse; work overload; history of abuse or neglect; and mental illness such as depression, anxiety, bipolar disorder, or posttraumatic stress disorder. No one is immune from stressors such as serious illness, unexpected death of a loved one, a family member's mental illness, or a natural disaster. Bearse and colleagues (2013) observe that it is not uncommon for people who go into psychology to be "trying to figure out their own issues" (p. 151).

Graduate students under supervision and graduates in practice deal with a range of situational and personal stressors, and of course practitioners and trainers must deal with major stressors too. Empathy for their colleagues and supervisees is one of the resources school psychologists can bring to the workplace. The following are examples of school psychologists' experiences with stress and burnout, as a preface to this chapter's discussion of self-knowledge and self-care. These examples do not depict any specific individual or situation but rather represent composites.

Janis was a 42-year-old practitioner who had been working as a school psychologist in a rural school district for 10 years. She was married and had three children, two in high school and one in elementary school. During her career, she had become friends with many of her colleagues in the school system, including teachers, administrators, counselors, and others. Further, she knew many of the parents and families in the community and was comfortable with her ability to navigate multiple relationships while providing ethical services. When her oldest son was arrested on the high school campus for drug possession and public intoxication, he also was expelled and cut from the football team. The ensuing educational, legal, and treatment interventions required Janis and her husband to be involved in meetings and legal proceedings and thus miss some work. Janis's younger child was upset by the reactions of children who knew about this event; the high school sibling was angry and embarrassed when she heard for the first time from peers a rumor that her brother had been selling drugs. Janis learned that her son's coach knew about his substance use but had not informed her and her husband. Janis felt emotionally overwhelmed by the stress on the family and felt exposed in her role as a school psychologist, perceiving others as judging her competence as a parent and mental health professional. In her counseling relationships with students, she wondered about limits of confidentiality when a counselor was aware of drug use among students.

In another example, Leo had been practicing school psychology for 3 years in an urban area. He maintained close contact with some of his graduate school colleagues, and those who were working nearby had formed a social support group that met regularly for dinner and conversation. A school shooting occurred on a campus where a member of his group, Richard, worked as a school psychologist. The shooter, who was killed when law enforcement arrived, had been Richard's counseling client. Richard was emotionally devastated by this event; in addition, he feared that he would face public judgment and possible legal problems because he had not been aware of the degree of this student's cognitive or emotional distress and had not anticipated the shooting. Leo wanted to support his friend during this crisis but also felt threatened by his own vulnerability to unexpected crises.

These are dramatic, but realistic, examples of stressors that occur in the lives of school psychologists. More commonly, school psychologists experience marriages, divorces, births, illnesses, injuries, and stressors such as administrative changes, campus realignments, changes in job duties, benefits concerns, personnel evaluations, compensation, and so on. How do school psychologists take care of themselves given that "school psychology relies heavily on the excellence of its practitioners in order to ensure the delivery of high-quality school-based services to students" (Schilling et al., 2018, p. 324).

Self-Knowledge and Self-Care

> "An empty lantern provides no light. Self-care is the fuel that allows your light to shine brightly." – Unknown

For school psychologists to be effective in their work, they must have knowledge about and take care of themselves. The question school psychologists may ask is: "How can we practice what we preach?" In training, practice, and in this book, working toward the goal of a productive and balanced life involves learning about the power of relationships, the need for belongingness, the value of mindfulness, and the necessity of addressing stress, depression, anxiety, and other mental health issues. Abuse of alcohol and other substances, unchecked anger, unresolved grief, and distorted thought processes can derail even the most committed and competent individuals. The health of their families, work environment, and community systems dynamically interact with their intrapersonal selves to both challenge and support their work efforts. In this book's discussion of cognitive–behavioral counseling approaches, it talks about encouraging students to describe and assess their "quality world," a technique used in reality therapy. Can school psychologists not do the same for themselves? This discussion may help with that, as it addresses both self-knowledge and self-care as essential elements of professional responsibility.

Self-Knowledge

Ethical guidelines for school psychologists encourage self-knowledge: monitoring personal fitness for practice, the bounds of competence, effects on clients with respect to "do no harm," equity, and justice. Although self-care is not part of any ethics documents or standards, school psychologists are clearly held accountable for monitoring their own mental health and preparation for any practice they undertake. As Gill Lopez (2016) eloquently states, "proactive self-care should be one of the ethical standards in its own right. In the same way that mental health is much more than the absence of mental illness, nurturing positive emotional states through self-care is not the same as alleviating harmful disruptive emotional states after the fact" (pp. 24–25). Rupert and Dorociak (2019) observe that self-care has been described as "an ethical imperative" (p. 343). Hence, school psychologists must be proactive rather than reactive in addressing their own well-being. This process starts with self-knowledge.

One of the basic premises of self-knowledge is that all people have blind spots and areas of personal sensitivity that may create discomfort. Graduate training programs would do well to encourage students to examine their own life experiences for any that may have created bias, presumption, anxiety, avoidance, distaste, or another negative mind-set that might interfere with their work. Examples include racial, cultural, or sexual orientation biases; gender presumptions; topic avoidance; or habitual patterns of response to authority. Other possible sources of interference might be a personal history or family history of substance abuse or addiction; physical, sexual, or emotional abuse; mental illness; psychiatric diagnoses; legal problems; school struggles; and others. At the same time, graduate students can be encouraged to reflect on their areas of strength, which might include tolerance for differences, empathy for individuals' struggles, willingness to listen and skills for listening, motivation for learning, among other strengths.

In graduate classes, such self-reflection is accomplished by writing about feelings in response to readings, having in-class discussion, and conducting self-assessment. Fostering a safe classroom space in which graduate students can openly discuss the process of exploring personal strengths and weaknesses is a faculty responsibility. Supervision in clinical and field experiences presents a prime opportunity for graduate students and early career practitioners to process their growing awareness of their personal dispositions in relation to work demands and to receive feedback. Gill Lopez (2016), citing Huebner, Gilligan, and Cobb (2002), advocated for faculty to model wellness, management of stress, and personal growth to encourage self-care. Such modeling includes respectful communication and supportive listening when sensitive content occurs in the classroom, in supervision, or in faculty–student meetings.

The relevant literature also provides guidance. Moore and colleagues (2019) advocate for the use of supervision to convey knowledge and the practice of self-care, stating that "Personal challenges may negatively impact psychological services, ultimately placing both the client's and the trainee's well-being in jeopardy. It is therefore imperative that supervisors teach and foster school psychology graduate students' use of effective self-care strategies to encourage ethical practice" (p. 30). Gill Lopez observed that both the American Counseling Association (ACA) and the American School Counselors Association (ASCA) include specific language in their ethical guidelines for self-knowledge and self-care:

> [C]ounselors engage in self-care activities to maintain and promote their own emotional, physical, and spiritual well-being to best meet their professional responsibilities. (ACA, 2014, p. 8)

> Professional school counselors . . . monitor their emotional and physical health and practice wellness to ensure optimal professional effectiveness. School counselors seek physical or mental health support when needed to ensure professional competence. (ASCA, 2016, B.3.f)

Monitoring of self-care can be informal, for example, through supervision or peer consultation, or formal. Rupert and Dorociak (2019) describe a tool developed by Dorociak and colleagues (2017) for psychologists to use to monitor their self-care. This measure is a 21-item Self-Care Assessment for Psychologists (SCAP) that includes five factors:

- Professional Support (cultivating supportive relationships with colleagues)
- Professional Development (seeking opportunities for professional growth and involvement in enjoyable professional activities)
- Life Balance (cultivating relationships and activities outside of work)
- Cognitive Awareness (monitoring workplace stress and reactions)
- Daily Balance (managing demands and structuring the work day). (p. 344)

Rupert and Dorociak (2019) conducted a study of archival survey data to examine how self-care increases life satisfaction and reduces burnout risk among practicing psychologists, using results from the SCAP completed by practitioners. They found that higher scores on all five aspects of self-care predicted lower stress, which in turn predicted lower burnout. Life balance, cognitive awareness, and daily balance emerged as particularly important to psychologists' professional and personal functioning. They further concluded that proactive self-care is most effective when "aimed at reducing stress and thereby avoiding the progression to negative outcomes" (p. 343).

These findings underscore the importance of school psychologists' ongoing self-assessment of well-being so that self-care can be proactive rather than reactive. Other factors in school psychologists' well-being include their personal relationships and activities outside of work, their reactions to stress at work, and their ability to structure the workday to manage demands. Faculty in training programs, university and field supervisors, and colleagues are responsible to each other to encourage such self-reflection and self-knowledge.

Self-Care

Self-knowledge and self-care are an ethical responsibility of the school psychologist, and willingness to conduct self-assessment and monitoring have been established. To help school psychologists fulfill those responsibilities, this section describes some practical considerations about self-care, including how they can pursue treatment when prevention has not worked.

Bearse and colleagues (2013) provide a helpful discussion of barriers experienced by psychologists who seek psychotherapy as a form of self-care. They surveyed 260 professional psychologists (52%

response rate) and acknowledged that self-selection by those who responded that may have affected findings. The problem most frequently identified by respondents as the reason for psychotherapy was burnout. The two most frequently encountered obstacles to getting treatment were difficulty finding a psychotherapist and lack of time. Other obstacles that emerged as less problematic were cost, difficulty admitting distress, and stigma (which had the least reported impact). Most clinical psychologists reported not seeking psychotherapy at times when they needed it (Bearse et al., 2013).

Gill Lopez (2017) defined self-care as the "intentional, proactive pursuit of integrated wellness through balancing mind, body, and spirit personally and professionally" (p. 4) and described a series of pro bono self-care workshops provided to school psychologists and teachers in public schools in Connecticut. The workshops, which were designed around the ADKAR model for change (Hiatt, Creasey, & the Change Management Learning Center, 2003), were provided to promote self-care. The following are elements of the model:

- Raise Awareness of need for change
- Nurture Desire to participate in change
- Provide Knowledge for how to change
- Develop the Ability to change
- Reinforce the change

Gill Lopez (2017) provided a neurobiological explanation of the importance of school psychologists being good role models for students, in that a child's perception of adults' nervous system, as expressed in behavior, has a significant influence on children and youth, even more so than what is said by that adult. She also explained that self-care, which allows individuals to be at their best, is best accomplished when strategies are customized for the individual and are shown to have long-lasting effects.

In their discussion of self-care in supervision, Moore and colleagues (2019) focus on graduate students, who are likely to experience stress that includes academic demands, financial obligation, time constraints, and poor work and school-life balance. This stress affects daily functioning, and graduate students may not reliably practice appropriate coping strategies. Graduate students who engage in self-care are more likely to have decreased psychological stress and increased self-compassion and life satisfaction, along with higher grades, according to research cited by Moore and colleagues (2019). They advocate for supervision to (a) encourage the use of individualized self-care strategies early in their education, reinforcing the importance of such strategies throughout graduate training; and (b) respond to supervisees' stress and related needs during times of personal crises. To create a safe and trusting supervisory relationship for disclosing personal stressors, supervisors can model transparent communication, provide clear expectations, and demonstrate empathy, without moving into a psychotherapy model. Moore and colleagues (2019) recommend that supervisors set aside regular times during supervision to discuss self-care, possibly by using self-care checklists and self-care planning worksheets (citing Kelly & Davis, 2017, pp. 105–108).

NASP (n.d.) provides an online list of resources for self-care, including articles, podcasts, websites, apps, and others. For example, a list of guidelines for developing support systems and managing stress (Bjorkman & the NASP Early Career Workgroup, 2010) includes tips on (a) establishing professional relationships (e.g., visibility in hall, keeping door open, meeting administrators); (b) reducing stress (e.g., making office a cozy, welcoming space; setting hours and sticking to them; making time for enjoyable activities; having a regular exercise routine); and (c) accessing social supports (informational, instrumental, emotional, and appraisal). Recommendations are made for responding to challenges, including (a) keeping clear boundaries between relationships that are friendships and those that are professional, (b) maintaining respectful resolve about one's position when there are differences of opinion, and (c) seeking support from social resources as needed. The webpage contains many other useful self-care resources, including websites with mindfulness activities and free access to yoga exercise programs.

Self-compassion has emerged as a construct of interest in both professional and popular literature. School psychologists are not protected from the real-life hardships, losses, disappointments, and insecurities that affect all humans. In the book *Self-Compassion* (Neff, 2015), the author begins with the question, "[H]ow many of us truly feel good about ourselves?" (p. 3). She goes on to observe that without the capacity to see themselves clearly, and to acknowledge their weaknesses, people can't grow. At the same time, the sense of not being good enough (in professional practice, a related construct is the *imposter syndrome*) is pervasive and makes dealing with everyday life challenging, with depression, anxiety, and insecurity very common. Her proposed solution is for people to accept themselves with an open heart, treating themselves with the same kindness, caring, and compassion they would show to others. This is self-compassion.

Actively practicing self-compassion is not simple, nor is it typically a part of the training of psychologists. Although the activities and exercises in Neff's book are probably more appropriate for individual use, it contains guidelines for beginning the practice of self-compassion that may be helpful to school psychologists who are seeking better self-care strategies. An example that relates directly to the kinds of strategies school psychologists might use as counselors is that of the *empty chair*, which involves role-playing by taking each of three chairs consecutively—one as the voice of the inner self-critic, one as the voice of the part of oneself that feels judged and criticized, and one as the wise, compassionate observer. A dialogue among the three parts of the individual is followed by reflection to develop insights so that individuals can relate to themselves in a kinder, healthier way.

Efforts to establish and maintain a self-care regimen can be buoyed by the many resources in both the popular and professional literature, such as resources and recommendations from the Mayo Clinic (2018) and other sources cited in this chapter. Essentially, self-care programs involve attention to an individual's own physical, emotional, cognitive, and spiritual well-being, with the premise that any self-care program must be individualized to the person's needs, circumstances, and preferences.

Contributing to a Healthy Work Environment

Not only do school psychologists have a responsibility for self-care; they also must commit to fair, safe, and just practices within the school systems that employ them. In a dynamic interplay, healthy systems promote healthy people, and healthy people promote healthy systems. This section focuses on the opportunities school psychologists have to serve school systems, personnel, families, and students by contributing to healthy practices through healthy channels of communication.

Lines of authority within school systems are not always clear. Many professional, paraprofessional, and other positions within different disciplines coexist in school systems. Given the widely diverse training and job duties of school personnel, at times it is hard for them to figure out who the decision makers are for staffing, work assignments, and resources for school psychologists (e.g., lead school psychologists, special education directors, head of psychological services, special education coordinators, and principals). Although administrative lines of authority are outside the scope of this section, modes of communication are central to healthy systems. School psychologists should have safe and clear guidelines to acknowledge and appropriately address personal issues and their effects on work. Parents need to know that their voices are heard, even when opinions and perspectives differ from those of school personnel. Students must have private and protected means for conveying their intrapersonal and interpersonal challenges. The goal of school psychologists is to promote positive school climates, reduce stress, and participate in efforts to establish effective interventions when needed. Some of the options they have available are advocacy through consultation and family work (Chapters 4 and 5, respectively), supervision of graduate students and trainees, and modeling of self-knowledge and self-care.

Advocacy

School psychologists who practice self-care are better able to advocate for school systems that promote the well-being of adults and students. As participants in tiered systems of support, in both development and implementation phases, school psychologists can promote empirically supported models for their own school districts. One of those, response to intervention (RTI), has to a large extent focused on prevention and intervention in the academic realm. However, efforts to develop and research effectiveness of social–emotional RTI are ongoing. The Boston school system model for multitiered systems of support has been well studied and disseminated. The Collaborative for Academic, Social, and Emotional Learning (CASEL; https://casel.org/) provides examples of model programs. According to their website, emotional learning "is how children *and adults* learn to understand and manage emotions, set goals, show empathy for others, establish positive relationships, and make responsible decisions" (italics added). School psychologists can inform themselves about efforts to establish positive behavioral supports at the system level and advocate for their school systems, if they haven't already, to develop similar models and to implement them with integrity.

Support for Colleagues

Supervision has already been discussed as a vehicle for promoting and supporting the self-knowledge and self-care of graduate students, trainees, and early practitioners. This confidential relationship between a more experienced school psychologist and one or more early career school psychologists has great power associated with modeling of appropriate communication, self-awareness, and self-care. Further, the supervision relationship can serve a preventive role, in that supervisees' stressors and their responses to them can be processed to bring about an appropriate resolution that is consistent with ethical responsibilities to self and others.

Group supervision (e.g., of two interns by an experienced supervisor) offers opportunities to normalize shared experiences, validate interpretations, and facilitate solutions. When personal issues exceed the bounds of supervision, the experienced supervisor can direct the supervisee to more intensive interventions or assist in reducing duties until the supervisee is better able to cope. Again, all humans, including school psychologists, experience life stressors that sometimes exceed their immediate capacity to maintain high-level work responsibilities. It is far preferable, and ethical, to acknowledge such occurrences and support appropriate interventions than to encourage them to continue providing psychological services when those providers are impaired. In most cases, promoting mental, emotional, and physical health are best done through prevention efforts, including healthy systems with clear lines of communication and reasonable caseloads and duties.

For example, Jamie is an intern in a rural school district. Her site supervisor is contracted with the school district because they do not employ a full-time school psychologist who is qualified to supervise. She sees her site supervisor for weekly visits. Jamie has access to her university supervisor through scheduled site visits and online meetings, telephone calls (including to her supervisor's direct line when not in the office), or additional site visits as needed. She is assigned counseling cases in addition to her assessment caseload. One of the students she is counseling, Jenny, discloses that her boyfriend has talked about bringing a gun to school and killing specified teachers and students. Jamie recognizes that this represents a major crisis and feels her heart pounding and her mind going blank while listening to this disclosure. What should she do next? Jamie's ethical responsibility to her client entails reminding her of the limits of confidentiality when imminent danger is disclosed and informing Jenny that she will contact others who can ensure the safety of students and teachers. In this instance, Jamie's campus administrators should also be alerted to follow established campus procedures when safety issues are paramount. Jamie's school and university supervisors should be immediately alerted; it is their role and ethical responsibility to be available for crises, and she needs to know that she is not alone in addressing this crisis.

Support among colleagues who are not in supervisor–supervisee relationships is also a powerful force for maintaining a sense of well-being. One school district uses group meetings on Friday afternoons in which all school psychologists in the district bring difficult cases for collegial discussion and problem solving, thus reducing any sense of isolation. Another school district employs an experienced psychologist who works with individuals with severe mental problems (e.g., psychotic disorders, bipolar disorder, addiction) to consult monthly with school psychologists who are providing counseling services. Collegial support is reinforced by social events, such as regularly scheduled lunches off campus and celebrations of colleagues' milestones. Such support is consistent with a positive psychology approach, which emphasizes strengths, resources, and enjoyment of life. Opportunities to openly express frustration, confusion, and even fear can help mental health practitioners gain the sense that their problems are shared and that solutions will be found. Group consensus on suggestions for professional advocacy (e.g., appropriate roles, caseloads, credibility, recommendations, resources) will strengthen participants' sense of resolve and support when they are faced with system stressors, thus reducing likelihood of burnout.

Positive Behavioral Interventions and Supports
PBIS, a federally funded initiative through the Office of Special Education Programs (OSEP), is defined as "an evidence-based three-tiered framework to improve and integrate all of the data, systems, and practices affecting student outcomes every day. PBIS creates schools where all students succeed" (https://www.pbis.org/). This aspirational goal assumes that those developing and implementing PBIS are reasonably healthy themselves. The stated broad purpose of PBIS is "to improve the effectiveness, efficiency, and equity of schools and other agencies. PBIS improves social, emotional, and academic outcomes for all students, including students with disabilities and

students from underrepresented groups" (https://www.pbis.org/). Moreover, the use of positive behavioral supports should apply to staff, including school psychologists, as well as to students. Employee assistance programs (EAPs) are one systemic means of providing staff with supports by organizing information and resources for employees.

In PBIS, Tier 1 supports are described as the foundation for the other, more intensive intervention tiers. At Tier 1, school personnel are expected to effectively teach appropriate behavior to all children and to intervene early before unwanted behaviors escalate. Three messages relevant to this discussion are that school psychologists must (a) recognize and value appropriate behavior, (b) be able to model it in order to teach it, and (c) acknowledge appropriate behavior in colleagues to increase the chance that the behavior will happen again. The values that are espoused for students should also be emphasized for staff. School psychologists, through their consultation role, can advocate for positive supports for themselves and their colleagues.

An example of a system-wide Tier 1 model is restorative discipline. According to the website of the Institute for Restorative Justice and Restorative Dialogue (https://irjrd.org/restorative-discipline-in-schools/), "[R]estorative Discipline is a whole-school, relational approach to building school climate and addressing student behavior that fosters belonging over exclusion, social engagement over control, and meaningful accountability over punishment. Its practices replace fear, uncertainty, and punishment as motivators with belonging, connectedness and the willingness to change because people matter to each other" (attributed to Dr. Marilyn Armour, n.d.). This foundational statement reinforces the assertion that all individuals in school systems, including school psychologists, respond to a positive school climate that emphasizes connectedness with others as essential to well-being. This section does not go into detail on restorative discipline but encourages readers to explore the website and the examples of implementation across the country.

Another aspect of PBIS, or any tiered system of support, involves school systems providing opportunities for professional development, which bolster adults' abilities to provide appropriate multitiered support to students. As described by Gill Lopez (2017), teachers and school psychologists are eager to learn about self-care, as evidenced in their participation in free workshops conducted across the state of Connecticut. Topics for professional development that are particularly relevant to school psychologists include psychopharmacology, given that many students are prescribed medication as an intervention for emotional–behavioral problems, and practices in mental health agencies, hospitals, and clinics where students may be served. Being well-informed about the practices of other mental health professionals in their communities strengthens the network of support for children, families, and staff. School psychologists themselves are equipped to provide professional development to colleagues on topics such as mindfulness, stress management, and mental health interventions.

As an example, when one of us was a special education teacher, a free, voluntary after-school exercise program (after students left, during work hours) was offered to all staff. Most teachers participated and greatly enjoyed the biweekly vigorous exercise after stressful teaching days, enthusiastically filling out evaluations at the end of the program. The exercise leader was a school psychology doctoral intern and participants' attendance and evaluation contributed to her doctoral dissertation research. What a great idea—prevention-oriented positive behavior support for teachers—advocated by a school psychologist in training with administrative sanction!

The point of the example and of including PBIS in this discussion of self-care is to emphasize the importance of ensuring the well-being of adults in providing such supports to students. To some extent, it is the responsibility of school systems to create positive supports for their staff. It is also the responsibility of school psychologists, particularly supervisors, to model and teach appropriate self-care to new career professionals. Further, it is the responsibility of individual school psychologists to practice preventive self-care, monitor stress and response, and intervene efficiently and effectively when needed. Well-established and effective tiered systems of support allow school psychologists to provide for others while they access needed supports for themselves in times of crisis.

School crises have expanded the need for schools and districts to establish response protocols and to bolster the self-care supports they provide to caregivers, both before and after such events. NASP (2017a) provides a handout for school crisis teams and administrators following a school crisis or tragedy. Given the number of school crises, including multiple school shootings, the well-being of school caregivers is a grave concern. The shocking spectacles replayed in extensive media coverage following school shootings, and the visible suffering, do not focus on school caregivers, perhaps because they are giving support to the students. Although some readers may have been on the front lines during school crises, others may know that secondary trauma—the stress resulting from listening to another's traumatic experience or from helping or wanting to help someone directly affected by the tragedy—produces the same general range of symptoms as those with firsthand experience.

The following list describes some of the physical, emotional, and social or interpersonal recommendations for self-care strategies for caregivers:

- Physical self-care—healthy diet, adequate sleep, exercise, relaxation, deep breathing
- Emotional health—fewer duties, good time management, practicing of spiritual or religious faith, hobbies and creative activities, calming self-talk, soothing music, visualization
- Social care and connection—normal routines and connections with trusted friends or family, activism, or advocacy work

Self-care in the context of school crises must be addressed through a system that provides preventive support for caregivers and allows them to engage in debriefing and stress reduction opportunities.

SUMMARY

In this chapter we reviewed the research documenting what all school psychologists know, that the job is difficult and risk for burnout is high. School psychologists are not immune from the stressors that affect all humans, and greater self-knowledge precedes effective self-care. Both should be addressed during graduate training and reinforced through field and university supervision. Practitioners have an ethical obligation to support self-care and well-being within their school by advocating for the profession at the systems level; by providing support for colleagues, including professional development; and by modeling appropriate self-care. By advocating for and participating in the development and implementation of positive behavioral interventions and supports within school districts, school psychologists support the profession as well as colleagues and students. When serving in the counseling role, the school psychologist's well-being, including the ability to tolerate stress and experience empathy and compassion, are essential to maintaining wellness supporting the retention and success of school psychologists in public schools.

KEY POINTS FOR DISCUSSION

1. In your training and practice, what systems stressors have you encountered that affect your work? Personal stressors?
2. How controllable are these external stressors? For those that can possibly be changed, what tools do you have to address systems stressors?
3. How will you avoid burnout for yourself? If you have the privilege to supervise, how will you incorporate self-knowledge and self-care into supervision?
4. What collegial activities have provided you with the most support? How has this support affected your work?
5. Consider either the case of Janis or Leo presented earlier.
   - What self-care issues are present?
   - Describe any ethical dilemmas that are present in this case.
   - How would you provide support to a colleague in this situation?
   - If you were the school psychologist Janis (or Leo), what steps would you take in support of your own well-being?
   - Describe PBIS efforts you have observed in schools, the involvement of school psychologists, and the effects of the program on system health.

REFERENCES

American Counseling Association. (2014). *2014 ACA code of ethics*. Retrieved from https://www.counseling.org/resources/aca-code-of-ethics.pdf

American School Counselor Association. (2016). *ASCA ethical standards for school counselors*. Retrieved from https://www.schoolcounselor.org/asca/media/asca/Ethics/EthicalStandards2016.pdf

Bearse, J. L., McMinn, M. R., Seegobin, W., & Free, K. (2013). Barriers to psychologists seeking mental health care. *Professional Psychology: Research and Practice, 44*(3), 150–157. https://doi.org/10.1037/a0031182

Bjorkman, S., & the NASP Early Career Workgroup. (2010). Developing support systems and managing stress. Retrieved from https://www.nasponline.org/resources-and-publications/early-career-professionals/developing-support-systems-and-managing-stress

Gill Lopez, P. (2016). Self-care: The missing link in best practice—Part 1. *Communiqué, 45*(4), 1, 24–25.

Gill Lopez, P. (2017). Self-care: The missing link in best practice—Part 2. *Communiqué, 45*(5), 4, 6–7.

Griffith, M. (2018, October 17). What is the cost of providing students with adequate psychological support? *Policy Matters Blog*. https://www.nasponline.org/research-and-policy/policy-matters-blog/what-is-the-cost-of-providing-students-with-adequate-psychological-support

Hiatt, J. M., Creasey, T. I., & the Change Management Learning Center. (2003). *Change management: The people side of change*. Loveland, CO: Prosci Research.

Huebner, E. S., Gilligan, T. D., & Cobb, H. (2002). *Best practices in preventing and managing stress and burnout*. In A. Thomas & J. Grimes, (Eds.), *Best practices in school psychology IV* (pp. 173–182). Bethesda, MD: National Association of School Psychologists.

Institute for Restorative Justice and Restorative Dialogue. (n.d). Restorative discipline in schools. https://irjrd.org/restorative-discipline-in-schools/

Kelly, K. K., & Davis, S. D. (2017). *Supervising the school psychology practicum: A guide for field and university supervisors*. New York, NY: Springer.

Maslach, C., & Jackson, S. E. (1986). *Maslach Burnout Inventory manual* (2nd ed.). Palo Alto, CA.

Mayo Clinic Staff. (2018, November 21). Job burnout: How to spot it and take action. Retrieved from https://www.mayoclinic.org/healthy-lifestyle/adult-health/in-depth/burnout/art-20046642

Moore, E. C., Jeglum, S., Young, K., & Campbell, S. M. (2019). Self-care in supervision: How do we teach others to care for themselves? *Communiqué, 47*(8), 1, 30–31.

National Association of School Psychologists. (n.d.). *Self-care for school psychologists*. https://www.nasponline.org/resources-and-publications/resources-and-podcasts/mental-health/self-care-for-school-psychologists

National Association of School Psychologists. (2017a). *Care for the caregiver: Guidelines for administrators and crisis teams [handout]*. Bethesda, MD: Author.

National Association of School Psychologists. (2017b). *Shortages in school psychology: Challenges to meeting the growing needs of U.S. students and schools* [Research summary]. Bethesda, MD: Author.

Neff, K. (2015). *Self-compassion: The proven power of being kind to yourself*. New York, NY: HarperCollins.

Rupert, P. A., & Dorociak, K. E. (2019). Self-care, stress, and well-being among practicing psychologists. *Professional Psychology: Research and Practice, 50*(5), 343–350. https://doi.org/10.1037/pro0000251

Schilling, E. J., Randolph, M., & Boan-Lenzo, C. (2018). Job burnout in school psychology: How big is the problem? *Contemporary School Psychology, 22*, 324–331. doi:10.1007/s40688-017-0138-x

Walcott, C. M., & Hyson, D. (2018). *Results from the NASP 2015 membership survey, Part one: Demographics and employment conditions* [Research report]. Bethesda, MD: National Association of School Psychologists.

Appendix A

Behavioral, Social, and Emotional Concerns
Guidance for Problem Solving and IEP Teams

DEFINING THE PROBLEM

1. How do you characterize the student's problems? Primarily…
_____ Behavioral   _____ Social   _____ Emotional

2. What are the specific target behaviors requiring intervention?

_____

_____

_____

3. How do these behaviors affect the student's educational progress?

_____

_____

_____

DOCUMENTING EXISTING INTERVENTIONS (PAST AND CURRENT)

Intervention	Dates, Details, Effectiveness
Increased structure	
Behavior plan/contract	
Monitoring by teacher/specialist	
Classroom guidance lessons	
General ed counseling (group/individual)	
Teacher/Parent consultation	
Interventions outside of school	
Medications	
Other	

ASSESSING THE APPROPRIATENESS OF IEP COUNSELING

1. Have past/current interventions been given sufficient time to judge their effectiveness? _____

2. Are the parents/guardians and student amenable to counseling at school? _____

3. Does the student attend regularly? _____

4. What competencies does the student have that would maximize the effectiveness of counseling?
   _____
   _____

OUTLINING A PLAN OF ACTION

Interventions	Person(s) Responsible	Timeline

Appendix B

Eligibility for Counseling as a Related Service

Student: Sally Sample
DOB: MM-DD-YY
Grade: 9

Date of Report: MM-DD-YY
School:
Examiner: Estefania Leal, NCSP

Sources of Data: Full Individual Evaluation (FIE) (MM-DD-YY)
Behavior Assessment System for Children-3
    Self-report
    Parent rating scale
    Teacher rating scale (from Geography and Math)
Classroom observations (MM-DD-YY and MM-DD-YY)
Interviews
    Student
    Parent
    Teacher (Geography and Math)

Reason for referral: Sally's parents and teachers have concerns about her behavior and requested an evaluation to determine whether she is eligible for counseling as a related service. Sally began receiving special education services earlier this year (Other Health Impairment: ADHD) but continues to struggle academically. Specifically, she appears to be disorganized and turns in homework inconsistently. Members of the IEP team requested this assessment to determine whether Sally needs counseling as a related service and, if so, to identify appropriate goals and objectives.

Background information: A more comprehensive history can be found in Sally's FIE (MM-DD-YY). A brief summary is provided here. Sally was born without complications, the product of a healthy and unremarkable pregnancy. Parents reported that during infancy Sally displayed a difficult temperament and was not soothed easily. Throughout childhood she was reportedly inattentive and easily distracted. She was diagnosed by a family physician with ADHD (primarily inattentive type) in September of YYYY, and this diagnosis was confirmed in her FIE. Otherwise, Sally has been in good health. She has no record of major illness and has never been hospitalized. Her academic performance had been satisfactory until middle school, at which point she began to have difficulties with organization and task completion.

A number of interventions have been tried to address the organizational and task completion challenges. Sally's parents hired an "academic coach" to meet with Sally individually once a week starting in August of YYYY. Her parents report that as long as school was in session, Sally met with her coach weekly through the end of the eighth grade (June of YYYY). Sally's parents and Sally reported that the academic coaching was unsuccessful, and Sally reported, "Nothing will make a difference because I simply can't stay organized." Sally's eighth grade homeroom teacher brought concerns to the MTSS team for consideration in February of YYYY. The MTSS team recommended a daily morning check-in with the guidance counselor to review assignments, organize materials, and so on. After 3 weeks, the intervention was discontinued because Sally reportedly did not consistently remember to attend the check-in meetings, and when she did attend, she did not have all of her materials. As a third approach to intervening, parents and teacher maintained contact by email to facilitate communication about assignments, due dates, and so on. This proved to be somewhat effective, but primarily only as a way of raising parental awareness.

The IEP team met in November of YYYY to evaluate the interventions that were tried and recommended that this current evaluation be conducted to determine whether Sally would be eligible for counseling as a related service.

Results: Parent and teacher ratings on the BASC-3 were remarkably consistent and indicated concern primarily in the areas of inattention and executive functioning. On the self-report BASC-3, Sally's responses indicated that she has a negative attitude about school and, at least with respect to academic work, an external locus of control (e.g., that success is beyond her control).

Sally was observed twice for this evaluation (once in Math, in 1st period, and once in Geography, in 6th period). During both observations, Sally appeared to be distracted and disengaged. The observer noted that she was off-task during most of each class and frequently talked to peers, used her phone to text, and doodled on her paper. When assignments were given, Sally did not write them down. When homework was collected, Sally did not turn any in.

Sally was interviewed for this assessment. During the interview she was polite, cheerful, and verbally expressive. She appeared to be aware of her academic difficulties, but reported that her challenges were beyond her control. She stated that she had tried to become better at paying attention and staying organized in the past, but that she did not find her efforts to be effective and gave up.

Teachers reported that Sally is a kind, generous, and friendly student. They stated that her inattention and disorganization have had a serious impact on her academic performance, noting that the behaviors observed by this examiner were "typical" of Sally's daily classroom behavior.

Eligibility: The results of this evaluation show that Sally is eligible for counseling as a related service. The following findings related directly to this eligibility:

1. Sally's ADHD affects her involvement and progress in the general education curriculum primarily in the area of inattention and poor task completion. Secondarily, she appears to have developed the belief that she is incapable of succeeding academically.
2. Sally has some competencies that suggest that counseling may be beneficial. She gets along well with adults, is verbally expressive, and is self-aware. Although she does not currently believe she is capable of succeeding academically, she would like to improve.

Goals: The IEP team must develop and approve an IEP for counseling. However, on the basis of this evaluation, the following general goals are recommended:

1. Improve on-task behavior in the classroom.
2. Improve homework completion.
3. Replace thoughts of helplessness with more adaptive thinking.

Estefania Leal, NCSP

Index

A

abuse, 98
academic systems, *57*
ACTION program, 155–156
addiction, 89–90, 97–98, 194
    medications, 208
    see also substance abuse
Addressing Behavioral, Social, and Emotional Concerns, 30
ADHD. *See* attention deficit hyperactivity disorder
ADKAR model, 244
administrators, 73, 79
adoption, 96
advocacy, 246
Affordable Care Act (ACA) of 2010, 8
alcoholic parent. *See* addiction
alliance, 103
American Psychological Association, ethics guidelines, 9–10, 19–20
antianxiety medications, 207
anticonvulsants, 207
antidepressants, 206
antipsychotics, 206, 208
anxiety, 4, 154–155
art techniques, 100–102, *103*
assessment, 17
    case example, 226–230
    eligibility for counseling, 33–36
    intervention and, 51–52
    assessment-only role, 240
attention deficit hyperactivity disorder (ADHD), 4, 94, 116–117, 151, 195
    medications, 207, 208
autism spectrum disorders (ASD), 4
    CBT and, 153
autonomy and self-determination, 10

B

behavior
    concerns, 253–254
    screeners, 53
    substance use disorders, 194
    systems, *57*
behavioral consultation, 69–70
    conjoint, 70–71, 79
belonging, 146
benefit, direct, 11
bibliotherapy, 221–222
book design, 3
boundaries, 89
brain, adolescent, 197–198
breathing, 130
    controlled, *135*
Bronfenbrenner model, *76*, 77
buprenorphine, 208
bupropion, 208
burnout, 238–239

C

cases, strategies for organizing, 42–44
CBT. *See* cognitive–behavioral therapy
Centers for Medicaid and CHIP Services (CMS), survey, 4
child-centered play therapy (CCPT), 113, 116–120, 124–125
    efficacy, 124–125
    outcomes evaluation, 121–122
choice theory, 145–146, 147
Coalition for Evidence-Based Policy, 21
cognitive abilities, 24
cognitive awareness, 243
cognitive–behavioral intervention for trauma in schools (CBITS), 177
cognitive–behavioral therapy (CBT), 90–91, 113, 139, 162, 203–204, 219
    applications, 150–153
    case examples, *226–230*
    OCD and, 151–152
    REBT and, 144
    trauma-focused (TF-CBT), 147–148, 152, 171, 177
collaboration, 59, 103, 210–211
    consultation, 68–69
    with families, 86–87
Collaborative for Academic, Social, and Emotional learning (CASEL), 136, 246
The Comprehensive Behavioral Health Model, 23, *24*
communication channels, blocked, 68
community
    resources, 74
    variables, crises and, 175
comorbidity, 197–198
compassion fatigue, 239
competence, 15–16, 239
concordance, 35
confidentiality, 11, 13–14, 78–79
conflict of interest, 19
    see also ethics
consultation
    conjoint behavioral consultation, 70–71, 79
    consultee-centered, 71
    defined, 68
    expert, 69
    models, 68–72, *72*

contingency therapy, 203–204
controlled breathing, *135*
Coping Cat, 154–156
Coping Power program, 204
counseling, 7
    defined, 5–6
    informed consent, 40
    need for, 4–5
    relationship, 22–23
    techniques, 203–204
counseling process, 29–46
    discussion points, 46
    objectives, 30–45
counseling role in school psychology, 3–27, 58–63, 68, 239–240
    discussion points, 25
    ethical guidelines, 9–20
    history, 6–9
    objectives, 4
    training standards, 9
countertransference, 239–240
crisis, 172–173
    communication, 176
    discussion points, 187
    intervention, 186
    objectives, 169–170
    prevention and preparation, 173
    response and counseling, 176–178
    Roberts's model, 180
    school, 249
    teams, 173–176
cultural variables
    crises, suicide, and grief, 186
    play-based interventions, 115
culturally relevant practices, 234

D

daily balance, 243
data, norm-referenced, 34–35
death, 184
    family member, 97
debriefing, 178
definitions, 5–6
delinquency, 193–217, 198–201
    causative factors, 199
    discussion points, 213–214

interventions, 201–206
    objectives, 193–194
    practice case, *212–213*
    prevention, 200
depression, 154–155
developmental disabilities, 185
developmental issues, 184, 197–198
dextromethorphan, 196
diagrams, 77
dialectical behavior therapy (DBT), 145
dignity and rights of all persons, 10, 14–15
    principles and standards, 10
direct benefit, 11
directive approaches, 139–167
    behavioral approaches, 140–142, *141*
    case examples, *158–161*
    CBT, 142–143
    CBT, trauma-focused, 147–148
    choice therapy, 145–146, 147
    DBT, 145
    discussion points, 162–163
    nondirective approaches vs., 112–113
    objectives, 139
    reality therapy, 145–146, 147
    REBT, 144
    theory and technique, 140
discipline/disciplinary action, 199, 201
    restorative, 248
dismissal, 44–45
disruptive behavior disorders, 4, 100
diversity factors, 14
divorce, 95–96
doing, 156
drugs
    off-label use, 206
    polypharmacy, 206
    prescription, 211
    see also psychopharmacology; psychotropic (psychoactive) medications

E

eating disorders, 4, 99
eclectic model, 140, *141*
ecological systems
    approach, 71
    framework, 93
    model, 75–76
Education for All Handicapped Children Act, 86
effective elements, 22–23
effects, 170
Elementary and Secondary Education Act (ESEA), 8
eligibility for counseling, 255–257
    assessment to determine, 33–36
EMOTION, 156
emotional concerns, 253–354
employee assistance programs (EAPs), 248
empty chair technique, 102–103
epigenetics, 197
equanimity, 130–131
equity in education, 86
ethics, 9–20, 78–79
    guidelines, 9–20, 242
    self-knowledge and self-care, 243
    see also informed consent
Ethics and Law for School Psychologists, 10
evaluation, 156, 157
    outcomes, 157–158
    progress, 102
event, 170
Every Student Succeeds Act (ESSA), 86–87
evidence-based practice, 4, 9, 20–22, 220
    barriers to, 21–22
    counseling relationship and, 22
    resources, 234
Evidence-Based Practices Resource Center, 21
executive functions, 140
experience, 170
expulsion, 199

F

fairness and justice, 14
family, 93
    blended, 96
    engagement with schools, 92–93
    extended, 73
    partnering, 186
    projection, 90
    special issues, 93–98
    structure, changes, 95

family interventions, 85–109, 203
  case study, *104–105*
  discussion points, 106
  objectives, 85
family–school partnering, 59–60
  practice, *62–63*
Family–School Partnerships, Task Force on, 59–60
family systems therapy, 89–90
family therapy, 89–92
  counseling techniques, 100
  multidimensional (MDFT), 90–91, 203
FDA approved, 206, 207
FEAR, 155
follow-through, 104
follow-up, 104
FRAMES, 149
freedom, 146

G

games therapy, 222, 234
gates 1, 2, 3. *See* Systematic Screening for Behavior Disorders (SSBD)
genogram, 77–78, 101–102, *101*
  community, 102
Glasser, William, 145–147
goal setting, 33
graduate students, 16–17
grief/grieving, 183–186
  counseling, 186
  see also loss
group counseling, individual counseling vs., 41–42
  competency, 42
  reasons for, 42

H

harm, confidentiality and, 14
heroin, 196
high cognitive/high verbal abilities, 24
high cognitive/low verbal abilities, 24
Hildreth, Gertrude, 7
history, school psychology, 6–9
homelessness, 98
homeostasis, 89
honesty, 18

I

IDEA. *See* Individuals with Disabilities Education Improvement Act
IEP. *See* Individualized Education Program
individual characteristics/differentiation, 24, 90
individual counseling, group counseling vs., 41–42
Individualized Education Program (IEP), 6, 16, 21, 29, 34, 35, 86, 221, 222
  annual goals, 37–38
  counseling, mindfulness and, 132–134
  counseling goals and objectives, 36–39
  reports, 35, 43–44
  teams, 46, 253–254
Individuals with Disabilities Education Improvement Act (IDEA), 21, 29, 33, 86, 87
informed consent, 11–13, 40–41, 104
  form, 11
  see also ethics
injustice, 14
integrative play therapy. *See* play therapy
integrity, 18
interpersonal dynamics, substance use disorders, 194
intervention, assessment and, 51–52

J

job satisfaction, 238
Joint Informational Bulletin, 4
juvenile delinquency. *See* delinquency
juvenile justice system, trauma-informed intervention and, 204
life balance, 243
loss, 169, 183–186
  discussion points, 187
  objectives, 170
  nonfinite, 184
  see also grief/grieving
love, 146
low cognitive/low verbal abilities, 24

M

manifestation determination, 202
mastery criteria, 38

materials that can be held or manipulated, 222
medications, 195, 196
    prescribed, 211
    use, 100
mental health needs, 60–61
military deployment, 94–95
mindfulness, 129–138
    activities, *134–135*
    benefits, 131–132
    case example, *133–134*
    discussion points, 136
    IEP and, 132–134
    objectives, 129
    rationale, 135–136
    research, 131–132
Model for Comprehensive and Integrated School Psychological Services, 9
modeling, 242, 244
Model Programs Guide, 203, 204
mood stabilizers, 207
motivational interviewing (MI), 148–149
multidimensional family therapy (MDFT), 90–91, 203
multifaceted client profile, case example, *230–234*
multiple relationships, 19–20
multisystemic therapy (MST), 91, 203
multitiered service delivery model, 56, *57*
multitiered systems of support (MTSS), 9, 23, 52–54, 136
    counseling within, 47–66
    discussion points, 63
    objectives, 47–48
    prevention orientation, 49

N

NASP
    membership survey, 8
    practice model, 8, 9
    professional standards, 9
nature basket, *134*
neglect, 98
No Child Left Behind Act of 2002 (NCLB), 86
nondirective approaches, 111–128
    case examples, *122–124*
    directive approaches vs., 112–113
    discussion points, 126
    empirical support for, 113
    objectives, 111
nondiscrimination, 14
nonjudgmental acceptance, 104

O

objects, 222
obsessive–compulsive disorder (OCD), 151–152
off-label use, 206
opioid agonist, partial, 208
oppositional defiant disorder (ODD), 151
organizational consultation, 71
outcomes evaluation, 157–158
    play-based therapy, 121–122

P

parent management training (PMT), 92
    Oregon model (PMTO), 92
parents, 73, 79
    alcoholic, 89–90
    referral and, 31
partnership-centered orientation, 86–87
PBIS. *See* positive behavioral intervention and support
peer-reviewed research, 21
performance level, statement of, 37
pharmaceuticals. *See* drugs; treatment
planning, 156, 157
play therapy, 125, 222, 223
    appropriate uses, 115–118
    case example, *223–226*
    cultural factors, 115
    evidence base, 115–118
    integrative, trauma-focused (TF-IPT), 171
    other interventions and, 115
    outcomes evaluation, 121–122
    research, 116–117
    theory and techniques, 100–102, *103*, 113–115, 118–122
    toys, 222
PMT. *See* parent management training
polypharmacy, 206
positive behavioral intervention and support (PBIS), 54–56, *55*, 200, 247–248, 249
positive psychology, 76–77, 131

posttraumatic stress disorder (PTSD), 177, 199
  CBT and, 152
poverty, 98
power, 146
practical applications, 219–235
  case examples, *223–233*
  discussion questions, 226, 230, 233–234
  objectives, 221–222
  techniques, methods, and tools, 221
PRECEDENT, 185
PREPaRE School Crisis Prevention and Intervention Training Curriculum, 172–173
prescription drugs, 211
prevention and preparation, crises, 186
Principles for Professional Ethics, 9–15, 18–20
privacy, 97
  see also confidentiality
private practice, 43
problem-solving approach, 48, 49–53
  case example, *50–51*
  decision-making questions, 49
  guidance, 253–254
  model, 75
professional development, 243, 248
Professional Ethics for School Psychologists: A Problem-Solving Casebook, 10
professionals
  other, 74
  support, 243
profile, multifaceted, case example, *230–234*
progress
  evaluation tools, 102
  report, *44*
Promising Practices Network on Children and Families, 21
psychiatric disorders, incidence, 4
Psychological Service for School Problems, 7
psychologists
  graduate, 242
  personal side, examples, *240–241*
  self-knowledge and self-care, 237–251
psychopharmacology, 193, 205–210
  discussion points, 213–214
  objectives, 193–194
  pediatric, 207–208
  practice case, 211–212
  practice case, 212
  scope of use, 207–208
psychosis, 4
psychotherapy, 7
  brief, 6
  defined, 5–6
psychotropic (psychoactive) medications, 206–210
  benefits and risks, 209–210
  ethical considerations, 210–211
  reference guide, 207
  side effects, 210
PTSD. *See* posttraumatic stress disorder

Q

quality world, 146

R

rational emotive behavior therapy (REBT), 144, 150
  effectiveness, 150–151
reality play therapy, 157
reality therapy, 103, 145–146, 147
  techniques, 156–157
records
  sole possession 17–18
  student's, 34
referrals, 18–19, 30–33
  case example, *32*
  framing, 33
  problem-solving meeting, 30–31
  substance abuse, 202
relationships, 79
  building, 74–75
  multiple, 19–20
reports, 43–44
  IEP, 35
  progress, *44*
resilience, 97–98
resources, 234
response to intervention (RTI), 9, 23, 136
  psychologists, 246
  Tier 1, 23, 52–53, *55*
  Tier 2, 23, 53–54, *55*
  Tier 3, 23, *55*

transition from general to special education
support, 55–57, *57*
responsibility, 16–20
psychologist, 20
restorative discipline, 248
rewards, 205
role-playing, 103

S

SAMHSA. *See* Substance Abuse and Mental Health Services Administration
sandtray therapy, 120–121
outcomes evaluation, 121–122
school
family partnering, 86–87, 92–93
staff, 73, 79
teachers, 72–73, 79
see also crisis, school; family–school partnering
school-based family interventions, 88–89
see also family–school partnering
school-based motivational interviewing (SBMI), 149
school psychologist
as councilor, 58–63
demands on, 43
intern, case example, *61–62*
role, 7–8, 58
School Psychology for the 21st Century: Foundations and Practices, 10
school-to-prison pipeline, effects, 199
school-wide positive behavioral interventions and supports, 55
SEL. *See* social–emotional learning
self-assessment, 242
self-care, 237–251
discussion points, 250, 237
monitoring, 243
objectives, 237–238
psychologists, 241, 243–245
regimen, 245
resources for, 244–245
strategies, 249
self-compassion, 245
self-evaluation, 154
self-healing, 114

self-knowledge, 237–251
psychologists, 241, 242–243
discussion points, 250, 237
premises, 242
self-regulation techniques, 153–154
sertraline, CBT and, 151
service delivery models, 87–89
sessions, first, 43
strategies for organizing, 42–44
siblings, 73, 79
SMART (self-management and recovery training) approach, 205
Smith, D.K., 7–8
social competence, 59
social concerns, 253–254
social–emotional learning (SEL), 52–53
models, 93
skills, 131, 136
social executive functioning model, 77
solution-focused brief therapy (SFBT), 149–150, 204–205
solution-focused orientation, 220
special education
general education vs., 48
RTI and, 55–57, *56*
services, 34
student, 202
standards, evidence-based interventions, 22
Standards for Graduate Preparation of School Psychologists, 9
Standards for the Credentialing of School Psychologists, 9
Standards of Accreditation for Health Service Psychology, 9
stimulants, 207
stress, 238–239
counseling role, 239–240
psychologists', 240–241
students
characteristics, 220
input, 35
substance abuse, 193–197
addiction, 89–90, 97–98, 194, 208
discussion points, 213–214
drugs, prescription, 211
objectives, 193–194

substance abuse (*Continued*)
  practice case, *212*
  precursors, 213
  school psychologists' roles, 211, 212–213
  treatment, 202, 208
  warning signs, 196
Substance Abuse and Mental Health Services Administration (SAMHSA)
  helpline, 202
  survey, 4
substance intoxication, 197
substance use disorder, 194
  risk, 194, 197–198
suicide, 178–183
  risk factors, 179–180
  stages of care, 181–182
support for colleagues, 246–247
suspension, 199
Systematic Screening for Behavior Disorders (SSBD), 54–55
  gates 1, 2, 3, 54–55
systems consultation, techniques for, 67–83
  applications, 72–74
  case examples, *79–81*
  discussion points, 82
  ethical considerations, 78–79
  objectives, 67–68
  specific techniques, 74–78
systems interventions, 203

T

talk therapy, 125
TARGET (Trauma Affect Regulation: Guide for Education and Therapy), 204
teachers, 72–73, 79
teamwork, 58
techniques, selection, 23–25
termination, 44–45
test and place model, 48
TF-CBT. *See* cognitive–behavioral therapy, trauma-focused
theme interference, 71
theories, 219–234
therapeutic modalities, selection, 220
therapy, 7
  defined, 5

single-session, defined, 6
Tier 1, 2, 3. *See* response to intervention
timelines, 102
topdog, 103
training
  intern, case example, *61–62*
  programs, 8
  standards, 8–9
trauma, 170–171, 198–199
  approaches, 148
  discussion points, 187
  objectives, 169
trauma-focused CBT. *See* cognitive–behavioral therapy, trauma-focused
trauma-informed care, 171
traumatization, vicarious, 239
treatment
  defined, 88
  drugs, prescription, 211
  planning, 39–40
triangulation, 89–90
trust, 103
12-step programs, 205

U

unanticipated negative outcomes, 16
underdog, 103

V

verbal abilities, low or high, 24
visual techniques, 100–102, *103*

W

wants, 156
WDEP (wants, doing, evaluation, and planning), 156–157, 162
websites, therapy, 234
wellness model, 76–77
What Works Clearinghouse, 21
workbooks and worksheets, 222
work environment, healthy, 245–249
working relationships, 214

Z

zero tolerance policies, 201